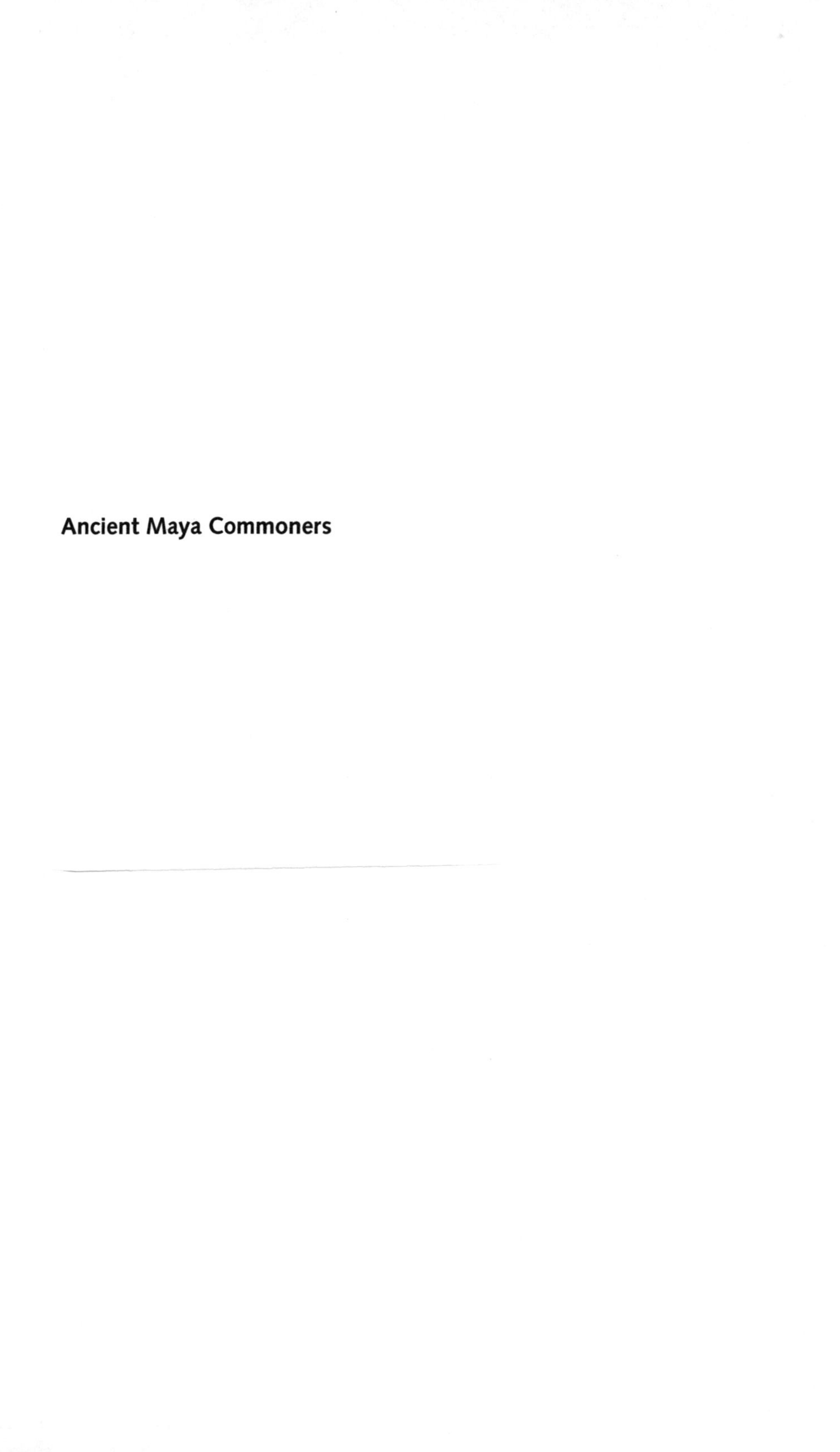

Ancient Maya Commoners

Ancient Maya Commoners

EDITED BY JON C. LOHSE AND FRED VALDEZ, JR.

University of Texas Press, Austin

Printed in the United States of America

First edition, 2004

♾ The paper used in this book meets the minimum requirements of ANSI/NISO Z39.48-1992 (R1997) (Permanence of Paper).

Library of Congress Cataloging-in-Publication Data

Ancient Maya commoners / edited by Jon C. Lohse and Fred Valdez, Jr.— 1st ed.
p. cm.
"Most of these papers were originally presented as part of a symposium organized for the 1999 American Anthropological Association meetings held in Chicago, IL"—Ack.
Includes bibliographical references and index.
ISBN 0-292-70571-9 (hardcover : alk. paper)
1. Mayas—Social conditions—Congresses. 2. Mayas—Antiquities—Congresses. 3. Working class—Central America—History—Congresses. 4. Social structure—Central America—History—Congresses. 5. Land settlement patterns—Central America—Congresses. I. Lohse, Jon C., 1968- II. Valdez, Fred. III. American Anthropological Association. Meeting (98th : 1999 : Chicago, Ill.)
F1435.3.S68A53 2004
972.81′01—dc22
2004004631

In memory of the late Professors Gordon R. Willey and Eric R. Wolf, pioneers whose achievements continue to advance our understanding of ordinary people, both past and present.

Contents

Acknowledgments ix

1. Examining Ancient Maya Commoners Anew 1
JON C. LOHSE AND FRED VALDEZ, JR.

2. Daily Life in a Highland Maya Community: Zinacantan in Mid-Twentieth Century 23
EVON Z. VOGT

3. The Role of Pottery and Food Consumption among Late Preclassic Maya Commoners at Lamanai, Belize 49
TERRY G. POWIS

4. Of Salt and Water: Ancient Commoners on the Pacific Coast of Guatemala 73
BÁRBARA ARROYO

5. Down on the Farm: Classic Maya "Homesteads" as "Farmsteads" 97
NICHOLAS DUNNING

6. Intra-Site Settlement Signatures and Implications for Late Classic Maya Commoner Organization at Dos Hombres, Belize 117
JON C. LOHSE

7. Heterogeneous Hinterlands: The Social and Political Organization of Commoner Settlements near Xunantunich, Belize 147
JASON YAEGER AND CYNTHIA ROBIN

8. The Spatial Mobility of Non-Elite Populations in Classic Maya Society and Its Political Implications 175
TAKESHI INOMATA

9. Commoners in Postclassic Maya Society: Social versus Economic Class Constructs 197
MARILYN A. MASSON AND CARLOS PERAZA LOPE

10. Methods for Understanding Classic Maya Commoners: Structure Function, Energetics, and More 225
NANCY GONLIN

11. Maya Commoners: The Stereotype and the Reality 255
JOYCE MARCUS

Contributors 285

Index 287

Acknowledgments

We are grateful to the many individuals who contributed in some measure to this edited volume. Most of these papers were originally presented as part of a symposium organized for the 1999 American Anthropological Association meetings held in Chicago, IL, and we appreciate the various contributors' efforts to revise their presentations into the chapters that follow. The chapters by Nancy Gonlin and Marilyn Masson were added subsequent to the conference to "fill in" important gaps in chronological, regional, or topical coverage; we appreciate these authors' willingness to contribute their studies to this collection. Evon Vogt, who served as the session discussant, graciously revised his contribution from a summary to an account of daily Zinacanteco life in the mid-twentieth century. Finally, we are indebted to Joyce Marcus, who, though also not a participant in the original session, prepared the excellent summary chapter for the volume.

At the University of Texas Press, we are grateful for the dedicated efforts of Theresa May and her assistant Allison Faust on our behalf in helping to steer early versions of this manuscript through the review and university committee approval process. Carolyn Wylie helped with the production of the volume, and Nancy Warrington did an excellent job as copyeditor. Linda Webster prepared the index, and Ellen Gibbs and Regina Fuentes served as proofreaders. Additionally, the help of designer Ellen McKie is acknowledged in working with the illustrations, particularly the cover. We appreciate the contributions of all these people.

Finally, we are indebted to Frank Cancian for allowing the use of one of his extraordinary photographs (© 1974, courtesy of Frank Cancian) taken during his tenure on the Harvard Chiapas Project as the cover illustration for this book. It serves, we think, as an appropriate reminder of the intimacy and vibrancy that defines the subject matter of this volume, and much else in the Maya world.

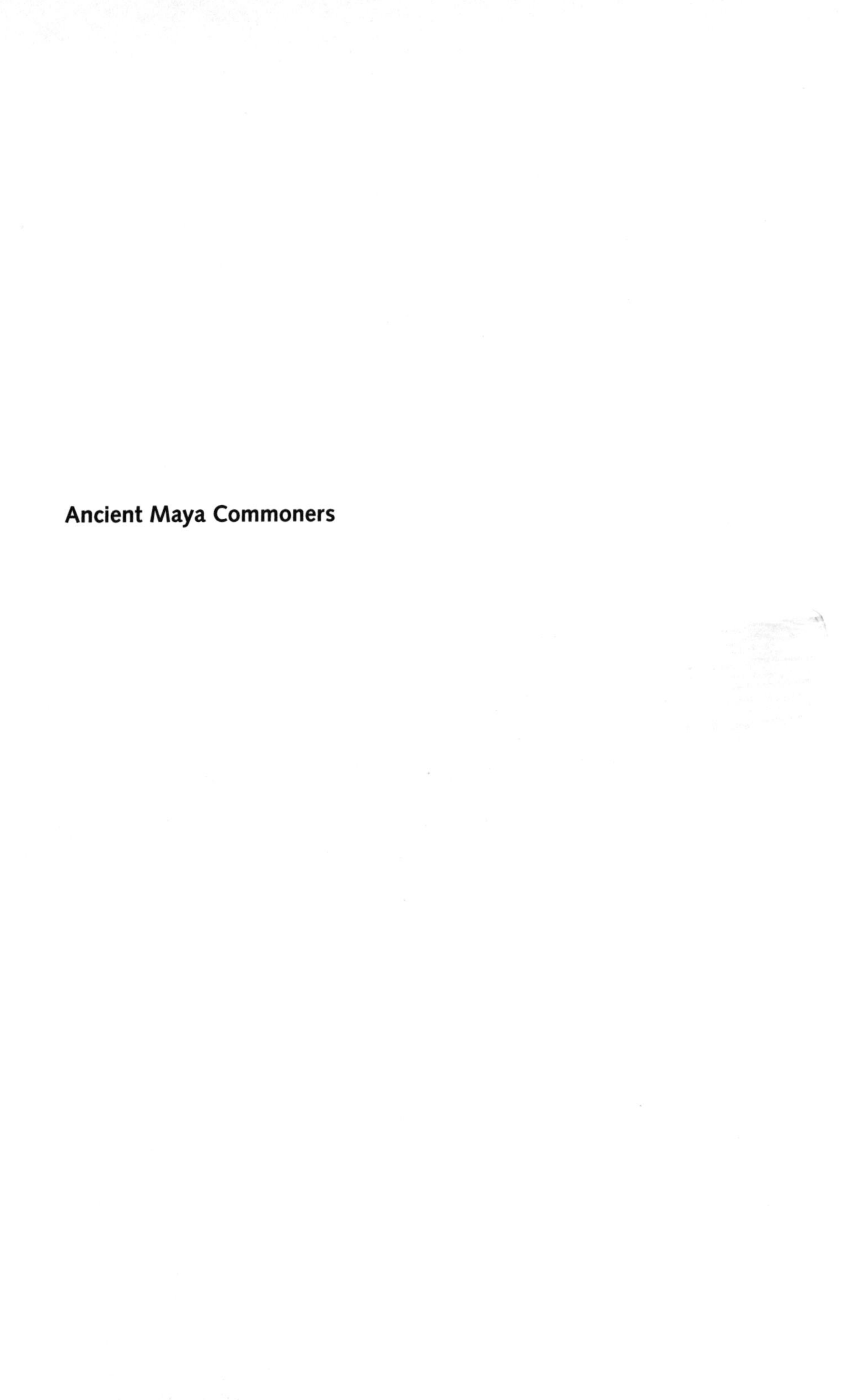

Ancient Maya Commoners

CHAPTER 1

Examining Ancient Maya Commoners Anew

JON C. LOHSE AND FRED VALDEZ, JR.

Studies of ancient complex societies are often charged with answering basic questions such as how such civilizations came about, how they adapted specialized strategies allowing them to contend with widely diverse environments, and why they ceased to exist. Archaeologists necessarily rely on theoretical models, sometimes using ethnographically or ethnohistorically based bridging arguments to provide humanistic explanations for these complex and dynamic processes. These accounts determine to a very large degree how social scientists and, ultimately, the general public come to understand ancient societies and the roles different people played in them.

An array of frameworks, approaches, and perspectives have been employed through the years to address questions such as these, particularly in the case of the prehistoric Maya of Central America, though the majority of these frameworks have tended to focus on the behavior of only a small segment of society. Highlighted individuals, many of whom are known to us by name thanks to advances in epigraphy, were community and polity leaders whose actions are perceived as influencing the course of culture history. Most people today are, quite understandably, comfortable with this picture; it accords well with the model of our own society. However, while the point that such individuals long ago played central roles seems beyond question, we suggest that much Maya scholarship traditionally has failed to account for the vast majority of historic and prehistoric populations.

It is our immediate goal to bring attention to the rich diversity that characterized social non-elites in Maya society. Looking into the future, we hope to encourage a thoughtful reconsideration of both the overt theoretical perspectives and implicit assumptions applied to the study of prehistoric elites and commoners alike. The most important theme underlying our approach, a theme that is reiterated throughout many of the chapters in this volume, involves examining commoners on *their* terms, according to the roles they *did* play in providing the economic base for the social, political, and ideological institutions in ancient Mesoamerica. This view is indispensable to the study of ancient civilizations such as the Maya, for, as has been noted by many, commoners "allowed the specialized division of labor that led to writing, metallurgy, monumental architecture, cities, and the great religious and artistic traditions we associate with civilization" (Peoples and Bailey 1997:146–147).

Seeing Ancient Maya Commoners

Even though individuals of non-elite status constituted anywhere between 80 and 98 percent of the population in pre-Columbian times, our perception and understanding of commoners are frequently based on comparisons with elites, in terms of both material well-being and behaviors undertaken in broader social contexts. Recently, Rosemary Joyce (1994:182) succinctly characterized some distinctions between commoners and elites: "Thus, the elite become those who use imported or elaborate goods, consume *more* of these goods in life (as seen in middens) and death (as seen in burials), draw on *greater* energy for the construction of their living sites, and have *less* evidence of malnutrition or poor health" (emphasis added). Focusing on what elites do (and by implication what commoners do not do), Arlen Chase and Diane Chase (1992:3) identify elites simply as "those who run society's institutions." Perspectives such as these, perfectly valid and with deep roots in Western anthropology, reflect something of an imbalance in the ways commoners of the past are approached, or not, in archaeology.

Qualities ascribed to the non-elite are often defined in reference to those displayed by paramount status holders in society. Archaeologists frequently see commoners as "small" (versus larger-than-life rulers often glorified on stone monuments), "impoverished" (when compared to elaborate palaces and grave offerings of the high and mighty), "unempowered" (in the face of elite decisions on most weighty social matters), and "anonymous" (in that none are known to us by name or individual deed). In her summary chapter to this volume, Joyce Marcus evaluates some additional stereotypes of commoners. Throughout the history of anthropology, commoners have been variously characterized as faceless, internally homogeneous, and relatively inert in terms of their impacts on cultural development and processes. Karl Marx (1971:230), for example, egregiously described the constituency of the nineteenth-century French countryside as "a smallholding, a peasant and his family; alongside them another smallholding, another peasant and another family. A few score of these make up a village, and a few score of villages make up a department. In this way, the great mass of the French nation is formed by simple addition of homologous magnitudes, much as potatoes in a sack form a sack of potatoes." While acknowledging that both the perceived quality and quantity of archaeological remains often favor investigations of social elites, we argue that these material biases, together with the weight of theoretical perspectives that traditionally lend understanding to the strategies and rationales of society's rulers, have resulted in incomplete, unbalanced, and, frankly, inaccurate views of the past. To paraphrase Eric Wolf (1982), in most realms of Maya scholarship, commoners remain the people without history.

The challenge, simply put, is to view the actions of elites and non-elites alike through the same lens of understanding, and to recognize the ways common-status individuals and family groups might have participated in social institutions. In this effort, relying on any single theoretical perspective will not suffice; problems with "seeing" commoners in the past (e.g., Dunning, this volume) crosscut *all* avenues of archaeological study: how we see them as initiating economic production or agricultural intensification, expressing individual agency, participating by different means in shared religious beliefs, and, collectively, affecting the course of historical change. Our point is that (and to paraphrase another eminent scholar) until archaeologists "see" ancient Maya commoners as people who at least sometimes had the ability and will to live their lives as they chose, they will remain "faceless blobs" (Tringham 1991:94) in our reconstructions of prehistory.

In charting an approach for investigating ancient Maya commoners, the authors of chapters in this volume ascribe two key components to the behavior of non-elites in complex societies. First, commoners are viewed as adapters to their social environments, responding to economic, political, and ideological pressures exerted on them by others. Second, they are seen as primarily responsible for engaging their surrounding biophysical environments for the production of food and many other goods. Several of the following chapters illustrate these themes, either singularly or in combination, while others highlight problems with archaeologists' ability to accurately distinguish between elites and commoners in the archaeological record, an important task when one begins ascribing social roles to one segment over another (Chase 1996:219). In sum, though, the studies presented herein offer a broad cross section of theoretical and methodological issues in the study of Maya commoners, and illustrate the potential contributions of commoner studies to our understanding of pre-Hispanic society.

Recognizing Ancient Maya Commoners

Several approaches lend themselves to recognizing and examining commoners in the archaeological record (Sharer 1993). These include the use of material remains recovered through archaeological investigations (Buttles 2002), ethnohistoric accounts of Contact period Maya (and Mesoamerican) society (see Marcus, this volume, for a detailed discussion of Maya terms used to refer to various social positions), and ethnographic explanations of the organization of modern communities (see Vogt, this volume). Many of the chapters in this collection discuss theoretical and procedural issues concerning the material record of ancient commoners.

Use of the archaeological record remains perhaps the most commonly used method for identifying ancient Maya socioeconomic units; indeed, Robert Sharer (1993:91) has argued that "the delineation of the social organization of the Classic Maya is fundamentally an archaeological problem." Many of the chapters in the important volume *Mesoamerican Elites* (D. Chase and A. Chase 1992) illustrate attempts to discern the "haves" from the "have nots" in the archaeological record by using evidence such as associated architecture, ritual paraphernalia, residential location, burial elaboration, and domestic material remains.

Although palace complexes found in site centers can easily be associated with elite occupation, and the "humble" mounds found by the scores in site peripheries suggest commoner abodes (Webster and Gonlin 1988), identifying the point in archaeological space where these two social units meet but do not overlap is no easy matter (see chapters by Masson and Peraza and Marcus, this volume). For example, as Terry Powis demonstrates for the Terminal Preclassic at Lamanai, local and regional trends in ceramic styles may vary geographically and through time. Moreover, domestic architecture found outside site centers varies widely in elaboration, supporting arguments for a "rural elite" (Adams and Smith 1981). Vagaries such as these have led some (Carmean 1991:163; Palka 1997:303) to suggest socioeconomic continuums on the basis of material remains. At the site of Caracol, tomb volume has been used to argue for the presence of a middle class (A. Chase 1992:40). Partial support for this argument is derived from the ethnohistoric term *azmen uinic*, which refers to "middle" or "medium men" (D. Chase 1992:121; cf. Roys 1943). Dialogue around the nature of class structure in ancient Maya society (A. Chase 1992:37; D. Chase 1992:121; Marcus 1983, 1992:221, this volume) holds implications for the study of ancient Maya commoners and for our ability to differentiate between high-status commoners and low-status elites.

We add to the arguments made by those such as Kenneth Hirth (1993:143), Michael Smith (1987:327), Barbara Stark and Barbara Hall (1993:252), and Marilyn Masson, Nancy Gonlin, and Joyce Marcus (this volume) in concluding that in instances where precise determinations between elite and commoner are unclear, multiple lines of material evidence must be used concurrently to assess differences between ancient Maya social strata. The value of this approach is *not* to compile some checklist of attributes that allows archaeologists to identify one segment over another, but to gain a more robust understanding of how social activities and behaviors were conditioned as a result of hereditary and institutionalized social inequality.

In truth, qualities of *eliteness* and *non-eliteness* were both forged and expressed in local, perhaps community settings that involved situationally negotiated expressions of wealth and power. It is unlikely, for example, that rulers at Tikal had any direct effect on most aspects of daily commoner life at Dos Hombres, Copán, or Sayil. These communities maintained their own unique systems of local economic production while also participating somewhat differently in regional trade and exchange systems, meaning that the specific material inventories available to people in the past for expressing their social standing varied from one end of the Maya world to the other. Further confounding the problem of recognizing commoners based on material means is that strategies for displaying or not displaying material standing and for expressing concepts of "value" and "importance" also are likely to have varied from one community and social context to another based on long-lived and deeply rooted local traditions and customs. These factors mean that in cases where it is difficult to separate out high-ranking commoners from low-ranking elites, distinctions must derive from case-by-case studies that allow archaeologists to recognize localized strategies employed for expressing social position, rather than rely on previously defined or generalized notions of "commoner" and "elite." This point makes community-focused research programs perhaps *the* key avenue for future studies of ancient Maya commoners (see Yaeger and Canuto 2000).

In addition to archaeology and ethnohistory, ethnographic studies have contributed significantly to the study of pre-Hispanic commoners in at least two key areas. First, descriptions of contemporary social structure offer another basis for modeling the Preclassic and Classic Maya. Work by scholars such as George Collier (1975), Charles Wisdom (1940), Sol Tax (1937), Robert Hill and John Monaghan (1987), Brian Hayden and Aubrey Cannon (1982), Evon Vogt (1969, this volume), and others has helped increase our awareness of multi-household corporate groups as focal units of social organization (see Dunning, this volume). These groups have been shown in agrarian societies to control access to important local resources; may have represented loci of intermediate political, economic, and religious administration (McAnany 1995); and perhaps even took precedence over class-endogamous socioeconomic distinctions as a basis for social differentiation in emergent complex societies (Joyce 1999).

Second, ethnographic accounts and ethnoarchaeology have proven extremely useful in elucidating many otherwise enigmatic aspects of ancient Maya lifeways. These have included the organization of both household (Hanks 1990; Vogt 1976, this volume) and community-wide (Cancian 1965) ritual behavior according to cosmological and calendric principles (Gossen 1986); recognizing the potential effects of economic, environmental, and ethnic factors on domestic architecture (M. Blake 1988; S. Blake 1988; Wilk 1983, 1988); and the use of an array of ritual paraphernalia, including pottery and household altars (Deal 1987, 1988, 1998).

Unfortunately for archaeologists, contemporary Maya society is far removed from that of pre-Hispanic times. The transformation from complex agrarian societies through the Spanish Conquest to modern nation-states has, without doubt, wrought tremendous change on nearly all facets of Maya culture. However, when used with caution, ethnographic accounts and perspectives can be particularly well suited to adding flesh to the bones of our archaeological understanding of ancient Maya commoners.

Approaches to the Study of Commoners

A number of archaeological approaches, some of which are discussed below and are highlighted in the following chapters (particularly those by Gonlin and Marcus), have been applied to the study of ancient Maya commoners. Taken individually, each of these approaches has the capacity to enhance our understanding of the local adaptations that constituted the economic foundation for pre-Columbian communities across the Maya region. However, our best view of Maya commoners and the social orders in which they were integral parts is likely to come about through research designs that simultaneously employ multiple perspectives.

Settlement Studies

Settlement pattern studies, which examine the "disposition of ancient remains across the landscape" (Ashmore and Willey 1981:3), represent perhaps the most frequently applied line of inquiry into Maya commoners. While such work (Bullard 1960, 1964; Eaton 1975; Haviland 1965; Kurjack 1974; Michels 1979; Puleston 1973; Sanders 1955; Smith 1962, 1972; Tourtellot 1988a; Vogt 1961; Willey et al. 1965; also see Marcus, this volume) had been conducted long before the publication of *Lowland Maya Settlement Patterns* (Ashmore 1981), that landmark volume firmly established settlement studies as an important focus of comprehensive research designs across the Maya area.

Influenced in part by work and ideas from outside the Maya area (Chang 1958, 1968; Phillips et al. 1951; Steward 1949, 1955; Trigger 1967; Willey 1953, 1956; and others), Maya settlement archaeology has and remains today focused principally on two issues. As Wendy Ashmore and Gordon Willey (1981:4) note, these include: "(1) those concerning people in their relationships to their natural ambience (ecological); and (2) those concerning people in their relationships to other people (social and political)." Such themes clearly are integral to our framework for the study of commoners, and they are highlighted in chapters by Nicholas Dunning, Jon Lohse, Jason Yaeger and Cynthia Robin, and Takeshi Inomata, which view the responses of commoners at both community and regional levels to differing conditions of available natural resources and political strategies for marshalling populations as bases of support.

Household Archaeology

Another line of inquiry well suited to the examination of commoners is household archaeology. While early accounts (Smith 1962; Thompson 1892; Wauchope 1934, 1940) described the arrangements of house mounds and their assemblages, the shift to an activity-based definition of household (Ashmore and Wilk 1988; Netting et al. 1984; Wilk and Rathje 1982) has allowed Mayanists to define, or at least hypothesize, discrete social units for comparative purposes (Inomata and Stiver 1999; Manzanilla and Barba 1990; Sheets et al. 1990; Webster and Gonlin 1988; Webster et al.

1997). These studies frequently involve commoner assemblages and have helped us examine different growth cycles of domestic groups (Haviland 1988; Tourtellot 1988b; Yaeger and Robin, this volume), compare status differences (Carmean 1991; Hendon 1991; Palka 1997; Smith 1987), and understand the use of space surrounding domestic units (Gonlin, this volume; Killion et al. 1989; Manzanilla 1987; Robin 2002).

Additional topics have been raised more recently pertaining to households that hold special promise to inform us about commoner behavior and organization. These include the symbolic meaning of domestic architecture (Johnston and Gonlin 1998:144–150; Robin 1999) and house-lots (Lohse 2000), and the effects of status and gender on power and the division of labor within households (Hendon 1996, 1997; Sweely 1999; Trachman 2003). The identification of the same cosmological principles expressed in commoner domestic caches, architecture, and house-lots (Lohse 2000; Mathews and Garber 2004; Robin 1999) as found in monumental site plans (Ashmore 1986, 1991) and elite residences (Webster et al. 1998) may require us to reconsider our models explaining the accessibility to ritual knowledge by all socioeconomic segments of Maya society (DeMarrais et al. 1996; Earle 1997). And examining the intra-household tensions that revolve around status and gender roles might represent our best opportunity to penetrate the "black box" (Wilk 1989) of household decision-making processes.

Subsistence Economy

In addition to settlement and household studies, the broadly encompassing field of subsistence economy (Flannery 1982; Pohl 1985) also holds great potential for increasing our understanding of ancient Maya commoners. As the component of society that articulated directly with the natural environment, commoners were responsible for fulfilling many of the food requirements for themselves, full-time craft specialists, and the ruling elite. Accordingly, it may be argued that cultivation techniques and agricultural systems (Lohse, Dunning, this volume) as well as other food-procurement or -production strategies (Miksicek 1991; Powis et al. 1999; Wing and Scudder 1991) were largely, if not exclusively, in the domain of commoners (see Marcus, this volume, for more discussion on sociopolitical aspects of food production).

The environment of the Maya lowlands has been described as a patchwork "mosaic" of resources (Fedick 1996; Graham 1987). This means that agricultural variables such as water availability, soil type, and slope can vary drastically from region to region or within a region (Dunning 1992; Dunning et al. 1997; Fedick 1989). Dunning (1996), however, has warned against predicting agricultural technologies for one region based solely on its geomorphic similarities to another. That is to say, not all wetlands underwent ditching or saw the construction of raised planting platforms, and not all hilly environs were terraced. Furthermore, the demands for food changed through time as populations approached, exceeded, and then returned below regional carrying capacities for swidden agriculture from the Preclassic through the Postclassic periods (see papers in Culbert and Rice 1990). Intensifying food production (Boserup 1965; Turner 1974; Wilken 1971) would therefore have required adaptive responses within highly variable geographic, temporal, sociopolitical, and demographic parameters (see Lentz 2000). Successful strategies for producing and procuring food would most likely have been those that were flexible and that could be implemented at various levels of social organization, from the independent farming household upward (Dunning, this volume).

In addition to cultigen production, a range of other foodstuffs should be included when piecing together the ancient Maya subsistence base. David Lentz (1991), for example, reconstructed elements of the diet at Copán based on paleoethnobotanical remains, including evidence for arboriculture. Paul Healy et al. (1990) have demonstrated the importance of fresh-water mollusks in the Maya diet in the Belize River valley. Nancy Hamblin (1984) presented evidence for the exploitation of both terrestrial and aquatic animals by the pre-Hispanic Maya of Cozumel Island. These studies serve only as examples of the diversity of subsistence resources available to the ancient Maya; numerous others have been conducted but are not mentioned here. Each resource would necessarily have involved its own unique technology and ideal labor arrangement for exploitation, all greatly affecting the complexity of daily commoner life.

While exploitation of the natural environment represents one of the roles of ancient commoners, there is also evidence suggesting the important effects of status differences on subsistence practices. William Folan et al. (1979) documented the patterned occurrence of trees useful for fruit, fiber, bark, and resin at the site of Cobá. These patterns were positively correlated with vaulted architecture at that site, suggesting that social groups of higher status may have controlled access to at least some economically valuable species. Leslie Shaw (1991) examined access to different fauna as an indication of status during the Preclassic period at the site of Colha. Focusing on changes in social complexity during this time period allowed her to document "modifications in the social aspect of food procurement and distribution, including exchange relationships" (Shaw 1991:x), and to argue that households of higher status were increasingly able to procure food through indirect means such as exchange or tribute.

Reconstructing the wide array of ancient Maya subsistence practices remains crucial to understanding how population growth and increasing social complexity were sustained, as well as what were the potential causes for the collapse of cultural systems. Given that Maya populations comprised a high percentage of commoners, better understanding subsistence economies seems particularly important to achieving a clearer view of the roles of non-elites and how these varied across time and space in the pre-Columbian Maya world. However, as Willey (1978:334) predicted when he stated that "working the sequence out is going to be very difficult and something that will be with us for a long time," our advances in this field may be in excruciatingly small steps.

Remainder of the Volume

The chapters in this volume all reflect some aspect of the issues discussed above. Though our coverage of the Maya area (Figure 1.1) is incomplete, with much of the data presented here coming from the southern lowlands, it is beyond our space limitations here to pursue the needed in-depth, region-specific examinations of the roles of commoners and of how these changed through time. With respect to the chapter by Evon Z. Vogt, we feel that although this study deals with daily Zinacanteco life of the mid-1900s rather than the archaeological past, the contributions of ethnographers, particularly those of the Harvard Chiapas Project, to archaeologists' understanding of the Maya (both past and present) cannot be underestimated. It is our hope that the inclusion of Vogt's chapter here will serve not only to encourage readers to question how such aspects of daily life as he reports might appear in the archaeological record, but also to acknowledge the importance and long-lasting contributions of those pioneering ethnographies to Maya studies.

Most of the chapters that follow focus primarily on presenting data cases from sites or regions of the Maya area. These include those by Terry Powis, Bárbara Arroyo, Nicholas Dunning, Takeshi Inomata, Jon Lohse, Marilyn Masson and Carlos Peraza, and Jason Yaeger and Cynthia Robin. These authors pursue different tracks to understanding commoners, resulting in a more comprehensive presentation of potential issues archae-

Figure 1.1. Map of Maya area showing sites discussed in this volume

ologists considering commoners elsewhere might face. It should be noted that not all the authors of this volume concur with positions adopted in other chapters. For example, both two- and three-class models for the organization of Maya society receive support in this volume, from Joyce Marcus and Marilyn Masson and Carlos Peraza, respectively. Masson and Peraza's chapter, in particular, places commoners in the Mesoamerican-wide mercantile system of the Postclassic and recognizes the opportunity for upwardly mobile traders and merchants to occupy the often-problematic middle stratum. Additionally, Inomata's chapter evaluates the residential mobility of commoners, but from the perspective of elite strategies for power building rather than from the archaeological record of commoners. However, we see these moderate divergences in approaches and viewpoints as one of the strengths of this volume, as they underscore the diversity of ancient Maya life and also highlight the multiplicity of perspectives capable of enhancing our understanding of social non-elites.

The final two chapters, by Nancy Gonlin and Joyce Marcus, complement each other well by discussing a host of issues to be considered as archaeologists undertake more systematic and comprehensive examinations of non-elites. Each chapter discusses relevant units of analysis, often blending ethnohistoric accounts with archaeological data from settlement and household studies in a manner that results in a more complete view of the past than can be compiled by either data set alone.

In summary, the chapters of this volume offer an array of approaches to the study of ancient Maya commoners, and together demonstrate the diversity of this important segment of society. It is clear that we can no longer neglect the inclusion of non-elites in our accounts of the past nor fail to integrate their roles and contributions into our frameworks for analyzing social complexity. The plea is often heard that the non-elite segment of society receives inadequate attention from archaeologists; the challenge from this point onward is to expand our perspectives beyond either top-down or bottom-up approaches to understanding the ancient Maya, and to undertake more complete and inclusive narratives that include the actions and behaviors of commoners and elite alike.

References

Adams, Richard E. W., and Woodruff D. Smith

1981 Feudal Models for Classic Maya Civilization. In *Lowland Maya Settlement Patterns*, edited by Wendy Ashmore, pp. 335–349. University of New Mexico Press, Albuquerque.

Ashmore, Wendy

1986 Peten Cosmology in the Maya Southeast: An Analysis of Architecture and Settlement Patterns at Classic Quirigua. In *The Southeast Maya Periphery*, edited by Patricia A. Urban and Edward M, Schortman, pp. 35–49. University of Texas Press, Austin.

1991 Site-Planning Principles and Concepts of Directionality among the Ancient Maya. *Latin American Antiquity* 2(3):199–226.

Ashmore, Wendy (editor)
1981 *Lowland Maya Settlement Patterns.* University of New Mexico Press, Albuquerque.

Ashmore, Wendy, and Richard R. Wilk
1988 Household and Community in the Mesoamerican Past. In *Household and Community in the Mesoamerican Past,* edited by Richard R. Wilk and Wendy Ashmore, pp. 1–27. University of New Mexico Press, Albuquerque.

Ashmore, Wendy, and Gordon R. Willey
1981 A Historical Introduction to the Study of Lowland Maya Settlement Patterns. In *Lowland Maya Settlement Patterns,* edited by Wendy Ashmore, pp. 3–17. University of New Mexico Press, Albuquerque.

Blake, Michael
1988 Household Features and Social Processes in a Modern Maya Community. In *Ethnoarchaeology among the Highland Maya of Chiapas, Mexico,* edited by Thomas A. Lee, Jr., and Brian Hayden, pp. 45–60. Papers of the New World Archaeological Foundation 56. Brigham Young University, Provo.

Blake, Susan
1988 House Materials, Environment, and Ethnicity in Southeastern Chiapas, Mexico. In *Ethnoarchaeology among the Highland Maya of Chiapas, Mexico,* edited by Thomas A. Lee, Jr., and Brian Hayden, pp. 21–37. Papers of the New World Archaeological Foundation 56. Brigham Young University, Provo.

Boserup, Ester
1965 *The Conditions of Agricultural Growth: The Economics of Agrarian Change under Population Pressure.* Earthscan Publications, London.

Bullard, William R., Jr.
1960 Maya Settlement Pattern in Northeastern Peten, Guatemala. *American Antiquity* 25(3):355–372.
1964 Settlement Patterns and Social Structures in the Southern Maya Lowlands during the Classic Period. In *XXXV Congreso Internacional de Americanistas,* vol. 1:279–287. N.p., Mexico City.

Buttles, Palma J.
2002 Material and Meaning: A Contextual Examination of Select Portable Material Culture from Colha, Belize. Ph.D. diss., University of Texas at Austin.

Cancian, Frank
1965 *Economics and Prestige in a Maya Community: The Religious Cargo System in Zinacantan.* Stanford University Press, Stanford.

Carmean, Kelli
1991 Architectural Labor Investment and Social Stratification at Sayil, Yucatán, Mexico. *Latin American Antiquity* 2(2):151–165.

Chang, Kwang-Chih

1958 Study of Neolithic Social Grouping: Examples from the New World. *American Anthropologist* 60(2):298–334.

Chang, K. C. (editor)

1968 *Settlement Archaeology*. National Press Books, Palo Alto.

Chase, Arlen F.

1992 Elites and the Changing Organization of Classic Maya Society. In *Mesoamerican Elites: An Archaeological Assessment*, edited by Diane Z. Chase and Arlen F. Chase, pp. 30–49. University of Oklahoma Press, Norman.

1996 The Organization and Composition of Classic Lowland Maya Society: The View from Caracol, Belize. In *Eighth Palenque Round Table, 1993*, edited by Martha J. Macri and Jan McHargue, pp. 213–221. The Pre-Columbian Art Institute, San Francisco.

Chase, Arlen F., and Diane Z. Chase

1992 Mesoamerican Elites: Assumptions, Definitions, and Models. In *Mesoamerican Elites: An Archaeological Assessment*, edited by Diane Z. Chase and Arlen F. Chase, pp. 3–17. University of Oklahoma Press, Norman.

Chase, Diane Z.

1992 Postclassic Maya Elites: Ethnohistory and Archaeology. In *Mesoamerican Elites: An Archaeological Assessment*, edited by Diane Z. Chase and Arlen F. Chase, pp. 118–134. University of Oklahoma Press, Norman.

Chase, Diane Z. and Arlen F. (editors)

1992 *Mesoamerican Elites: An Archaeological Assessment*. University of Oklahoma Press, Norman.

Collier, George

1975 *Fields of the Tzotzil*. University of Texas Press, Austin.

Culbert, T. Patrick, and Don S. Rice (editors)

1990 *Precolumbian Population History in the Maya Lowlands*. University of New Mexico Press, Albuquerque.

Deal, Michael

1987 Ritual Space and Architecture in the Highland Maya Household. In *Mirror and Metaphor: Material and Social Constructions of Reality*, edited by Daniel W. Ingersoll, Jr., and Gordon Bronitsky, pp. 172–198. University Press of America, Lanham.

1988 Recognition of Ritual Pottery in Residential Units: An Ethnoarchaeological Model of the Family Altar Tradition. In *Ethnoarchaeology among the Highland Maya of Chiapas, Mexico*, edited by Thomas A. Lee, Jr., and Brian Hayden, pp. 61–89. Papers of the New World Archaeological Foundation 56. Brigham Young University, Provo.

1998 *Pottery Ethnoarchaeology in the Central Maya Highlands*. University of Utah Press, Salt Lake City.

DeMarrais, Elizabeth, Luis Jaime Castillo, and Timothy Earle

1996 Ideology, Materialization, and Power Strategies. *Current Anthropology* 37(1):15–31.

Dunning, Nicholas P.
1992 *Lords of the Hills: Ancient Maya Settlement in the Puuc Region, Yucatán, Mexico.* Monographs in New World Archaeology 15. Prehistory Press, Madison.
1996 A Reexamination of Regional Variability in the Pre-Hispanic Agricultural Landscape. In *The Managed Mosaic: Ancient Maya Agricultural and Resource Use*, edited by Scott L. Fedick, pp. 53–68. University of Utah Press, Salt Lake City.

Dunning, Nicholas, Timothy Beach, and David Rue
1997 The Paleoecology and Ancient Settlement of the Petexbatun Region, Guatemala. *Ancient Mesoamerica* 8(2):255–266.

Earle, Timothy
1997 *How Chiefs Come to Power: The Political Economy in Prehistory.* Stanford University Press, Stanford.

Eaton, Jack D.
1975 Ancient Agricultural Farmsteads in the Río Bec Region of Yucatán. *Contributions of the University of California Archaeological Research Facility* 27: 56–82. University of California, Berkeley.

Fedick, Scott L.
1989 The Economics of Agricultural Land Use and Settlement in the Upper Belize Valley. In *Prehistoric Maya Economies of Belize*, edited by Patricia A. McAnany and Barry L. Isaac, pp. 215–253. Research in Economic Anthropology Supplement 4. JAI Press, Greenwich.

Fedick, Scott L. (editor)
1996 *The Managed Mosaic: Ancient Maya Agriculture and Resource Use.* University of Utah Press, Salt Lake City.

Flannery, Kent V. (editor)
1982 *Maya Subsistence: Studies in Memory of Dennis E. Puleston.* Academic Press, New York.

Folan, William J., Lorraine A. Fletcher, and Ellen R. Kintz
1979 Fruit, Fiber, Bark, and Resin: Social Organization of a Maya Urban Center. *Science* 204(4394):697–701.

Gossen, Gary H. (editor)
1986 *Symbol and Meaning beyond the Closed Community: Essays in Mesoamerican Ideas.* Institute for Mesoamerican Studies, State University of New York, Albany.

Graham, Elizabeth Ann
1987 Resource Diversity in Belize and Its Implications for Models of Lowland Trade. *American Antiquity* 52(4):753–767.

Hamblin, Nancy L.
1984 *Animal Use by the Cozumel Maya.* University of Arizona Press, Tucson.

Hanks, William F.
1990 *Referential Practice: Language and Lived Space among the Maya.* University of Chicago Press, Chicago.

Haviland, William A.
1965 Prehistoric Settlement at Tikal, Guatemala. *Expedition* 7(3):14–23.
1988 Musical Hammocks at Tikal: Problems with Reconstructing Household Composition. In *Household and Community in the Ancient Mesoamerican Past*, edited by Richard R. Wilk and Wendy Ashmore, pp. 121–134. University of New Mexico Press, Albuquerque.

Hayden, Brian, and Aubrey Cannon
1982 The Corporate Group as an Archaeological Unit. *Journal of Anthropological Archaeology* 1(2):132–158.

Healy, Paul F., Kitty Emery, and Lori E. Wright
1990 Ancient and Modern Maya Exploitation of the *Jute* Snail (*Pachychilus*). *Latin American Antiquity* 1(2):170–183.

Hendon, Julia A.
1991 Status and Power in Classic Maya Society: An Archaeological Study. *American Anthropologist* 91:894–918.
1996 Archaeological Approaches to the Organization of Domestic Labor: Household Practice and Domestic Relations. *Annual Review of Anthropology* 25:45–61.
1997 Women's Work, Women's Space, and Women's Status among the Classic-Period Maya Elite of the Copán Valley. In *Women in Prehistory: North America and Mesoamerica*, edited by Cheryl Claassen and Rosemary A. Joyce, pp. 33–46.

Hill, Robert M., II, and John Monaghan
1987 *Continuities in Highland Maya Social Organization: Ethnohistory in Sacapulas, Guatemala.* University of Pennsylvania Press, Philadelphia.

Hirth, Kenneth G.
1993 Identifying Rank and Socioeconomic Status in Domestic Contexts: An Example from Central Mexico. In *Prehispanic Domestic Units in Western Mesoamerica*, edited by Robert S. Santley and Kenneth G. Hirth, pp. 121–146. CRC Press, Boca Raton.

Inomata, Takeshi, and Laura R. Stiver
1999 Floor Assemblages from Burned Structures at Aguateca, Guatemala: A Study of Classic Maya Households. *Journal of Field Archaeology* 25(4):432–452.

Johnston, Kevin J., and Nancy Gonlin
1998 What Do Houses Mean? Approaches to the Analysis of Classic Maya Commoner Residences. In *Function and Meaning in Classic Maya Architecture*, edited by Stephen Houston, pp. 141–185. Dumbarton Oaks, Washington, D.C.

Joyce, Rosemary A.
1994 Review of *Mesoamerican Elites: An Archaeological Assessment. Latin American Antiquity* 5(2):182–183.
1999 Social Dimensions of Pre-Classic Burials. In *Social Patterns in Pre-Classic Mesoamerica*, edited by David C. Grove and Rosemary A. Joyce, pp. 15–47. Dumbarton Oaks, Washington, D.C.

Killion, Thomas W., Jeremy A. Sabloff, Gair Tourtellot, and Nicholas P. Dunning
1989 Intensive Surface Collection of Residential Clusters at Terminal Classic Sayil, Yucatán, Mexico. *Journal of Field Archaeology* 16(2):273–294.

Kurjack, Edward B.
1974 *Prehistoric Lowland Maya Community and Social Organization: A Case Study at Dzibilchaltun, Yucatán, Mexico.* Middle American Research Institution Publication 38. Tulane University, New Orleans.

Lentz, David L.
1991 Maya Diets of the Rich and Poor: Paleoethnobotanical Evidence from Copán. *Latin American Antiquity* 2(3):269–287.

Lentz, David L. (editor)
2000 *Imperfect Balance: Landscape Transformations in the Precolumbian Americas.* Columbia University Press, New York.

Lohse, Jon C.
2000 Ancient Maya House-lots as Landscapes at Dos Hombres, Belize. Paper presented at the 99th Annual Meeting of the American Anthropological Association, San Francisco.

Manzanilla, Linda (editor)
1987 *Cobá, Quintana Roo: Análisis de dos unidades habitacionales mayas del horizonte Clásico.* Instituto de Investigaciones Antropológicas, Universidad Nacional Autónoma de México, Mexico City.

Manzanilla, Linda, and Luis Barba
1990 The Study of Activities in Classic Households: Two Case Studies from Coba and Teotihuacan. *Ancient Mesoamerica* 1(1):41–49.

Marcus, Joyce
1983 Lowland Maya Archaeology at the Crossroads. *American Antiquity* 48(3):454–488.
1992 Royal Families, Royal Texts: Examples from the Zapotec and Maya. In *Mesoamerican Elites: An Archaeological Assessment,* edited by Diane Z. Chase and Arlen F. Chase, pp. 221–241. University of Oklahoma Press, Norman.

Marx, Karl
1971 Peasantry as a Class. In *Peasants and Peasant Societies,* edited by Teodor Shanin, pp. 229–237. Penguin Books, Harmondsworth.

Mathews, Jennifer P., and James F. Garber
2004 Models of Cosmic Order: Physical Expression of Sacred Space among the Ancient Maya. *Ancient Mesoamerica* 15:49–59.

McAnany, Patricia A.
1995 *Living with the Ancestors: Kinship and Kingship in Ancient Maya Society.* University of Texas Press, Austin.

Michels, Joseph W. (editor)
1979 *Settlement Pattern Excavations at Kaminaljuyu, Guatemala.* Pennsylvania State University Press, University Park.

Miksicek, Charles H.
1991 The Ecology of Cuello: The Natural and Cultural Landscape of

Preclassic Cuello. In *Cuello: An Early Maya Community in Belize*, edited by Norman Hammond, pp. 70–84. Cambridge University Press, Cambridge.

Netting, Robert McC., Richard R. Wilk, and Eric J. Arnould
1984 Introduction. In *Households: Comparative and Historical Studies of the Domestic Group*, edited by Robert McC. Netting, Richard R. Wilk, and Eric J. Arnould, pp. xiii–xxxviii. University of California Press, Berkeley.

Palka, Joel W.
1997 Reconstructing Classic Maya Socioeconomic Differentiation and the Collapse at Dos Pilas, Petén, Guatemala. *Ancient Mesoamerica* 8(2):293–306.

Peoples, James, and Garrick Bailey
1997 *Humanity, An Introduction to Cultural Anthropology.* West/Wadsworth, New York.

Phillips, Phillip, James A. Ford, and James B. Griffin
1951 *Archaeological Survey in the Lower Mississippi Alluvial Valley, 1940–1947.* Papers of the Peabody Museum of Archaeology and Ethnology 25. Harvard University, Cambridge.

Pohl, Mary D. (editor)
1985 *Prehistoric Lowland Maya Environment and Subsistence Economy.* Papers of the Peabody Museum of Archaeology and Ethnology 77. Harvard University, Cambridge.

Powis, Terry G., Norbert Stanchly, Christine D. White, Paul F. Healy, Jaime J. Awe, and Fred Longstaff
1999 A Reconstruction of Middle Preclassic Maya Subsistence Economy at Cahal Pech, Belize. *Antiquity* 73(280):364–376.

Puleston, Dennis E.
1973 Ancient Maya Settlement Patterns and Environment at Tikal, Guatemala: Implications for Subsistence Models. Ph.D. diss., Department of Anthropology, University of Pennsylvania, Philadelphia.

Robin, Cynthia
1999 Towards an Archaeology of Everyday Life: Maya Farmers of Chan Nòohol and Dos Chombitos Cik'in, Belize. Ph.D. diss., Department of Anthropology, University of Pennsylvania.
2002 Outside of Houses: The Practices of Everyday Life at Chan Nòohol, Belize. *Journal of Social Archaeology* 2(2):245–268.

Roys, Ralph L.
1943 *The Indian Background of Colonial Yucatan.* Carnegie Institution of Washington Publication 548. Carnegie Institution, Washington, D.C.

Sanders, William T.
1955 An Archaeological Reconnaissance of Northern Quintana Roo. *Current Reports* 2, no. 24. Carnegie Institution, Washington, D.C.

Sharer, Robert J.
1993 The Social Organization of the Late Classic Maya: Problems of Defini-

tion and Approaches. In *Lowland Maya Civilization in the Eighth Century A.D.: A Symposium at Dumbarton Oaks*, edited by Jeremy A. Sabloff and John S. Henderson, pp. 91–109. Dumbarton Oaks, Washington, D.C.

Shaw, Leslie C.

1991 The Articulation of Social Inequality and Faunal Resource Use in the Preclassic Community of Colha, Northern Belize. Ph.D. diss., Department of Anthropology, University of Massachusetts at Amherst.

Sheets, Payson D., Harriet F. Beaubien, Marilyn Beaudry, Andrea Gerstle, Brain McKee, C. Dan Miller, Hartmut Spetzler, and David B. Tucker

1990 Household Archaeology at Cerén, El Salvador. *Ancient Mesoamerica* 1(1):81–90.

Smith, A. Ledyard

1962 Residential and Associated Structures at Mayapan. In *Mayapan, Yucatan, Mexico*, by Harry E. D. Pollock, Ralph L. Roys, Tatiana Proskouriakoff, and A. Ledyard Smith. Carnegie Institution of Washington Publication 619. Carnegie Institution, Washington, D.C.

1972 *Excavations at Altar de Sacrificios: Architecture, Settlement, Burials, and Caches*. Papers of the Peabody Museum of Archaeology and Ethnology, vol. 62, no. 2. Harvard University, Cambridge.

Smith, Michael E.

1987 Household Possessions and Wealth in Agrarian States: Implications for Archaeology. *Journal of Anthropological Archaeology* 6(4):297–335.

Stark, Barbara L., and Barbara Ann Hall

1993 Hierarchical Social Differentiation among Late to Terminal Classic Residential Locations in La Mixtequilla, Veracruz, Mexico. In *Prehispanic Domestic Units in Western Mesoamerica*, edited by Robert S. Santley and Kenneth G. Hirth, pp. 249–273. CRC Press, Boca Raton.

Steward, Julian H.

1949 Cultural Causality and Law: A Trial Formulation on the Development of Early Civilizations. *American Anthropologist* 51(1):1–27.

1955 *Theory of Culture Change: The Methodology of Multilinear Evolution*. University of Illinois Press, Urbana.

Sweely, Tracy L.

1999 Gender, Space, People, and Power at Cerén, El Salvador. In *Manifesting Power: Gender and the Interpretation of Power in Archaeology*, edited by Tracy L. Sweely, pp. 155–171. Routledge Press, New York.

Tax, Sol

1937 The *Municipios* of the Midwestern Highlands of Guatemala. *American Anthropologist* 39:423–444.

Thompson, Edward E.

1892 The Ancient Structures of Yucatan not Communal Dwellings. *Proceedings of the American Antiquarian Society* 8:262–269.

Tourtellot, Gair, III

1988a *Excavations at Seibal, Department of Peten, Guatemala: Peripheral Surveys and Excavation, Settlement and Community Patterns.* Memoirs of the Peabody Museum of Archaeology and Ethnology 16. Harvard University, Cambridge.

1988b Developmental Cycles of Households and Houses at Seibal. In *Household and Community in the Mesoamerican Past*, edited by Richard R. Wilk and Wendy Ashmore, pp. 97–120. University of New Mexico Press, Albuquerque.

Trachman, Rissa

2003 "Archaeology of Everyday Life: Social Reproduction among Three Households in the Dos Hombres Settlement of Northwestern Belize." Ph.D. diss. prospectus, Department of Anthropology, University of Texas at Austin.

Trigger, Bruce G.

1967 Settlement Archaeology—Its Goals and Promise. *American Antiquity* 32(2):149–160.

Tringham, Ruth E.

1991 Households with Faces: the Challenge of Gender in Prehistoric Architectural Remains. In *Engendering Prehistory: Women and Prehistory*, edited by Joan M. Gero and Margaret W. Conkley, pp. 93–131. Basil Blackwell, Oxford.

Turner, B. L. II

1974 Prehistoric Intensive Agriculture in the Mayan Lowlands. *Science* 185:118–124.

Vogt, Evon Z.

1961 Some Aspects of Zinacantan Settlement Patterns and Ceremonial Organization. *Estudios de Cultural Maya* 1:131–145.

1969 *Zinacantan: A Maya Community in the Highlands of Chiapas.* Belknap Press of Harvard University Press, Cambridge.

1976 *Tortillas for the Gods: A Symbolic Analysis of Zinacanteco Rituals.* University of Oklahoma Press, Norman.

Wauchope, Robert

1934 *House Mounds of Uaxactun, Guatemala.* Carnegie Institution of Washington Publication 436. Contributions to American Archaeology, vol. 2, no. 7:107–171. Washington, D.C.

1940 Domestic Architecture of the Maya. In *The Maya and Their Neighbors*, pp. 232–241. D. Appleton-Century Company, New York.

Webster, David, Barbara Fash, Randolph Widmer, and Scott Zelenik

1998 The Skyband Group: Investigation of a Classic Maya Elite Residential Complex at Copán, Honduras. *Journal of Field Archaeology* 25:319–343.

Webster, David, and Nancy Gonlin

1988 Household Remains of the Humblest Maya. *Journal of Field Archaeology* 15(2):169–190.

Webster, David, Nancy Gonlin, and Payson Sheets

1997 Copan and Cerén: Two Perspectives on Ancient Mesoamerican Households. *Ancient Mesoamerica* 8(1):43–61.

Wilk, Richard R.

1983 Little House in the Jungle: The Causes of Variation in House Size among Modern Maya. *Journal of Anthropological Archaeology* 2(2):99–116.

1988 Maya Household Organization: Evidence and Analogies. In *Household and Community in the Mesoamerican Past*, edited by Richard R. Wilk and Wendy Ashmore, pp. 135–151. University of New Mexico Press, Albuquerque.

1989 Decision Making and the Resource Flows within the Household: Beyond the Black Box. In *The Household Economy: Reconsidering the Domestic Mode of Production*, edited by Richard R. Wilk, pp. 23–52. Westview Press, Boulder.

Wilk, Richard R., and William L. Rathje

1982 Household Archaeology. *American Behavioral Scientist* 25(6):617–639.

Wilken, Gene C.

1971 Food-Producing Systems Available to the Ancient Maya. *American Antiquity* 36(4):432–448.

Willey, Gordon R.

1953 *Prehistoric Settlement Patterns in the Viru Valley, Peru.* Bureau of American Ethnology, Smithsonian Institution Bulletin 155. Washington, D.C.

1978 Pre-Hispanic Maya Agriculture: A Contemporary Summation. In *Pre-Hispanic Maya Agriculture*, edited by Peter D. Harrison and B. L. Turner II, pp. 325–335. University of New Mexico Press, Albuquerque.

Willey, Gordon R. (editor)

1956 *Prehistoric Settlement Patterns in the New World.* Viking Fund Publications in Anthropology 23. Wenner-Gren Foundation for Anthropological Research, New York.

Willey, Gordon R., William R. Bullard, Jr., John B. Glass, and James C. Gifford

1965 *Prehistoric Maya Settlements in the Belize Valley.* Papers of the Peabody Museum of Archaeology and Ethnology 54. Harvard University, Cambridge.

Wing, Elizabeth S., and Sylvia J. Scudder

1991 The Ecology and Economy of Cuello: The Exploitation of Animals. In *Cuello: An Early Maya Community in Belize*, edited by Norman Hammond, pp. 84–97. Cambridge University Press, Cambridge.

Wisdom, Charles

1940 *The Chorti Indians of Guatemala.* University of Chicago Press, Chicago.

Wolf, Eric R.

1982 *Europe and the People without History.* University of California Press, Berkeley.

Yaeger, Jason, and Marcello A. Canuto

2000 Introducing an Archaeology of Communities. In *The Archaeology of Communities: A New World Perspective*, edited by Marcello A. Canuto and Jason Yaeger, pp. 1–15. Routledge Press, London.

CHAPTER 2

Daily Life in a Highland Maya Community: Zinacantan in Mid-Twentieth Century

EVON Z. VOGT

This chapter purposely focuses on Zinacanteco culture in the 1950s, when I first engaged in field research in the highlands of Chiapas in southeastern Mexico (Vogt 1994). The reason: it is being published in a volume on the culture of Maya commoners in pre-Columbian times, and I decided that the earliest systematic description I could provide of Zinacantan would be closest to the daily life of those ancient Maya commoners studied by the archaeologists. Now, a half century later, these Zinacantecos drive automobiles; keep their accounts with calculators; possess and utilize computers, TV sets, and cell phones; and engage in a variety of economic enterprises that are a far cry from the subsistence maize farming I observed in the 1950s.

Daily life for a Zinacanteco family ordinarily begins an hour or two before dawn when the father awakens and goes outside to urinate. He takes a reading on the predawn constellations rising in the east and judges when it is time to awaken the women of the household. This traditional time reckoning is amazingly accurate. A Zinacanteco who later possessed a watch and who was interviewed in mid-July reported that Shonob (Pleiades) rises at 4 A.M. and Osh-lot (Orion's Belt) rises at 5 A.M. (Vogt 1997). It is time to awaken the women because it will take them at least an hour to gently blow the smoldering embers into a fire burning on the floor-hearth inside the square thatched-roof house; give the maize kernels (which have been soaking in lime water on the fire during the night) a grinding on the mano and metate and bake the tortillas on the clay *comal* (round griddle) resting on three hearthstones in the fire (Figure 2.1); warm up the beans; boil the coffee; and have breakfast ready to serve the men just at sunrise, which comes quickly after a very short dawn at this tropical latitude of sixteen degrees north.

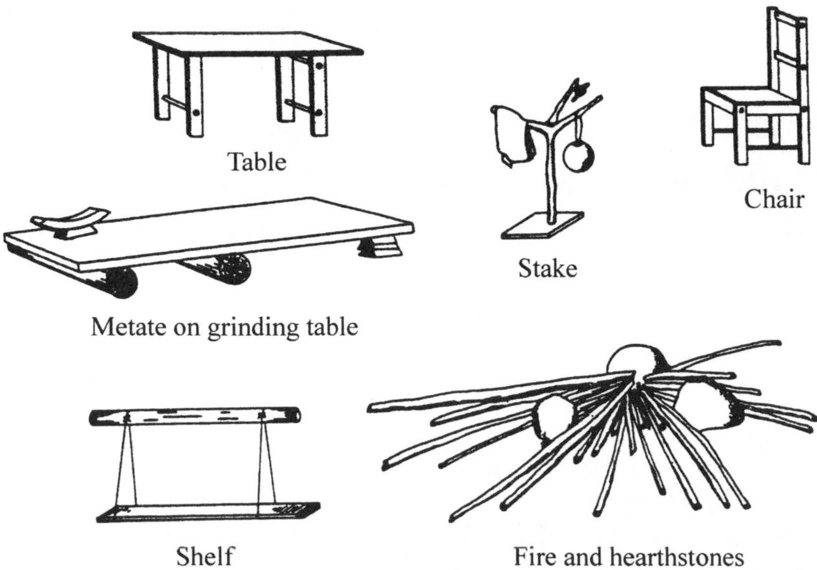

Figure 2.1. Zinacanteco domestic furniture

Having watered and changed the grazing location of the horses or mules, which are carefully staked with a long rope to prevent their breaking into nearby fields of maize, the men are now seated on small wooden chairs or stools on the eastern side of the fire (the men's domain toward the rising sun), wearing their woolen *chamarras* (ponchos) and warming themselves. Zinacantan is located in the highlands of Chiapas at an elevation of 7,000 feet, and it is always cold in the early morning.

The women (including the mother, her unmarried daughters, and perhaps a recently married daughter-in-law or two) are kneeling on *petates* (reed mats) around the west side of the fire (the women's domain toward the setting sun), forming the tortillas from the ground maize dough by slapping them back and forth between their hands (an unmistakable percussive sound in traditional Mexican communities) and then placing them on the *comal*, turning them, and removing them when cooked. There is usually a division of labor, with one or more of the women grinding while others pat the tortillas and place them on the *comal*. The tortillas are kept warm in a gourd container by the fire that is covered with a handwoven cotton cloth.

The men (including the father, his unmarried sons, and perhaps a newly married son or two) are served first, accompanied by some eating rituals that constitute good etiquette in a Zinacanteco home. First comes a ceramic bowl of warm water with which to wash their hands; then a bowl to rinse their mouths. Next a bowl of beans is placed on the earthen floor before each man in rank order (i.e., the eldest man first, then next eldest, etc.) as the woman politely asks "*Mi chave' chenek'?*" ("Will you eat beans?"). Next comes the gourd of warm tortillas with "*Mi chave' vah?*" ("Will you eat maize tortillas?"). Finally, a cup of sweetened coffee is presented with "*Mi chavuch' kahve?*" ("Will you drink coffee?"). In each case, the man will politely respond, "I will eat beans, thank you," and so forth. A tiny dish of salt is always set down after the food, and each man sprinkles a bit on his beans before he takes a bite. While tortillas and beans are the most common foods served, sometimes mushrooms or greens or even eggs cooked on the *comal* are dished up.

When the men have finished, they hand each container back to the women, who finish any bits of food the men may have left. The women nibble as they cook and finish their informal "meals" after the men have left, for they, in contrast to the men, tend to see food as a continuous stream of tidbits throughout the day. The younger children in the household often sleep through the morning meal, but if they awaken, the women put a small bowl of beans and some tortillas before older children (ages five to ten) and wrap beans in a tortilla for younger ones to eat. The children usually sit on the floor between the women's and men's side of the fire.

Shortly after sunrise, the men of the household set out on foot for the market in San Cristóbal de las Casas or for their maize fields. A trip to the market, which is two to three hours away, to sell corn and purchase items from hardware stores—such as nails for houses or sheep corrals, or copal incense, candles, and cane liquor for an impending ceremony—is begun promptly after breakfast. The men are usually accompanied by one or more women of the family, who help to carry the bags of corn and assist with the shopping. The group walks single file along the mountain trails or on the edge of the Pan-American Highway—men in front, women and children behind. The men wear sandals, but the women and children walk barefoot.

Meanwhile, there are many tasks for the women left at home. Water must be carried from the waterhole or spring belonging to their waterhole group. Using tumplines attached to special ceramic jugs with two handles on the sides, two or more young women will make the trip to the waterhole, carrying laundry to be done at the same time. The clothes are washed by rubbing them with stones or slapping them against a flat stone by a waterhole designated for the laundry. Many waterholes have three openings: one for household water, one for laundry, and one for watering the livestock. At the waterhole, women often wash their hair and their legs, as well as doing the laundry. At home, the clothes are spread over bushes and rocks to dry in the sun.

One or more of the women may also tend to the garden plot in the patio outside the house where they grow herbs and where the chickens and turkeys forage. One of the women is designated as the sheepherder for the day. She takes the family herd out to graze and takes her portable backstrap loom along to attach to a tree and weave some item of clothing while keeping close watch on the sheep to prevent them from breaking into a cornfield and eating the neighbors' maize.

Another group of women go with their machetes into the nearby hills or mountains to cut and bring home firewood carried in heavy loads on tumplines. The long sticks of wood, which have been cut from green or recently felled trees, are placed upright against the house to dry underneath the wide eaves of the thatched roof. As the sticks are needed for the fire in the hearth, they are brought into the house and their ends placed in the fire, then pushed farther into the hearth as they burn. Also stored under the eaves are the pots of various types that are not needed on a daily basis, such as the enormous cooking pots used for preparing food for weddings or for *cargo* (ritual position) ceremonies.

In all these tasks the younger boys and the girls are an additional labor supply. For example, a girl of eight to ten will often be given the duty of carrying an infant in a shawl while the mother engages in other tasks.

The men who leave in the morning for the fields must carry food with them. If the fields are close by, they carry only some maize dough, which will be mixed with water in a gourd to provide a corn gruel for nourishment at midday. Since the men do not know how to make tortillas, the trips to distant fields in the lowlands always involve carrying fresh tortillas, maize dough, and sacks of toasted tortillas (toasted by the women beside the open fire), which are carried with a tumpline and last for several days before they begin to mold. The men do know how to boil beans in ceramic pots to eat with the tortillas.

The men also carry the metal heads of their hoes to fit into wooden handles they have hidden beside their fields. These work parties, consisting of the men in the extended family, including sons as young as ten years of age, typically remain in the lowlands for a week or more, eating and sleeping next to their fields in small thatched shelters. Older sons are often dispatched to carry back more toasted tortillas.

All of the farming operations—cutting and burning; planting with planting sticks; weeding the maize, beans, and squash fields during the summer; doubling over the maize when ripe (to hasten the formation of hard kernels and keep out the late summer and early autumn rains); husking and shelling the corn; and carrying the heavy sacks of maize and beans home to be stored in their granaries—are highly patterned in ways that make the process maximally efficient from start to finish (for details, see Vogt 1969:35–65; also Cancian 1972; Collier 1975). I have always been impressed with many of these procedures. For example, to burn the brush in the spring and ensure that the fire does not get out of control, a firebreak is made around a maize field, and if the field is on a slope, the fire is set at the top of the field, rather than on the bottom, to keep the fire from roaring up the slope and jumping the firebreak. The seed corn for planting (six kernels to a hole made with a planting stick) is carried in an armadillo shell. Weeding is always done (twice a summer) by hoeing up the slope, which places less pressure on the back than moving across the slope or downhill. The husking is done with the ear still on the stalk; the husking instrument, made from deer bone and carried tied by a string to the farmer's belt, is used to open the husk from bottom to top; then the husk is peeled back and the ear is twisted off and tossed into a pile. The shelling of the corn is done beside the field so that only the kernels of corn make up the load carried on human backs with tumplines (or sometimes on horses and mules) to the granaries in the home villages. These granaries are separate buildings or, in the case of poorer families, the maize may be stored in bins in the corner of their houses. A small wooden cross, surrounded by several unhusked "father" and "mother" ears of maize (Vogt 1969:57), is always erected on top of the corn to keep an evil spirit from entering the bin and eating the maize. Ears of seed corn are hung from the rafters of the house.

The family compounds are surrounded by fences, and besides the houses, there is usually a sweat house in a corner of the compound as well as a granary for storing the corn. The sheep corral is located outside the compound, and it is periodically moved to provide fertilizer for the soil in the small fields cultivated nearby (Figure 2.2).

By midafternoon at the family compound, the men and women who traveled to the market return with their purchases, and the men working in nearby fields also come home. Before sunset, the herders bring the sheep back to the small corrals built of upright poles near the house compound. Shortly thereafter the chickens and turkeys roost in a nearby tree. By dark, the evening meal of beans and tortillas is served by the hearth.

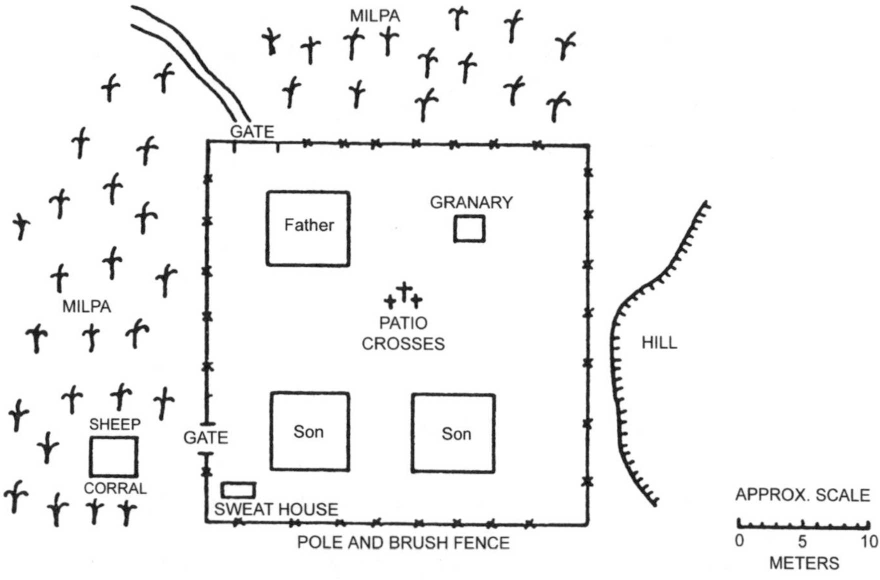

Figure 2.2. A Zinacanteco house compound

After sharing their experiences of the day by the fire and relating a story or two about the ancestors, the Zinacantecos go to sleep either on reed mats on wooden platform beds or on mats on the earthen floor and covered with blankets. During the night, if a member of a family has a dream, he or she will awaken the rest of the family and relate the dream, which is discussed and commented upon, paying attention to information that may foretell the future or provide a solution to a family problem. Then they all go back to sleep during the long night (for details, see Laughlin 1976).

Ritual Ceremonies

If ethnographers observe groups of Zinacantecos up and around during the night, they can be certain that a ceremony is in progress. These ceremonies, such as for a curing or the dedication of a new house, permeate Zinacanteco life and often add different routines to their daily life.

The ceremonies always involve one or more ritual meals, for which the setting and etiquette are much more formal than those of an everyday meal. The members of the domestic group (ordinarily a patrilineally extended family including the sons and their wives and children living in adjacent houses within the compound) are always invited.

A ritual meal is always served on a rectangular table oriented along the daily path of the sun and covered by a red-and-white cotton cloth (Figure 2.3). At the center of the rising sun end of the table are placed a bottle of sugarcane liquor (called *posh* in Tzotzil), a shot glass, and a bowl of salt. It is here at the head of the table that the *tot'il-me'iletik* (fathers-mothers), the ancestral gods of the patrilineage, are believed to be seated. These ancestors inhabit hills or mountains above the lands on which their descendants live, but they come to participate in the ceremony.

The ancestral deities are responsible for installing an inner soul in the embryo of every unborn Zinacanteco child. Interaction between the living Zinacantecos and the ancestors takes place via these inner souls located in the hearts and bloodstreams of persons. The Zinacanteco soul is composed of thirteen parts, and a person who loses one or more parts must have a curing ceremony to recover them. But the inner soul, though temporarily divisible into parts, has some special attributes and is believed to be indestructible and eternal. At death, this soul leaves the body and joins a pool of inner souls kept by the ancestors. It is later utilized for another person, often a grandchild, but while the person is alive, the inner soul as a unit can leave the body during sleep and go visiting with the inner souls of other Zinacantecos or the deities. It can drop out of the body temporarily in periods of intense excitement, such as the point of orgasm in sexual intercourse. During life, soul loss can also occur from falling down (mothers are very concerned about their children falling) or because of bad behavior, such as fighting with kinsmen or mistreating maize, which is punished by the ancestors causing the person to fall down or, more dramatically, sending a lightning bolt to knock out several parts of the soul.

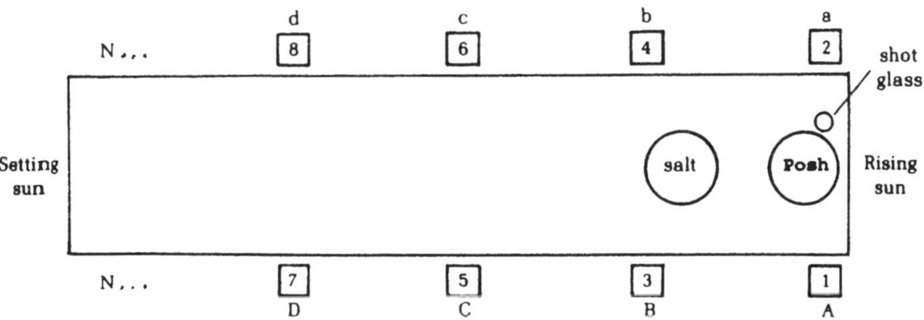

Figure 2.3. The rank order of participants in a ritual meal

Soul loss can also occur when an evil person performs a witchcraft ritual in a cave to "sell" the inner soul to the Earth Lord, who then uses the person as a servant.

At the same time the ancestors install the inner soul in the human embryo, it is also installed in the embryo of a wild animal, such as a jaguar, ocelot, coyote, or smaller animal, like a squirrel. These animal spirit companions are kept in four corrals inside the "Senior Large Mountain," a large volcano rising majestically to over 9,000 feet east of Zinacantan Center. Throughout life, the inner soul of a person is shared with the animal companion; anything that happens to the person happens to the animal and vice versa. When the ancestors are really provoked with the behavior of a living person, they will let his/her animal spirit companion out of the corral to wander alone in the woods. The life of the living person is then in genuine peril, and an elaborate curing ceremony must take place promptly to round up the animal companion and place it back in its corral.

During a ritual meal, the living participants are seated on small chairs in a strict rank order. The highest-ranking person sits at the southeast corner, and the next-highest-ranking person sits opposite him or her at the northeast corner. The ranking pattern proceeds in symmetrical pairs down the length of the table (A,a, B,b . . .), simultaneously expressing two basic principles of the culture: the primacy of the rising sun and the primacy of the right over the left hand (see Figure 2.3).

In many ceremonies, especially the public rites for *cargo* holders, the participants are all male. The women remain in the cooking area by the hearth. However, in domestic ceremonies, some of the participants are women, who take their places in appropriate rank order at the table while the rest of the women remain by the hearth.

The meal includes sugarcane liquor, maize tortillas, chicken cooked in a broth with chile, salt, and epazote (Mexican tea, *Chenopodium ambrosioides*), coffee, and small round wheat-flour rolls made by Ladinos. The senior man signals the young man designated as the drink pourer to serve the first round of liquor from the bottle at the head of the table. (Here the participants are symbolically drinking with the ancestors, and the liquor is believed to open the circuits of communication with these supernaturals.) The senior man prays over the shot of liquor before he drinks it:

Well, then, I drink first Father,
Drink first Mother,
Thank you a little.
In the divine name of God, Jesus Christ, my Lord,

Take this, then Father,
Take this, then Lord.
There is still a little left,
There is still a drop left.
Of this dew of your holy mouth,
Of this dew of your holy lips,
I will share with you,
I will stand in your shadows [under your cover . . .].

Today, the supernaturals are called by loan words from Spanish, and the syncretism of Maya with Catholic symbols is evident; but when interviewed, the Zinacantecos described these ancestors as elderly Zinacanteco men and women.

A shot glass of liquor is then served to each in rank order and is accompanied by bowing-and-releasing behavior in which a junior person (in age) bows and says "*Kich'ban*" ("I drink") plus an appropriate term of respect, such as "Totik" or "Me'tik" (derived from the terms for "father" or "mother," but best translated as "Sir" or "Madam"), to a senior person and is released with the back of the right hand of the senior person, who says "*Ich'o*" ("Drink then") as the junior person downs the strong liquor in one gulp.

One of the young men designated as the server places a gourd of warm water in the center of the table. Beginning with the senior man, who says "Let's wash our hands," all wash their hands. Next comes the gourd of warm water for rinsing the mouth, which all do in rank order after the senior man initiates with "Come, let's rinse our mouths."

The server places a bowl of chicken parts in broth before each participant, always in rank order. A stack of tortillas is placed in the center of the table. Saying "Please take your salt," the senior man leads the eating sequence by putting a pinch of salt into his bowl of chicken; the others do the same. (While the liquor opens the circuits to the supernaturals, the salt serves as an "insulator," protecting living Zinacantecos from too much exposure to the gods' supernatural heat.) Taking a tortilla in his right hand, the senior man says "Come, fall to!", shifts the tortilla to his left hand, tears off a small piece with his right, dips it in the broth, and eats it. The others follow as the senior man signals "Drink the broth, please," picks up his bowl with his right hand, and drinks the broth.

"Please take the chicken to make the tortillas taste better" signals the eating of the chicken itself, each person following the lead of the senior man, who takes a piece of chicken in his right hand, places it in the tortilla, and eats it a small bite at a time. The bowls and gourds are then returned to the women by the server. All of the chicken must either be eaten or wrapped in a tortilla to be taken home. A second round of liquor is served, followed by a cup of coffee topped by a wheat-flour roll across the rim of the cup. The tablecloth is then removed and the hand washing and mouth rinsing are repeated. The third round of liquor follows. The bottle, now empty if the drink pourer has been careful with his measurements, is returned to the host's collection of empty bottles in the corner of the house. This marks the formal end of the meal, and the table is removed.

These patterned sequences of behavior apply to ritual meals at all levels of the social system. For small domestic ceremonies, a very small table is used for four or five people. For the ceremonies for patrilineages or waterhole groups, larger tables are used, seating in rank order the senior members, followed by the shamans and ritual assistants. The maximum is reached in Zinacantan Center at the Fiesta of San Sebastián, the major winter ceremony occurring in late January, when the entire religious hierarchy of *cargo* holders plus the Presidente and his assistants sit down in shifts at an enormous table and are served a whole chicken per person.

New House Dedication Ceremonies

In the 1950s, Zinacantecos reported that a generation or two before, most people lived in what were called *vakash na* (from Spanish *vaca* and Tzotzil *na*, meaning "cow houses"), with gable roofs of gradual pitch, walls of split logs or sometimes of flat planks, and a back wall often rounded. The roof was of thatch. The shape resembled the fireworks-spouting reed-mat frameworks carried by men in fiestas to impersonate bulls—hence the name of these older houses.

Most of the Zinacanteco houses in the 1950s were square structures constructed of wattle-and-daub walls and steep roofs thatched with grass, *Muhlenbergia macroura*, which is called *hobel* (a term also used for all grasses). Grasses formerly grew abundantly in the valley of San Cristóbal, which is appropriately named Hobel in Tzotzil (Vogt 1969, chapter 4).

Houses are built during the winter dry season by groups of related men in the lineage. The construction is always accompanied by two ceremonies, whose purposes are (1) to compensate the Earth Lord for all the materials (woods, mud, thatch, and so on) from his domain that are needed in the process, and (2) to give the house an "inner soul" and incorporate it into the sacred belief system, making it a living part of Zinacanteco culture.

One ceremony occurs when the walls are completed and the roof rafters are in place. This simple rite does not require a shaman; the workers building the house direct and perform it themselves. They suspend a long rope from the peak of the house and tie four black chickens (one for each corner) to it by their feet. The chicken heads are cut off and buried in the center of the floor. Later the women cook the chickens. Then two men climb up onto the framework of the roof and "feed" the four corners of the joists the chicken broth and cane liquor by pouring both liquids at each of the three levels and the peak of the roof, called *ka'* in Tzotzil (Figure 2.4). The rite culminates with the workers eating the chickens and drinking the cane liquor.

The second ceremony is performed after the completion of the house and requires the services of a shaman. The participants include the house owner and his immediate family as well as his father and brothers and their wives and children. The ritual begins with the planting of the house cross in the patio. It is placed near the center of the compound and most commonly oriented so that prayers to the shrine will be offered in the direction of the rising sun. The shaman continues the ritual inside the house by praying to the table that holds the ritual candles. An assistant hangs a rope from the peak of the house, and one black rooster and several other roosters and hens (the number and sex corresponding to the house owner and the members of his family) are hung by their feet at the end of the rope. All except the large black rooster have their heads cut off, and their blood is drained into a hole in the center of the floor. They are then plucked and cooked for eating. The shaman censes the black rooster, kills it by pulling its neck, and pours a shot of liquor and a handful of earth over him. He then buries the entire bird in the center "grave," with its head toward the rising sun. After a prayer, the shaman leads a counterclockwise procession to each of the four corners, where he plants three pine-tree tops in each corner and decorates them with red geraniums and then places and lights three candles (two white wax, symbolically "tortillas" for the ancestral gods, and one tallow, symbolically "meat" for the Earth Lord) and prays at each corner. Assistants then perform another "feeding" of chicken broth and liquor to the peak and four corners of the roof. After lighting white wax and tallow candles at the center of the house, the shaman bathes all who will live in the house, and they put on freshly washed and censed clothing. Next comes a visit to four holy mountains of the

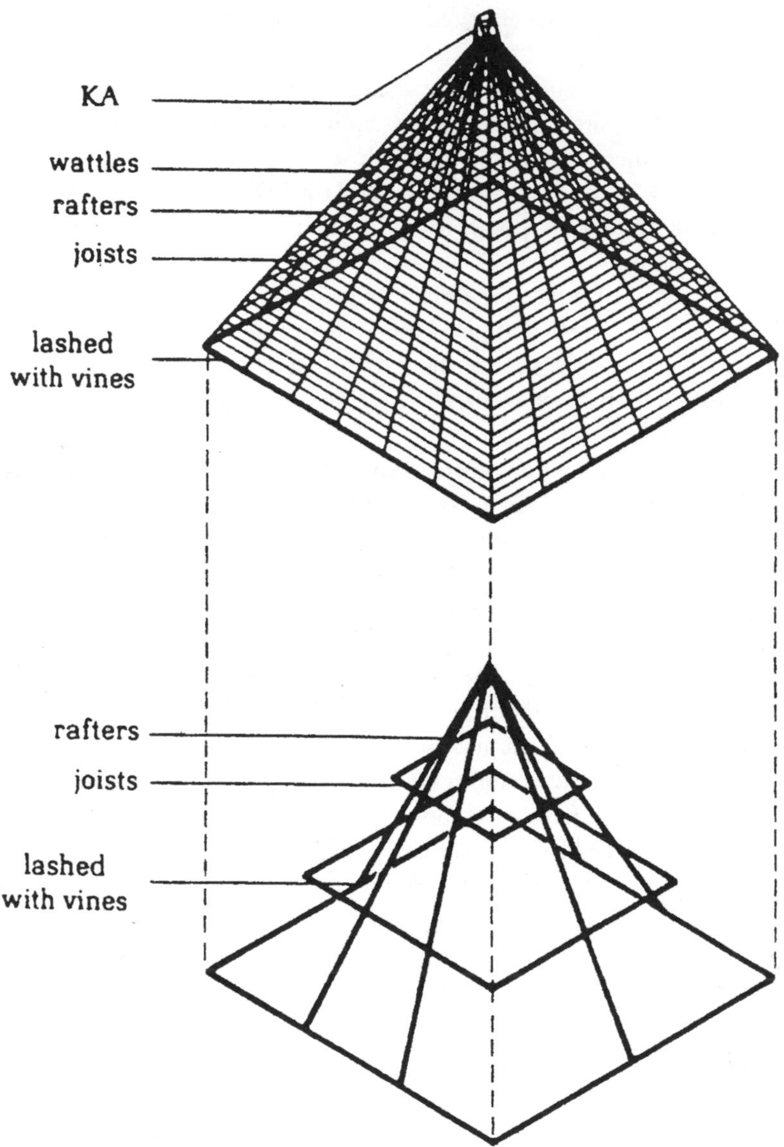

Figure 2.4. Framework for a thatched roof

community, where offerings are made to the ancestral gods. Returning to the house, the men don their black ceremonial robes and hats and dance to the music of violin, harp, and guitar. The formal part of the ceremony ends with a ritual meal. But for the next three days, the home must be carefully tended, for it now possesses an innate soul and requires special care, "just like a sick person" following a curing ceremony or a newborn infant. The members of the family place their hair combings in cracks in the walls, signifying their occupancy and symbolizing their belonging (for more details, see Vogt 1998).

Domestic Group Hierarchy and Related Ceremonies

While Zinacanteco domestic groups are ordinarily composed of extended families living in their separate compounds, over time they go through a developmental cycle (see Goody 1958). An elder son and his family set up an independent household on land near that of his father's house. As the sons bring home wives from other lineages, the couples live at first in the father's house. As they grow older and have more children, each married son will build his own house within the compound. Later in the cycle, all the older sons and their families may live in separate houses, but the youngest son remains in the house of the father and mother, pays the funeral expenses of the parents when they die, and inherits the house. Finally, one or more of the older sons may split off from the domestic group within the compound and establish his own budding extended family.

These domestic groups are embedded in two other crucial social units: the localized lineage and the waterhole group. Although the lineage unit does not have an abstract name in Tzotzil, the Zinacantecos talk about them as being the "houses of," or "*sna* of," a particular lineage. For example, Sna Akovetik refers to the "Houses of the Wasp Nests" and Sna Ok'iletik, the "Houses of the Coyotes," which are two important lineages in one of the waterhole groups in the hamlet of Paste'. These *sna*s live on adjacent lands they have inherited from their ancestors. The composition of the group is made operationally clear by the *k'in krus* performed each May and each October for the ancestral gods and the Earth Lord. *K'in* is a Tzotzil word that means "fiesta" or "ceremony" to the Zinacantecos, but it is derived from an ancient Maya word that means "sun," "day," or "time." It is therefore the "day" or "time" of the "cross" in a ritual that is obviously merged in meaning with the Catholic Day of the Cross. Significantly, it is also related to the beginning of the rainy season in May and the end of the rainy season in October, and may also be related to the zenith transit of the sun, which in Zinacantan occurs on May 5.

Each lineage maintains a series of cross shrines. Some are erected on nearby mountains and serve as channels of communication with the ancestors from whom their lands were inherited. Others are erected in caves and are channels of communication with the Earth Lord. All the shamans who live in the lineage assemble in rank order to perform the lineage ritual.

The lineage ceremony has four basic parts. First, there is a formal meal in the house of the outgoing Senior Mayordomo, who is designated each year to serve as host for the ceremony. The expenses are shared by the Junior Mayordomo and the heads of the various domestic groups in the lineage. Second, a long prayer is recited over the candles and flowers that will be offered by the shamans, who pray in rank order, holding censers with burning copal incense. Third, an all-night ceremonial circuit proceeds counterclockwise around the lands belonging to the lineage, and stops are made at all the cross shrines to make offerings of music, liquor, candles, incense, and prayers to the ancestors and the Earth Lord. The ceremony ends the following morning back at the house of the Senior Mayordomo with a closing ritual meal. This ceremonial circuit is a symbolic expression of the rights the lineage members have to the lands they have inherited from their patrilineal ancestors, and it emphasizes the unity of the lineage as a structurally significant unit of Zinacanteco society (Figure 2.5).

A waterhole group, the next unit of ascending size in Zinacanteco social structure, is composed of a series of lineages that share a common water source. The waterholes are highly sacred, and myths are told about each of them, describing the circumstances under which the ancestors found the water and the way in which the waterhole acquired its distinctive name. For example, in the mythological past, a waterhole known as Vom Ch'en was the domain of an ancestor who was one of the first to live in this area of the hamlet. Some people passed by the waterhole unmolested, but others were stopped by this ancestor. The people started discussing this extraordinary situation and decided to have a meeting and investigate. Two of the men fell into the waterhole as they approached, and the others were afraid to go any closer. Instead, they left to bring back candles, which they then lighted as offerings and began to pray. As they prayed, the waterhole began to bark like a dog—"Vom, Vom"—which is why it is called Vom Ch'en. (When I protested that dogs do not bark like this, but make sounds like

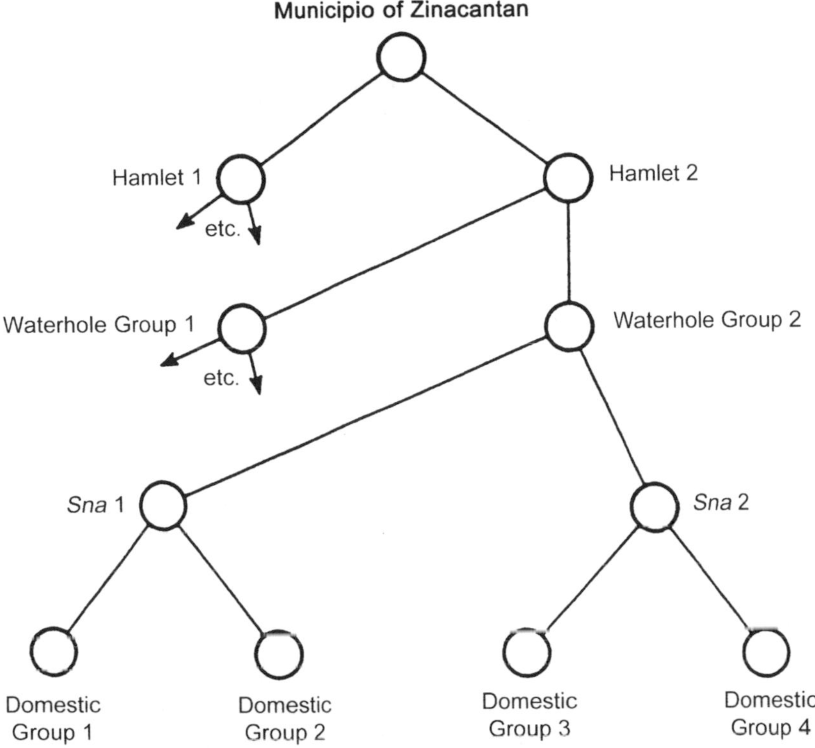

Figure 2.5. Social structural levels in Zinacanteco society

"Bowwow" or "Arf, Arf," my informants laughed and said that any fool knows a dog's bark sounds like "Vom, Vom!")

Each waterhole group maintains a series of cross shrines, one of which is beside the waterhole and another is on a hill above the waterhole and is designated as the meeting place of the ancestors of the whole waterhole group. The *k'in krus* for the waterholes ordinarily precedes by a few days the various rituals for the lineages that compose the waterhole group.

The waterhole ceremony is performed by all the shamans who live in the waterhole group. It follows the same pattern as the ceremonies for the lineages, except that before the initial ritual banquet, the men assemble to clean out the waterhole, repair fences around the openings, and fix up the cross shrines. During the all-night ceremonial circuit, rituals are performed at the waterhole, at the houses of the Mayordomos, and at the meeting place, where the assembled ancestors are waiting for their offerings of incense, candles, and liquor. The ceremony expresses the rights that members of the waterhole group have to draw water from their waterhole and their obligations to care for it properly.

Control of rights to water is crucial for human and animal life in the Chiapas highlands, especially during the long dry season from October to May when supplies of water are strictly limited. By including rituals for the deities associated with the waterhole, the ceremony also links together all the lineages that compose a waterhole group and hence symbolizes the unity of the waterhole group as another structurally significant unit in Zinacanteco society.

In the ascending scale in the social structure, the hamlet is composed of a number of these waterhole groups, and a series of fifteen hamlets and a Ceremonial Center make up the *municipio* of Zinacantan. The *municipio* is governed by a civil hierarchy consisting of a *presidente*, a *síndico*, and four *alcalde jueces*. One of the major duties of this hierarchy, which sits in rank order on a bench each day in front of the town hall, is to resolve quarrels and disputes among Zinacantecos (for details, see Collier 1973).

Curing Ceremonies

When a Zinacanteco falls ill, a shaman is summoned to diagnose the illness and to perform a curing ceremony. The Tzotzil term for "shaman" is *h'ilol*, literally "seer." Zinacantecos believe that in ancient times all people could "see" into the mountains and observe their ancestral gods directly, but that now only shamans can accomplish this miracle. There are at least 150 shamans in Zinacantan; most are men, but some are women, and some are as young as fifteen years of age. Prospective shamans dream of being attacked by a cow or bull that they have to subdue to qualify as a shaman; each then dreams three times that his/her inner soul has been called before the ancestral gods in the Senior Large Mountain. In the first dream, which usually comes at ten or twelve years of age, the inner soul of a supernatural messenger appears and directs the inner soul of the novice to come with him to the house of the Big Alcalde (named after the Big Alcalde who is the highest-ranking official in the *cargo* system) inside the mountain. Upon arrival, the novice is conducted inside the house, where the Big Alcalde is seated at the head of a long table that is flanked by all the shamans of Zinacantan in order of rank. The novice kneels at the west end of the table after bowing to all of those present. The Big Alcalde asks if the novice is prepared to become a shaman. The novice has to say "yes," otherwise he or she will die. Then the novice receives all the types of candles and flowers required for a curing ceremony and is given instructions on how to say the proper prayers and perform the ritual. He/she is given a black ceremonial robe to wear, and he/she kneels again while the Big Alcalde makes the sign of the cross on his/her forehead to swear him/her in. A patient is then brought in, and the novice must diagnose the illness and perform the proper ceremony while the Big Alcalde and all the shamans observe his or her performance.

In the second and third dreams, which usually occur about a year apart, the process is repeated, but the patients that the novice must cure are different. For example, if the patient in the first dream was an old man, it may be a woman in the second dream, a child in the third dream. The novice now possesses the necessary knowledge, and he/she makes his/her public debut as a shaman sometime afterward, typically when he/she him/herself falls ill and knows by this signal that he/she must respond to the "call." To make his/her public debut, the novice visits the highest-ranking shaman in the hamlet in which he/she lives and tells him the dreams and asks permission to reveal him/herself as a shaman. The older shaman prays to all the ancestral gods in the sacred mountains before giving permission. A male novice then goes to the lowlands to cut a bamboo (*Otatea fimbriata*) staff, which he will henceforth always carry in his left hand as a symbol of his office and as protection from the dog that may guard a patient's house. (The staff is buried with him when he dies.) Female shamans carry another species of bamboo (*Olmeca reflexa*) as a staff. Returning home, the shaman tells relatives about his/her new ritual power, and they begin to call upon him/her to perform ceremonies. The novice thus becomes a full-fledged shaman.

All the male shamans in Zinacantan are ranked, not upon age or power, but upon time in service, that is, the number of years elapsed since the shaman made his public debut. Reliable operational measures determine rank. For example, the marching order in ceremonial processions always places the junior person in front and the senior person in the rear. It is worth noting that this marching order is a reversal of that used in secular processions, such as the single-file travel to market or to distant fields, in which the senior person walks in front, the junior person at the rear. The ritual order of processions flows from the Tzotzil Maya concept that sacred processions proceed along the daily path of the sun, from rising sun to setting sun. Since the senior person is conceived as having the most "heat" and the junior person the least "heat," the seniors march at the end of the procession, closest to the rising sun (Gossen 1972).

Shamans diagnose illness by "listening to the blood," which they do by feeling the pulse of the patient at the wrist and the elbow on the right arm, then the left. It is believed that the blood "talks" and furnishes messages that the shaman can understand and interpret. A common ailment is "soul loss" of parts of the inner soul, or sometimes the animal spirit companion has been released from its corral in the Senior Large Mountain. The shaman then prescribes what type of curing ceremony will be necessary to restore the patient to good health. In the case of the animal spirit being let out of its corral, the necessary ceremony is called Muk'ta Ilel ("The Great Seeing," referring to the large number of ancestral gods that will be "seen" in the mountains by the shaman) and lasts about thirty-six hours, continuing day and night.

The family requests that either the same shaman or a different one perform the ceremony, and the shaman will be fetched at sundown. Upon arrival, the shaman first prays to the household cross in the patio, since this shrine is regarded as the ritual entrance to the house. Inside, the shaman sits on a small chair at the foot of the ritual table and inspects the candles purchased in San Cristóbal, the wild plants from "the gardens of the gods," and the gourds of water from the sacred waterholes at which the ancestral gods are believed to take their baths. After censing the ritual objects with copal, the shaman chants a long prayer known as "Looking at the Candles," which in part goes like this:

Divine Kalvaryo, Divine Father
Kalvaryo, Divine Mother.
Holy Kalvaryo, holy Ancient Ones,
Holy Kalvaryo, holy Yellow Ones.
Holy seas,
Holy Ancient Ones,
Holy gathering place,
Holy meeting place.
Holy place of recovery,
Holy place of rest.
I shall visit your shrines a little,
I shall entrust my soul to you a little.
To your feet,
To your hands.
For your sons,
For your children.
For your flowers,
For your sprouts.

For these I beseech divine pardon,
For these I beg divine forgiveness.

Then the shaman bathes the patient in water containing ritual plants, and the patient dons clothes freshly washed in the sacred waterholes. Next comes the bathing of two black chickens, the same sex as the patient, in the same wash water. The chicken that is to be sacrificed later as a "substitute" for the patient is then bled from the jugular vein in the neck, and the blood is collected in a bowl. The patient drinks some of the blood, and the shaman daubs the blood on the forehead and arms of the patient.

After a ritual meal, the patient and the shaman and his assistants set out for the mountain shrines around the valley in which the Ceremonial Center of Zinacantan is located. The order of march is always shaman in the rear, preceded by the patient and the assistants of the shaman as this small procession proceeds along the path of the sun. At Kalvaryo (from the Spanish "Calvario"), which is the meeting place of the ancestral gods in a supernatural mirror image of the town hall where the civil officials sit in rank order, the black chicken is killed by pulling of the neck, placed on a ceramic plate, and left in an enclosure for the ancestors to consume. After visiting three other sacred mountains, the procession makes its final stop at the shrine on top of the Senior Large Mountain. This shrine is regarded as the patio cross of the house of the supernatural Big Alcalde, who is in charge of the four corrals with the animal spirit companions of all the Zinacantecos.

Upon returning to the house, the patient is placed in a platform bed decorated with thirteen bundles of sacred plants and now called a *koral*. The second black chicken is killed and placed beside the patient. (It is later cooked for the patient to eat.) The moment the patient enters this *koral* (corral), the animal spirit companion is believed to be herded into its corral by the ancestral gods, and health is restored to the patient.

If the patient has been diagnosed as losing only part of his soul, the ritual upon return from the mountain shrines consists of a "soul calling." First, grains of maize of the four colors (red, black, white, yellow) are tossed into a gourd of salt water. The number of grains whose "mouths" (the part of the kernel originally attached to the ear) are pointed upward represent lost parts of the soul; the grains "seated" (resting quietly on the bottom of the bowl) are parts still safely in the body of the patient. The shaman, carrying a small gourd with kernels of maize in salt water and accompanied by an assistant who carries a gourd whistle, exits the house. They walk to where a soul loss has occurred. While the assistant blows an eerie sound on the whistle, the shaman beats the ground with a wand of pine and oak brush and calls "Come, please! Come, please!" The process is repeated at other locations, then the shaman brings the parts of the soul back inside the house and into the body of the patient. Holding water from the summoner gourd in his mouth, the shaman sucks noisily in two places (the wrist and under the elbow) on the patient's arms "to prepare the blood to receive the soul." The gourd with salt water and wand are placed in bed with the patient. Thus, health and harmony are restored to the patient. In each ceremony there is a final ritual meal, and then the patient stays secluded in the house for a prescribed number of days before resuming usual activities.

The other types of ceremonies that affect Zinacanteco daily life are those performed by the *cargo* holders in the Ceremonial Center. The ritual power and knowledge of these specialists do not come from dreams but from learning from older Zinacantecos who have served previously in the *cargo* system, especially from the ritual advisors who guide each important *cargo* holder through the rituals he must perform. The sacristans, who have the duty of opening and closing the churches and ringing the church bells and who serve in their positions for many years, are also important sources of guidance for *cargo* holders.

A key feature of the Zinacanteco Ceremonial Center is a religious hierarchy, organized around the two Catholic churches and one chapel and the saints. When a Zinacanteco speaks of *abtel ta hteklum*, he is referring to important "work" or "service" that is provided by men who hold positions in this hierarchy. *Abtel* is conceived of as bearing a burden, much as a Zinacanteco carries a heavy sack of maize on his back. But in the context of carrying burdens in the Ceremonial Center, the concept is probably related to the ancient Maya idea of the "Year Bearer," especially since the positions are held for a year. Like the ancient Maya gods who carried the "year" with a tumpline and passed it along to their successors, a contemporary Zinacanteco carries the burden of office for a year and then passes it along to his successor. In Spanish, these positions came to be called *cargos*. Although the positions are conceived of as burdens, especially since they take a great deal of time and heavy expenses, all of which must be paid by the *cargo* holder, they also provide enormous prestige and are much sought after by Zinacanteco men.

The *cargo* system in Zinacantan consists of fifty-six positions in four levels in a ceremonial ladder (Figure 2.6; for more details, see Cancian 1965). To pass through this ceremonial ladder, a man must serve a year at each level, and during the time he holds a *cargo* he is expected to move from

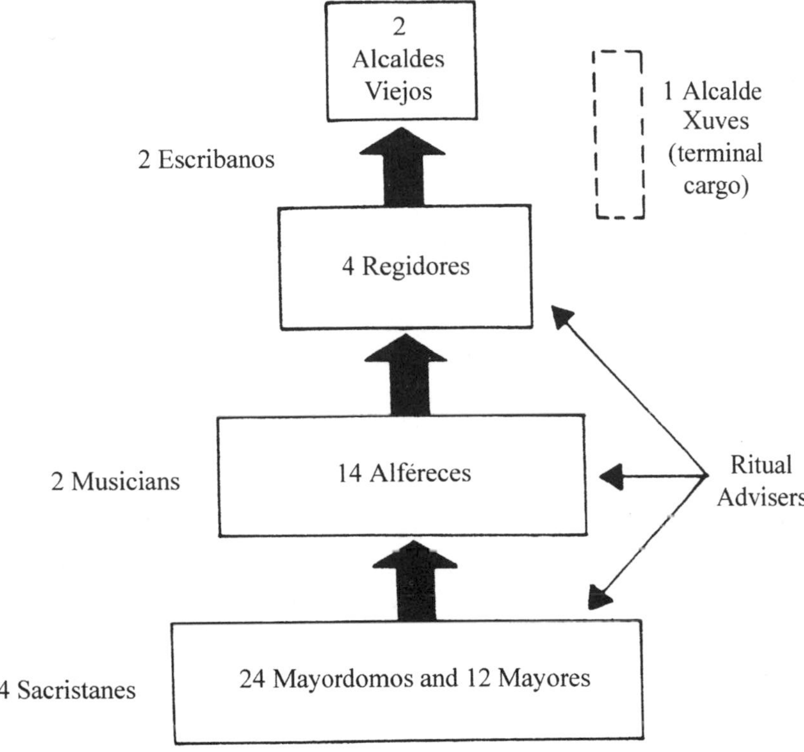

Figure 2.6. The *cargo* system in Zinacantan Center

his hamlet into the Ceremonial Center and engage in a complex round of ceremonies.

While he fills the role, the *cargo* holder wears special costumes and enjoys special prestige. At the end of the year, he turns the post over to the next incumbent and moves back to his hamlet to become a full-time maize farmer again. Some years must elapse before he can work himself out of debt and accumulate enough wealth to ask for a *cargo* position on the next higher level. When he completes all four *cargos*, he becomes an honored elder who has passed through the system.

The first level contains two alternatives; for the sake of simplicity, I have divided these into *mayores* and *mayordomos*. The twelve *mayores*, who are ranked from one to twelve, serve as policemen and errand boys for the civil officials at the town hall, but they also have important ceremonial duties during the Fiesta of San Sebastián in January. The twenty-four *mayordomos* care for particular saints in the Catholic churches in the Ceremonial Center or in one of the chapels of the outlying hamlets. Their *cargos* are named after the principal saint they serve, and in the Ceremonial Center, they are organized into two orders, Senior and Junior, which are ranked from one to twelve.

On the second level, the fourteen *alféreces* are also named for saints and organized into Senior and Junior orders. The third level has four *regidores*, ranked from one to four. Together with the two *alcaldes* at the fourth level ranked into "Big" and "Little" *alcaldes*, the *regidores* form a group at the top of the hierarchy known collectively as the *moletik*, the "elders." It is the duty of these elders to manage the *cargo* system. For an old man who has not managed to serve at each level, the position of *alcalde xuves* is available as a terminal cargo when it is evident he is not going to achieve a top *alcalde viejo* post.

Since the Zinacanteco way of life emphasizes ceremony, hardly a day passes in Zinacantan Center without some ritual being performed. The complex and colorful ceremonies are scheduled by a calendar that coincides closely with the calendar of the Catholic saints. On the most important saints' days (such as Epiphany, San Sebastián, San Pedro Mártir, San Lorenzo, Virgen de Natividad, and Virgen del Rosario), major ceremonies last three "official" days and involve repetitive ritual sequences that renew the flower decorations for the house and church altars; place sacred necklaces on the saint's images; install incoming *cargo* holders and remove outgoing *cargo* holders; provide processions, dances, and fireworks; and feed all the *cargo* holders and their assistants special food and sugarcane rum. Three days of preparation precede the actual fiesta and involve many male helpers as well as the work of the women in cooking and serving the enormous quantities of food required to feed the *cargo* holders.

The Zinacantecos find this life in the Ceremonial Center exciting, but it is also tension ridden because of the heavy expenses and work and because they are living in the Ceremonial Center among people from many different hamlets whom they do not know and may not trust. There is always the danger, for example, that harmful witchcraft rituals may be carried out by envious members of other lineages.

In addition to the repeating ritual sequences listed above, there are five occasions during the year—Christmas–New Year, San Sebastián in January, Easter, San Lorenzo in August, and Virgen de Rosario in October—when the *cargo* holders also perform special ceremonies with very distinctive rituals that are as complicated and interesting as any that occur in the Maya highlands (for more details, see Vogt 1993; Vogt and Bricker 1996).

Other important rites are the Year Renewal Ceremonies that are performed so that the year may pass in happiness and contentment, without sickness or death. They are performed by the shamans and *cargo* holders in most of the hamlets twice a year—for the "New Year" and "End of the Year"—and three times a year in the Ceremonial Center—"New Year," "Middle of the Year," and "End of the Year." The dates for each are set by the highest-ranking shaman in consultation with the civil Presidente and the top *cargo* holders. The New Year rite is set for a date following the Fiesta of San Sebastián in late January; the Middle of the Year rite is performed shortly after San Juan Day on June 24; and the End of the Year follows All Saints' Day in November (during which the ancestors come back to visit their former homes).

For the hamlets, the essence of the ceremony, performed by all the male shamans who are resident in a hamlet, is a pilgrimage to the Ceremonial Center to offer candles and copal incense at the foot and on top of the sacred mountains around the Center. The ceremony appears to be a symbolic way of relating the outlying hamlets to the tribal ancestral gods and the saints in the churches in the Center.

For the Year Renewal in the Center, the ritual is performed by all the shamans who live in the Center plus two from each hamlet. The shamans from the hamlets are not of high rank, but rather are the new and more junior members of the group, who are sent to the Center and then on the most arduous pilgrimages. The shamans assemble on Sunday at the Chapel of Esquipulas, where they count the money collected in each hamlet for the expenses of the ceremony. On Monday, ritual assistants are dispatched to San Cristóbal to purchase the candles, incense, and liquor; others are sent out to renew the decorations on all the cross shrines. At sundown the shamans and the top members of the *cargo* hierarchy and the civil hierarchy assemble in the house of the Big Alcalde, the highest-ranking *cargo* holder, who is the host for the ritual. A lengthy prayer begins at about 7 P.M. and lasts until 4 A.M. the following morning. The first four shamans in the rank order stand with smoking copal censers and pray while moving the censers in a counterclockwise direction; then come the next four shamans, who stand, receive the censers, and pray in the same way. This procedure is repeated by the third group of four shamans and so on until all have prayed. The prayers are followed by a ritual meal, and then at sunrise all the important tribal shrines are visited by shamans in groups of two. The more junior shamans are dispatched to the most distant shrines; the more senior shamans divide into six pairs, each of which is accompanied by one of the six elders of the *cargo* hierarchy, to visit the saints in the churches and the nearby mountain shrines.

The climax comes in the late morning when the entire assemblage of ritualists gathers at Kalvaryo (the meeting place of the ancestral gods with its six crosses). Here the shamans and elders of the *cargo* hierarchy pray in unison to all the tribal ancestral gods, turning counterclockwise in kneeling position to face and address each mountain and church in turn. The ceremony ends with a final ritual meal at the house of the Big Alcalde.

These Year Renewal Ceremonies are unique in the ritual life of Zinacantan in that they are the only rites that renew all of the community's tribal shrines and unite all crucial parts of the official structure—the shamans, the *cargo* holders, and the civil officers. Indeed, they focus attention on the two peaks of sacred power—the Senior Shamans and the Big Alcalde—and the peak of civil power, the Presidente.

Acknowledgments

The major sources I relied upon in writing this article were Vogt 1969, 1990, 1993, 1994, but I have also cited other Harvard Chiapas Project publications when appropriate in the text. I deeply appreciate the detailed critique and suggestions made by Jane F. Collier, Robert M. Laughlin, Joyce Marcus, and Nan Vogt on the first draft of the article.

References

Cancian, Frank

1965 *Economics and Prestige in a Maya Community: The Religious Cargo System in Zinacantan.* Stanford University Press, Stanford.

1972 *Change and Uncertainty in a Peasant Economy: The Maya Corn Farmers of Zinacantan.* Stanford University Press, Stanford.

Collier, George A.

1975 *Fields of the Tzotzil: The Ecological Bases of Tradition in the Highlands of Chiapas.* University of Texas Press, Austin.

Collier, Jane F.

1973 *Law and Social Change in Zinacantan.* Stanford University Press, Stanford.

Goody, Jack (editor)

1958 *The Developmental Cycle in Domestic Groups.* Cambridge University Press, New York.

Gossen, Gary H.

1972 Temporal and Spatial Equivalents in Chamula Ritual Symbolism. In *Reader in Comparative Religion: An Anthropological Approach*, 3rd ed., edited by William A. Lessa and Evon Z. Vogt, pp. 135–149. Harper and Row, New York.

Laughlin, Robert M.

1976 *Of Wonders Wild and New: Dreams from Zinacantan.* Smithsonian Contributions to Anthropology 22. Smithsonian Institution Press, Washington, D.C.

Vogt, Evon Z.

1969 *Zinacantan: A Maya Community in the Highlands of Chiapas.* Harvard University Press, Cambridge.

1990 *The Zinacantecos of Mexico: A Modern Maya Way of Life.* Holt, Rinehart and Winston, Fort Worth.

1993 *Tortillas for the Gods: A Symbolic Analysis of Zinacanteco Rituals.* University of Oklahoma Press, Norman.

1994 *Fieldwork among the Maya: Reflections on the Harvard Chiapas Project.* University of New Mexico Press, Albuquerque.

1997 Zinacanteco Astronomy. *Mexicon* 19(6):110–117.

1998 Zinacanteco Dedication and Termination Rituals. In *The Sowing and the Dawning*, edited by Shirley Boteler Mock, pp. 21–30. University of New Mexico Press, Albuquerque.

Vogt, Evon Z., and Victoria R. Bricker

1996 The Zinacanteco Fiesta of San Sebastián: An Essay in Ethnographic Interpretation. *Res* 29/30:203–222.

CHAPTER 3

The Role of Pottery and Food Consumption among Late Preclassic Maya Commoners at Lamanai, Belize

TERRY G. POWIS

In recent years, ceramic research in the Maya area has adopted a number of approaches to help describe and explain ancient economic, social, political, and ideological organization. New trends in classification as well as those in chemical, statistical, petrographic, and iconographic studies have allowed researchers to expand beyond defining and refining site chronologies to examining more fully the socioeconomic aspects of ancient Maya life (Valdez et al. 1999). Many of these lines of inquiry focus on pottery as a tool for understanding increasing economic differentiation. Maya ceramicists have become concerned with pottery primarily as a form of wealth and for the role it played in promoting and maintaining social power among elite individuals (for example, see LeCount 1999). With an emphasis placed on the sociopolitical significance of ceramics for a small segment of the population, little recognition has been given to how Maya commoners, those who formed the majority of ancient Maya society, used pottery in their daily social and ritual activities.

One of the main goals of this study is to define the pottery inventory and the range of activity sets (both domestic and ritual) present in Late Preclassic (300 BC–AD 250) commoner households at the Maya center of Lamanai, located in northern Belize (Figure 3.1). To attempt this, however, there must be some discussion of what constitutes the pottery inventory for an elite household. This is necessary because so much more ceramic research has already been directed toward defining the archaeological signatures of elite households than toward non-elite ones, particularly during the Classic period (see Chase and Chase 1992).

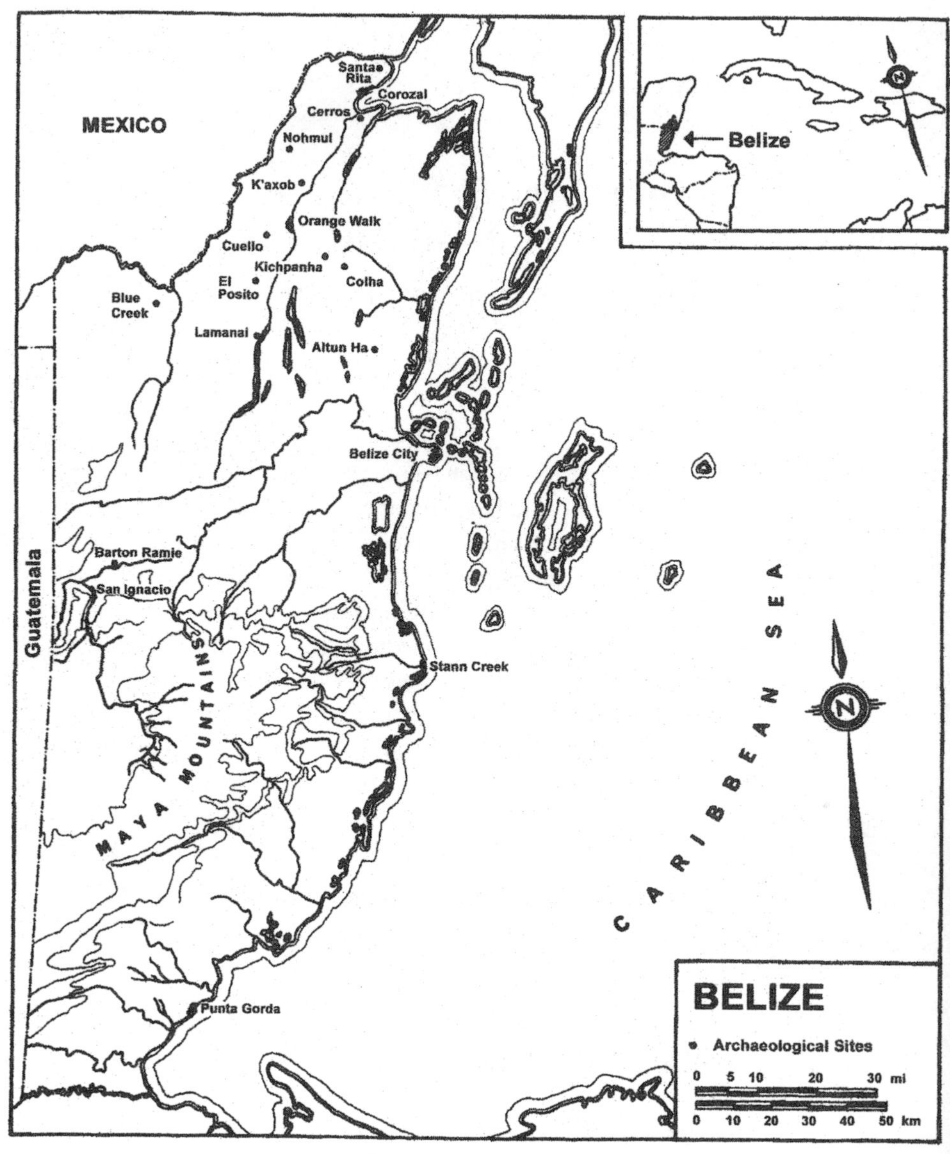

Figure 3.1. Map of Belize showing location of Lamanai (after Pendergast 1981a: Fig. 1)

Previous Research on Vessel Function

Although functional studies have been performed on Classic period assemblages, few attempts have been made to examine vessel function as a means of gaining insight into the variability and patterning of pottery at the household level during the Preclassic period. Some notable exceptions include Altar de Sacrificios (Adams 1971), Cerros (Robertson 1983), Chalchuapa (Sharer 1978), Cuello (Kosakowsky 1983), and K'axob (McAnany and López 1999). In particular, the material from Cerros has been subjected to a formal functional analysis. At Cerros, Robin Robertson (1983) looked at function based primarily on context, but also vessel form, surface treatment, paste, modes (e.g., medial ridges), and evidence of use (e.g., fire blackening and wear patterns). From this analysis, she developed nine functional categories: stationary storage vessels, soaking vessels, mixing bowls, water vessels, dry storage vessels, serving dishes for hot and cold foods, buckets, eating and ritual offering bowls, and ritual vessels. Robertson (1983:140) was able to determine a functional significance of the Late Preclassic (300 BC–AD 150) pottery with respect to social status, namely, that elites used ceramics to express social differentiation.

Generally speaking, ceramicists working in the Maya area have tended to establish only broad functional categories based on form and use-wear patterns. These types of functional studies are limited because they focus too strongly on vessel form and the nature of the ceramic type itself, which may limit or even suggest the possibilities of usage (Adams 1971:138). Therefore, rather than focusing too much on determining vessel function from vessel form, as has been the trend in the past, the attempt with the Lamanai material was to work from the contextual data to the establishment of ceramic categories or classes, an approach similar to that performed on the Cerros material (Robertson 1983). The analysis of the Lamanai pottery relies primarily on context, vessel form, surface treatment, paste, and use-wear patterns to determine the functional nature of the Preclassic ceramics. A concerted effort was made to use location within the community, degree of elaboration in architecture and burials, and presence/absence of luxury goods to provide information on distinguishing non-elite from elite and domestic from ritual areas of the site.

Lamanai Data

The site of Lamanai, located on the northwestern shore of the New River Lagoon in northern Belize (Figure 3.2), was excavated between 1974 and 1986 under the direction of David Pendergast of the Royal Ontario Museum (Pendergast 1981a). Analyses of the material remains recovered during those twelve years of investigation are now being directed by Elizabeth Graham of the Institute of Archaeology at University College London in England.

A total of 718 structures were mapped at Lamanai, of which 37 were excavated (Pendergast 1981a, 1981b, 1981c). Primary deposits dating to both the Middle Preclassic (900–300 BC) and Late Preclassic (300 BC–AD 250) periods were exposed in 11 of these sampled structures, over 25 percent of the total surveyed. Most of the Preclassic settlement is dispersed within a 2 km strip along the lagoon. To date, it appears that the Preclassic settlements were located in the north (close to the Harbour area), with a shift southward in later times as changes in the lagoon environment made the northern area less attractive for habitation (David Pendergast, personal communication 1999).

The ceramic analysis of the Late Preclassic assemblage began by enumerating types using the type-variety system of classification commonly used in the Maya lowlands (Gifford 1960, 1976; Sabloff and Smith 1969; Smith et al. 1960; Wheat et al. 1958; Willey et al. 1967). Additionally, a detailed ware or modal approach was employed on each pot to complement the types defined for each ceramic phase (Powis 2000). Functional inferences of the Lamanai ceramic types are based primarily on archaeological context and ethnographic data. The use of ethnographic data is particularly important for gaining knowledge about possible Preclassic household functional requirements, potting activities, and use and re-use strategies (Deal 1998; Reina and Hill 1978; Thompson 1958).

A total of 132 whole ceramic vessels were used in this study; these were recovered from mainly primary contexts (Powis 1999, 2000). The Late Preclassic assemblage at Lamanai is derived from a number of different contexts, shown in Table 3.1. Vessels from middens, burials, and caches were recovered from both commoner and elite contexts. However, the ceramic material from the hearth, rock feature, and *chultun* (subterranean storage feature) are considered commoner contexts only, whereas the pottery from the sherd feature represents an elite context.

In analyzing the Late Preclassic ceramic assemblage, I have been able to identify two, possibly three separate facets: an early, a late, and a ter-

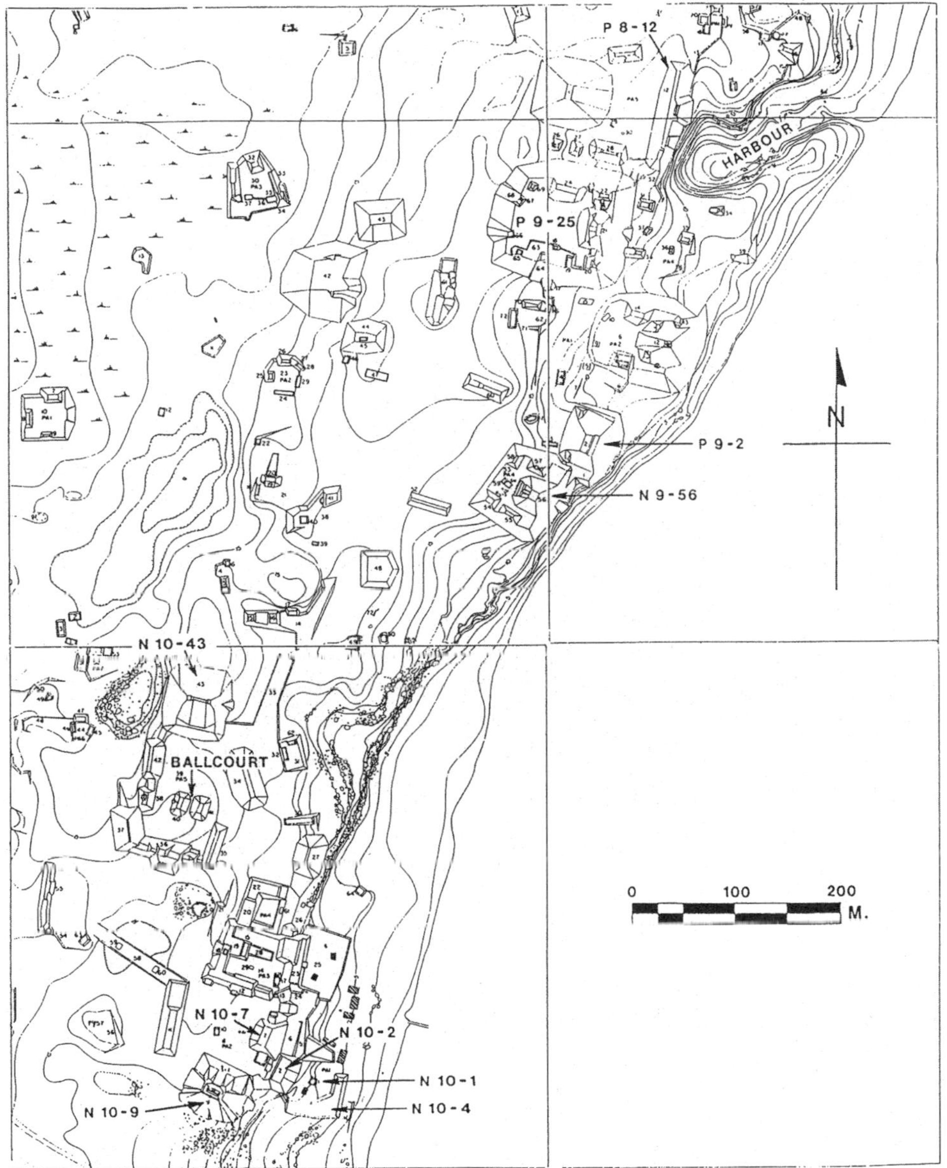

Figure 3.2. Plan of central portion of Lamanai, Belize (after Pendergast 1981a: Fig. 2)

Table 3.1. Late Preclassic domestic and ritual activity areas for elite and commoner structures at Lamanai, Belize

Structure	*Context*	*Function for Deposit*	*Time Period*
N10-2	Sherd Feature #1	Domestic/Elite	Protoclassic
N10-9	Lowest Floor	Domestic/Elite	Late Preclassic
N10-27	N10-27/3	Ritual	Late Preclassic
N10-43	Cache N10-43/2	Ritual	Protoclassic
	Hearth #1	Domestic/Non-elite	Late Preclassic
	Rock Feature #1	Domestic/Non-elite	Late Preclassic
	Cache N10-43/6	Ritual	early Late Preclassic
P8-2	Chultun	Domestic/Non-Elite	Late Preclassic
P8-9	Surface	Domestic/Elite	Late Preclassic
	Burial P8-9/1, 2, 3, and 5	Ritual	early Late Preclassic
	Cache P8-9/1	Ritual	early Late Preclassic
P8-11	Core material	Domestic/Non-elite	Late Preclassic
	Midden	Domestic/Non-elite	Protoclassic
P8-14	Lower Core	Domestic/Non-elite	Late Preclassic
	Cache P8-14/1	Ritual	Late Preclassic
P8-27	Core	Domestic/Non-elite	Protoclassic
P8-103	Burial P8-103/1 and 2	Ritual	Middle Preclassic
P9-2	Core material	Domestic/Elite	Protoclassic
YDL II-7	Cache YDL-7	Ritual	Late Preclassic

minal facet—the last two corresponding to the Protoclassic/Floral Park complex. The early facet is a long, relatively homogeneous one, which is followed by two shorter, more variable later ones (Table 3.2). The identification of the two later facets is based on the addition of a few new ceramic types to the earlier facet as well as the appearance of new modes. The three facets for the Late Preclassic period are based on stratigraphic position, modal comparisons, technological development, and relative cross-dating with other northern Belize sites. Beginning and ending dates are approximated.

The early facet dates to the early part of the Late Preclassic (300–100/50 BC), and the late facet (100/50 BC–AD 150) and terminal facet (AD 150–250) are dated to the end of the Late Preclassic, a ceramic stage known as the Protoclassic period. It was first identified as the Floral Park complex at Barton Ramie (Gifford 1976). During the Protoclassic period, a broad series of ceramic attributes begin to appear across the Maya area, including mammiform tetrapod dishes and bowls and wavy and nonwavy positive and negative painting (Brady et al. 1998; Pring 1977). Technological experimentation and artistic expression mark this period of ceramic development across the Maya region. The Protoclassic period likely terminates about AD 400, depending on the site (Brady et al. 1998). Not all sites produced the same quantity or quality of these wares. Why some sites exhibited a stronger Protoclassic component compared to others, even within the same region, is not fully understood by Maya archaeologists and ceramicists (Forsyth 1993). In northern Belize, many sites produced Protoclassic pottery, including Blue Creek, Colha, Cuello, El Posito, K'axob, Kichpanha, Nohmul, and Santa Rita. The site of Lamanai also has a significant Protoclassic component (Powis 2001). The ceramic material dating to the late and terminal facets forms a major part of this study of identifying the pottery inventories for both elite and non-elite structures.

Identifying Elite and Commoner Contexts

The question of identifying "elite" versus "commoner" contexts must be briefly addressed before proceeding with a functional interpretation of the Lamanai Preclassic pottery assemblage. Traditionally, the criteria used by archaeologists to distinguish elite pottery from commoner pottery have been: (1) the superior quality of manufacture of the vessels; (2) the relative density of whole vessels recovered; (3) the execution of design and technique; (4) the variation of types; (5) the esoteric form (such as masks, drums, and effigy vessels) of the pottery; and (6) the evidence of vessel forms that are analogous to modern wealth/status forms (see Chase and Chase 1992). Additionally, Adams (1971:139) defined ceremonial and status pottery as "all finely made pottery whose decoration, by its symbolic nature, may indicate ritual or status functions." He included the following type classes: mortuary vessels, drums, incense burners, cult effigies, and trade exotics (Adams 1971:139).

Table 3.2. Facets represented in the Late Preclassic ceramic assemblage at Lamanai, Belize

Early facet (Chicanel ceramic sphere)	300–100/50 BC
Late facet (Floral Park ceramic sphere)	100/50 BC–AD 150
Terminal facet (Floral Park ceramic sphere)	AD 150–250

During the course of my study, it became obvious that using these traditional criteria to identify elite pottery from commoner pottery may not be possible for the Lamanai data set. While some of the traits listed in Chase and Chase (1992) for the Classic period could be used to a certain degree (e.g., numbers 1–3, 6), the other two (numbers 4 and 5) presented problems, as elite and commoner pottery exhibited both of these traits. Furthermore, a few of the pottery types (e.g., drums and incense burners) listed by Adams (1971:139) could not be employed because these forms were not recovered in the Lamanai Preclassic assemblage. Therefore, aspects of both trait lists mentioned above are used in my study in concert with degree of associated architectural and burial elaborateness.

Using a combination of approaches has alleviated potential problems with identifying elite and commoner pottery at Lamanai. Based on excavations in residential structures from the Classic period at the site, it appears that "elite" vessels were not restricted to elite individuals; quite elaborate ceramics occurred in distinctly "non-elite" contexts. Because of this distribution, it can be dangerous to define a structure as an elite residence on the basis of ceramic content alone, and equally dangerous to identify the depositors of the material as elite (David Pendergast, personal communication 1999). As a result, it may be better to identify elite contexts on the basis of architecture, although this approach is not devoid of problems. In some cases, a deposit is clearly associated with an elite structure. For example, in a major temple, whatever the nature of the ceramics may be, one can assume the deposit was placed there by members of the elite. The opposite is probably to be assumed in "low-status" structures, in which the structure suggests that the users were non-elite, no matter how elaborate the pots may be.

Difficulty arises in structures that are of considerable size and complexity in form but are clearly residential. Where is the dividing line between commoner and elite when it comes to architectural characteristics such as size and complexity? Echoing a theme repeated throughout this volume, I submit that determining whether a structure was the residence of members of the elite or of commoners is quite likely to be somewhat arbitrary, and it is hard in such circumstances to avoid being affected by the ceramics, which may not be a good basis for decision making. This is why every effort has been taken in this study to use architectural context, degree of elaboration in architecture and burials, and the presence/absence of luxury goods in burials and caches to provide information on distinguishing Preclassic elite from commoner structures.

Functional Data

Sierra Red is the dominant ceramic type during all three facets of the Late Preclassic, making up 65 percent of the total assemblage (Tables 3.3 and 3.4). All other groups, including Aguacate, Coconut Walk, Polvero, Flor, and Matamore, consist of less than 10 percent each (see Gifford 1976 and Graham 1994 for ceramic type descriptions). Of the 132 vessels, 37 were recovered from seven elite structures (N10-2, N10-9, N10-27, N10-43, P8-9, P9-2, and YDL II-7), and 96 were recovered from three commoner structures (P8-11, P8-14, and P8-27) and a midden in Chultun P8-2. The *chultun* contained significant amounts of late- and terminal-facet pottery (i.e., true Protoclassic wares).

Eight general vessel forms are present in the Preclassic Lamanai assemblage. There are sixty-six open bowls and dishes, twenty jars, eighteen open plates, eleven crudely fashioned bowls, nine restricted-rim bowls, three deep basins and buckets, three vertical-walled bowls, and three vases. Of the forms present, open bowls, dishes, and plates are the most common, making up approximately two-thirds (63 percent) of the Preclassic assemblage. Jars are also common, forming 21 percent (twenty out of ninety-six), and are represented by both spouted and unspouted forms. Only two of the twenty jars had handles. All unspouted ones were striated.

In the commoner assemblage of ninety-six vessels, all eight vessel forms are represented, with open bowls, plates, and dishes being found with the highest frequency—at 60 percent (fifty-seven out of ninety-six) of this subassemblage. Both bowls and dishes in the commoner assemblage have a rim diameter range of 11–46 cm and a height range of 3–35 cm. Elite bowls and dishes, on the other hand, have a rim diameter range of 10–42 cm and a height range of 3–18 cm. In Tables 3.5 and 3.6, both bowls and dishes in the commoner and elite assemblages are not significantly different in terms of diameter or height, regardless of whether the vessels were found in domestic or ritual activity areas. Additionally, vessel forms like basins, open plates, and jars are even larger, on average, in commoner contexts than those recovered from elite ones. In a domestic context, this information further suggests that both groups utilized a wide variety of vessel sizes for serving and eating individual-sized and family-sized meals. For example, the volume, in milliliters (ml), for twenty-six Late Preclassic vessels (eighteen elite and eight commoner) demonstrates the range of serving sizes or portions for the different vessel categories at the site (Table 3.7).

Table 3.3. Occurrence of ceramic types over the functional loci at Lamanai, Belize

Ceramic Type	*Elite*	*Non-elite*	*Ritual*
Sierra Red Variety	16	20	x
Sierra Red-and-Black	1	3	
Sierra Red Usulutan	0	5	
Society Hall Red	9	4	x
Society Hall Grooved	0	1	
Society Hall Red Punctated	0	1	
Laguna Verde Incised	2	2	
Laguna Verde Grooved	1	2	x
Laguna Verde Usulutan	0	1	
Puletan Red-and-Unslipped	0	8	
Dawson Creek Composite	0	1	
Rio Bravo Red	0	1	
Cabro Red	0	1	
Composite Red-on-Orange	0	1	
Unnamed Red-Rimmed	0	1	
Unnamed Red-Brown	0	1	
Unnamed Red-on-Buff	1	2	
Unnamed Red-and-Buff	0	1	
Polvero Black	2	2	x
Lechugal Incised	2	0	x
Lechugal Grooved	0	4	
Flor Cream	2	2	x
Accordion Incised	0	1	
Indian Church White	0	1	
Matamore Dichrome	0	1	
Matamore Dichrome Usulutan	0	2	
Monkey Falls Striated	0	1	
Coconut Walk Incised	0	11	
Ixcanrio Orange Polychrome	0	1	
Gavilan Black-on-Orange	0	1	
Unnamed Black and Red-on-Orange	0	1	
Unnamed Buff	0	5	
Unnamed Buff-Orange	1	0	
Unnamed Buff Usulutan	0	2	
Unnamed Orange Usulutan	0	1	
Ramgoat Red	0	1	x
Chunhinta Black	0	1	x
Guitara Incised	0	1	x
Consejo Red	0	1	x
Total	37	96	

Table 3.4. Ceramic groups represented in the Late Preclassic assemblage at Lamanai, Belize

Ceramic Group	*Total*	*Percentage*
Sierra	86	64.7
Aguacate	12	9
Coconut Walk	11	8.27
Polvero	10	7.51
Flor	6	4.51
Matamore	3	2.25
Monkey Falls	1	0.75
Ramgoat	1	0.75
Consejo	1	0.75
Chunhinta	1	0.75
Joventud	1	0.75
Total	133	99.99

About 51 percent of the commoner vessels are decorated compared to 38 percent of the elite vessels during all three facets. Both assemblages are generally highly polished and slipped red, black, cream, or a combination of the three. They are decorated with incisions, grooves, and punctations. The Late Preclassic assemblage exhibited a number of modeled vessels in the zoomorphic shapes of birds, bats, frogs, and crocodiles. The crocodile effigy vessel (Figure 3.3a), dating to the early facet, is important because it represents the first evidence of crocodile imagery at the site, perhaps related to the name Lama'anayin ("submerged crocodile"), which was the ancient name of the site and community (Pendergast 1981a:32). Three effigy vessels in the shape of birds, including a Lechugal Grooved-Incised (early-facet) bowl (Figure 3.3b) and an Unnamed Buff-and-Modeled (terminal-facet) spouted jar (Figure 3.3c), were recovered from commoner midden contexts, and compared to the crocodile effigy bowl recovered from an elite burial, the bird vessels are rather finely made. In late-facet times, surface decorations applied to commoner vessels included concentric horizontal streaky marks painted on the surfaces of Society Hall Red bowls and dishes as well as red crosses painted on the base of Sierra Red plates. According to McAnany et al. (1999:139–140), these cross motifs could represent an early example of the quadripartite motif or Kan cross. At Lamanai, two of the five vessel bottoms with red crosses also exhibited a painted circle creating a five-pointed cross, like the

Table 3.5. Mean diameter (in centimeters) of vessel forms for Late Preclassic elite and commoner pottery at Lamanai, Belize

Vessel Form	*Elite*	*Commoner*
Open bowls and dishes	24	26
Vertical-walled bowls	n/a	24
Restricted-rim bowls	20.4	20.2
Basins/buckets	23	42.5
Jars	15	17
Vases	14.3	12
Open plates	26.2	24.3

Table 3.6. Mean height (in centimeters) of vessel forms for Late Preclassic elite and commoner pottery at Lamanai, Belize

Vessel Form	*Elite*	*Commoner*
Open bowls and dishes	7.47	7.44
Vertical-walled bowls	11.6	9.5
Restricted-rim bowls	9.7	11.8
Basins/buckets	13	15.1
Jars	14.5	17.6
Vases	20.2	12.1
Open plates	3.7	4.2

vessels recovered from Late Preclassic burials at K'axob (McAnany et al. 1999:140). Freidel et al. (1993:59–122) have interpreted variations of this motif in Classic period monumental art as symbolic of the World Tree and the Milky Way. Interestingly, none of these Kan crosses at Lamanai were found on vessels recovered from elite contexts.

Ethnographic data from the Yucatán Peninsula and the Guatemalan highlands indicate that open bowls, dishes, and plates likely functioned as serving and eating vessels (Deal 1998; Reina and Hill 1978; Thompson 1958), and they may have done so during the Late Preclassic period as well. Many of these forms had broad, horizontal, everted rims, which likely made it easier to serve hot foods like soups and stews. Some of the flaring-walled bowls with convex interior bases and direct rims appear to have been used as mixing bowls. The interiors of some show horizontal scoring and the exterior basal break is worn in many cases, probably through contact with a hard surface. Such patterns of wear would be produced if pressure were applied to the vessel while it was rotated, as is commonly done when mixing food (Fred Valdez, personal communication 1999). The convex base would reduce the area of contact, making it easier to rotate due to less friction.

The large, restricted-necked, striated jars were probably used to store

Table 3.7 Volume (in milliliters) of Late Preclassic elite and commoner vessels at Lamanai, Belize

	Elite	*Commoner*
Bowls	970	775
	1,160	1,705
	1,845	
	1,885	
	3,715	
Mean	1,915	1,240
Dishes	1,005	730
	1,340	1,155
	1,585	1,265
		2,345
Mean	1,310	1,374
Plates	385	
	2,265	
Mean	1,325	
Spouted jars	560	390
	2,175	1,205
	2,405	
Mean	1,713	798
Buckets	1,665	
	4,235	
Mean	2,950	
Vases	3,225	
Vertical-walled jars	2,695	

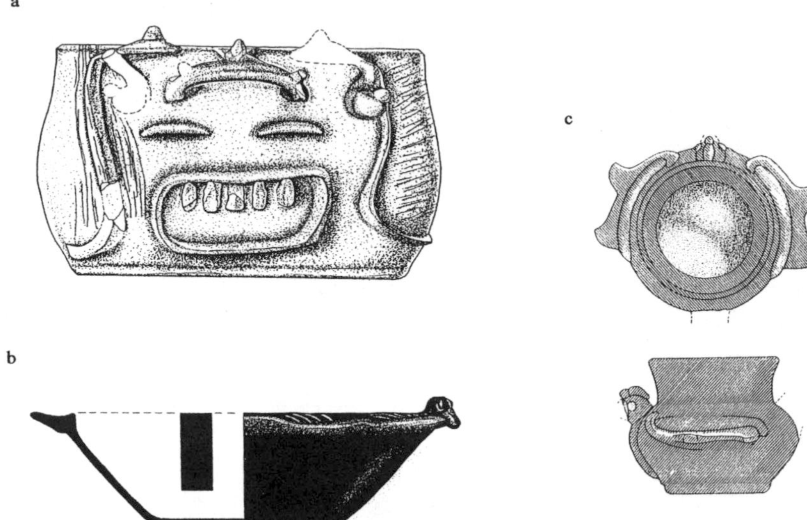

Figure 3.3. (a) Stylized crocodile effigy bowl from an elite burial in Str. P8-9; illustration drawn by Ruth Dickau; (b) bird effigy bowl from a commoner midden in Str. P8-11; illustration drawn by Ruth Dickau; and (c) bird effigy spouted jar from a commoner midden inside Chultun P8-2; illustration drawn by Louise Belanger.

water, whereas smaller versions may have been used to carry it. The jars with low, wide necks would have been better utilized for dry storage. Their low necks make it difficult to pour liquid contents and would thus not inhibit spilling.

Throughout all three facets of the Late Preclassic, spouted jars with and without bridge-supports likely functioned to hold liquid contents, like soup bowls and drinking cups (Figures 3.4a and 3.4b). Recent residue analyses conducted on spouted vessels have confirmed that these vessel types did indeed contain liquids. At the site of Colha, located to the northeast of Lamanai in northern Belize, preliminary data have revealed that some of the vessels found in Middle and Late Preclassic burials contained substantial amounts of liquid theobromine, a distinct marker for cacao or chocolate (Hurst et al. 2002; Powis et al. 2002). During the Classic period, cacao was typically associated with the elite as a luxury drink, trade item, tribute item, and currency (Coe and Coe 1996; McAnany 2000; Reents-Budet 1994: Stuart 1988). Why, then, during the Late Preclassic period at Lamanai, do we find spouted vessels recovered from a midden inside a *chultun*, a commoner context?

Other vessels that may have held liquids were double-slipped bowls and dishes found in both elite and commoner household contexts. Four Sierra Red vessels showing this double interior slip, along with a limited number of vertical-walled bowls and restricted-rim bowls, may indicate that specific forms served specific functions. Another form present in the commoner assemblage was one very large medial hip basin with a high vertical rim dating to the late facet (see Figure 3.4c). This basin may have served a similar function to the large buckets (Figure 3.5a) found in elite burials. From a functional point of view, the unrestricted orifices make all of them ideal for serving large quantities of food, such as soups and stews with a high liquid content.

Two out of the three vases found in Late Preclassic deposits come from

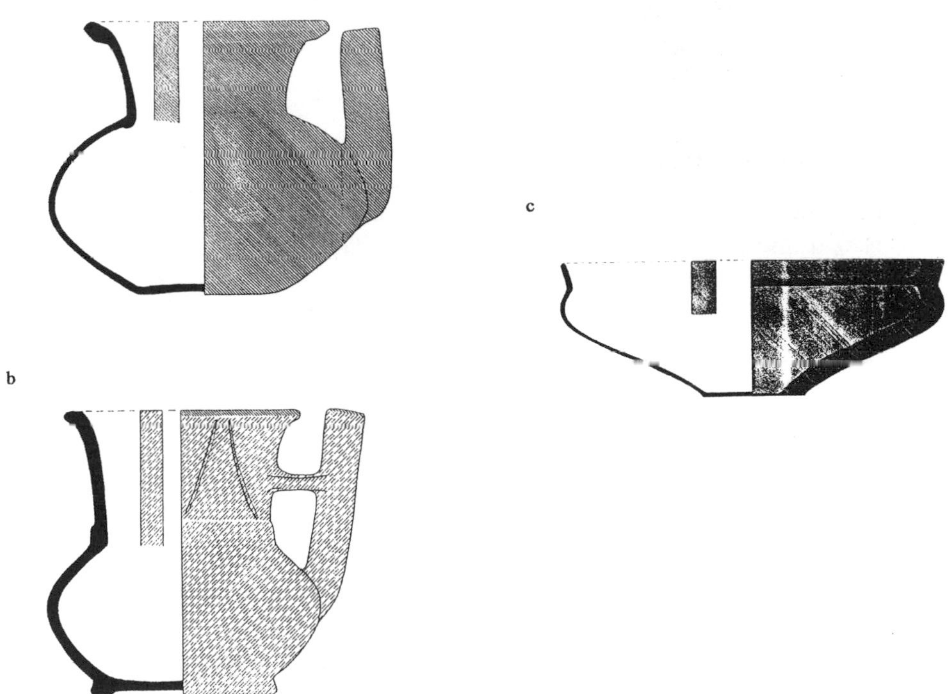

Figure 3.4. (a) Example of a spouted jar from an elite burial in Str. P8-0; (b) Unnamed Red-Rimmed Buff spouted jar with bridge-support from a commoner midden inside Chultun P8-2; and (c) a large medial hip basin from a commoner midden inside Chultun P8-2. Illustrations drawn by Louise Belanger.

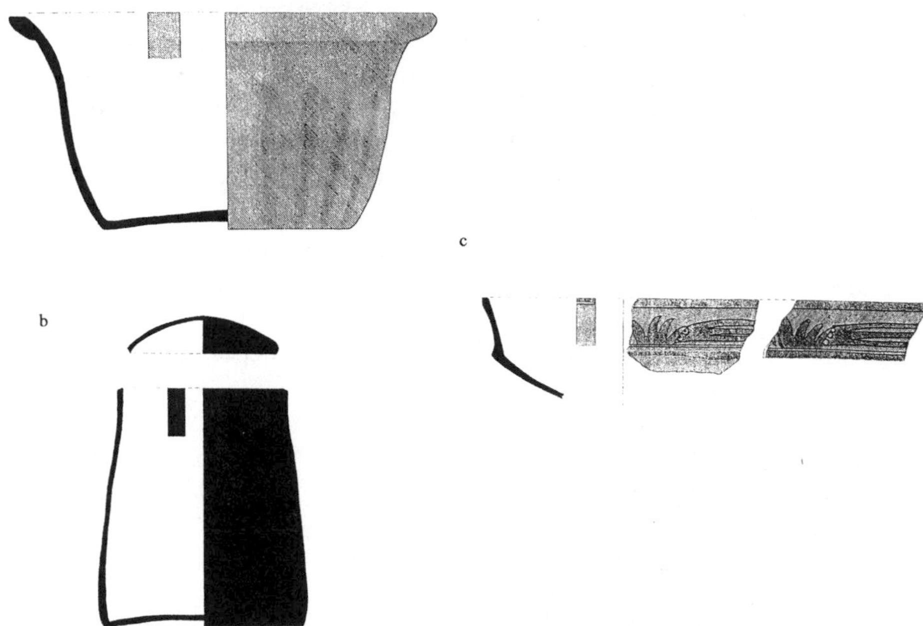

Figure 3.5. (a) A large bucket or "flower pot" from an elite burial in Str. P8-9; (b) a black-slipped cylinder lidded vase from an elite cache in Str. N10-43; and (c) a polychrome bowl with geometric designs and stylized images of birds (macaws?) from a commoner midden inside Chultun P8-2. Illustrations drawn by Louise Belanger.

non-elite middens. In the Classic period, vases are typically associated with elite contexts (Adams 1971:139), so it is important to note that two of them occur in non-elite midden locations. Functionally, the vases were probably used for storing liquids because of the slipped interior and the constriction of the vessel walls, which inhibited evaporation. Neither of the commoner ones is as finely made as the Polvero Black cylindrical lidded vessel dating to the early facet (see Figure 3.5b). This vessel was excavated from an elite cache found on top of the 33 m tall High Temple, designated as Structure N10-43 (Pendergast 1998:57).

The final vessel category to be discussed is the crude open bowls called Coconut Walk Unslipped. Eleven of these unslipped vessels were found alongside elaborate polychrome Usulutan-style wares and spouted jar vessels inside the *chultun* (P8-2). They are well smoothed on the interior, but their exterior surface is rough, showing grass impressions. They are thin-walled (mean average = 4 mm) and have large rim diameters ranging from 34 to 40 cm. There is also evidence of spalling on their interiors. Their function is somewhat puzzling, but they may have been used to line pits, given the grass impressions; however, similar forms have been recovered by Elizabeth Graham (1994) in the Stann Creek region of Central Belize. She thinks that these kinds of vessels might have been used for soaking purposes, perhaps the soaking of corn in lime or the mixing of lime with water for construction purposes (Graham 1994:155).

Discussion

During the Preclassic at Lamanai there was a considerable variety of vessels that satisfied many domestic and ritual requirements for both elites and non-elites. Each vessel form was associated with a specific range of functions. Certain groups of vessels were likely used in distinct activity sets, as seen with contemporary Maya highland groups. Today, as in the past, activity sets consisted of a group of vessels that served a specific activity, were associated with a specific activity area, and were stored together near their area of use (Deal 1998:84; Sheets 1992). Generally speaking, in modern Maya households there are vessels for three kinds of activity sets: food preparation and serving, water procurement and storage, and ritual functions (Culbert 1965; Deal 1998). At Lamanai, the variety of vessels used in each of these three kinds of activity sets has been observed for the Preclassic period.

A number of fine-quality vessels are found in both elite and non-elite contexts at Lamanai, such as in household middens and burials. They are typically bowls and jars, and their predominance is consistent with the situation today, indicating they may have served a similar range of domestic and ritual functions. The abundance of fine-quality wares probably reflects the highly developed ritual system that required most Preclassic households to keep on hand quantities of finer serving vessels (Evon Vogt, personal communication 1999). In the Protoclassic, this is exemplified with the production of Usulutan-style and polychrome wares. Some of the finest vessels of these types were recovered from a midden context—the *chultun*. The Protoclassic polychrome bowls, dishes, and jars, for example, exhibit geometric designs and stylized images of birds painted in red, black, and orange (see Figure 3.5c). Given the amount of excavation at Lamanai, it is surprising to see that few polychromes have been excavated from Protoclassic elite contexts.

One explanation for this may be sampling bias or error. It may also be that the principle of placing cached offerings along the primary axis of ceremonial buildings was not followed in the Lamanai community during the Preclassic. As Pendergast (1998:56) has stated, "Neither architectural size and complexity nor the degree of change wrought by modifications was necessarily reflected in primary axis offerings of an appropriately sumptuous nature, or even the presence of an offering in any form."

Another explanation for a lack of elaborate pottery in elite contexts may be that variations in activity sets, the use of pots for ritual and domestic functions, did not seem to be markedly different within structures during the Late Preclassic. Additionally, the variations in the types of vessels represented within these activity sets may be minor between elite and non-elite groups. For example, there has been the tendency in Maya archaeology to equate the presence of polychrome pottery with high status later on in the Classic period. This inference probably has resulted from the prominent place of polychromes in high-status burials and in ceremonial contexts such as caches (Beaudry 1983:183). Nevertheless, there is evidence that polychromes were not restricted to the elite but were available to commoner households not closely associated with any one particular major center. At the Classic period sites of Barton Ramie (Willey et al. 1965:350–351), Cerén (Beaudry 1983:183), Copán (Webster and Gonlin 1988:187), and Tikal (Culbert 1974:183), polychrome pottery has been recovered from numerous commoner households. According to Culbert (1974:65), even the most remote households at Tikal during the Late Classic regularly used hand-painted polychrome pottery for serving food, and the vessels used for domestic activities like food storage and carrying water were the products of specialized manufacturers.

The viewpoint here is that certain types of pottery, like polychrome vessels for the Classic, may not be the best marker of wealth in Maya society (see Haviland and Moholy-Nagy 1992:54). Although polychrome decorations are often found in high-status contexts, such as burials, when using ceramics to try to distinguish between elites and commoners, the criteria should be amplified and qualified to include such differences as execution of design and technique of the painted and printed surfaces.

Generally, there is a positive correlation between status-level context and pictorial/hieroglyphic complexity and artistic (painting) quality of polychrome pottery. However, this does not hold true when we are discussing the quality of vessel formation and firing. The ability to manufacture vessels of the highest quality is seen in pottery from all socioeconomic and political contexts (Dorie Reents-Budet, personal communication 2001). Furthermore, there are anomalies in the archaeological record where we find sherds with elaborately painted designs in less than elite contexts. Likewise, we find poorly painted "commoner" service wares in the highest socioeconomic and political contexts. The site of Buenavista, located in western Belize, is one of the best examples of this inverse correlation (Reents-Budet et al. 2000). So, the picture is much too complicated to support simplistic statements about ancient Maya polychrome pottery as evidence of elite status. Given the variety of contexts in which polychrome pottery occurs, other indicators such as better construction, size, and elaborateness of architecture; presence of multiple structures within a household; percentage of polychrome wares versus percentage of plain wares; involvement in craft activities; inclusion of imported ceramic wares and exotic items such as jade in burials; and burial construction may be better measures reflecting household wealth (Chase and Chase 1992:54; Flannery and Marcus 1994:333–339; Hendon 1991; Smith 1987).

Conclusions

In conclusion, the preliminary data on the Late Preclassic whole vessels from Lamanai suggest that there was considerable variability in ceramic content within commoner and elite households. Based on ceramic content, there does not seem to be a significant difference in the frequency and variety of ceramic types and forms identified in elite and commoner contexts and domestic and ritual contexts at the site during the Late Preclassic. From commoner structures occupied during the Protoclassic (late and terminal facets), polychrome dishes have been recovered in midden deposits, and crude bowls have been found in a burial and a cache. In elite structures, finely made serving bowls and plates have been found in middens, and plainware has been recovered from caches and burials.

It may be, as recent ethnoarchaeological investigations in the Maya highlands of Chiapas have indicated, that most domestic ritual pottery types are undecorated plainwares and that finely made decorated wares served both ritual and domestic functions (Deal 1998:61). Therefore, the distribution of fine-quality decorated pottery versus plainware, which has often been used by archaeologists as an indicator of economic status, may not be a reliable indicator for status or wealth in ancient Maya society. Michael E. Smith (1987) has demonstrated the potential problems associated with making simple correlations between household wealth and status. He states that there are a large number of complicating factors such as family size, developmental cycle, and the professions or specialized activities of household members (Smith 1987). Other factors, such as patterns of use and re-use and the borrowing of pottery by family and neighbors for both short-term and long-term periods, should also be considered.

Future Research

Although using a single line of evidence like ceramics as a material indicator to try to distinguish between elites and commoners at a single site for a single time period does not appear to work well at Lamanai, the current study could offer important leads for other researchers who are facing similar problems. Examining pottery has the potential of allowing us to discern social status, but certain criteria must be amplified and qualified to include such differences as execution of design and technique. For example, polychrome pottery could be used as an important marker of wealth if researchers recognize pictorial/hieroglyphic complexity and artistic quality as the superior criteria.

If a hierarchy of criteria is established (and maintained) for pottery, then it could be utilized as an equally important line of argument as architectural context, the degree of elaboration in architecture and burials, and the presence/absence of luxury goods in burials and caches for determining wealth in Maya society.

References

Adams, Richard E. W.

1971 *The Ceramics of Altar de Sacrificios.* Papers of the Peabody Museum of Archaeology and Ethnology, vol. 63, no. 1. Harvard University, Cambridge.

Beaudry, Marilyn P.

1983 The Ceramics of the Zapotitán Valley. In *Archaeology and Volcanism in Central America: The Zapotitán Valley of El Salvador*, edited by Payson D. Sheets, pp. 161–190. University of Texas Press, Austin.

Brady, James E., Joseph W. Ball, Ronald L. Bishop, Duncan C. Pring, Norman Hammond, and Rupert A. Housley

1998 The Lowland Maya "Protoclassic": A Reconsideration of Its Nature and Significance. *Ancient Mesoamerica* 9:17–38.

Chase, Diane Z., and Arlen F. Chase (editors)
1992 *Mesoamerican Elites: An Archaeological Assessment.* University of Oklahoma Press, Norman.

Coe, Sophie D., and Michael D. Coe
1996 *The True History of Chocolate.* Thames and Hudson, London.

Culbert, T. Patrick
1965 *The Ceramic History of the Central Highlands of Chiapas, Mexico.* Papers of the New World Archaeological Foundation 19. Brigham Young University, Provo.
1974 *The Lost Civilization: The Story of the Classic Maya.* Harper and Row, New York.

Deal, Michael
1998 *Pottery Ethnoarchaeology in the Central Maya Highlands.* University of Utah Press, Salt Lake City.

Flannery, Kent V., and Joyce Marcus
1994 *Early Formative Pottery of the Valley of Oaxaca, Mexico.* Memoirs of the Museum of Anthropology 27. University of Michigan, Ann Arbor.

Forsyth, Donald W.
1993 The Ceramic Sequence at Nakbe, Guatemala. *Ancient Mesoamerica* 4:31–53.

Freidel, David A., Linda Schele, and Joy Parker
1993 *Maya Cosmos: Three Thousand Years on the Shaman's Path.* William Morrow, New York.

Gifford, James C.
1960 The Type-Variety Method of Ceramic Classification as an Indicator of Cultural Phenomena. *American Antiquity* 25(3):341–347.
1976 *Prehistoric Pottery Analysis and the Ceramics of Barton Ramie in the Belize Valley.* Peabody Museum of Archaeology and Ethnology Memoir 18. Harvard University, Cambridge.

Graham, Elizabeth
1994 *The Highlands of the Lowlands: Environment and Archaeology in the Stann Creek District, Belize, Central America.* Monographs in World Archaeology 19. Prehistory Press, Madison.

Haviland, William A., and Hattula Moholy-Nagy
1992 Distinguishing the High and Mighty from the Hoi Polloi at Tikal, Guatemala. In *Mesoamerican Elites: An Archaeological Assessment*, edited by Diane Z. Chase and Arlen F. Chase, pp. 50–60. University of Oklahoma Press, Norman.

Hendon, Julia A.
1991 Status and Power in Classic Maya Society: An Archaeological Approach. *American Anthropologist* 91:894–918.

Hurst, W. Jeffrey, Stanley M. Tarka, Terry G. Powis, Fred Valdez, Jr., and Thomas R. Hester
2002 Cacao Usage by the Earliest Maya Civilization. *Nature* 418:289–290.

Kosakowsky, Laura J.

1983 Intrasite Variability of the Formative Ceramics from Cuello, Belize: An Analysis of Form and Function. Ph.D. diss., Department of Anthropology, University of Arizona, Tucson.

LeCount, Lisa J.

1999 Polychrome Pottery and Political Strategies in Late and Terminal Classic Lowland Maya Society. *Latin American Antiquity* 10(3):239–258.

McAnany, Patricia A.

2000 Praise the Ahaw and Pass the Kakaw: Xibun Maya and the Luxury Economy of the Petén. Paper presented at the Annual Symposium of the University of Texas at Austin Maya meetings, Austin.

McAnany, Patricia A., Rebecca Storey, and Angela K. Lockard

1999 Mortuary Ritual and Family Politics at Formative and Classic K'axob, Belize. *Ancient Mesoamerica* 10:129–146

McAnany, Patricia A., and Sandra Varela López

1999 Re-creating the Formative Maya Village of K'axob: Chronology, Ceramic Complexes, and Ancestors in Architectural Context. *Ancient Mesoamerica* 10:147–168.

Pendergast, David M.

1981a Lamanai, Belize: Summary of Excavation Results, 1974–1980. *Journal of Field Archaeology* 8:29–53.

1981b The 1980 Excavations at Lamanai, Belize. *Mexicon* 2(6):96–98.

1981c A Regular Three-Ring Circus. *Royal Ontario Museum Archaeological Newsletter* 192. Toronto.

1998 Intercession with the Gods: Caches and Their Significance at Altun Ha and Lamanai, Belize. In *The Sowing and the Dawning: Termination, Dedication, and Transformation in the Archaeological and Ethnographic Record of Mesoamerica*, edited by Shirley B. Mock, pp. 55–63. University of New Mexico Press, Albuquerque.

Powis, Terry G.

1999 The Role of Pottery and Food Consumption among Late Preclassic Maya Commoners at Lamanai, Belize. Paper presented at the 98th Annual Meeting of the American Anthropological Association, Chicago.

2000 A Preliminary Report on the Preclassic Ceramics of Lamanai, Belize. In *Lamanai Field Reports 1997 to 1999*, edited by Elizabeth Graham and H. Ritscher, pp. 26–37. Manuscript on file, Institute of Archaeology, University College London, England.

2001 Technological Experimentation and Artistic Expression at Lamanai during the Protoclassic Period. Paper presented at the 66th Annual Meeting of the Society for American Archaeology, New Orleans.

Powis, Terry G., Fred Valdez, Jr., Thomas R. Hester, W. Jeffrey Hurst, and Stanley M. Tarka

2002 Spouted Vessels and Cacao Use among the Preclassic Maya. *Latin American Antiquity* 13(1):85–106.

Pring, Duncan C.

1977 Influence or Intrusion? The "Protoclassic" in the Maya Lowlands. In *Social Process in Maya Prehistory: Studies in Honour of Sir Eric Thompson*, edited by Norman Hammond, pp. 135–166. Academic Press, London.

Reents-Budet, Dorie

1994 *Painting the Maya Universe: Royal Ceramics of the Classic Period.* Duke University Press, Durham.

Reents-Budet, Dorie, Ronald L. Bishop, Jennifer T. Taschek, and Joseph W. Ball

2000 Out of the Palace Dumps: Ceramic Production and Use at Buenavista del Cayo. *Ancient Mesoamerica* 11:99–121.

Reina, Ruben E., and Robert M. Hill

1978 *The Traditional Pottery of Guatemala.* University of Texas Press, Austin.

Robertson, Robin

1983 Functional Analysis and Social Process in Ceramics: The Pottery from Cerros, Belize. In *Civilization in the Ancient Americas: Essays in Honor of Gordon R. Willey*, edited by Richard M. Leventhal and Alan L. Kolata, pp. 105–142. University of New Mexico Press, Albuquerque.

Sabloff, Jeremy A., and Robert E. Smith

1969 The Importance of Both Analytic and Taxonomic Classification in the Type-Variety System. *American Antiquity* 34(3):278–285.

Sharer, Robert J. (editor)

1978 Pottery and Conclusions. In *The Prehistory of Chalchuapa, El Salvador*, Vol. 3. Museum Monographs, University of Pennsylvania Press, Philadelphia.

Sheets, Payson D.

1992 *The Cerén Site: A Prehistoric Village Buried by Volcanic Ash in Central America.* Harcourt Brace Jovanovich, Fort Worth.

Smith, Michael E.

1987 Household Possessions and Wealth in Agrarian States: Implications for Archaeology. *Journal of Anthropological Archaeology* 6(4): 297–335.

Smith, Robert E., Gordon R. Willey, and James C. Gifford

1960 The Type-Variety Concept as a Basis for the Analysis of Maya Pottery. *American Antiquity* 25(3):330–340.

Stuart, David

1988 The Río Azul Cacao Pot: Epigraphic Observations on the Function of a Maya Ceramic Vessel. *Antiquity* 62:153–157.

Thompson, Raymond H.

1958 *Modern Yucatecan Maya Pottery Making.* Memoirs of the Society for American Archaeology 15. Salt Lake City.

Valdez, Fred, Lauren A. Sullivan, and Andrew Manning

1999 Old Problems, New Perspectives: Ceramic Analyses in the Northeastern Petén and Northern Belize. Paper presented at the 63rd Annual Meeting of the Society for American Archaeology, Chicago.

Webster, David L., and Nancy Gonlin

1988 Household Remains of the Humblest Maya. *Journal of Field Archaeology* 15:169–190.

Wheat, Joe B., James C. Gifford, and William W. Walsey

1958 Ceramic Type, Type Cluster, and Ceramic System in Southwestern Pottery Analysis. *American Antiquity* 32(3):289–315.

Willey, Gordon R., William R. Bullard, John B. Glass, and James C. Gifford

1965 *Prehistoric Maya Settlements in the Belize Valley*. Papers of the Peabody Museum of Archaeology and Ethnology 54. Harvard University, Cambridge.

Willey, Gordon R., T. Patrick Culbert, and Richard E. W. Adams

1967 Maya Lowland Ceramics: A Report from the 1965 Guatemala City Conference. *American Antiquity* 32(3):289–315.

CHAPTER 4

Of Salt and Water: Ancient Commoners on the Pacific Coast of Guatemala

BÁRBARA ARROYO

The study of commoners poses several problems in archaeology. First, the definition for commoners is a very broad one, normally referring to a person not of the nobility, a member of the common people, and second, it is difficult to clearly identify them on the archaeological record. Arlen and Diane Chase mentioned that the actual identification of ". . . commoners can be accommodated using traditional archaeological data, but with a bit more rigor than has sometimes been used in the past" (1992:12). Specifically for the Maya, they further argue that concepts such as egalitarian and two-class complexes are broad categories that are not overly helpful in interpreting the archaeological record. Contributions from this volume may help us understand useful ways to approach the study of commoners in Maya prehistory.

Commoners Research on the Pacific Coast

Almost every archaeological project carried out on the Pacific coast of Guatemala has focused on a general problem: aspects such as the origins and evolution of complex societies (Arroyo 1994; Coe 1961; Pye and Demarest 1991), the role of the Olmec and Teotihuacán on the Pacific coast (Love 1989), and the transition of chiefdoms to states (Bove et al. 1993). While the role of commoners is important to help understand the questions just mentioned, most projects have focused on single sites or regional surveys (Bove 1989; Chinchilla 1996). This has been done to gain a general perspective on the settlement hierarchy of a particular area and chronology and to obtain a wide sample of material that can provide information on ancient settlement patterns. Here, I present data from the

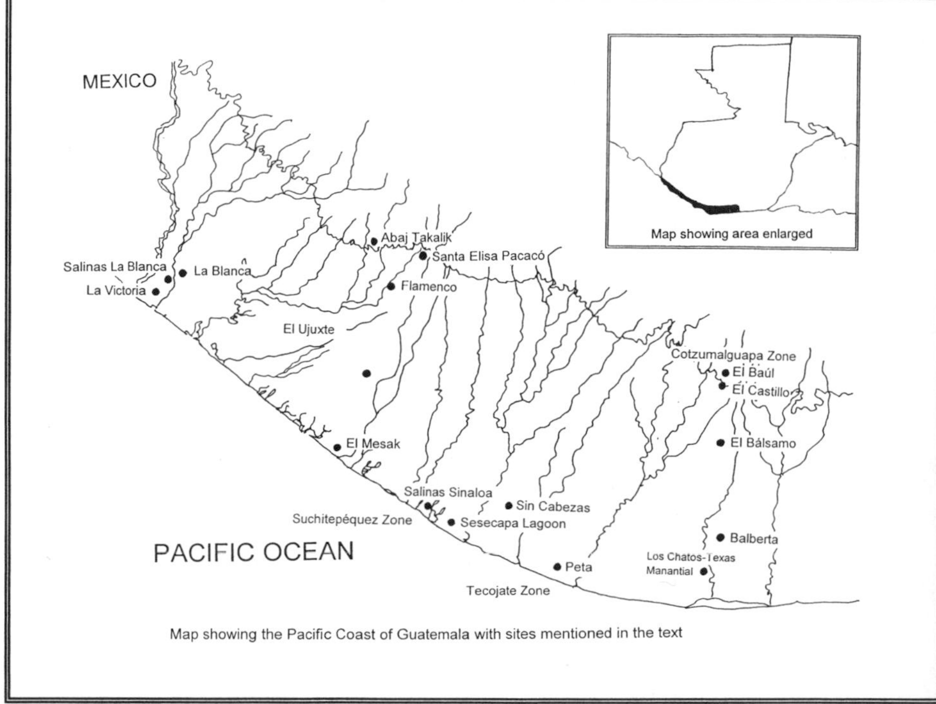

Figure 4.1. Map of the Pacific coast of Guatemala showing the location of sites mentioned in the text

Early Formative to the Postclassic that provide information on coastal commoners.

Early Formative Commoners

The earliest occupation documented to date on the Pacific coast of Guatemala corresponds to the Early Formative (1500–800 BC) period. We now have an ample perspective of the early occupation covering the regions between La Victoria and the Tecojate Zone and farther to the east (Figure 4.1). It is known that population density was low, the settlement was concentrated on the edges of estuaries and mangroves, and each region developed differently. There is a need to address regions individually to understand the different levels of social complexity and the role of commoners by region. Although a developed chiefdom may have existed in

Chiapas, and perhaps along the western Pacific coast, the remaining section seems to have been organized in a less complex manner.

La Victoria, Salinas La Blanca, and El Mesak

The sites of La Victoria, Salinas La Blanca, and El Mesak (see Figure 4.1), located in a rich area of estuaries and swamps, have been identified as fishing hamlets (Coe 1961; Coe and Flannery 1967; Pye and Demarest 1991). Excavation findings include living floors and associated features such as postholes, hearths, ceramics, and subsistence remains. The inhabitants subsisted on a variety of aquatic resources and mangrove fauna, demonstrating the importance of estuary products as food. Crude milling stones are present and, with them, inferential evidence for agriculture. Textile art is partly preserved through decorative impressions on pottery. Cordage of agave and cotton fibers is impressed on pottery.

The only evidence for ritual activity at La Victoria is illustrated by the presence of figurines. In contrast, at El Mesak, excavations uncovered a ceremonial construction dating to 1090±60 BC, suggesting a greater degree of social complexity than earlier research had revealed (Pye et al. 1999), hence showing the diverse social dynamics of the Early Formative society. At Salinas La Blanca, dating to the end of the Early Formative, there is a slightly different pattern from that of La Victoria and El Mesak. Michael Coe and Kent Flannery (1967:71) proposed a self-sufficient and totally sedentary hamlet, well adapted to coastal farming life.

Although more research in this region is needed to better understand the Early Formative, groups that settled on the western Pacific coast of Guatemala evidence relatively complex behavior. Archaeological sites consist of two or more mounds, and large buildings suggest some kind of ceremonial activity.

Suchitepéquez and Escuintla

Most of the archaeological sites found in the area of Suchitepéquez and Escuintla are single mounds, probably representing extended family households. They are located approximately 1 km from each other, suggesting a low population density. Excavations have revealed a superposition of living floors made of compact clay and a mixture of clay and shell. These deposits likely reflect the mobile nature of the Early Formative society in the region, with alternating periods of temporary occupation, abandonment, and re-occupation. All sites are located next to major estuaries and mangroves where horizontal movement on the coast was very easy. It is likely that once an extended family had exhausted all of the resources available at a specific zone, they would move to another, coming back to the original area once some time had passed and resources had replenished.

There is evidence for specific domestic activities, including the use of figurines (usually naked female representations) and of simple and bipolar flakes, which are often employed in a simple economy.

The mobile nature of the society may account for the lack of social differentiation at the sites near this part of the coast. Exceptions can be seen at Salinas Sinaloa, Suchitepéquez, and at Peta in the Tecojate Zone (see Figure 4.1), and these consist of platforms with large hearths and middens with animal remains, suggesting a more diverse function. At Peta, figurines were recovered, and because of the particular traits limited to these sites on the central coast, two explanations can be posited. One is that Peta was a public building where communal rituals and feasts took place, such as a location for celebrating a good fishing trip or a successful hunt. However, another possibility may be that it was the house of a leader who gained authority through becoming a successful hunter or fisherman. He may have gained prestige because of his expertise in hunting/fishing techniques or perhaps from knowledge of the best places to fish and hunt. Arlen Chase (1992) has mentioned that status in a noble society was determined by membership in a social group based on kinship and descent. However, relative position in society could have been affected by other factors, such as line of work or achievements, which could be the case for the Early Formative example. If there was social differentiation at Peta and Sinaloa, these sites would clearly have two groups: commoners and a leadership (possibly an elite). Here, we would not expect to see several levels of commoners because of low population density and a lack of marked centralization. Without a centralized structure, the Early Formative coastal society was flexible and adaptive, able to persist with relatively little change over long periods of time. And, importantly, evidence for commoners is just emerging at some sites but will need more archaeological work in the future.

Middle Formative Commoners

By the end of the Early Formative, the coastal society was changing dramatically due to the development and intensification of agriculture and sedentism. The number of villages grew, and sites extended from the mangrove swamp shores to the interior of the coastal plains. For the first time, planned ceremonial centers were constructed with clay platforms and pyramidal mounds. Most buildings showed a north-south orientation, as identified at Monte Alto, Cristóbal, Las Morenas, Los Cerritos-Sur, Pilar, Vista Hermosa, and Reynosa—all in Escuintla (Bove 1989).

Frederick Bove (1989) and others (e.g., Love 1991) have proposed the presence of a hierarchy of sites with regional and secondary sites. The most important sites of this period include La Blanca in San Marcos, Abaj Takalik in Retalhuleu, and El Bálsamo in Escuintla. Unfortunately, we have information for domestic activity only from La Blanca, as research on the other sites is limited to the main centers. At La Blanca, the main center was destroyed by the building of the road to Tilapa, but a small portion of the domestic area was studied by Michael Love, who sees a trend in intensification of food production (corn and dogs) from the previous period. He mentions that economic intensification was driven by the demands of emerging social inequality and competition for social status, processes that began in the Early Formative but became more clearly manifested by the Middle Formative (Love 1991).

While the construction of houses at La Blanca does not seem to differ one from another, Love noticed that two households had higher occurrences of certain valued goods than did other households at La Blanca and La Victoria. This difference suggests that some occupants were of higher rank than others of Conchas period society in the Middle Formative (850–650 BC; Love 1991:61). Love sees that some of these goods served to define groups in daily interaction. An important fact is that although the excavations took place on domestic structures, these were located very close to the main center, providing access to a particular and select sector of the site.

In contrast with Love's information from La Blanca, the site of La Victoria, just 35 km south, presents a different situation. Here, excavations at Mound III contain the remains of a Conchas house (Figure 4.2; Coe 1961). Foundations varied from shell layers to actual clay floors. The structure was rectangular and oriented to true north. Postholes indicate a structure's outline that included rounded corners, and it is probable that a thatch roof was utilized.

Houses were arranged at random in the village, and Coe proposes a social structure of a multilineage system (Coe 1961:116). Subsistence strategies were simple yet self-sufficient and included fishing, hunting, collecting, and agriculture. As with La Blanca, many figurines were recovered.

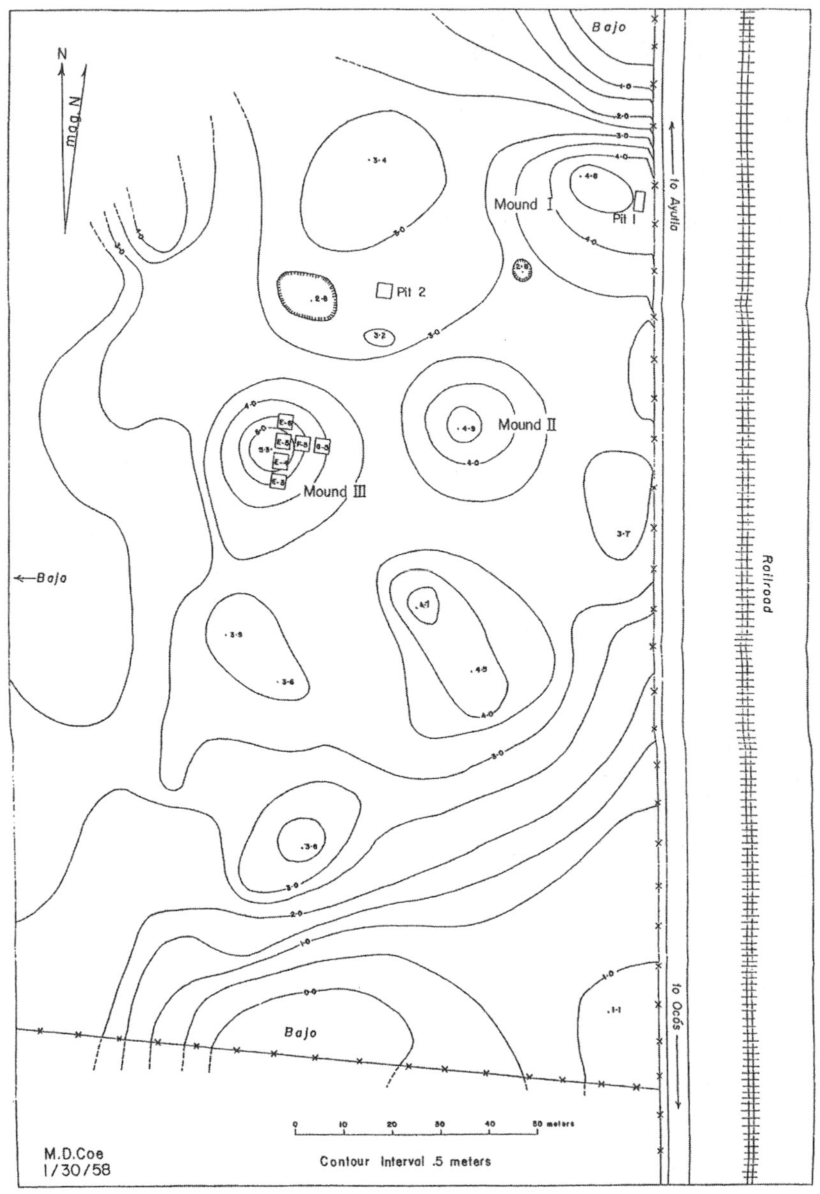

Figure 4.2. Map of La Victoria showing location of excavations, published by the Papers of the Peabody Museum of Archaeology and Ethnology, vol. LIII, courtesy of Michael D. Coe

They represent mostly naked women, some of which are pregnant. A variety of coiffures and headdresses are present. Burials at La Victoria were few and deficient in offerings, and some were encountered in midden deposits below the house floors (Arroyo 2002; Coe 1961:119; Love 2002). By comparing La Blanca with La Victoria, it seems that the latter site may represent a commoners' hamlet, while La Blanca represents the main center and probably the elite. Most of the households at La Blanca represent residences of ranked individuals, as determined from differential distribution of exotic goods.

According to Love, La Blanca had the first regional government on the Pacific coast during the Middle Formative, but at the end of this period, it collapsed. A new center emerged at El Ujuxte, located a short distance from La Blanca. El Ujuxte was larger and more powerful than La Blanca and survived longer (Love and Castillo 1996:144). At El Ujuxte, excavations were conducted at the main center and at the outskirts of the site (Figure 4.3). The mounds at the center suggest that they served as residences of the elite because of the presence of ornamental jade and obsidian and the density of animal bones. Large vessels at elite households suggest the presence of storage. The great density of obsidian indicates that the elite may have controlled the exchange of this product. Excavations at commoners' houses discovered few occurrences of obsidian and none of the other goods.

Another important aspect is that of household ritual. The absence of figurines at El Ujuxte, in contrast with the enormous amount at La Blanca and La Victoria, suggests changes in household ideology at the end of the Middle Formative and the beginning of the Late Formative. This may be due to the increase in labor needed for the building of public structures, suggesting that public rituals become more important than household ones.

Burials placed underneath the house floors are very common at El Ujuxte. Such a practice was not clearly defined for the previous periods. As a specific (uniform) pattern that begins by the end of the Middle Formative and continues for hundreds of years, this practice shows an important change in the nature of social identity of the period (Love and Castillo 1996:148).

Commoners in the Late Preclassic and Early Classic

The coastal society during the Late Preclassic comprised several regional chiefdoms. Some consider that by the end of the period a transition be-

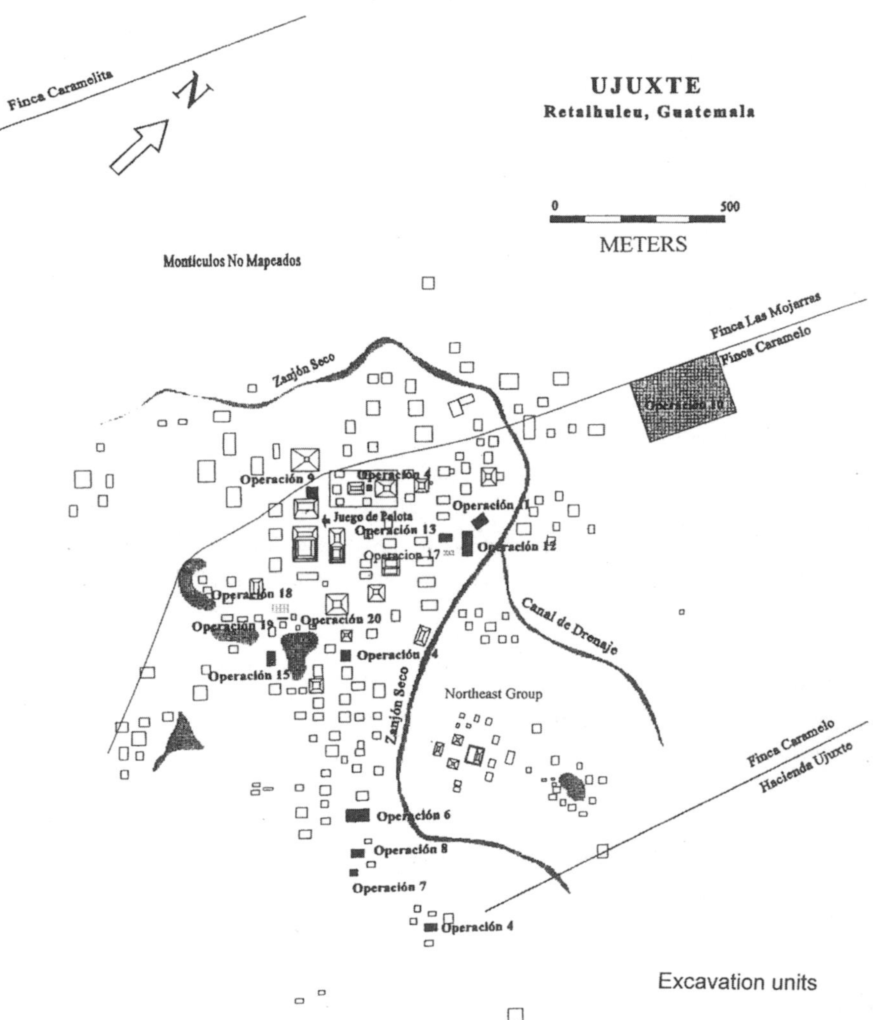

Figure 4.3. Map of Ujuxte, Retalhuleu, Guatemala, showing location of excavations, courtesy of Michael W. Love

tween chiefdom- and state-like organization was already occurring, as illustrated with the Balberta site (Bove et al. 1993). Balberta is located on the lower coast of the department of Escuintla (see Figure 4.1), near the modern town of La Gomera, and it was extensively excavated by Bove (Bove et. al. 1993). The main center and a large number of households dating to the Late Preclassic were documented (Figure 4.4). Households embody and underlie the organization of a society at its most basic level;

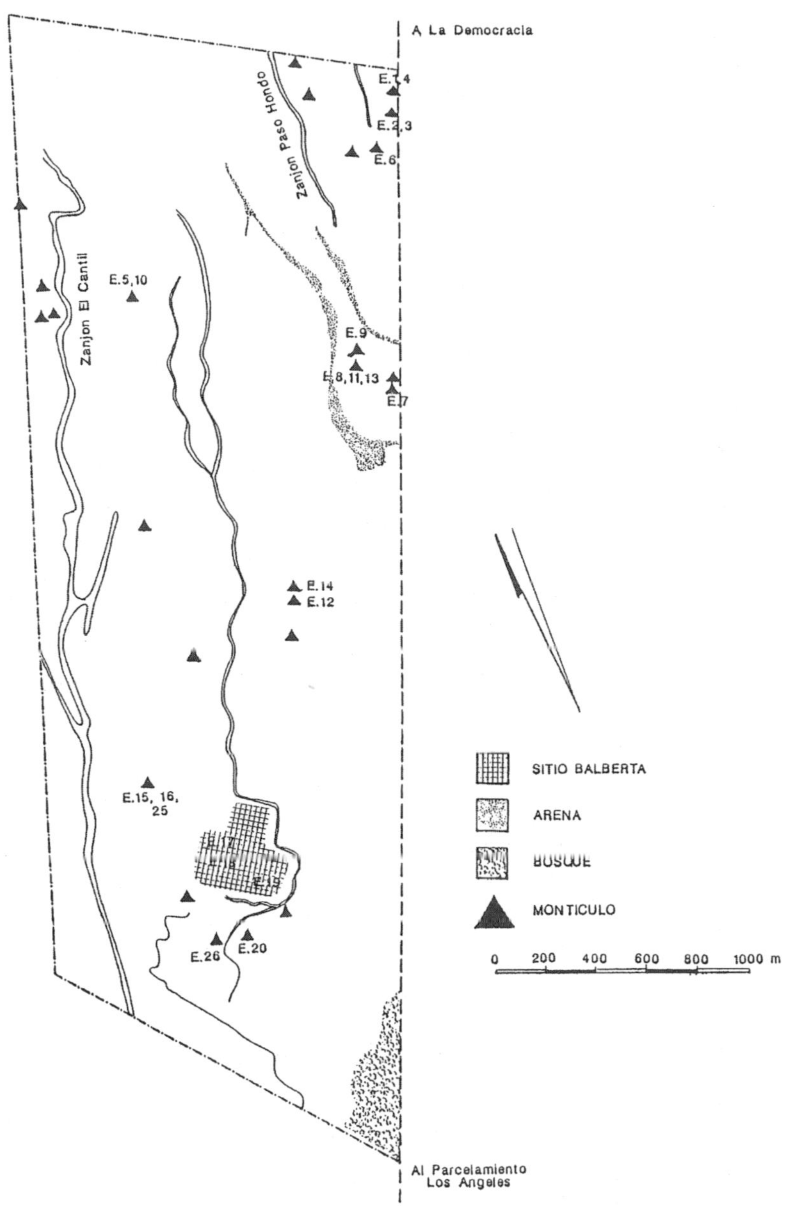

Figure 4.4. Map of Balberta showing location of the center and periphery, published by Bove et al. 1993, p. 111, © University of Pittsburgh Latin American Archaeology Publications, Memoir No. 6, 1993, courtesy of University of Pittsburgh Latin American Archaeology Publications

they can therefore serve as sensitive indicators of evolutionary change in social organization (Ashmore and Wilk 1988). Most households at the periphery of Balberta have clay surface floors with refuse that shows their domestic nature and perhaps even low status. They consist of very low platforms without formal architecture. Some of the excavations exposed clay floors with postholes and hearths. Almost every excavated household had a burial at the center of the structure (Arroyo 1990). Most burials contained simple offerings showing the low status of their ancient inhabitants. However, a few examples had jade beads or other artifacts, normally placed in the mouth. This is a tradition that Diego de Landa (1938) refers to as a way of assuring a person's way to the afterlife. It may be that jade was the only precious object kept by these commoners and is therefore not necessarily a reflection of high status. Information from the burials is critical, as treatment of the dead may provide information on their social position in life.

In contrast with the periphery, two burials excavated at the center contribute information on the wealth differences between the center and the periphery. Burial 25 corresponds to an individual that had a special role in Balberta's society. This individual was not buried at the main center, but was placed in a structure just north of the main plaza. The offering of nine vessels and a jade fragment suggests that this was an important person. One of the vessels had a smaller one inside it filled with red pigment, suggesting a specialized role in the society and thus explaining the larger number of offerings. The structure where the burial was placed shares the same characteristics of other houses excavated at the site.

The other important example is Burial 17, which was placed in the enormous clay platform at the center of the site. This was the only individual with dental modification and an offering of five vessels. The placement of this individual inside the platform, which is the largest construction at the site, suggests a very important person in the society. The platform seems to have housed specialized artisans that were controlled by the elite. This individual may have been a member of the elite responsible for supervising the work of the specialists. We know of specialized activities at Balberta because of the findings of a large number of spindle whorls, a cacao effigy offering associated with a deposit of green obsidian artifacts, and several storage vessels. Bove et al. (1993) suggest that these artifacts are related to the importance of the site, its control over cotton and cacao production, and trade along the Pacific coast. The periphery housed the commoners who were responsible for cultivating the land and caring for the orchards. Their residences were within 1 km of the main center. Apart from the commoners being responsible for cultivating the land, other members of the society had a higher status level because of their ability to carry out special work, such as the case of the individual in Burial 25. The location of his residence close to the main center is another argument to support such an idea. The layout of the main center seems to indicate that access to it may have been restricted as yet another way to show the differences between elite and commoners.

Although Sin Cabezas in Tiquisate is contemporaneous with Balberta, most of the excavations there were carried out at the main center, and the information pertains to the elite, so little can be said about the commoners at that site.

Commoners of the Middle Classic, Late Classic, and Postclassic

Again, we have little information on the role of commoners during the Classic and Postclassic periods. However, following is some analysis of research carried out at the sites of Los Chatos–Texas–Manantial, Escuintla; Flamenco and Santa Elisa Pacacó in Retalhuleu; and those in the Cotzumalguapa area—all of which have pertinent data.

Los Chatos-Texas-Manantial

The Los Chatos–Texas–Manantial area is an extensive archaeological region covering approximately 100 km² along the southern portion of Escuintla (see Figure 4.1). This significant area has several sites of great proportion and complex architecture. Part of it was excavated by Bove and others in 1991 and 1992 (Figure 4.5; Bove 1992). While most of the excavations were carried out at the main centers, some were done in the outskirts. The materials recovered are currently under analysis and may be available for future interpretations on the role of commoners.

Flamenco

The Flamenco site, excavated by Mark Johnson and Erick Ponciano, is located in Retalhuleu (see Figure 4.1) and dates to the Late Classic. Excavations outside the site show the daily life of commoners. In contrast with the other examples we have seen from the coast, houses are built from clay and wattle and daub, or *bajareque.* Interestingly, this site has foundations of unworked boulders that measure between 5 and 8 m in length and 3 to

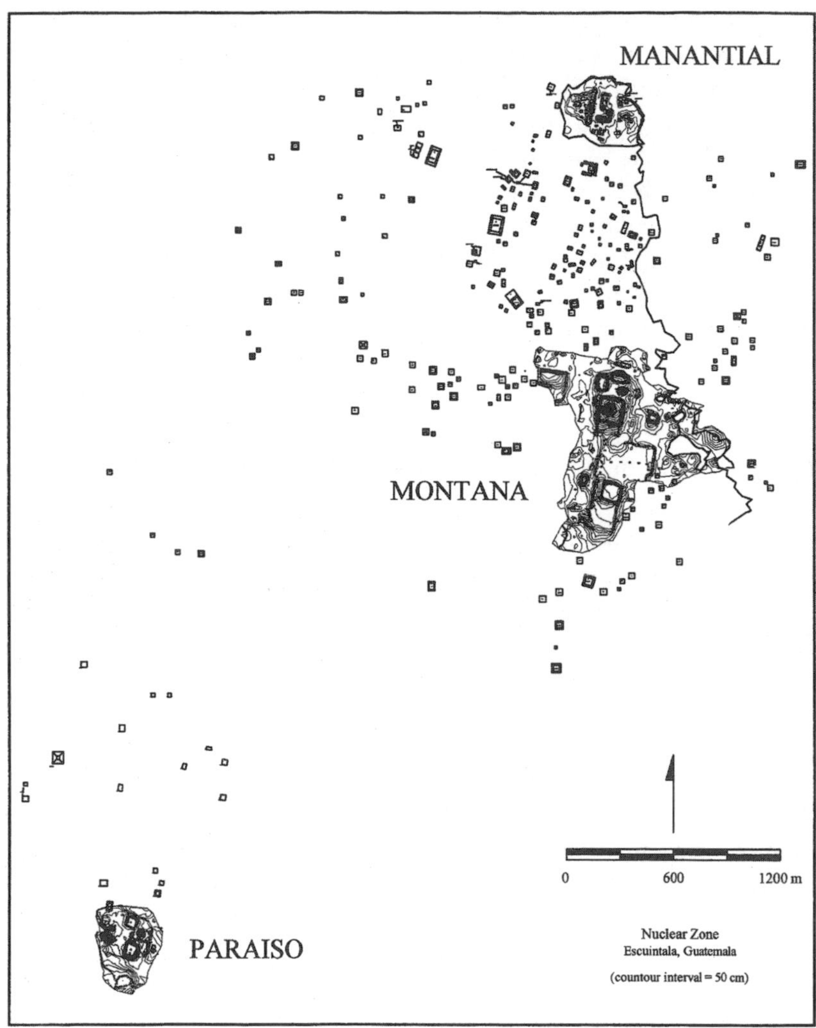

Figure 4.5. Sketch map of Montana-Paraíso-Manantial complex courtesy of Frederick J. Bove.

5 m in width (Figure 4.6). Houses are rectangular and have a packed or rammed clay floor. No postholes were identified, and a few walls were constructed of stone (up to 80 cm high), with perishable material completing the wall height. Some used *bajareque* as construction material.

Commoner structures were located 300 m south of the main center at Flamenco. Two small patio groups were identified, and three houses were excavated. Most artifacts were recovered from inside the structures, whereas the patio areas were completely clean of any items, demonstrating that the area shared by the groups was kept clear of debris. The domestic function of the structures is varied. A series of utilitarian pottery was recovered, together with manos, metates, bark beaters, and obsidian tools (blades, flakes, knives, etc.). Ponciano (1996) proposes that some areas were used for the preparation or storage of food. Various figurines and musical instruments were recovered, and examples of stone sculpture suggest the practice of household rituals.

An interesting finding at the site was the presence of 106 spindle whorls in one of the structures, suggesting specialization at the commoner level. It is likely that the residents at Structure D-1 enjoyed relative wealth and perhaps had a "middle position" in the local society. This is confirmed partly by the presence of luxury items such as Plumbate pottery, ear spools, beads, and greenstone objects (Ponciano 1996).

A problem with the site is that only D-1 was excavated and it is assumed to be a commoner's residence because of its distance from the main center

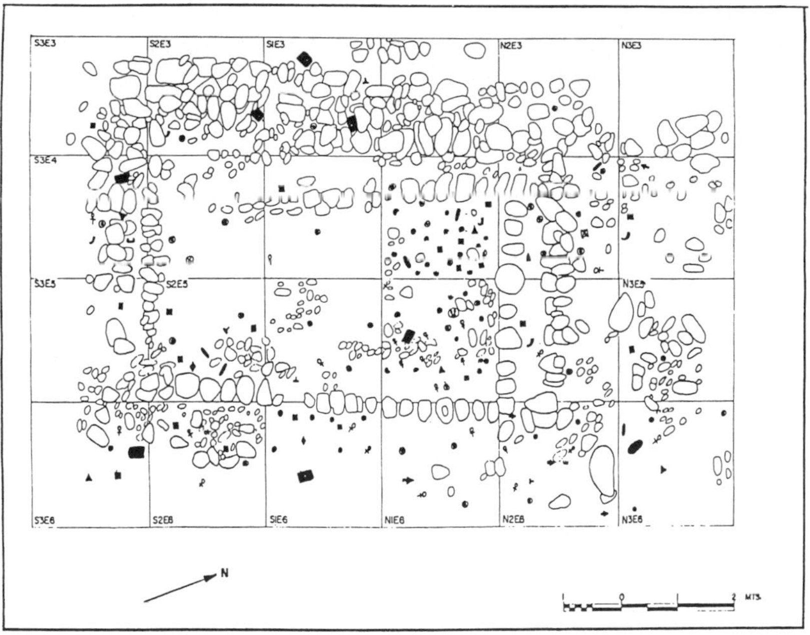

Figure 4.6. Plan view of a house at Flamenco, Retalhuleu, Guatemala, courtesy of Erick Ponciano

(Figure 4.7). Unfortunately, there are no other excavations at the site with which to compare artifacts and use patterns. Thus, the center is not compared directly with the periphery, making the definition of commoners a difficult assessment.

Cotzumalguapa

In the late 1990s, Oswaldo Chinchilla (1996) and collaborators began excavating sites in the Cotzumalguapa heartland. This is particularly important because they have excavated in domestic groups close to the main sites of El Baúl, El Castillo, and Bilbao (see Figures 4.1, 4.8). Prior to their work, all the excavations in the area were limited to the main centers (Parsons 1967; Thompson 1948). Part of this effort has been done as rescue projects because of the destruction of sites due to urbanization and modern agriculture.

A difficulty with the identification of house structures in the area is that the landscape is affected by volcanic phenomena, and the domestic structures are buried (Chinchilla and Antillón 1998). As part of Chinchilla's research, a systematic survey identified possible domestic areas. Later, a Ground-Penetrating Radar was used to identify deeply buried groups.

Four domestic groups have been excavated: G8-I (northwest of Baúl); K13-I (El Varal); K18-I (Figure 4.9; 200 m west of Baúl Acropolis); and J-107 (a short distance from K18-I).

GROUP G8-I Group G8-I is a rectangular structure constructed of stones, with two corners and parts of benches on the north and south sides. The floor is made of clay with a base of pebbles. The structure had Late Classic and Postclassic occupations.

GROUP K13-I Group K13-I consists of two platforms forming a patio made of stones. The platforms and associated benches were constructed of stone. One of the structures does not have a corner, just a stone bench at the front. The floor is made of clay. At the base of one house was an entrance step where a Plumbate vase, dating to the Late Classic, was recovered that was perhaps an offering for the construction of the house.

GROUP K18-I Very few artifacts were found during the surface survey of Group K18-I. However, shovel testing revealed a cobblestone floor. An extensive excavation followed that uncovered the floor measuring 10 × 11 m. This floor continues to a platform that is 55 m in height and has

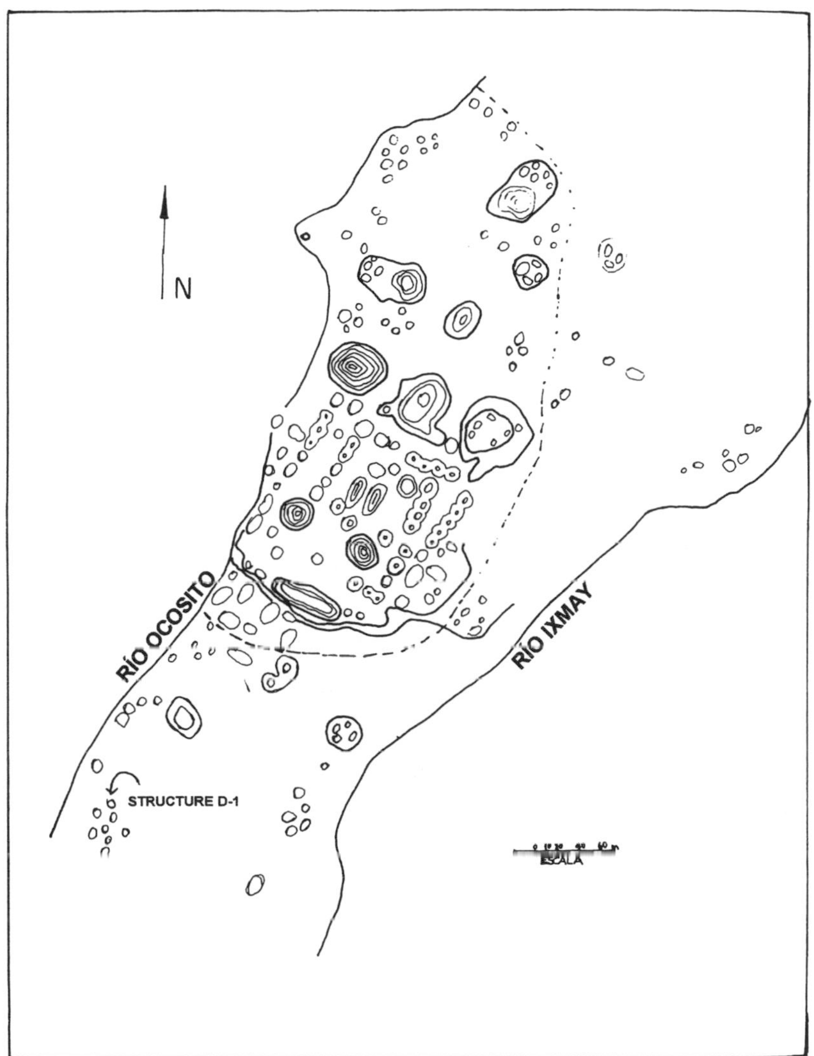

Figure 4.7. Map of the site of Flamenco courtesy of Erick Ponciano

a stairway as access (see Figure 4.9). On top of the platform, walls still remain on the east and south sides.

GROUP J-107 A short distance from the K18-I group was another cobblestone floor in Group J-107. The find indicates a much more complex zone of development than indicated by surface survey.

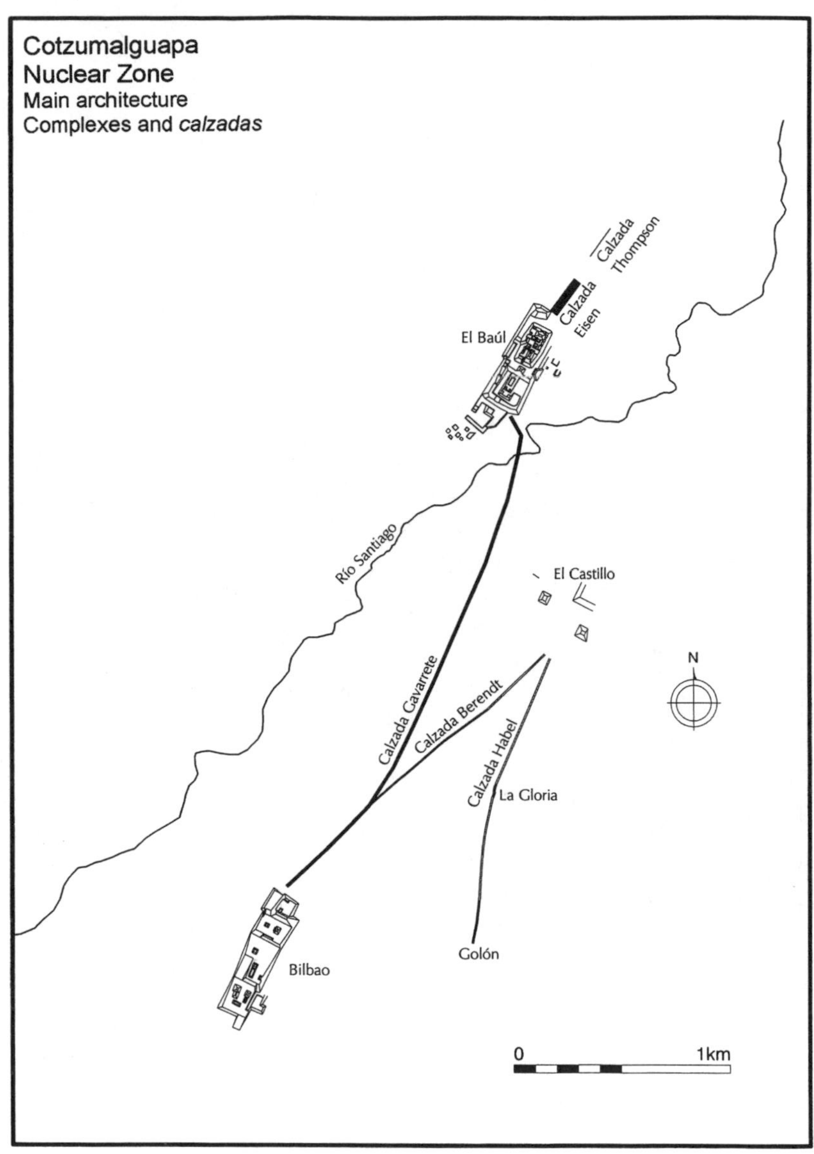

Figure 4.8. Map of the Cotzumalguapa Nuclear Zone, Guatemala, courtesy of Oswaldo Chinchilla

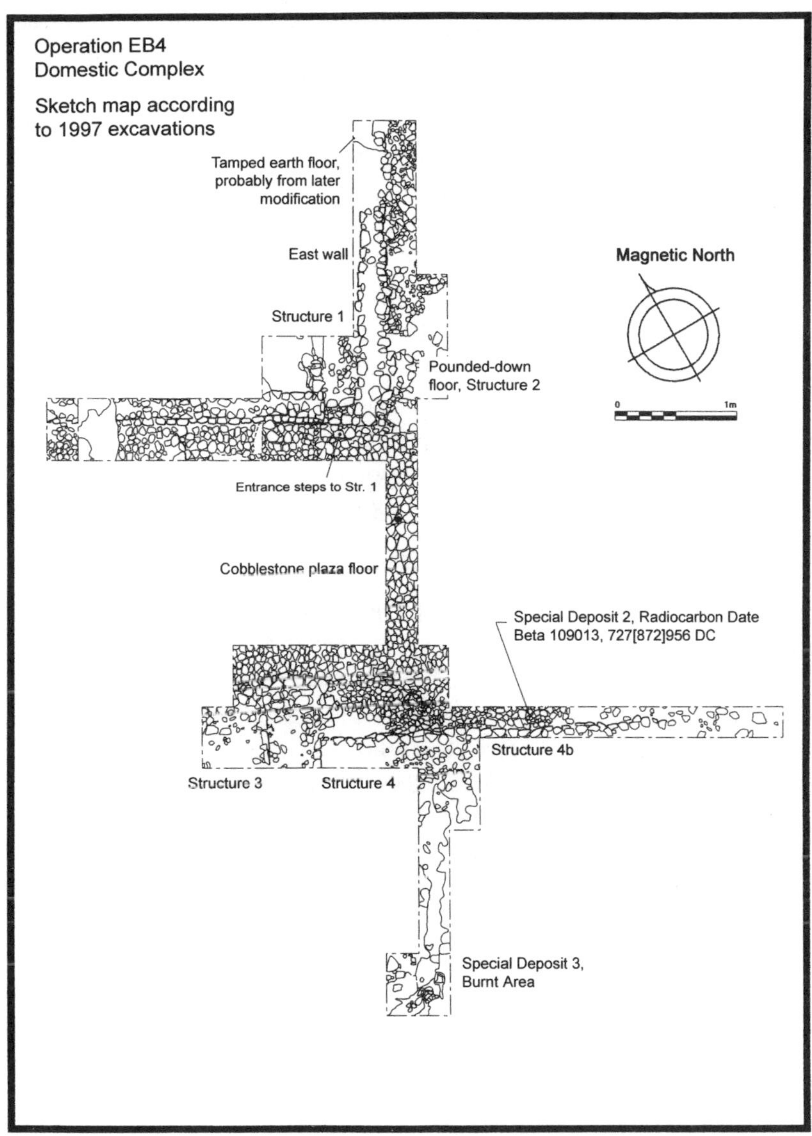

Figure 4.9. Map of El Baúl and sketch map of Group K18-I courtesy of Oswaldo Chinchilla

In summary, there is a sampling problem with the Cotzumalguapa area, as many sites have not had their domestic structures identified or excavated. While the presence of cobblestone floors characterizes El Baúl, none have been found at Bilbao or El Castillo. There is a tendency to use stone for the walls, floors, and benches in all three sites. Domestic structures are placed around patios, and there seems to be a continuity of occupation from the Late Classic to the Postclassic (Chinchilla and Antillón 1998).

As always, more analyses of the household artifacts are needed to understand their distribution and the differential consumption between elites and commoners. Previously, Bove (1989) carried out rescue excavations in the outskirts of the Cotzumalguapa heartland, finding obsidian workshops and several domestic structures. The results of those efforts may enhance our knowledge of commoners for that region.

Santa Elisa Pacacó

Excavations at Santa Elisa Pacacó were carried out as part of a rescue project at the Santa Elisa farm in Retalhuleu (see Figure 4.1). Sonia Medrano's (1996) research showed that during the Late Classic the site was a peripheral hamlet with a small temple, one household for "important" people, and other dispersed households. All the structures had foundations constructed of river cobbles, with *bajareque* walls and clay floors (Figure 4.10). They are rectangular in shape, measuring between 6 and 12 m long, and 3 to 8 m wide. There are no exotic artifacts, but Medrano interprets a different status based on the size of the living areas.

Medrano also suggests that there was a hamlet at the site during the Late Postclassic. The households excavated represent living areas of individuals of higher rank on the northern part of the site, with a platform measuring 10 × 16 m. Because of the number of structures excavated for this period, she proposed that population increased and that the commoners were dedicated to agriculture to fulfill their tribute obligations in cacao and *pataxte* (*Theobroma bicolor*, a species similar to cacao). She suggests that because of the presence of spindle whorls, some people were weaving and producing cloths.

As with other projects, excavations were limited and little information is known about the distribution of artifacts from elite versus non-elite contexts.

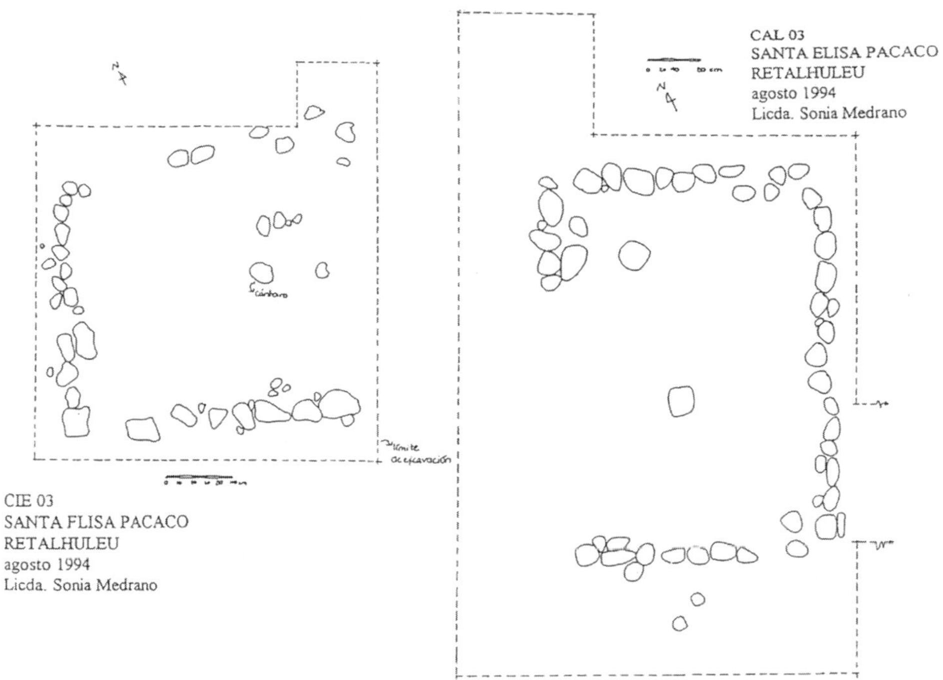

Figure 4.10. Plan view of houses at Santa Elisa Pacacó courtesy of Sonia Medrano

Some Thoughts and Concluding Remarks

Most of the research focusing on commoners from the Pacific coast of Guatemala is scant. By far, the majority of the research comes from projects carried out on the lower coast. Commoners seem to have lived in houses built with perishable materials, appearing very similar to the *ranchos* people live in today. Floors often consisted of pounded-down clay surfaces, and the walls were made of cane, sometimes with a mixture of clay and grass (forming *bajareque*). Roofs consisted of palms or other leaves. The exact shapes of the houses are unknown for the Preclassic because of the lack of extensive excavations and stone foundations. Human burials were generally placed underneath the house floors.

The presence of certain artifacts such as figurines can provide information on important ideological aspects of commoners' lives in ancient societies. These artifacts appear in households during the Early Formative and continue until the Middle Formative. During the Late Formative, the figurine cult disappears and does not show up again until the Classic period. This reflects important events in the society's ideological construction. However, this pattern occurs at both the elite and commoner levels and probably indicates certain common practices.

Households with stone foundations appear in the Late Classic period and are better illustrated with examples from sites on the piedmont, such as Flamenco and the Cotzumalguapa Zone. Here, there is a tendency for rectangular-shaped houses, arranged individually or in small informal groups. However, since some of them are ground-level dwellings, it is hard to understand the household distribution unless a systematic sampling strategy is utilized. This problem plagues the study of commoner houses elsewhere as well (see discussions by Gonlin and Marcus, this volume). At the site of Itzán, for example, Kevin Johnston (1994) refers to invisible domestic structures. These were constructed directly on the ground with perishable materials, sometimes indicated by posthole patterns and clay floors. Other examples include platforms that represent the size of the structure and are defined by retention walls made of stone. Most examples also have plastered floors. This contrasts with the information from the coast, where floors are made from pounded-down (or rammed) clay.

The use of stones in the piedmont occurs because of access to such building materials, whereas the lower coast had to import all its stone from farther inland. Therefore, examples of elite residences such as those at El Ujuxte reflect the ability of these groups to procure such unusual items. House sizes vary according to the status of the individuals, but house shapes seem to have been the same for commoners and elites (at least during the Classic and Postclassic).

House shapes along the Pacific coast contrast greatly with those seen in the Maya lowlands. Early Formative coastal commoners seem to have had ellipse-shaped houses, which changed to rectangular houses in the Classic period. In contrast, the Maya lowlands seem to have had a more stable pattern, as seen on dwelling platforms with benches, terraces, retaining walls, altars, and shrines that are rectangular and square in shape and can be seen from as early as the Cunil phase at Cahal Pech in the Early Formative (Cheetham 1990). There are also platformless dwellings associated with exterior, ground-level open patios constructed of hard plaster, as in the case of Cerros, Belize (Cliff 1988:206). These are presumably associated with a small egalitarian community. An example from Cerén shows the presence of a round structure at the site, illustrating the diversity of household shapes outside the Maya lowlands (Webster et al. 1997).

More extensive excavations are needed on the Pacific coast to understand commoners' roles and distribution. Most research projects have focused on the main centers and their residents, and little is known of other society members. This is also true for the Maya lowlands, as illustrated in this volume.

References

Arroyo, Bárbara

1990 *Enterramientos en Balberta, Escuintla: Inferencias sobre su organización social.* BAR International Series 559. Oxford, England.

1994 The Early Formative in Southern Mesoamerica: An Explanation for the Origins of Sedentary Villages. Ph.D. diss., Department of Anthropology, Vanderbilt University, Nashville.

2002 Appendix I: Classification of La Blanca Figurines. In *Early Complex Society in Pacific Guatemala: Settlements and Chronology of the Río Naranjo, Guatemala*, edited by Michael W. Love, pp. 205–235. Papers of the New World Archaeological Foundation 66. Provo, Utah.

Ashmore, Wendy, and Richard R. Wilk

1988 Household and Community in the Mesoamerican Past. In *Household and Community in the Mesoamerican Past*, edited by Richard R. Wilk and Wendy Ashmore, pp. 1–27. University of New Mexico Press, Albuquerque.

Bove, Frederick J.

1989 *Formative Settlement Patterns on the Pacific Coast of Guatemala: A Spatial Analysis of Complex Societal Evolution.* BAR International Series 493. Oxford, England.

1992 *Objetivos y algunos resultados del Proyecto Los Chatos–Manantial.* Informe entregado al Instituto de Antropología e Historia de Guatemala.

Bove, Frederick J., Sonia Medrano, Brenda Lou, and Bárbara Arroyo (editors)

1993 *The Balberta Project: The Terminal Formative–Early Classic Transition on the Pacific Coast of Guatemala.* University of Pittsburgh Memoirs in Latin American Archaeology 6. University of Pittsburgh and Asociación Tikal, Pittsburgh and Guatemala.

Chase, Arlen F.

1992 Elites and the Changing Organization of Classic Maya Society. In *Mesoamerican Elites: An Archaeological Assessment*, edited by Diane Z. Chase and Arlen F. Chase, pp. 30–49. University of Oklahoma Press, Norman.

Chase, Arlen F., and Diane Z. Chase

1992 Mesoamerican Elites: Assumptions, Definitions, and Models. In *Mesoamerican Elites: An Archaeological Assessment*, edited by Diane Z. Chase and Arlen F. Chase, pp. 3–17. University of Oklahoma Press, Norman.

Chase, Diane Z., and Arlen F. Chase (editors)

1992 *Mesoamerican Elites: An Archaeological Assessment.* University of Oklahoma Press, Norman.

Cheetham, David

1990 Interregional Interactions, Symbol Emulation, and the Emergence of Socio-Political Inequality in the Central Maya Lowlands. Master's thesis, Department of Anthropology and Sociology, University of British Columbia.

Chinchilla, Oswaldo

1996 Settlement Patterns and Monumental Art at a Major Pre-Columbian Polity: Cotzumalguapa, Guatemala. Ph.D. diss., Department of Anthropology, Vanderbilt University, Nashville.

Chinchilla, Oswaldo, and Julio Antillón

1998 Investigaciones en áreas habitacionales de la Zona Nuclear Cotzumalguapa. In *XI Simposio de Investigaciones Arqueológicas en Guatemala*, edited by Juan Pedro Laporte and Héctor Escobedo, pp. 387–396. Ministerio de Cultura y Deportes, IDAEH, Asociación Tikal, Guatemala City.

Cliff, Maynard B.

1988 Domestic Architecture and Origins of Complex Society at Cerros. In *Household and Community in the Mesoamerican Past*, edited by Richard R. Wilk and Wendy Ashmore, pp. 199–226. University of New Mexico Press, Albuquerque.

Coe, Michael

1961 *La Victoria, an Early Site on the Pacific Coast of Guatemala.* Papers of the Peabody Museum of Archaeology and Ethnology 53. Harvard University, Cambridge.

Coe, Michael, and Kent V. Flannery

1967 *Early Cultures and Human Ecology in South Coastal Guatemala.* Smithsonian Contributions to Anthropology 3. Smithsonian Institution, Washington, D.C.

Hoopes, John W.

1991 The Isthmian Alternative: Reconstructing Patterns of Social Organization in Formative Costa Rica. In *The Formation of Complex Society in Southeastern Mesoamerica*, edited by William R. Fowler, Jr., pp. 171–192. CRC Press, Boca Raton.

Johnston, Kevin J.

1994 The "Invisible" Maya: Late Classic Minimally-Platformed Residential Settlement at Itzán, Petén, Guatemala. Ph.D. diss., Department of Anthropology, Yale University.

Landa, Diego de

1938 *Relación de las cosas de Yucatán.* Edición Yucateca. Mérida, Mexico.

Love, Michael W.

1989 Early Settlements and Chronology of the Río Naranjo, Guatemala. Ph.D. diss., University of California, Berkeley.

1991 Style and Social Complexity in Formative Mesoamerica. In *The Formation of Complex Society in Southeastern Mesoamerica*, edited by William R. Fowler, Jr., pp. 47–76. CRC Press, Boca Raton.

2002 *Early Complex Society in Pacific Guatemala: Settlements and Chronology of the Río Naranjo, Guatemala.* Papers of the New World Archaeological Foundation 66. Provo, Utah.

Love, Michael, and Donaldo Castillo

1996 Excavaciones en zonas residenciales en El Ujuxte, Retalhuleu. In *X Simposio de Investigaciones Arqueológicas en Guatemala*, edited by Juan Pedro Laporte and Héctor Escobedo, pp. 143–154. Ministerio de Cultura y Deportes, IDAEH, Asociación Tikal, Guatemala City.

Medrano, Sonia

1996 La población de Santa Elisa Pacacó, Retalhuleu. In *IX Simposio de Investigaciones Arqueológicas en Guatemala, 1995*, edited by Juan Pedro Laporte and Héctor L. Escobedo, pp. 601–617. Ministerio de Cultura y Deportes, IDAEH, Asociación Tikal, Guatemala City.

Parsons, Lee A.

1967 *Bilbao, Guatemala.* Vol. 1. Milwaukee Public Museum Publications in Anthropology 11.

Ponciano, Erick

1988 Un sector habitacional Clásico Tardío, Flamenco, Retalhuleu, Guatemala. Master's thesis, Universidad de San Carlos de Guatemala, Guatemala City.

1996 Evidencia arqueológica sobre una especialización económica en la costa sur de Guatemala en el Clásico Tardío: El Caso Flamenco. *Los Investigadores de la Cultura Maya* (Universidad Autónoma de Campeche, Mexico) 4:268–289.

Pye, Mary, and Arthur A. Demarest

1991 The Evolution of Complex Societies in Southeastern Mesoamerica: New Evidence from El Mesak, Guatemala. In *The Formation of Complex Society in Southeastern Mesoamerica*, edited by William R. Fowler, Jr., pp. 77–100. CRC Press, Boca Raton.

Pye, Mary, Arthur A. Demarest, and Bárbara Arroyo

1999 Early Formative Societies in Guatemala and El Salvador. In *Pacific Latin America in Prehistory*, edited by Michael Blake, pp. 75–88. Washington State University Press, Pullman.

Thompson, Eric H.

1948 *An Archaeological Reconnaissance in the Cotzumalhuapa Region, Escuintla, Guatemala.* Carnegie Institution of Washington Publication 574.

Webster, David, Nancy Gonlin, and Payson Sheets

1997 Copan and Cerén: Two Perspectives on Ancient Mesoamerican Households. *Ancient Mesoamerica* 8:43–61.

Whitley, Tamara

1989 Excavaciones en 1986, Montículo FD-4. In *Investigaciones arqueológicas en la costa sur de Guatemala*, edited by D. S. Whitley and Marilyn P. Beaudry, pp. 98–106. Institute of Archaeology, Monograph 31. University of California, Los Angeles.

CHAPTER 5

Down on the Farm: Classic Maya "Homesteads" as "Farmsteads"

NICHOLAS DUNNING

Several years ago, while interviewing Maya farmers about indigenous soil terms, I was often asked: "What is the land like where you live? Is it good for milpa?" (Dunning 1992a). Such questions underscore a fundamental aspect of Maya life. Both historically and in the more distant past the large majority of Maya have been farmers, a fact that influences almost all aspects of their worldviews and lives. While this fact is, of course, a truism, we sometimes overlook its importance in our pursuit of a more esoteric understanding of the Maya.

In early colonial Yucatán, Maya society was self-divided into two basic classes: *almehenob* (nobility) and *mazehualob* (commoners). This simple categorization, however, belies a more complex reality in which there were clearly subclasses of nobility as well as of commoners, and the boundary between the lower and upper tier of *almehen* and *mazehual* respectively was somewhat fluid (Restall 1997:88–92). Both nobility and commoners were generally farmers, but their ownership and access to farmland was unequal, a situation paralleling pre-Hispanic times.

As farmers, most Maya have lived lives dependent on (among other things) their ability to understand the nuances of their environment and to successfully cultivate the earth. Over time, Maya farmers transformed the lands on which they toiled, often consciously, sometimes unwittingly. Adaptation to a changeable physical environment and to shifting social circumstances was necessary for sustained well-being. Risk management, on the part of both individual farmers and the corporate groups and communities of which they were a part, was a key aspect of successful adaptation. Corporate groups are viewed here simply as hierarchically organized social units (Hayden and Cannon 1982). The nature of these groups and their changeability will be discussed further in the concluding section. For present, suffice it to say that the nature and structure of these groups appear to have changed through time, at least partially in relation to shifting requirements of agricultural production.

In the archaeological record, remnants of the built environment created by the ancient Maya offer many clues concerning both the function and meaning of Maya places (Webster 1998). Following Amos Rapoport (1990), Stephen D. Houston (1998) advises that the meaning of architecture, including houses, needs to be understood as part of the total built environment or cultural landscape. In the case of the Maya of the Classic period, such an understanding would involve a wide range of elements, including centralized areas of monumental architecture, the dwellings of commoners, and the human-modified "natural" environment (Dunning et al. 1999). So where in this totality of landscape do we best come to terms with the lives of Maya commoners? Many have suggested that the archaeological investigation of households offers an insightful entry point into Maya daily life (e.g., Wilk and Ashmore 1988). I would further suggest that from the vantage point of landscape archaeology, approaching Maya homesteads (both houses and house-lots) as farmsteads offers a number of advantages.

Homesteads as Farmsteads

As William F. Hanks (1990:316) has noted for many contemporary Yucatec Maya: "The homestead and the *milpa* . . . [are] two embodiments of a single spatio-temporal system." This "landedness" of Maya reality was likely true in pre-Hispanic times as well (McAnany 1995; Restall 1997). I here define Classic Maya farmsteads as the household, including both its material manifestations and the social group that created and used them, and the totality of their landholdings. Jack D. Eaton (1975) suggested the use of this term in the Río Bec region of the Central Hills physiographic zone to describe distinctly bounded areas that included residential groups and agricultural terraces. However, such clearly demarcated farmsteads are comparatively rare in the archaeological record of the Maya lowlands. Nevertheless, the house-lots (near-residential "open" space) of most urban residences apparently comprised a variety of activity areas, often including areas of significant agricultural production (Tourtellot 1993).

Of course, tying all landholdings to particular households in an archaeological context is an impossible task, particularly during times of relatively low population pressure when field systems likely included spatially distinct and widely distributed "in-field" and "out-field" components (see Ewill and Merrill-Sands 1987; Sanders 1981; Vogt 1969, this volume). However, it is likely that as population levels increased, the distinction between in-field and out-field was progressively blurred and intensive forms of cultivation came to characterize large areas (Drennan 1988; Killion 1992; Turner 1983). For most subregions of the Maya lowlands, this scenario of mounting population pressure and agricultural intensification peaked during the Late or Terminal Classic periods (Dunning et al. 1998). In many areas, the boundary between urban and rural space also became quite blurred, with a notable agricultural component to many urban areas and an increasingly populated countryside. Under these conditions, the close spatial association between residences and probable agricultural fields strongly suggests direct occupation of significant landholdings. In many cases, the farmstead as an organizational unit can easily be detected in both urban and rural contexts (where these contexts are even distinguishable). Farming households needed to be adaptable to both constants and perturbations in social and environmental systems. At times their responses became manifest in the landscape. Examination of several areas of the Maya lowlands from the perspective of adaptive farmsteads may serve to illustrate how changes within larger social and environmental contexts transformed the cultural landscape.

La Milpa and Environs

The ancient city of La Milpa is located in the Three Rivers region toward the eastern edge of the Petén Karst Plateau in what is today northwestern Belize (Figure 5.1). Like many Maya cities in the Petén, La Milpa is situated in proximity to several upland *bajos*, large karst depressions that today contain seasonal swamp forests and agriculturally problematic Vertisol soils. Over the past several years, geo-environmental archaeological investigations have revealed that as late as the Protoclassic period some of these *bajos* contained perennial wetlands and shallow lakes (Dunning et al. 2002), habitats similar to those known to have been highly attractive to early Maya settlers (Pohl et al. 1996). Over the course of several centuries, erosion on surrounding uplands choked the *bajos* with huge quantities of clayey sediment, hydrologically transforming them into seasonal swamps (Dunning et al. 1999). While similar environmental degradation may have contributed to the demise of the large Preclassic urban centers of Nakbe and El Mirador (Jacob 1995), at La Milpa and many other southern lowland centers, the Maya successfully adapted to their changing environment. One adaptation was the construction of centralized reservoirs within the urban area (Scarborough et al. 1995). This development probably contributed to growing social and economic inequalities in Maya society by vesting symbolic and, to a limited degree, actual control over a vital resource (water) as well as by increasingly skewing land values in favor of the site center and elite landholders (Dunning 1995). Nevertheless, smaller-scale water management features and more soil- and water-conserving forms of agriculture came to characterize the cultivated areas of the La Milpa urban area (Hammond et al. 1998) as well as rural farmsteads throughout the region (Hughbanks 1998; Lohse, this volume; Lohse and Findlay 2000), particularly as population growth accelerated in the Late Classic.

Notably, many of the areas of highest rural population concentration in the Three Rivers region were along ecotonal boundaries such as escarpment edges and *bajo* margins (Dunning et al. 2003). For example, the Barba Group, an apparent corporate group settlement (mapped, excavated, and identified as a lineage compound by Hageman 1999a), is situated along the Río Bravo Escarpment, potentially giving residents access to the water and land resources of both the Río Bravo floodplain and the lands of the flanking karst uplands, as well as terrace systems on the escarpment itself (Figure 5.2). This rural settlement pattern is one that might best be predicted on the basis of risk management: a strategy of resource diversification that minimized risk (in the event of the failure of one resource) and maximized group resource control (see Levi 1996). In the settlement areas around the major site of Dos Hombres, Jon C. Lohse (2001, this volume) identifies two distinct types of settlement patterns: (1) hierarchically structured corporate groups, and (2) densely settled, structurally more homogeneous "micro-communities." Notably, both types of settlement organization are viewed as specific adaptations to environmental circumstances and the requirements of local agriculture.

Petexbatún/Río de la Pasión Region

The Petexbatún region lies within the Río de la Pasión lowlands of southwestern Petén, Guatemala (see Figure 5.1). It is a strongly divided landscape of elevated limestone horst uplands and swamp-filled grabens separated by steep fault scarps. Though it was once thought that the region's

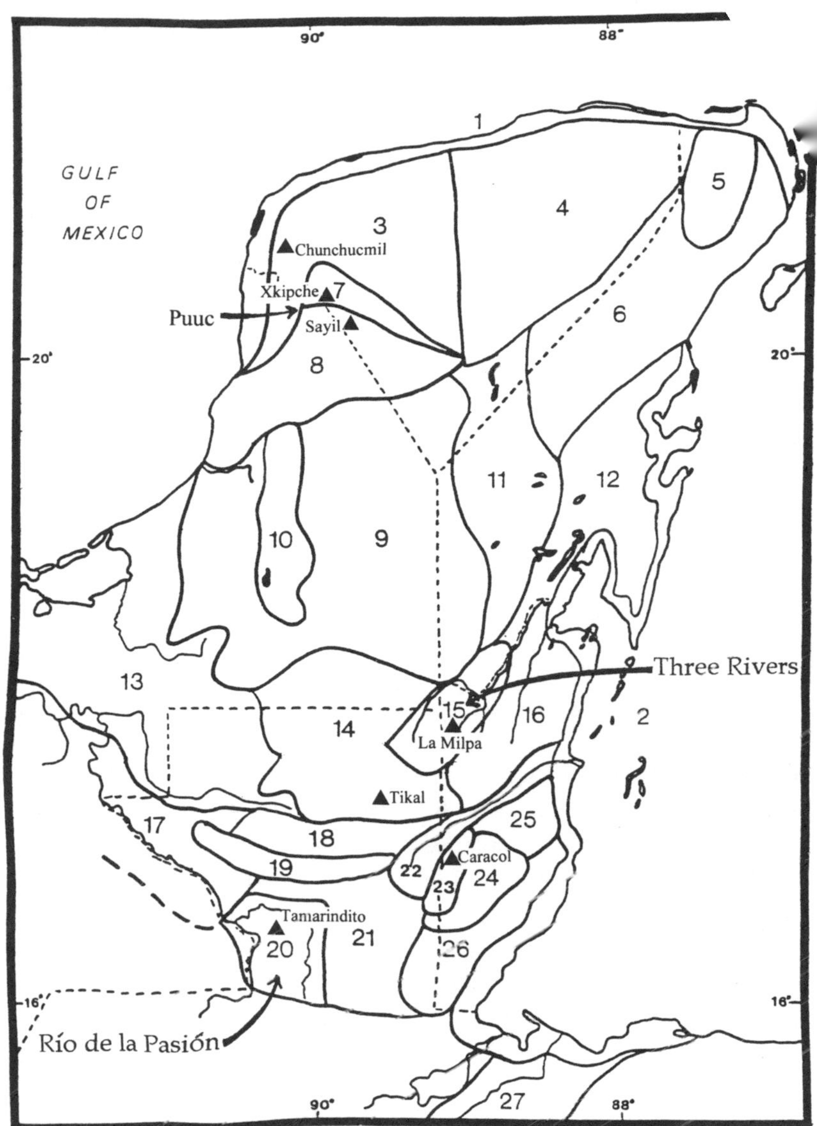

Figure 5.1. Adaptive regions of the Maya lowlands: (1) North Coast, (2) Caribbean Reef and Eastern Coastal Margin, (3) Northwest Karst Plain, (4) Northeast Karst Plain, (5) Yalahau, (6) Cobá-Okop, (7) Puuc-Santa Elena, (8) Puuc-Bolonchen Hills, (9) Central Hills, (10) Edzna-Silvituk Trough, (11) Quintana Roo Depression, (12) Uaymil, (13) Río Candelaria-Río San Pedro, (14) Petén Karst Plateau, (15) Three Rivers, (16) Río Hondo, (17) Lacandón Fold, (18) Petén Itzá Fracture, (19) Libertad Anticline, (20) Río de la Pasión, (21) Dolores, (22) Belize River Valley, (23) Vaca Plateau, (24) Maya Mountains, (25) Hummingbird Karst, (26) Karstic Piedmont, (27) Motagua and Copán Valleys (modified from Dunning et al. 1998: Fig. 1)

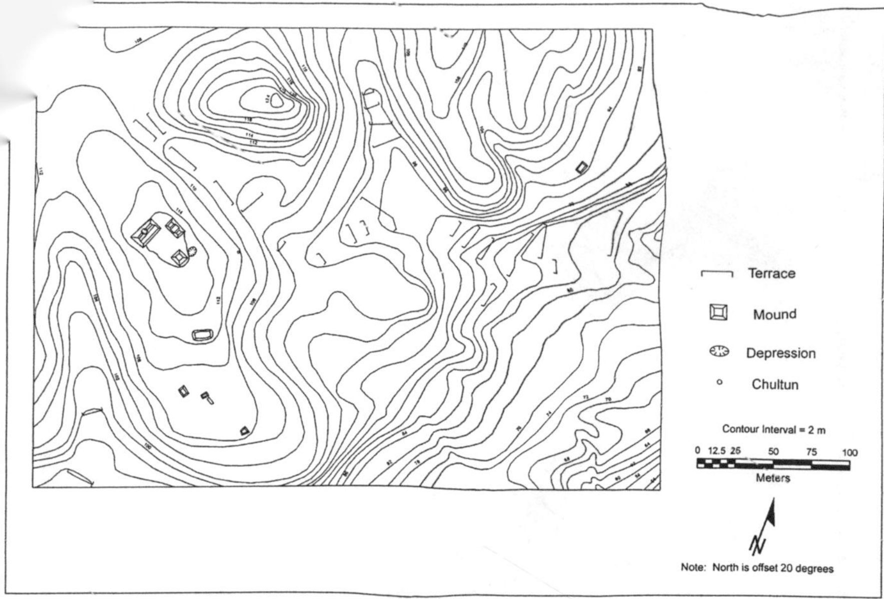

Figure 5.2. Map of the Barba Group, Programme for Belize (after Hageman 1999a)

swamps could have been the focus of intensive wetland cultivation (Adams 1983), evidence for such land use has proven elusive, whereas evidence for intensive cultivation on the uplands is abundant (Dunning 1996; Dunning and Beach n.d.; Dunning et al. 1997). A remarkable aspect of the Petexbatún region is the abundance of epigraphic and archaeological evidence for endemic and escalating Late Classic warfare associated with the rise and fall of the Petexbatún kingdom centered on the twin capitals of Dos Pilas and Aguateca (Demarest 1997; Houston 1993). One effect of this warfare was to increasingly concentrate settlement onto defensible positions on the uplands. Rural landscapes of the uplands were demarcated by wall systems as population concentrated and land use intensified during the Late Classic (Dunning et al. 1997; Killion et al. 1991). Initially, property wall systems parceled land between corporate group residential compounds, often tying in agricultural terrace complexes (Figure 5.3). Later, hilltop residential compounds were ringed by defensive walls, in essence creating a landscape of fortified farmsteads (Demarest et al. 1997; Dunning and Beach n.d.). The fortification of these rural settlements appears to correspond to a period when larger-scale political authority and organization was disintegrating (Demarest 1997). At this point in time, defense of life and property in the Petexbatún may have fragmented to the farmstead level. Analysis of human skeletons recovered from burials individuals of apparently highly varied status indicates that although, o average, the diet of Petexbatún Maya did not suffer during the period of endemic warfare, there was an increasing disparity in the quality of the diet between richer and poorer people (Wright and White 1996).

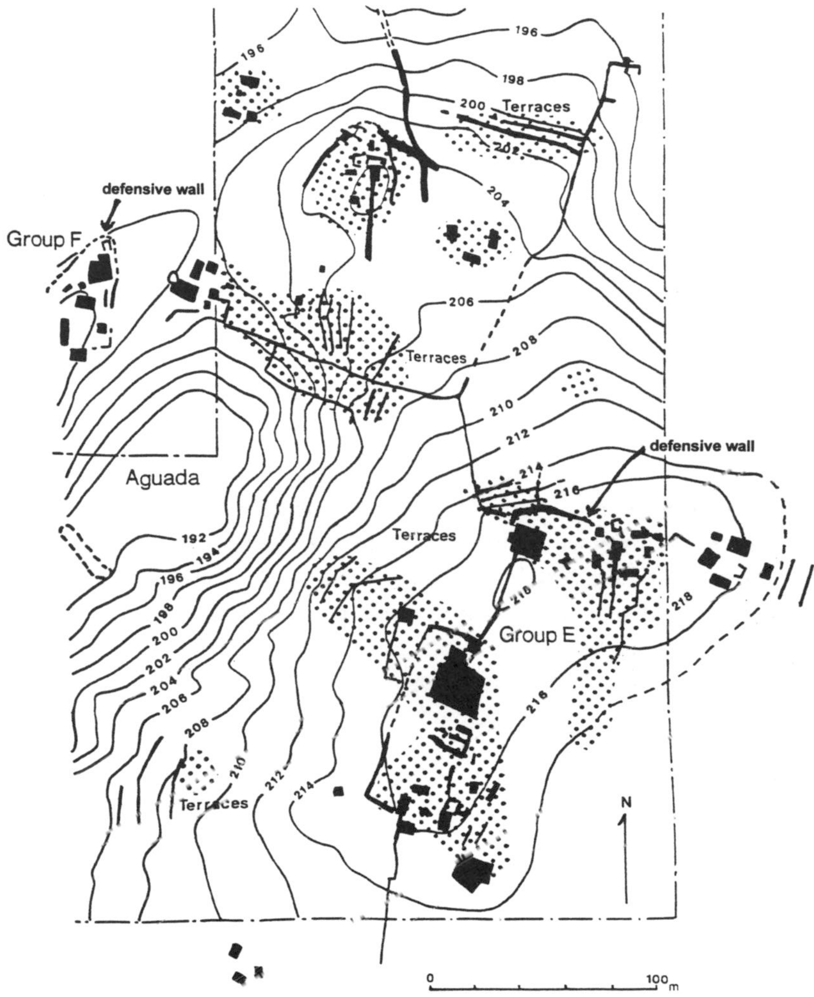

Figure 5.3. Partial map of Petexbatún Intersite Settlement Transect 2 showing rural farmsteads and wall and terrace systems. Stippled areas indicate high concentrations of soil phosphates (after Dunning and Beach n.d., adapted from Killion et al. 1991).

Figure 5.4. Urban farmstead at Tamarindito, Petén, Guatemala (after Demarest and Dunning 1990)

Within urban zones, areas of intensive cultivation are sometimes indicated by the presence of agricultural terrace systems tied to residential groups (Figure 5.4). Based on architectural elaboration and midden deposits, these "urban farmsteads" include residential groups that appear to be elite or middle class in status, but with lower-status residences in close association and probably occupied by members of the same corporate group (Dunning and Beach n.d.; Valdés 1997).

Puuc Region

The Puuc, or "hill country," lies in southern Yucatán and northern Campeche, Mexico (see Figure 5.1), an area that feels the full brunt of the annual winter-spring dry season and desiccates severely. However, it is also home to some of the best agricultural land in the northern Maya lowlands (Dunning 1992b, 1996). Combined archaeological and pedological investigations indicate that the Late and Terminal Classic Maya communities of the Puuc were indeed "garden cities" with large amounts of urban space devoted to agricultural production (Dunning 1992b, 2003; Farrell

1997; Killion et al. 1989; Smyth et al. 1995). At Sayil, residential areas contained numerous urban farmsteads (Figure 5.5), with a high correlation between large gardens and in-fields and high-status residential complexes with prime land probably having been occupied and controlled at an early date in accordance with the first founder principle. (In Yucatec Mayan, the phrase *yax chibal way tiluum*, or "first founding lineage of the land," expressly illustrates this principle whereby the first settlers of land claim it as their own [see McAnany 1995:96–97].) All of these farmsteads included one or more *chultunes*, large, subterranean cisterns used to store rainwater needed to survive the dry season. Notably, what appear to be small rural farmsteads in the Puuc region generally lack *chultunes*, indicating that these places were likely only inhabited during the rainy season (Figure 5.6; Dunning 1992b, 2003). This aspect of Puuc rural farmsteads has possible implications for other parts of the Maya lowlands where water-storage *chultunes* were not ubiquitously associated with permanent residences, and seasonal occupation may be much more difficult to detect. Control of outlying land was also maintained by the late creation of outlying minor centers situated to manage other pockets of prime land and to control frontiers with neighboring polities (Dunning 1992b).

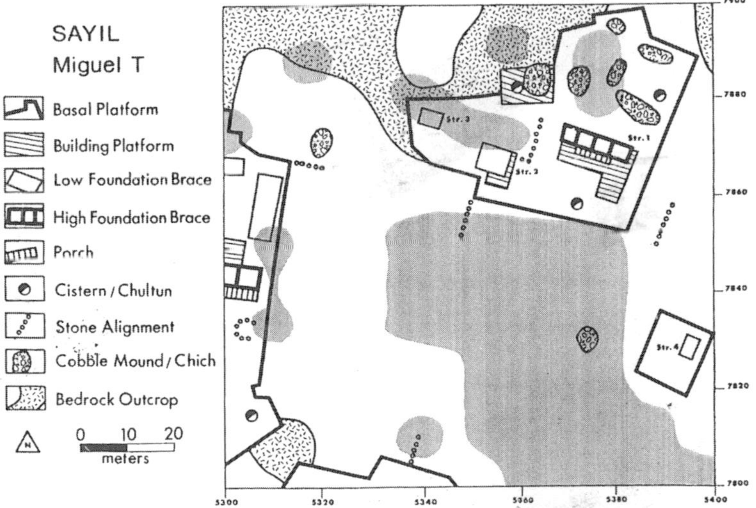

Figure 5.5. Map of the Miguel T Quadrangle at Sayil, Yucatán, Mexico. Shaded areas indicate elevated soil phosphate values. The large shaded area south of the Structure 1 platform is believed to represent an intensively cultivated urban garden (after Dunning 1992b and Killion et al. 1989).

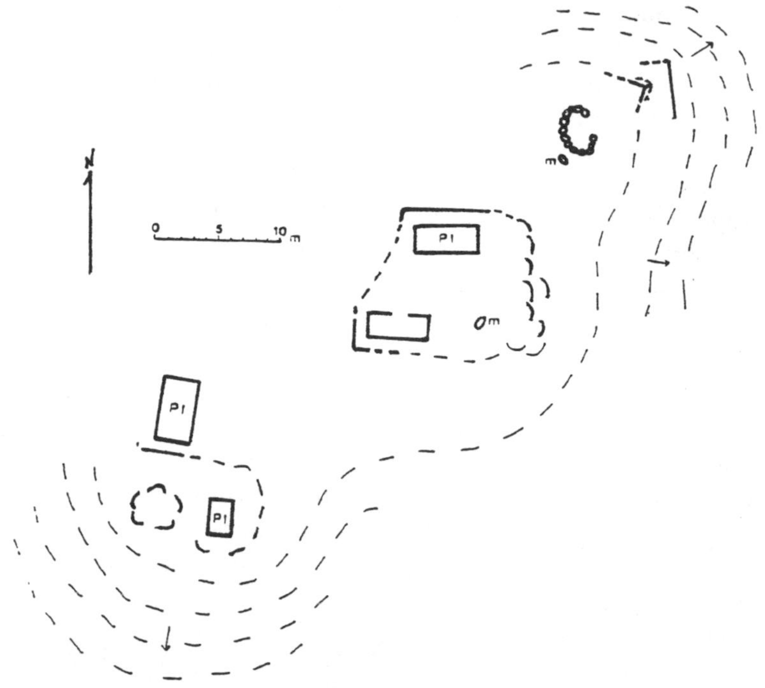

Figure 5.6. Xkipché Project Regional Extended Settlement Survey (XPRESS) Group C-1, a probable seasonally occupied rural farmstead west of Xkipché, Yucatán, Mexico (after Dunning 2003)

Notably, the socioeconomic hierarchy of residences seen in the large centers was replicated in smaller, presumably subordinate centers. This replication of hierarchy and the apparent stringent control of rural occupation evident in the seasonal nature of rural farmsteads both indicate that once the unequal control of the Puuc's prized farmland was established, it was apparently strictly maintained.

Discussion

In the preceding pages, I have intentionally referred to the residents of many farmsteads as undefined corporate groups. This is simply because the precise identity of such groups is not always clear. Broadly speaking, in the archaeological record corporate groups are manifestations of localized, hierarchically organized social units (Hayden and Cannon 1982). In the case of the Classic period Maya, many households apparently underwent accretionary growth such as one might expect of co-resident extended families (Tourtellot 1993; see Yaeger and Robin, this volume). However, there are numerous exceptions to this pattern. In a critique of the functional approach traditionally used in Maya settlement pattern studies, Kevin Johnston and Nancy Gonlin (1998:153) note:

> What the approach cannot explain is why some Maya families were extended and others were nuclear, nor can it account for variation in family development cycles as evidenced by the idiosyncratic architectural histories of individual residences.

It is likely that the social organization of ancient Maya farmsteads and other residential complexes varied across space and time. In some cases, such variation probably represents adaptive responses, but in other cases politically enforced changes may have occurred. Nevertheless, the most typical residential grouping in both rural and urban areas during the Classic is that of the multiple household cluster, probably the locus of lineage-based settlement (McAnany 1995; Tourtellot 1993).

Jon B. Hageman (1999b) has noted the close correspondence between the lineage-organized settlement documented for the Tzotzil Maya (Vogt 1969) and archaeological settlement patterns in parts of the Maya lowlands. Matthew Restall (1997) has painstakingly documented the lineage-based nature of Yucatec Maya society during the Colonial period. Individuals and their families were relegated by birth to a hierarchically assigned place within both *chibal* (lineage) and *cah* (community)—with one's position in the *cah* partly determined by one's lineage identity. This birth identity and status were closely tied to land wealth. Patricia McAnany (1995) has aptly referred to the Maya lineage as "a crucible of inequality." This can be seen in the disparity in land wealth between lineages in a given area, with "first families" generally enjoying privileged positions. However, it can also be seen within lineages, particularly as land became increasingly scarce and inheritance of land more problematic. In such a system, the potential for tyranny by lineage elders was strong. "Commoners" in this system were likely both members of relatively land-poor lineages as well as the disenfranchised members of large, dominant lineages. Commoners were, of course, the principal labor force in this system, likely working land they had only a small hope of inheriting or otherwise acquiring.

Agglomeration into multifamily compounds and dispersal into nuclear family units are variously evident in the archaeological settlement record (Johnston and Gonlin 1998). In some cases, such changes may be attributable to changing social and economic contexts. At the huge urban center of Caracol, the patterned and apparently deliberate distribution of nuclear family compounds at intervals within the fabric of an expanding landscape of intensive agricultural terracing may have been orchestrated as part of a "master" land-use/agricultural-production plan at a centralized or supralineage level (Chase and Chase 1998). Similarly, the singular, highly dense, and "center-less" Late Classic settlement pattern found on Albion Island, Belize, may represent the establishment of an agricultural "colony" by a large political entity such as Tikal (Pyburn 1998). At the huge urban center of Chunchucmil on an almost soil-less portion of the northwestern coastal plain, social forces apparently created a "garden city" in an ill-suited environment by importing huge quantities of organic mucks from coastal savannas to build thousands of garden beds (Beach 1998; Farrell 1997). The conflict-induced changes in rural farmsteads in the Petexbatún and the manipulation of farmsteads as part of land control in the Puuc have already been discussed above. In all cases, it was likely the lot of commoners to be shifted to the outskirts of expanding urban field systems, to frontier agricultural colonies, and in and out of seasonal farmsteads. However, in at least some cases, Maya commoners may have chosen to migrate rather than endure oppressive political-economic conditions. Such movements of people may help explain the rise and fall of some Classic polities (see Inomata, this volume, for discussion of factors relating to population mobility).

Changes in farming systems were also likely the result of adaptive responses to changing environmental contexts. On a panlowlands scale, it is likely that the "mosaic" of habitats provided by environmental variability across space likely favored particular kinds of adaptive responses in some areas (see Figure 5.1; Dunning et al. 1998; Fedick 1996). However, the heterogeneity found within environmental regions also promoted flexibility in adaptive response on more localized scales. Such responses often may well have been initiated within lineages as part of risk-minimization strategies. For example, as discussed above, the positioning of farmsteads across ecotones in northwestern Belize can be seen as an adaptive risk-management response, as can the development of water and soil conservation strategies as the result of environmental degradation. Similarly, sea-level changes may have induced adaptive responses in agricultural systems in low-lying riparian areas (Pohl et al. 1996). Whether broader, panregional environmental changes (such as increasing drought frequency;

Whitmore et al. 1996) may have defeated other attempts at ac sponse remains problematic.

The adaptive responses made by Maya farmers through time clearly nonlinear in nature (Denevan 1983). As in most farming system such responses were typically conservative, favoring risk-minimization strategies (Butzer 1996). The study of ancient Maya farmsteads offers an important key to understanding how adaptations were implemented, potentially shedding light on the interactions of Maya commoners within changeable social and environmental contexts. Farmsteads played a critical adaptive role at the intersection between the natural world and human society and were the nexus between the relatively powerful and powerless members of Maya society. Farmsteads should be examined in their entirety, including both architectural features and landholdings (Ball and Kelsay 1992; Gleason 1994; Johnston and Gonlin 1998; Killion 1992; Robin 1998). Additionally, in order to understand the nature of changes occurring within farmsteads, they must also be analyzed as part of broader landscape contexts (Fedick 1996).

As David Webster (1998) has noted, Classic Maya monumental architecture was characterized by its intentional conspicuousness, in which scale equated with power. At the other end of the social/architectural spectrum, the modest dwellings of commoners are conspicuous only in their large number. Nevertheless, these features are all part of the same landscape, a landscape in which the tremendous disparities in wealth and power were given both material and symbolic expression. The "voices" of Maya rulers still speak loudly to us from the crumbling monuments erected to reify their high-status world. However, the voices of those who toiled in the fields have become even more muted by the passage of time. To hear them, we must take care to listen more closely.

Acknowledgments

An earlier version of this study was presented in the symposium "A- cient Maya Commoners (*Mazehualob*)," organized by Jon Lohse and F Valdez, Jr., at the 98th Annual Meeting of the American Anthr- logical Association, Chicago, November 17–21, 1999. Useful com- its on that paper were received from the organizers and from Lau- evi, Cynthia Robin, and Vernon Scarborough. Some of the work rted here was carried out as part of the Programme for Belize Ar- ologi- cal Project, under the general supervision of Fred Valdez, d with ous cooperation of both the Department of Archaeology, Min- of Tourism and the Environment, and the Programme for Belize. estigations during 1997 and 1998 were carried out with the generous support of the National Science Foundation (Grant No. SBR-963-1024 to Vernon Scarborough and Nicholas Dunning). Earlier work was supported by funds from a Heinz Family Foundation grant to Dunning in 1994, and from the University of Cincinnati and University of Texas. Work was undertaken in 1996 as part of Boston University's La Milpa Archaeological Project, headed by Norman Hammond and Gair Tourtellot. Hammond and Tourtellot are to be thanked for their cooperation and friendly exchange of ideas over the past several years. Numerous personnel of the Programme for Belize Archaeological Project have contributed to the work reported here, in particular, Timothy Beach, Jon Hageman, Paul Hughbanks, John Jones, Julie Kunen, Jon Lohse, Sheryl Luzzadder-Beach, Vernon Scarborough, and Fred Valdez, Jr. My work in the Petexbatún region was undertaken as part of Vanderbilt University's Petexbatún Regional Archaeological Project under the general direction of Arthur Demarest, and in cooperation with the Instituto de Antropología e Historia de Guatemala. Research undertaken in the Petexbatún was supported by funds from the United States Agency for International Development, the National Endowment for the Humanities, the National Geographic Society, the Swedish International Development Agency, and the Guggenheim Foundation. Numerous personnel from the Petexbatún Project contributed to the research reported here, in particular, Timothy Beach, Arthur Demarest, Stephen Houston, Thomas Killion, Matt O'Mansky, and Juan Antonio Valdés. My work on the regional settlement patterns of the Puuc region was supported by grants from the Organization of American States and the University of Minnesota. This research benefited immensely from collaboration with the Sayil Project under the direction of Jeremy Sabloff and Gair Tourtellot, the continuing Sayil and Chac Projects under the direction of Michael Smyth, and the Xkipché Project under the direction of Hanns J. Prem.

ferences

, Richard E. W.

Ancient Land Use and Culture History in the Pasión River Region. In *Prehistoric Settlement Patterns*, edited by Evon Vogt and Richard Leventhal, pp. 319–336. University of New Mexico Press, Albuquerque.

Whitmore et al. 1996) may have defeated other attempts at adaptive response remains problematic.

The adaptive responses made by Maya farmers through time were clearly nonlinear in nature (Denevan 1983). As in most farming systems, such responses were typically conservative, favoring risk-minimization strategies (Butzer 1996). The study of ancient Maya farmsteads offers an important key to understanding how adaptations were implemented, potentially shedding light on the interactions of Maya commoners within changeable social and environmental contexts. Farmsteads played a critical adaptive role at the intersection between the natural world and human society and were the nexus between the relatively powerful and powerless members of Maya society. Farmsteads should be examined in their entirety, including both architectural features and landholdings (Ball and Kelsay 1992; Gleason 1994; Johnston and Gonlin 1998; Killion 1992; Robin 1998). Additionally, in order to understand the nature of changes occurring within farmsteads, they must also be analyzed as part of broader landscape contexts (Fedick 1996).

As David Webster (1998) has noted, Classic Maya monumental architecture was characterized by its intentional conspicuousness, in which scale equated with power. At the other end of the social/architectural spectrum, the modest dwellings of commoners are conspicuous only in their large number. Nevertheless, these features are all part of the same landscape, a landscape in which the tremendous disparities in wealth and power were given both material and symbolic expression. The "voices" of Maya rulers still speak loudly to us from the crumbling monuments erected to reify their high-status world. However, the voices of those who toiled in the fields have become even more muted by the passage of time. To hear them, we must take care to listen more closely.

Acknowledgments

An earlier version of this study was presented in the symposium "Ancient Maya Commoners (*Mazehualob*)," organized by Jon Lohse and Fred Valdez, Jr., at the 98th Annual Meeting of the American Anthropological Association, Chicago, November 17–21, 1999. Useful comments on that paper were received from the organizers and from Laura Levi, Cynthia Robin, and Vernon Scarborough. Some of the work reported here was carried out as part of the Programme for Belize Archaeological Project, under the general supervision of Fred Valdez, Jr., and with the gracious cooperation of both the Department of Archaeology, Ministry of Tourism and the Environment, and the Programme for Belize. Investigations during 1997 and 1998 were carried out with the generous support of the National Science Foundation (Grant No. SBR-963-1024 to Vernon Scarborough and Nicholas Dunning). Earlier work was supported by funds from a Heinz Family Foundation grant to Dunning in 1994, and from the University of Cincinnati and University of Texas. Work was undertaken in 1996 as part of Boston University's La Milpa Archaeological Project, headed by Norman Hammond and Gair Tourtellot. Hammond and Tourtellot are to be thanked for their cooperation and friendly exchange of ideas over the past several years. Numerous personnel of the Programme for Belize Archaeological Project have contributed to the work reported here, in particular, Timothy Beach, Jon Hageman, Paul Hughbanks, John Jones, Julie Kunen, Jon Lohse, Sheryl Luzzadder-Beach, Vernon Scarborough, and Fred Valdez, Jr. My work in the Petexbatún region was undertaken as part of Vanderbilt University's Petexbatún Regional Archaeological Project under the general direction of Arthur Demarest, and in cooperation with the Instituto de Antropología e Historia de Guatemala. Research undertaken in the Petexbatún was supported by funds from the United States Agency for International Development, the National Endowment for the Humanities, the National Geographic Society, the Swedish International Development Agency, and the Guggenheim Foundation. Numerous personnel from the Petexbatún Project contributed to the research reported here, in particular, Timothy Beach, Arthur Demarest, Stephen Houston, Thomas Killion, Matt O'Mansky, and Juan Antonio Valdés. My work on the regional settlement patterns of the Puuc region was supported by grants from the Organization of American States and the University of Minnesota. This research benefited immensely from collaboration with the Sayil Project under the direction of Jeremy Sabloff and Gair Tourtellot, the continuing Sayil and Chac Projects under the direction of Michael Smyth, and the Xkipché Project under the direction of Hanns J. Prem.

References

Adams, Richard E. W.

1983 Ancient Land Use and Culture History in the Pasión River Region. In *Prehistoric Settlement Patterns*, edited by Evon Vogt and Richard Leventhal, pp. 319–336. University of New Mexico Press, Albuquerque.

Ball, Joseph, and Richalene G. Kelsay

1992 Prehistoric Intrasettlement Land Use and Residual Soil Phosphate Levels in the Upper Belize Valley, Central America. In *Gardens of Prehistory*, edited by Thomas W. Killion, pp. 234–262. University of Alabama Press, Tuscaloosa.

Beach, Timothy

1998 Soil Constraints on Northwest Yucatán: Pedo and Agricultural Archaeology of Chunchucmil. *Geoarchaeology* 13:759–791.

Butzer, Karl W.

1996 Ecology in the Long View: Settlement Histories, Agrosystemic Strategies, and Ecological Performance. *Journal of Field Archaeology* 23:141–150.

Chase, Arlen F., and Diane Z. Chase

1998 Scale and Intensity in Classic Period Maya Agriculture: Terracing and Settlement at the "Garden City" of Caracol, Belize. *Culture and Agriculture* 20:60–77.

Demarest, Arthur A.

1997 The Vanderbilt Petexbatún Regional Archaeological Project 1989–1994: Overview, History, and Major Results. *Ancient Mesoamerica* 8:209–227.

Demarest, Arthur A., and Nicholas P. Dunning

1990 Ecología y guerra en la Región de la Pasión. In *Proyecto Arqueológico Regional Petexbatún, Informe #2, Segunda Temporada 1990*, edited by Arthur A. Demarest and Stephen D. Houston, pp. 595–604. Department of Anthropology, Vanderbilt University, Nashville.

Demarest, Arthur A., Matt O'Mansky, Claudia Wolley, Dirk Van Tuerenhout, Takeshi Inomata, Joel Palka, and Héctor Escobedo

1997 Classic Maya Defensive Systems and Warfare in the Petexbatún Region: Archaeological Evidence and Interpretation. *Ancient Mesoamerica* 8:229–254.

Denevan, William M.

1983 Adaptation, Variation, and Cultural Geography. *Professional Geographer* 35:399–407.

Drennan, Robert D.

1988 Household Location and Compact versus Dispersed Settlement in Prehispanic Mesoamerica. In *Household and Community in the Mesoamerican Past*, edited by Richard R. Wilk and Wendy Ashmore, pp. 273–293. University of New Mexico Press, Albuquerque.

Dunning, Nicholas P.

1992a The Implications of Folk Soil Taxonomies for Agricultural Change in Middle America. In *Conference of Latin Americanist Geographers: Benchmark 1990*, edited by Tom L. Martinson, pp. 243–248. Auburn University Press, Auburn.

1992b *Lords of the Hills: Ancient Maya Settlement in the Puuc Region, Yucatán, Mexico.* Monographs in World Archaeology 15. Prehistory Press, Madison.

1995 Coming Together at the Temple Mountain: Environment, Subsistence, and the Emergence of Classic Maya Segmentary States. In *The Emergence of Lowland Maya Civilization*, edited by Nikolai Grube, pp. 61–70. Acta Mesoamericana 8. Verlag von Flemming, Möckmühl.

1996 An Examination of Regional Variability in the Prehispanic Maya Agricultural Landscape. In *The Managed Mosaic: Ancient Maya Agriculture and Resource Management*, edited by Scott L. Fedick, pp. 53–68. University of Utah Press, Salt Lake City.

2003 A lo largo de la quijada de la culebra: Ambiente y asentamiento en Xkipché, Yucatán. Appendix 1 in *Xkipché: Una ciudad maya Clásica en el corazón del Puuc*, edited by Hanns J. Prem and Michael Vallo. Instituto Nacional de Antropología e Historia de México, Mexico City. In press.

Dunning, Nicholas P., and Timothy Beach

n.d. An Ancient Maya Landscape: Environmental Archaeology and Ancient Settlement in the Petexbatun Region, Petén, Guatemala. Vanderbilt University Press, Nashville. [In initial editing.]

Dunning, Nicholas P., Timothy Beach, Pat Farrell, and Sheryl Luzzadder-Beach

1998 Prehispanic Agrosystems and Adaptive Regions in the Maya Lowlands. *Culture and Agriculture* 20:107–120.

Dunning, Nicholas P., Timothy Beach, and David Rue

1997 The Paleoecology and Ancient Settlement of the Petexbatun Region, Guatemala. *Ancient Mesoamerica* 8:255–256.

Dunning, Nicholas P., John G. Jones, Sheryl Luzzadder-Beach, and Timothy Beach

2003 Ancient Maya Landscapes in Northwestern Belize. In *Heterarchy, Political Economy, and the Ancient Maya: The Three Rivers Region of the East-Central Yucatán Peninsula*, edited by Vernon Scarborough, Fred Valdez, Jr., and Nicholas P. Dunning, pp. 14–24. University of Arizona Press, Tucson.

Dunning, Nicholas P., Sheryl Luzzadder-Beach, Timothy Beach, John G. Jones, Vernon Scarborough, and T. Patrick Culbert

2002 Arising from the Bajos: The Evolution of a Neotropical Landscape and the Rise of Maya Civilization. *Annals of the Association of American Geographers* 92:267–283.

Dunning, Nicholas P., Vernon Scarborough, Fred Valdez, Jr., Sheryl Luzzadder-Beach, Timothy Beach, and John G. Jones

1999 Temple Mountains, Sacred Lakes, and Fertile Fields: Ancient Maya Landscapes in Northwestern Belize. *Antiquity* 73(281):650–660.

Eaton, Jack D.

1975 Ancient Agricultural Farmsteads in the Río Bec Region of Yucatan. In *Contributions of the University of California Archaeological Research Facility* 27, pp. 56–82. University of California, Berkeley.

Ewill, Peter T., and Deborah Merrill-Sands

1987 Milpa in Yucatan: A Long-Fallow Maize System and Its Alternatives in the Maya Peasant Economy. In *Comparative Farming Systems*, edited by

B. L. Turner II and Stephen Brush, pp. 95–129. Guilford Press, New York.

Farrell, Patrice M.
1997 The Garden City Hypothesis in the Maya Lowlands. Ph.D. diss., Department of Geography, University of Cincinnati.

Fedick, Scott L.
1996 Conclusion: Landscape Approaches to the Study of Ancient Maya Agriculture and Resource Use. In *The Managed Mosaic: Ancient Maya Agriculture and Resource Use*, edited by Scott L. Fedick, pp. 335–347. University of Utah Press, Salt Lake City.

Gleason, Kathryn L.
1994 To Bound and to Cultivate: An Introduction to the Archaeology of Gardens and Fields. In *The Archaeology of Garden and Field*, edited by Naomi F. Miller and Kathryn L. Gleason, pp. 1–24. University of Pennsylvania Press, Philadelphia.

Hageman, Jon B.
1999a Ideology and Intersite Settlement among the Late Classic Maya. Paper presented at the 64th Annual Meeting of the Society for American Archaeology, Chicago.
1999b Were the Late Classic Maya Characterized by Lineages? Paper presented at the Tercera Mesa Redonda de Palenque (New Series), Palenque, Chiapas.

Hammond, Norman, Gair Tourtellot, Sarah Donaghey, and Amanda Clarke
1998 No Slow Dusk: Maya Urban Development and Decline at La Milpa, Belize. *Antiquity* 72:831–837.

Hanks, William F.
1990 *Referential Practice: Language and Lived Space among the Maya*. University of Chicago Press, Chicago.

Hayden, Brian, and Aubrey Cannon
1982 The Corporate Group as an Archaeological Unit. *Journal of Anthropological Archaeology* 1(2):132–158.

Houston, Stephen D.
1993 *Hieroglyphs and History at Dos Pilas: Dynastic Politics of the Classic Maya*. University of Texas Press, Austin.
1998 Finding Function and Meaning in Classic Maya Architecture. In *Function and Meaning in Classic Maya Architecture*, edited by Stephen D. Houston, pp. 519–538. Dumbarton Oaks, Washington, D.C.

Hughbanks, Paul J.
1998 Settlement and Land Use at Guijarral, Northwest Belize. *Culture and Agriculture* 20:107–120.

Jacob, John S.
1995 Archaeological Pedology in the Maya Lowlands. In *Pedological Perspectives in Archaeological Research*. Soil Science Society of America Special Publication 44, pp. 51–79. Madison.

Johnston, Kevin J., and Nancy Gonlin

1998 What Do Houses Mean? Approaches to the Analysis of Classic Maya Commoner Residences. In *Function and Meaning in Classic Maya Architecture*, edited by Stephen D. Houston, pp. 141–184. Dumbarton Oaks, Washington, D.C.

Killion, Thomas W.

1992 The Archaeology of Settlement Agriculture. In *Gardens of Prehistory*, edited by Thomas W. Killion, pp. 1–13. University of Alabama Press, Tuscaloosa.

Killion, Thomas W., Jeremy A. Sabloff, Gair Tourtellot, and Nicholas Dunning

1989 Intensive Surface Collection of Residential Clusters at Terminal Classic Sayil, Yucatán, Mexico. *Journal of Field Archaeology* 16(2):273–294.

Killion, Thomas W., Inez Verhagen, Dirk Van Tuerenhout, Daniela Triadan, Lisa Hamerlynck, Mathew McDermott, and José Genoves

1991 Reporte de la temporada 1991 del recorrido arqueológico intersitio de Petexbatún. In *Proyecto Arqueológico Regional Petexbatún, Informe #3, Tercera Temporada 1991*, edited by Arthur Demarest, Takeshi Inomata, Héctor Escobedo, and Joel Palka, pp. 588–645. Department of Anthropology, Vanderbilt University, Nashville.

Levi, Laura J.

1996 Sustainable Production and Residential Variation: A Historical Perspective on Prehispanic Domestic Economies in the Maya Lowlands. In *The Managed Mosaic: Ancient Maya Agriculture and Resource Use*, edited by Scott L. Fedick, pp. 92–106. University of Utah Press, Salt Lake City.

Lohse, Jon C.

2001 The Social Organization of a Late Classic Maya Community: Dos Hombres, Northwestern Belize. Ph.D. diss., Department of Anthropology, University of Texas at Austin.

Lohse, Jon C., and Patrick N. Findlay

2000 A Classic Maya House-Lot Drainage System in Northwestern Belize. *Latin American Antiquity* 11(2):175–185.

McAnany, Patricia A.

1995 *Living with the Ancestors: Kinship and Kingship in Ancient Maya Society.* University of Texas Press, Austin.

Pohl, Mary D., Kevin O. Pope, John G. Jones, John S. Jacob, Dolores R. Piperno, Susan D. deFrance, David L. Lentz, John A. Gifford, Marie E. Danforth, and J. Kathryn Josserand

1996 Early Agriculture in the Maya Lowlands. *Latin American Antiquity* 7:355–372.

Pyburn, K. Anne.

1998 The Albion Island Settlement Pattern Project: Domination and Resistance in Early Classic Northern Belize. *Journal of Field Archaeology* 25:37–62.

Rapoport, Amos
1990 *History and Precedent in Environmental Design*. Plenum Press, New York.

Restall, Matthew
1997 *The Maya World: Yucatec Culture and Society, 1550–1850*. Stanford University Press, Stanford.

Robin, Cynthia
1998 Where People Really Live: Methods for Identification of Household Spaces and Activities. Paper presented at the 63rd Annual Meeting of the Society for American Archaeology, Seattle.

Sanders, William T.
1981 Classic Maya Settlement Patterns and Ethnographic Analogy. In *Lowland Maya Settlement Patterns*, edited by Wendy Ashmore, pp. 351–369. University of New Mexico Press, Albuquerque.

Scarborough, Vernon L., Matthew E. Becher, Jeffrey L. Baker, Garry Harris, and Fred Valdez, Jr.
1995 Water and Land at the Ancient Maya Community of La Milpa. *Latin American Antiquity* 6(2):98–119.

Smyth, Michael P., Christopher Dore, and Nicholas Dunning
1995 Interpreting Prehistoric Settlement Patterns: Lessons from the Maya Center of Sayil, Yucatán. *Journal of Field Archaeology* 22:321–347.

Tourtellot, Gair, III
1993 A View of Ancient Maya Settlements in the Eighth Century. In *Lowland Maya Civilization in the Eighth Century A.D.*, edited by Jeremy A. Sabloff and John S. Henderson, pp. 219–242. Dumbarton Oaks, Washington, D.C.

Turner, B. L., II
1983 *Once beneath the Forest: Prehistoric Terracing in the Rio Bec Region of the Maya Lowlands*. Westview Press, Boulder.

Valdés, Juan Antonio
1997 Tamarindito: Archaeology and Regional Politics in the Petexbatún Region. *Ancient Mesoamerica* 8:321–336.

Vogt, Evon Z.
1969 *Zinacantan: A Maya Community in the Highlands of Chiapas*. The Belknap Press of Harvard University Press, Cambridge.

Webster, David
1998 Classic Maya Architecture: Implications and Comparisons. In *Function and Meaning in Classic Maya Architecture*, edited by Stephen D. Houston, pp. 5–47. Dumbarton Oaks, Washington, D.C.

Whitmore, Thomas J., Mark Brenner, Jason Curtis, Bruce Dahlin, and Barbara Leyden
1996 Holocene Climate and Human Influences on Lakes of the Yucatán Peninsula, Mexico: An Interdisciplinary Paleolimnological Approach. *The Holocene* 6:273–287.

Wilk, Richard, and Wendy Ashmore (editors)
1988 *Household and Community in the Mesoamerican Past.* University of New Mexico Press, Albuquerque.

Wright, Lori, and Christine White
1996 Human Biology in the Classic Maya Collapse: Evidence from Paleopathology and Paleodiet. *Journal of World Prehistory* 10:147–198.

CHAPTER 6

Intra-Site Settlement Signatures and Implications for Late Classic Maya Commoner Organization at Dos Hombres, Belize

JON C. LOHSE

Mayanists have come a long way in their assessments of pre-Hispanic food production since Sylvanus Morley (1946) argued for the ubiquity of slash-and-burn agriculture. Today, there is a greater awareness of environmental variability and its effect on both agriculture and settlement systems (Fedick 1996b; Pohl 1985; Sanders 1977). However, although our appreciation of the natural "mosaic" within which the ancient Maya were situated has increased, it could be argued that our sensitivity to potential changes in the way people organized themselves to exploit different resources has not kept pace.

The goal of this chapter is to present a model of Late Classic (ca. AD 600–850) community organization for the site of Dos Hombres, located in northwestern Belize.[1] This work examines the distribution and organization of the supporting population in what is considered the Dos Hombres suburban area, consisting of the inner 2.5 km of settlement surrounding the site core. The primary assumption underlying this examination is that a large percentage, if not the majority, of those who might have been "commoners" in the Dos Hombres community were engaged either directly or peripherally in food production. Therefore, this study focuses on the economics of agricultural production by examining how intensification strategies and settlement distribution vary across the different environmental zones in the project area. Taking the arrangement of residential elements and other features such as terraces and field walls as an indication of social unit boundaries, I argue for two concurrent, though alternative, forms of social organization arising from the opportunities and requirements for managing environmental elements such as soil, water, space, and surface geometry (Wilken 1987:3) that constrain agricultural activities.

The remainder of this chapter is organized into three parts. First is a brief overview of the intellectual progress in grappling with Maya agricultural production over the past thirty years. Next, I present data collected from a settlement survey around Dos Hombres (Lohse 2001), beginning with a discussion of the project area and its environmental zones. I also describe two distinct settlement patterns, referred to as the "corporate group" and the "micro-community" patterns, taken to reflect different forms of social organization. A reconstruction of how agricultural production was organized and carried out in these areas is inferred in part from landscape modification features such as terraces, ground-level cobble surfaces, and even possible wetland canals. Finally, I offer brief conclusions concerning the role of commoners at Dos Hombres during the Late Classic. These conclusions hold implications for the study of commoners at other sites in the Maya area and in Mesoamerica.

Recent Developments Linking Maya Agriculture and Environmental Diversity

Beginning in the 1970s, models of Maya agriculture based on labor-intensive, rather than land-extensive, production have steadily gained support (e.g., Flannery 1982; Harrison and Turner 1978; Netting 1977). It may have been the recognition of pre-Hispanic exploitation of lowland wetlands (Adams et al. 1981; Pohl 1990a; Siemens and Puleston 1972; Turner and Harrison 1983), in particular, that helped fuel awareness that environmental diversity can serve as either a key component in or obstacle to agricultural intensification. The last three decades of the twentieth century witnessed an increase in studies attempting to tie large-scale settlement systems to regional environmental variability (Ashmore 1981:59; Dunning 1992; Dunning et al. 1997; Fedick 1989, 1995; Ford 1986, 1990; Ford and Fedick 1992; Rice 1976; Rice and Rice 1990; Scarborough 1993; Turner 1974, 1983; also see Dunning, this volume).

More recently, several scholars (e.g., Hughbanks 1998; Kepecs and Boucher 1996; Levi 1996; Liendo Stuardo 1999; Scarborough et al. 1995) have turned their attention to variations in soil, vegetation, water, and even topographic conditions at the site level. This shift in focus has allowed researchers to suggest resource management strategies, account for status differences among households, and explain localized diachronic shifts in residential distribution.

One thing that has become clear through these studies is that our understanding of the pre-Hispanic exploitation of any landscape depends in large part on the spatial scales of our analyses (Fedick 1996a:335–336; see Yaeger and Robin, this volume). Regional-level investigations yield insights into sociopolitical systems that operate at that scale, and site-level analyses can help us to understand the organization of a given community, or even the behavior of individual households. Each perspective has its particular strengths and weaknesses. Regional analyses can easily gloss over fine-grained environmental variations that might pose an important constraint to agricultural production, thereby overlooking the decision-making capacity of smaller social units. Small-scale analyses, on the other hand, may not explain how individual groups participated in a broader economy, as would a regional analysis, though they are more likely to help demonstrate the depth of ancient "local knowledge" and the "mechanics" of how societies adapted to diverse environments. This becomes important as we examine the roles individual households, especially those at the commoner level, played in larger polities.

As we have begun to appreciate the possible array of environmental niches in the Maya Lowlands (e.g., Fedick 1996b), the strength of our small-scale analyses has also grown. However, such analyses are often conducted under one of two competing theoretical paradigms. In the first, decision-making agents are frequently presumed to have been independent farming households. This perspective has a strong historical and cross-cultural basis in ethnography (e.g., Chayanov 1986; Killion 1990; Netting 1968; Sahlins 1972) and is deeply rooted in Mesoamerican studies through the popularity of household archaeology (Ashmore and Wilk 1988; Santley and Hirth 1993). In the second paradigm, centralized control of resources and production strategies is often presumed a priori (e.g., Ford 1996; Pohl 1990b; see discussion by Brumfiel and Earle [1987] regarding elite control over economy). Intensified agricultural systems in particular are often seen as the product of elite management and supervision (e.g., Adams and Culbert 1977; Sanders 1977).

I argue that it is unlikely and the available data are unconvincing that any single decision-making structure—be it an underclass of independently farming households or an overarching elite superstructure—is an adequate explanation for the degree of specialized environmental adaptation evidenced for the Late Classic period. I suggest that both "bottom-up" and "top-down" approaches, though each potentially useful, when employed by themselves may be too inflexible to allow us to fully understand the capacity held by different levels of society to make decisions for the exploitation of particular environmental niches. Put another way,

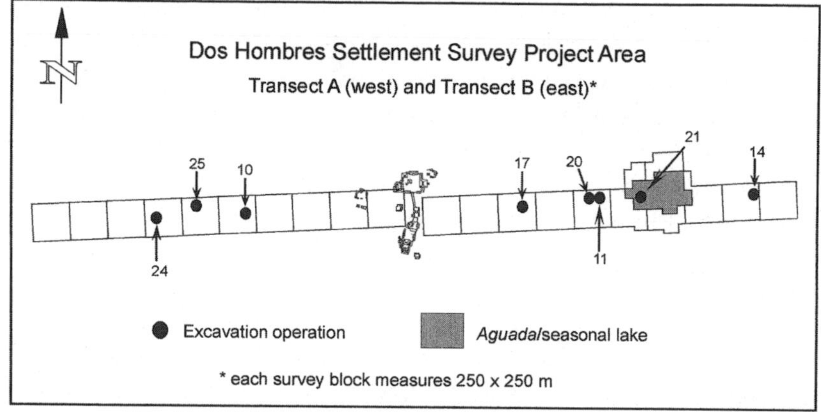

Figure 6.1. Survey Transects A (west) and B (east) showing excavation operations mentioned in the text

while our research designs have become relatively dynamic in terms of operating at different environmental scales, our understanding of how different levels of social organization might have acted simultaneously as agricultural agents has remained, by and large, static.

The Dos Hombres Data

Between 1996 and 1998, a survey was undertaken to study the settlement and biophysical environment around the ancient Maya site of Dos Hombres (Lohse 2001). The project area consisted of two transects, each measuring 2.5 km × 250 m and oriented at 267° (Transect A) and 87° (Transect B), respectively (Figure 6.1). Objectives of the survey and subsequent excavations were to investigate and identify social, political, and/or economic structures that might have existed at the site during the Late Classic period. Particular attention was given to correlating the distribution of residences with evidence for different forms of agricultural production. Analysis of settlement and environmental data has revealed a strong correlation between residential nucleation and the suitability of the localized environment for sustaining highly intensified food production.

Environmental Setting of the Study Area

The Dos Hombres center lies within the Río Bravo Embayment zone of the Programme for Belize property (Brokaw and Mallory 1993: Figure 4).

This area is largely composed of relatively flat, poorly draining terrain referred to as *bajo* (Brokaw and Mallory 1993:23). The Río Bravo Embayment zone is bounded on the west by the steep Río Bravo Escarpment, a north-south running fault or fold in the Eocene limestone bedrock that rises 80 to 90 m in elevation (Brokaw and Mallory 1993:12–13). On the eastern margin of the Embayment, a slight elevation rise followed by a steep decline marks the beginning of the Booth's River Upland. The escarpment to the west and the rise to the east define a broad "trough" measuring approximately 4 km across, with the Dos Hombres central precinct situated 1.4 km from the base of the escarpment (Figure 6.2).

The Embayment landscape is broken only by a few small, discontinuous limestone ridges that run north to south and are generally under 30 m in height. These ridges represent localized geographic features that, along with the presence and nature of surface water, result in a number of micro-

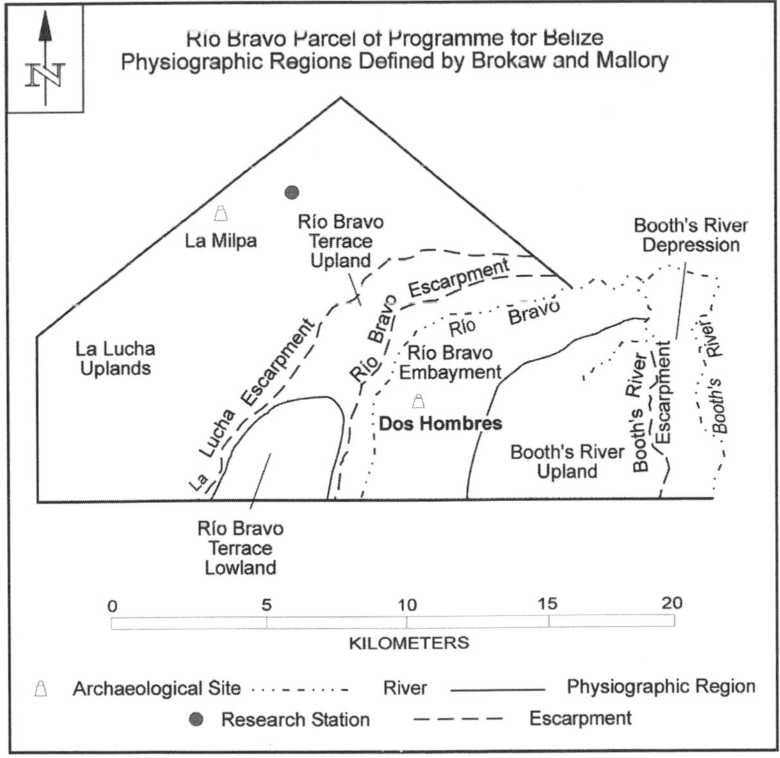

Figure 6.2. Environmental zones defined by Nicholas Brokaw and Elizabeth Mallory (1993), showing Dos Hombres site center

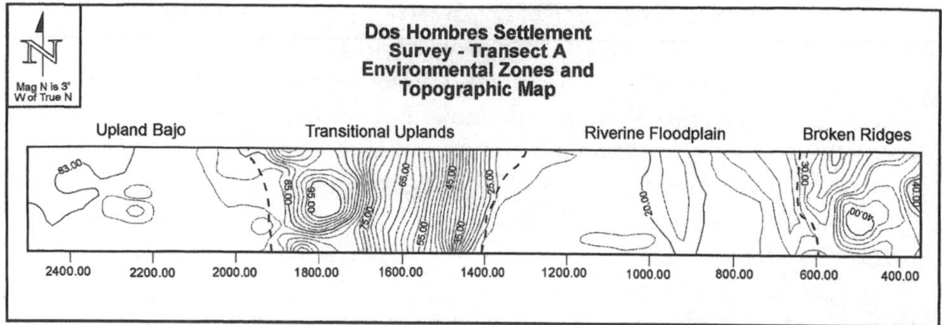

Figure 6.3. Topographic and environmental zone map of Transect A (contour interval 2 m)

environmental zones, or "ecozones" within the larger Embayment (Figures 6.3, 6.4).

THE UPLAND BAJO The Upland Bajo environmental zone lies at the far western end of the overall project area and is situated in Brokaw and Mallory's (1993: Figure 4) Río Bravo Terrace Uplands. This area represents a transitional zone between scrub swamp forests to the east and upland forests to the west. Soils here are thick clays that saturate quickly during the rainy season, leaving the area poorly suited for habitation. Indeed, not a single cultural feature was recorded in the Upland Bajo. Vegetation is generally low, with a dense understory and an overhead canopy of between 3 m and 8 m in height (Brokaw and Mallory 1993: Figure 9).

Given the poorly draining soils of the Upland Bajo, the area may be considered best suited for seasonally based dry farming techniques, such as slash and burn. The absence of either residential or agricultural features in this area makes a poor case for arguing for more intensive forms of production.

THE TRANSITIONAL UPLANDS The Transitional Uplands extend from the crest of the Río Bravo Escarpment to its base and are also found at the east end of Transect B. Vegetation in this zone compares most favorably with the Upland Forest described by Brokaw and Mallory (1993:19–22) and is dominated by tall (up to 25 m) hardwoods (Brokaw and Mallory 1993: Figure 7). These trees create a relatively dense overhead canopy blocking most sunlight from penetrating to the forest floor, thereby restricting the development of an understory.

Transitional Uplands soils are placed into two categories. In areas of steep (up to 20 percent) surface gradients, soils are very shallow, gravelly, and of moderate fertility (Brokaw and Mallory 1993:19). However, some level areas are produced by natural stair-step bedrock or cultural modifications such as terraces and platforms. Through colluvial deposition, prehistoric cultural activity, or natural pedogenesis, soils in these areas can attain depths of up to 50 cm. Remains of habitation are frequently found in these level areas.

Evidence for agricultural production in the Transitional Uplands zone is seen primarily in the form of dry-slope or contour terracing (Dunning and Beach 1994:58–59; Fedick 1994:119). Terraces run perpendicular to the topography and create level planting beds upslope. Dry-slope terraces occur in a variety of sizes, with several ranging up to 50 m in length. In these cases, the distribution of nearby house mounds suggests shared labor inputs for the construction and maintenance of the planting surfaces.

Evidence of specialized adaptation to these environmental conditions by individual households is also seen. A dry-slope terrace, measuring only a few meters long, was exposed at one residential excavation (Operation 24) and is taken to represent a house-lot garden. This terrace was completely buried by colluvial slope wash and was invisible from the surface prior to excavation. At another excavation (Operation 25), we recorded evidence of sophisticated soil and water management techniques (Lohse and Findlay 2000). During our work at Operation 25, a medium-sized patio group situated at the base of the escarpment, we documented a small

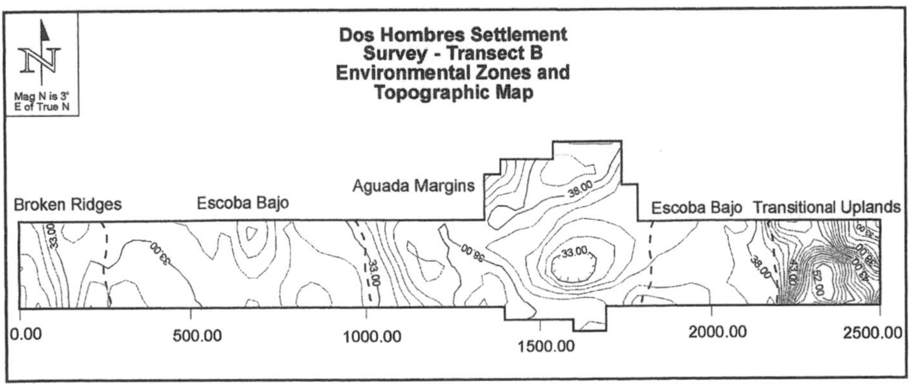

Figure 6.4. Topographic and environmental zone map of Transect B (contour interval 1 m)

channel that had been excavated into the limestone bedrock directly behind one of the structures. The channel was associated with naturally occurring depressions in the bedrock, one of which had been artificially augmented. Unit profiles revealed that this system was designed to operate beneath the planting bed. Its purpose appears to have been to allow excess soil moisture to drain away (downslope) during the rainy season, and also to help retain soil moisture in the dry season. These two finds, suggesting kitchen gardens, help demonstrate the high degree of household adaptability in overcoming localized conditions in the Transitional Uplands.

RIVERINE FLOODPLAIN Only three perennial water sources were noted in the entire survey area, and all are located in the Río Bravo floodplain. The Río Bravo itself parallels the base of the Río Bravo Escarpment, running between 300 and 500 m to the east. For most of the year the river is only a small stream a few meters wide. During heavy rains, either locally or upstream, the river floods its banks and covers an area of several hundred meters across (Dunning, Jones, et al. 1999:7). Additionally, a number of springs feed a second, smaller waterway at the escarpment base.

The eastern margin of the Riverine Floodplain terminates at a series of limestone ridges. At the base of the westernmost of these is the third perennial water source, an oxbow lake referred to as Laguna de Juan Piojo (Dunning, Scarborough, et al. 1999) that holds water through the dry season. This lagoon measures approximately 200 m north to south, and is 60 to 70 m at its widest point. The lake is recharged by seasonal floodwaters of the Río Bravo, by rainwater, and by surface water runoff from the adjacent limestone ridges to the east.

Vegetation in the Riverine Floodplain varies from open stands of cohune palms at the base of the escarpment to dense and impenetrable bamboo grass. The area around Laguna de Juan Piojo is well-developed secondary-growth forest (Jones 1999:4). Soils in this zone are deep organic clays that originate partially from low-energy seasonal flood events of the Río Bravo.

Because of impenetrable undergrowth, the floodplain was not included in the pedestrian survey. However, information on the ancient exploitation of this setting comes from two soil cores taken from Laguna de Juan Piojo (Dunning, Scarborough, et al. 1999; Jones 1999) and a soil profile from the floodplain that revealed a buried paleosol (Beach et al. 2000). Beginning soon after 820 BC, the pollen record indicates dramatic vegetation changes around this lagoon (Figure 6.5). Maize pollen ap-

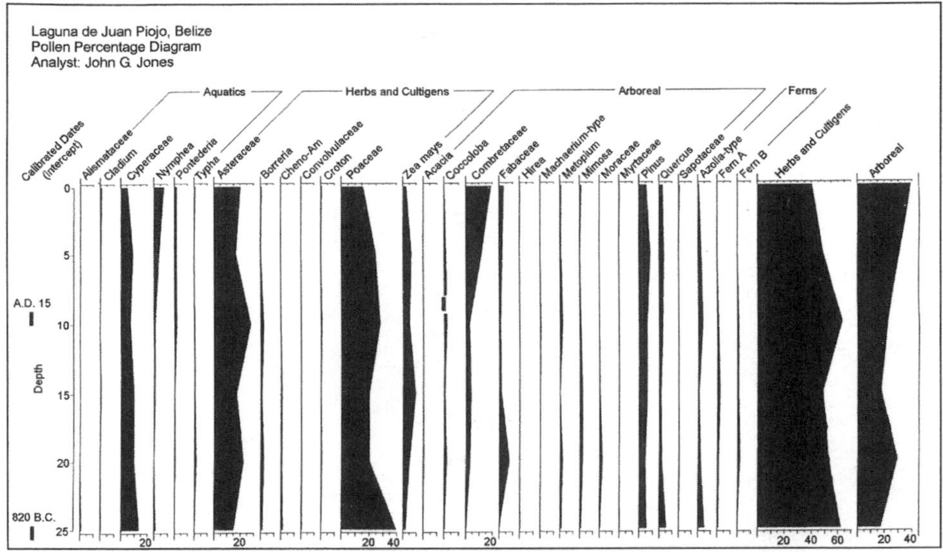

Figure 6.5. Pollen analysis from Laguna de Juan Piojo (after Jones 1999)

pears at this time, as do disturbance indicators such as grasses, composites, sedges, and *Borreria*, described as "a field weed commonly encountered in pollen samples from cultivated areas" (Jones 1999:6). Arboreal species were gradually replaced by grasses, herbs, and cultigens, but maize pollen grains were recovered in relatively high frequencies from throughout the core.

The soil profile (Figure 6.6) reveals a buried paleosol at a depth of approximately 85–90 cm below the surface. This buried horizon is described as "a black, 25–30 cm thick Ab horizon that gradually transitions below to a highly mottled, redoximorphic, Cg horizon, which extended down to over 2 m deep" (Beach et al. 2000). A calibrated radiocarbon date of 205 BC to AD 240 (2 sigma confidence rate) was derived from the top of this paleosol, indicating Late Preclassic–age soil formation buried by later alluvium. The core and profile sequences indicate that the surrounding area was probably used for agricultural production during the entire history of occupation at Dos Hombres, from the early Middle Preclassic (ca. 820 BC) to the Terminal Classic (ca. AD 850–900).

In spite of the pollen evidence for maize and the buried Late Preclassic soil horizon, Late Classic cultivation techniques used in the Riverine Floodplain are unknown. It is conceivable that the construction of canals would have helped to drain excess water during the wet season and to

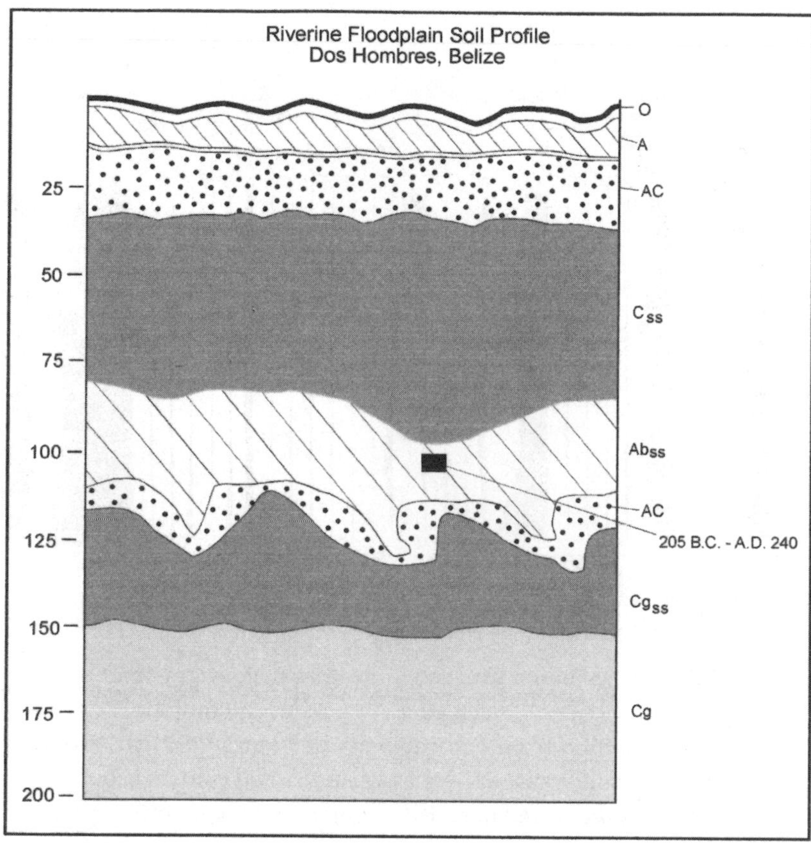

Figure 6.6. Soil profile from Operation 10 on the Río Bravo Floodplain (after Beach et al. 2000)

provide water for irrigation during the dry season. Such systems have been reported from *bajos* in Guatemala (Culbert et al. 1990; Kunen and Culbert 1997), riverine environs along the Río Hondo (Pohl 1990a), and large swamps in northern Belize (Turner and Harrison 1983). However, we failed to recover any evidence indicating agricultural intensification in this floodplain. Considering the seasonal inundation of the area, pollen evidence for forest clearance, and the lack of evidence for intensified food production, it is likely that a short-fallow system, such as recessional field agriculture, was employed here.

BROKEN RIDGES The Broken Ridges zone begins with the low (under 30 m) limestone ridges that appear immediately to the east of the Riverine

Floodplain and extend east through the site core. The primary characteristic of this zone is dramatic variation in topography; the steep ridges are separated by broad, shallow "basins" that measure some 30 to 50 m across, and that grade gently downslope to the north. Although residential features (mounds and low platforms) were recorded both on the ridges and in the basins, agricultural features were documented only between the ridges. In one case, a basin graded into a shallow drainage that had a pair of cross-channel terraces.

Vegetation patterns vary markedly between the basins and ridgetops. Mixed hardwoods, including *ramón*, my lady, and sapote are found together with copal, ceiba, cabbage bark, and fig trees across the ridges. The overhead canopy of the ridges is significantly higher than elsewhere, where vegetation is often impenetrable. Disturbance vegetation dominates many of these low-lying areas, indicating that they have been cleared in the past couple of decades by modern *milperos*.

During heavy rains, water and soil wash off the ridges into the intervening basins, yielding fertile colluvial deposits. By comparison, soils on the ridges themselves were virtually nonexistent, with deposits of any extent located primarily at the summits. Because of these localized soil conditions, the ridges are poorly suited for agricultural production, though house-lot gardening could certainly have been carried out on the ridgetops where sufficient soils have accumulated. By contrast, intervening basins are ideal for food production on a modest scale. Surface gradients in these troughs are very level (generally less than 1 percent), so topsoil erosion is not likely to have been a problem faced by the ancient Maya.

ESCOBA BAJO The Escoba Bajo constitutes the largest percentage of the survey area, covering nearly half of Transect B. This zone corresponds to the scrub swamp forest described by Brokaw and Mallory (1993:22) as a "seasonally wet swamp forest, occurring in clay-filled, poorly drained, slight depressions that are scattered over the Río Bravo [research area]." Vegetation in this zone is fairly dense, with a low (4–5 m) overhead canopy and only occasional emergent trees. Species include poisonwood, gumbolimbo, bullhorn acacia, and numerous *escoba* palms. Mahogany stumps are often present, indicating that though this species is largely absent now due to logging, it was formerly present.

Soils in the Escoba Bajo are thick clays that quickly swell with moisture as they become saturated during the rainy season. The poor drainage capacity of these clays, combined with a nearly level slope gradient, results in very few well-defined water courses in the area. After soils become saturated and as rainwater continues to accumulate, it gathers in low-lying areas and slowly moves northward. As clays dry out, they shrink and crack, producing a hummocky microtopography. This cycle of shrinking and swelling creates an unstable ground surface and subsurface that is marked by moderate vertisolic action. Profiles from soil test units failed to reveal any evidence of buried stable horizons that might correspond with ancient Maya settlement or exploitation of the area.

Another result of the poor drainage capacity of these clays is that the area is not well suited for habitation without substantial labor-intensive improvements. Only four isolated mounds were recorded between 200 and 750 m east along Transect B. One of these was tested (Operation 17), and the limited ceramic data recovered (Lauren Sullivan, personal communication 1998) suggest it to have been a field hut associated with agriculture or other activities, not a residence. At the 750 m point, the terrain begins to rise slightly, though the consistency of the soils remains the same. Beginning with this rise in elevation, surveyors recorded an increase in both settlement and landscape modification features such as dry-slope terracing and ground-level cobble surfaces or pavements (Lohse 1997). Many of the residences in this zone were not built on basal platforms, but on such cobble surfaces. Prior to the 1999 season, the function of these pavements could only be guessed. However, recent excavations in this area have shown that the cobble matrix facilitates drainage, thereby making the otherwise uninhabitable area suited for settlement (Trachman 2000).

AGUADA MARGINS Two *aguadas*, or enclosed depressions that fill with water during the rainy season, are located approximately 1.4 km east of the Dos Hombres site core. These natural, irregularly shaped depressions measure some 200 to 300 m across. One of these is located squarely in the center of Transect B, and the survey area was offset so as to encompass it. Vegetation undergoes a transition from the Escoba Bajo to resemble the Transitional Uplands. Trees are larger, with more hardwoods present, and undergrowth thins out somewhat from adjacent low-lying areas. Escoba palms and other lower species remain present.

Overall elevations rise noticeably out of the surrounding Escoba Bajo toward the *aguadas*, and bedrock frequently outcrops through the leaf litter on the forest floor. Within this general trend, localized topography in the Aguada Margins is varied, with elevation changes of several meters at the ecotonal boundary between these two zones. Soils are also more variable here; thin loamy deposits overlie shallow limestone bedrock in elevated places, and pockets of clay characterize areas of low relief. Soils within the *aguada* are organic rich clays that have washed in from the surrounding terrain. These clays have also undergone shrink-swell cycles, similar to those of the *bajo*.

These *aguadas* remain dry during the spring and early summer. Once the summer rains begin, however, they can fill with water in only a few days. It is therefore probable that the *aguadas* represented large, seasonal wetlands during the Late Classic, and likely were significant natural features in terms of the exploitable resources they offered. As an indication of the richness of this environmental niche, settlement density in this area is among the highest yet documented in northwestern Belize (Lohse 1998).

Due to the localized variation in soils and relief in the Aguada Margins, intensifying agricultural production appears to have required a variety of techniques. Several large dry-slope terraces are associated with residential groups in the ecotone between the Escoba Bajo and Aguada Margins where the topography is irregular. The enormous extent of these terraces suggests that (1) farming was carried out at a scale somewhat larger than house-lot gardening; and (2) many of these terraces were not associated with a single residence, suggesting that cooperative labor was required to construct and maintain these features.

A box terrace (Operation 11) was documented adjacent to one particularly large domestic group referred to as Las Terrazas (Operation 20 in Figure 6.1). Box terraces have been described in the Belize River Valley (Fedick 1994:119–120) and the Petexbatún region of Guatemala (Dunning and Beach 1994:58), where they are found with ancient residences. They have been interpreted as seedbeds, where crops are started and then transplanted to fields after achieving a state of maturity (Netting 1993:52; Wilken 1987:257–261). By starting crops in seedbeds and then transplanting them to fields as they mature, plants are allowed to germinate in a space-efficient manner. This method for growing food can also yield higher returns, as it enables farmers to provide more care to the plants through moisture control, protection against pests, and fertilization of soil during early stages of their lives, thereby minimizing risks of early crop loss. The significance of this possible seedbed and its association with the Las Terrazas group is discussed below.

In the *aguada* itself, we recorded evidence of potential soil modification by humans. Soil profiles of a test unit (Operation 21) close to the western margin of the *aguada* revealed highly altered stratigraphy. Beach et al. (2000) describe this sequence as "highly contorted Vertisol horizons beneath a topsoil of ca. 35 cm, including Ab_{ss}, AC_b, Cg_{ss}, and in situ limey masses." A soil core was taken from the bottom of the excavation unit, and microstratigraphic analyses performed by Paul Goldberg of Boston University indicate that the organic-rich AC_b stratum extends an additional 35 cm or so to the weathered limestone bedrock. A calibrated radiometric date of 195 BC to AD 430 (Beta-135555; 2 sigma rate of confidence) derived from the associated Ab_{ss} clay suggests a probable Late Preclassic/Early Classic origin for these anthropogenic strata. Explanations for the stratigraphic cut include either extreme Vertisol action, an in-filled canal that would have elevated planting beds above the *aguada*'s seasonal water table, or some combination of natural and cultural factors. In any case, it seems clear that the *aguada* represented an attractive locale that was well suited for intensive, sustainable agricultural production.

Intra-Site Settlement Patterns at Dos Hombres

Noting the distribution of settlement across the six ecozones as potential residences per hectare demonstrates the degree to which small-scale environmental variability played a key role in the arrangement of residences at Dos Hombres (Figure 6.7). These figures indicate the significantly higher carrying capacity of Aguada Margins, which has better than three times as much settlement per area as the next most densely settled ecozone, the Transitional Uplands. However, by closely examining the type and nature of settlement across the project area, two distinct patterns emerge that suggest important differences in the organization of farming households into localized coalitions. I refer to these as the *corporate group pattern* and the *micro-community pattern.*

THE CORPORATE GROUP PATTERN Examples of a distinctive pattern of settlement referred to as the corporate group pattern were documented in both transects. Characteristics defining this pattern are as follows:

1. Hierarchical ranking of settlement within cluster
2. Light to moderate density of settlement
3. Evidence for hierarchical use of or access to agricultural soils
4. First Tier groups reflect "special purpose" role
5. Cluster occupies poor to moderate agricultural zone

In each of the three examples of this pattern, one particular courtyard group, termed the First Tier group, is clearly larger and more formal than all others. Each First Tier group is an east-focused patio group, similar

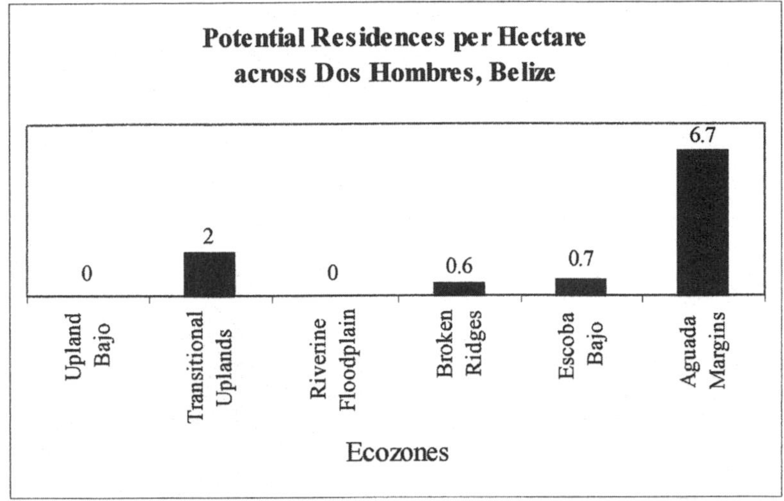

Figure 6.7. Distribution of potential residences per hectare of area across Dos Hombres

to Tikal's Plaza Plan 2 (Becker 1971, 1991) and reported at other southern Lowland centers such as La Milpa (Kunen 1999; Robichaux 1995; Tourtellot et al. 2003), Seibal (Tourtellot 1988a), and Caracol (Chase 1996; Chase and Chase 1994). The possible role of these east-focused groups is discussed in more detail below. A second tier is identified by a limited number of slightly smaller residential groups. Two or three successive tiers may be further defined, each in turn characterized by an increasing number of groups or isolated mounds that decrease in size.

The three cases were recorded in the Broken Ridges, the peripheral areas of the Aguada Margins, and the Transitional Uplands in Transect B. In each instance, First Tier groups occupy the most agriculturally advantageous location in the area, or appear to otherwise exert some control over localized food production. The best evidence for this was found in the peripheral areas of the Aguada Margins zone. Here, the First Tier residence Las Terrazas is associated with the box terrace described above (Figure 6.8). By controlling seedbed production, occupants of the Las Terrazas group would also have been able to oversee local agricultural production by monitoring the growth and subsequent distribution of seedling plants. This would have allowed residents of this group to determine when and where maturing crops were to be transplanted in surrounding fields.

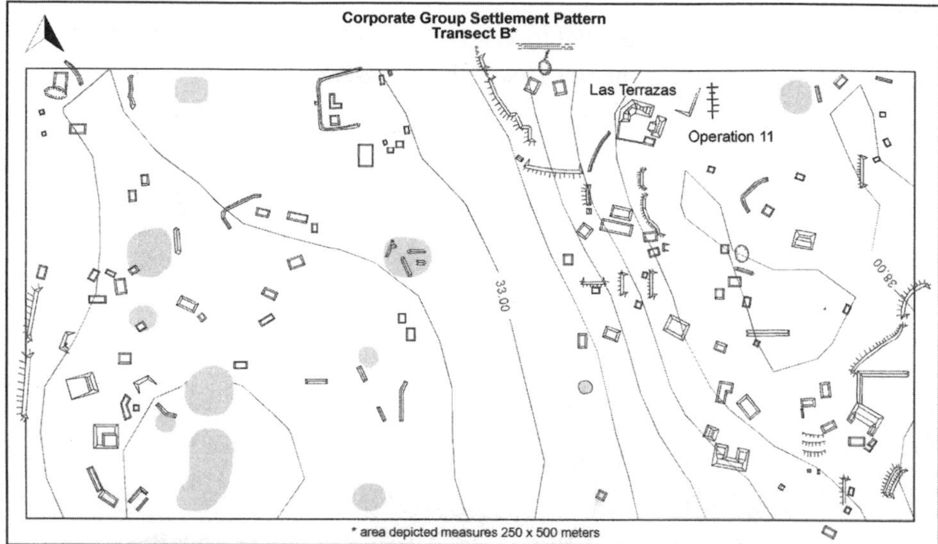

Figure 6.8. Corporate group settlement pattern from Aguada Margins environmental zone, showing the box terrace (Operation 11) in association with First Tier group Las Terrazas

Though evidence for the First Tier group at the eastern end of Transect B (named Cerro Zaro; Operation 14 in Figure 6.1) is less clear, this two-courtyard compound still ranks above the others in terms of its architectural elaboration. Cerro Zaro occupies a position immediately at the base of a low ridge (Figure 6.9), where it has direct access to both the fertile colluvial deposits at the base of that ridge and to the moderately fertile Escoba Bajo clays to the west. Other residential groups in this cluster occupy less favorable positions on the ridgetop or slopes, where labor-intensive terracing was required to transform otherwise marginal spaces into agriculturally productive land.

I interpret the corporate group settlement patterns to represent multifamily groups, perhaps arranged around lines of descent (after McAnany 1995; see also Schele and Mathews 1999:329) but that almost certainly cohered through their common reliance on an agricultural resource base of limited scale. These groups appear to have operated as relatively autonomous social units within the broader Dos Hombres community. Corporate groups that pass down rights to land have been proposed as the fundamental unit of social organization for the pre-Hispanic (Hageman 1999a; Hendon 1991; Schele and Freidel 1990), historic (Tozzer 1941), and contemporary Maya (Dunning, this volume; McAnany 1995; Sharer 1993:97–100; Vogt 1969, this volume). The architectural plans of First Tier groups, dominated by an isolated temple on their east sides, are distinctive enough from other residential groups to suggest that they may have been designed to fulfill special roles in their local communities (e.g., Chase and Chase 1997). If this turns out to have been the case, then their role in overseeing localized food production may be better understood.

THE MICRO-COMMUNITY PATTERN The example of a micro-community settlement pattern in the study area is located around the *aguadas* east of the site (Figure 6.10). Settlement in this area is characterized by two factors: (1) a very dense clustering of residences that (2) are not easily ranked in terms of size or architectural elaboration. While size differences are evident among mounds around the *aguada*, these are attributed to different stages in a developmental cycle (Goody 1958; cf. Neff et al. 1995:150–153; Tourtellot 1988b; also see Dunning and Yaeger and Robin, this volume) rather than to differences in status. There is also a sharp increase in the number of field walls in the Aguada Margins zone, indicating a conscious effort to define individual family compounds or house-lots. In contrast, these boundary markers are largely absent from

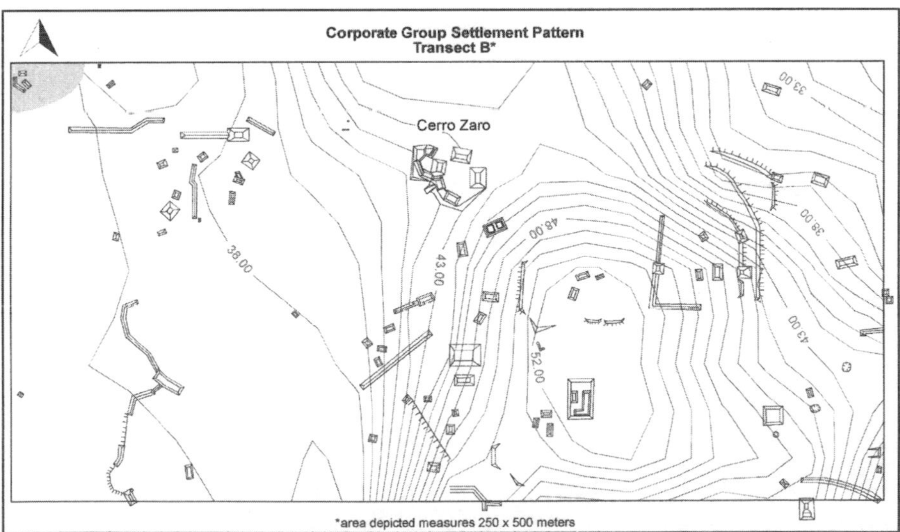

Figure 6.9. Corporate group settlement pattern at east end of Transect B. Cerro Zaro is First Tier group.

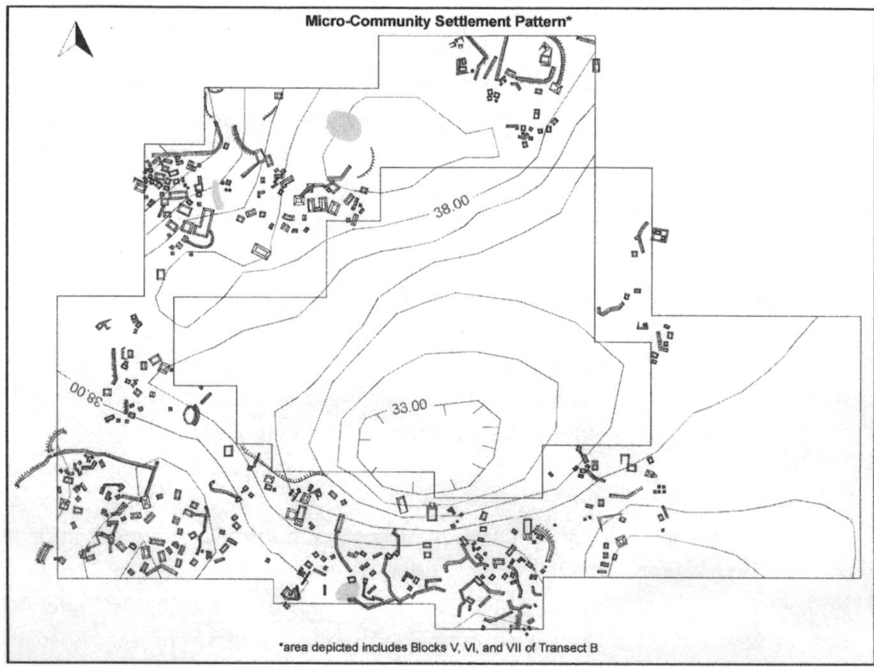

Figure 6.10. Micro-community settlement pattern around *aguada* in Transect B

the corporate group patterns, where intervening space is instead given to agricultural production.

The current impression garnered from the densely packed settlement around the *aguada* is that it is fundamentally different in character from the corporate group clusters, and that it may reflect a correspondingly different form of social organization. I suggest that this nucleated settlement represents a resource-specialized community (following Scarborough et al. 1999), focused on exploiting the *aguada* and its surrounding environs. Residents of the *aguada* community are viewed as agricultural specialists whose domestic economies were collectively bound and inextricably tied to production within the *aguada* (see Mabry's [1996] discussion of irrigation communities). The absence of a residential hierarchy around the *aguada*, as characterizes other areas of the Dos Hombres settlement system, and the compact nature of the settlement are suggestive of a cooperative, communally based decision-making structure. Elsewhere, "collective action" resource management and exploitation strategies (Mabry 1996:12) have been reported in complex societies as an alternative to strictly hierarchical decision making (McCay and Acheson

1987), though they remain underreported in the Maya area. Their possible role in the management of agricultural resources at Dos Hombres holds important implications for models of intensification without centralized or overarching bureaucracy.

Summary Discussions

By focusing attention across a relatively small spatial scale, this study has shown that adaptation to environmental factors such as soil, water availability, space, and surface geometry (Wilken 1987) takes place at different levels of social organization. This focus permits a better understanding of the degree to which individual households, as well as different types of producer coalitions (e.g., Wolf 1966:81–89), adapted to different conditions. Many individual households managed water runoff and soil erosion by constructing small terraces or modifying bedrock. In some cases, households aggregated into slightly larger corporate groups rather than implement their own farming strategies. Corresponding with unusually productive environmental resource areas, yet another form of social organization, which I refer to as the micro-community, appears to have engaged in specialized food production. These data offer compelling evidence for the complexity of the Dos Hombres community during the Late Classic period.

The distribution of residences within the corporate group patterns suggests a circumscribed, hierarchical decision-making process regarding direct access to and production from localized soil resources. Differences in status are also evident in these areas, and seeking to understand such differences provides lines for future inquiry. I have suggested that agricultural production by these groups may have been coordinated at least in part by First Tier residences, though carried out through the cooperative efforts of surrounding households. I derive some support for this argument from Kelli Carmean's (1998) study of Late to Terminal Classic period religious and political leadership at Sayil, Yucatán. Her work has indicated that certain domestic groups (not necessarily east-focused) distributed across that site may have served in the capacity of decision makers and administrators over adjacent residential groups. While the focus in the current study is on agricultural production rather than religious or political leadership, I propose a similar role for the First Tier groups identified at Dos Hombres.

Evidence suggests the presence of resource-specialized communities

(Scarborough et al. 1999) within the larger Dos Hombres political system during the Late Classic period. I have inferred from the absence of a residential hierarchy in the *aguada* community that agricultural production was structured horizontally, and carried out through "collective action" (Mabry 1996:12) rather than under direct elite supervision.

Other archaeologists working in the Lowlands (King and Potter 1994; MacKinnon and Kepecs 1989; Potter and King 1995; Scarborough 1991; Shafer and Hester 1983; Valdez and Mock 1991) have presented data arguing for the development of communities specialized in the exploitation of a particular resource. Vernon Scarborough (1991; Scarborough et al. 1999) proposes that many of these resource-specialized communities arose as early as the Late Preclassic period and were autonomous political entities. Given the *aguada* community's proximity to the Dos Hombres site center, and its lack of a discernible hierarchical structure, however, I suggest that this settlement was somehow embedded within a preexisting Dos Hombres political network. Ceramic data recovered from excavations around the *aguada* indicate that an overwhelming majority of the occupation dates to the Late Classic period (Lauren Sullivan, personal communication 1998), well after Dos Hombres was already an established community in northwestern Belize (Houk 1996).

Conclusions

Small-scale examinations of environmental variability and settlement patterning, such as the one presented here, provide important perspectives to the study of the pre-Hispanic Maya. They allow archaeologists both to recognize localized social groups and to define their roles in broader economic, political, and environmental contexts. I suggest that views of Lowland Maya society as having been strictly hierarchical are in part outgrowths of site-center-focused studies that have hindered our ability to recognize alternative social structures (e.g., Crumley 1995) that may directly implicate Maya commoners.

Intriguingly, work at Dos Hombres to date has found no evidence of agricultural schemes that were controlled by the ruling members of that ancient community. Instead, these finds place commoners squarely in the role of managing decentralized food production systems. Differences in status, in the form of architectural variation and proximity to favorable slope or soil conditions, are evident within localized groups. Also, at least in northwestern Belize during the Late Classic, particularly prime agricultural resources can be associated with alternative or "new" social configurations, referred to as micro-communities. The model presented here holds implications for our understanding of both ancient Maya agricultural production and certain aspects of social organization. It also allows us to better understand the role of commoners in each.

Acknowledgments

The site of Dos Hombres is but one focus of the Programme for Belize Archaeological Project, conducted under the general direction of Dr. Fred Valdez, Jr. The data and analyses presented here are a result and a reflection of the research goals of the larger regional project; I am grateful for the support of the PfBAP in facilitating this fieldwork. Also, it is with particular gratitude that I acknowledge the Institute of Archaeology (formerly the Department of Archaeology) of the Government of Belize, especially then-acting commissioners John Morris and Brian Woodye, for granting permission to work in their country.

Financial support for this work was provided by the University of Texas at Austin in the form of summer archaeological field schools, individual travel grants (Study Abroad Office), and a Faculty Sponsored Dissertation Research grant (Institute of Latin American Studies). The Programme for Belize Archaeological Project provided field and logistical support during the 1996–1998 seasons without which this work would not have been possible. In addition, the study benefited greatly from the National Science Foundation's award (Grant no. SBR-963-1024) to Vernon Scarborough and Nicholas Dunning of the University of Cincinnati. Information from soil analyses was graciously provided by Timothy Beach, who drafted the profile shown in Figure 6.6, and Nicholas Dunning. Finally, I would like to thank Fred Valdez, Jr., Vernon Scarborough, Jon B. Hageman, and Paul J. Hughbanks for reading earlier versions of this piece. Their comments have helped clarify many of the points made herein, but oversights and errors are my own.

Note

1. The data upon which these discussions are based were collected between 1996 and 1998. Additional survey and excavations are ongoing around the site of Dos Hombres as well as the surrounding areas. The results of these ongoing investigations may warrant refinements to some of my conclusions.

References

Adams, Richard E. W., W. E. Brown, and T. Patrick Culbert

1981 Radar Mapping, Archaeology, and Ancient Maya Land Use. *Science* 213:457–463.

Adams, Richard E. W., and T. Patrick Culbert

1977 The Origins of Civilization in the Maya Lowlands. In *The Origins of Maya Civilization*, edited by Richard E. W. Adams, pp. 3–24. University of New Mexico Press, Albuquerque.

Adams, Richard E. W., Hubert R. Robichaux, and Ruth Matthews

1997 Urban and Community Patterns in the Three Rivers Region. Paper presented at the 62nd Annual Meeting of the Society for American Archaeology, Nashville.

Ashmore, Wendy

1981 Some Issues of Method and Theory in Lowland Maya Settlement Archaeology. In *Lowland Maya Settlement Patterns*, edited by Wendy Ashmore, pp. 37–69. University of New Mexico Press, Albuquerque.

Ashmore, Wendy, and Richard R. Wilk

1988 Household and Community in the Mesoamerican Past. In *Household and Community in the Mesoamerican Past*, edited by Richard R. Wilk and Wendy Ashmore, pp. 1–27. University of New Mexico Press, Albuquerque.

Beach, Timothy, Nicholas Dunning, Vernon Scarborough, and Sheryl Luzzadder-Beach

2000 Environmental Change in the Bajos of the Three Rivers Region, Northwestern Belize. Paper presented at the 65th Annual Meeting of the Society for American Archaeology, Philadelphia.

Becker, Marshall J.

1971 The Identification of a Second Plaza Plan at Tikal, Guatemala, and Its Implications for Ancient Maya Social Complexity. Ph.D. diss., Department of Anthropology, University of Pennsylvania, Philadelphia.

1991 Plaza Plans at Tikal, Guatemala, and at Other Lowland Maya Sites: Evidence for Patterns of Culture Change. *Cuadernos de Arquitectura Mesoamericana* 14:11–26.

Brokaw, Nicholas V. L., and Elizabeth P. Mallory

1993 *Vegetation of the Río Bravo Conservation and Management Area, Belize.* Report on file at the Manomet Bird Observatory, Manomet.

Brumfiel, Elizabeth M., and Timothy K. Earle

1987 Specialization, Exchange, and Complex Societies: An Introduction. In *Specialization, Exchange, and Complex Societies*, edited by Elizabeth M. Brumfiel and Timothy K. Earle, pp. 1–9. Cambridge University Press, New York.

Carmean, Kelli

1998 Leadership at Sayil: A Study of Political and Religious Decentralization. *Ancient Mesoamerica* 9(2):259–270.

Chase, Arlen F.
1996 The Organization and Composition of Classic Lowland Maya Society: The View from Caracol, Belize. In *Eighth Palenque Round Table, 1993*, edited by Martha J. Macri and Jan McHargue, pp. 213–221. The Pre-Columbian Art Institute, San Francisco.

Chase, Arlen F., and Diane Z. Chase
1994 Maya Veneration of the Dead at Caracol, Belize. In *Seventh Palenque Round Table, 1989*, edited by Merle G. Robertson and Virginia M. Fields, pp. 53–60. The Pre-Columbian Art Institute, San Francisco.
1997 Spatial Dynamics and Household Size and Composition at Caracol, Belize. Paper presented at the 62nd Annual Meeting of the Society for American Archaeology, Nashville.

Chayanov, Alexander V.
1986 *The Theory of Peasant Economy*, edited by Daniel Thorner, Basile Kerblay, and R. E. F. Smith. University of Wisconsin Press, Madison.

Crumley, Carole L.
1995 Heterarchy and the Analysis of Complex Societies. In *Heterarchy and the Analysis of Complex Societies*, edited by Robert M. Ehrenreich, Carole L. Crumley, and Janet E. Levy, pp. 1–5. Archaeological Papers of the American Anthropological Association 6. Washington, D.C.

Culbert, T. Patrick, Laura J. Levi, and Lionel Cruz
1990 Lowland Maya Wetland Agriculture: The Río Azul Agronomy Program. In *Vision and Revision in Maya Studies*, edited by Flora S. Clancy and Peter D. Harrison, pp. 115–124. University of New Mexico Press, Albuquerque.

Dunning, Nicholas P.
1992 *Lords of the Hills: Ancient Maya Settlement in the Puuc Region, Yucatán, Mexico.* Monographs in World Archaeology 15. Prehistory Press, Madison.

Dunning, Nicholas P., and Timothy Beach
1994 Soil Erosion, Slope Management, and Ancient Terracing in the Maya Lowlands. *Latin American Antiquity* 5(1):51–69.

Dunning, Nicholas, Timothy Beach, and David Rue
1997 The Paleoecology and Ancient Settlement of the Petexbatún Region, Guatemala. *Ancient Mesoamerica* 8(2):255–266.

Dunning, Nicholas, John G. Jones, Timothy Beach, and Sheryl Luzzadder-Beach
1999 Ancient Maya Landscapes of Northwestern Belize. Paper presented at the 64th Annual Meeting of the Society for American Archaeology, Chicago.

Dunning, Nicholas P., Vernon Scarborough, Fred Valdez, Jr., Sheryl Luzzadder-Beach, Timothy Beach, and John G. Jones
1999 Temple Mountains, Sacred Lakes, and Fertile Fields: Ancient Maya Landscapes in Northwestern Belize. *Antiquity* 73(281):650–660.

Fedick, Scott L.
1989 The Economics of Agricultural Land Use and Settlement in the Upper

Belize Valley. In *Prehistoric Maya Economies of Belize*, edited by Patricia A. McAnany and Barry L. Isaac, pp. 215–253. Research in Economic Anthropology Supplement 4. JAI Press, Greenwich.

1994 Ancient Maya Agricultural Terracing in the Upper Belize River Area. *Ancient Mesoamerica* 5(1):107–127.

1995 Land Evaluation and Ancient Maya Land Use in the Upper Belize River Area, Belize, Central America. *Latin American Antiquity* 6(1):16–34.

1996a Conclusion: Landscape Approaches to the Study of Ancient Maya Agriculture and Resource Use. In *The Managed Mosaic: Ancient Maya Agriculture and Resource Use*, edited by Scott L. Fedick, pp. 335–347. University of Utah Press, Salt Lake City.

Fedick, Scott L. (editor)

1996b *The Managed Mosaic: Ancient Maya Agriculture and Resource Use.* University of Utah Press, Salt Lake City.

Flannery, Kent V. (editor)

1982 *Maya Subsistence: Studies in Memory of Dennis E. Puleston.* Academic Press, New York.

Ford, Anabel

1986 *Population Growth and Social Complexity: An Examination of Settlement and Environment in the Central Maya Lowlands.* Anthropological Research Papers 35. Arizona State University, Tempe.

1990 Maya Settlement in the Belize River Valley Area: Variations in Residence Patterns of the Central Maya Lowlands. In *Precolumbian Population History in the Maya Lowlands*, edited by T. Patrick Culbert and Don S. Rice, pp. 167–181. University of New Mexico Press, Albuquerque.

1996 Critical Resource Control and the Rise of the Classic Period Maya. In *The Managed Mosaic: Ancient Maya Agriculture and Resource Use*, edited by Scott L. Fedick, pp. 297–303. University of Utah Press, Salt Lake City.

Ford, Anabel, and Scott L. Fedick

1992 Prehistoric Maya Settlement Patterns in the Upper Belize River Area: Initial Results of the Belize River Archaeological Settlement Survey. *Journal of Field Archaeology* 19(1):35–49.

Goody, Jack (editor)

1958 *The Developmental Cycle in Domestic Groups.* Cambridge University Press, Cambridge.

Hageman, Jon B.

1999a Ideology and Intersite Settlement among the Late Classic Maya. Paper presented at the 64th Annual Meeting of the Society for American Archaeology, Chicago.

1999b Were the Late Classic Maya Characterized by Lineages? Paper presented at the Tercera Mesa Redonda de Palenque (New Series), Palenque, Chiapas.

Harrison, Peter D., and B. L. Turner (editors)

1978 *Pre-Hispanic Maya Agriculture.* University of New Mexico Press, Albuquerque.

Hayden, Brian, and Aubrey Cannon

1982 The Corporate Group as an Archaeological Unit. *Journal of Anthropological Archaeology* 1(2):132–158.

Hendon, Julia A.

1991 Status and Power in Classic Maya Society: An Archaeological Study. *American Anthropologist* 91:894–918.

Houk, Brett A.

1996 The Archaeology of Site Planning: An Example from the Maya Site of Dos Hombres, Belize. Ph.D. diss., Department of Anthropology, University of Texas at Austin.

Hughbanks, Paul J.

1998 Settlement and Land Use at Guijarral, Northwest Belize. *Culture and Agriculture* 20(2/3):107–120.

Jones, John G.

1999 Analysis of Fossil Pollen from Aguada Juan Pistola and Laguna Juan Piojo, Belize. Manuscript on file at Palynology Laboratory, Department of Anthropology, Texas A&M University, College Station.

Kepecs, Susan, and Sylviane Boucher

1996 The Pre-Hispanic Cultivation of Rejolladas and Stone-Lands: New Evidence from Northeast Yucatán. In *The Managed Mosaic: Ancient Maya Agriculture and Resource Use*, edited by Scott L. Fedick, pp. 69–91. University of Utah Press, Salt Lake City.

Killion, Thomas W.

1990 Cultivation Intensity and Residential Site Structure: An Ethnographic Examination of Peasant Agriculture in the Sierra de los Tuxtlas, Veracruz, Mexico. *Latin American Antiquity* 1(2):191–215.

King, Eleanor M., and Daniel R. Potter

1994 Small Sites in Prehistoric Maya Socioeconomic Organization: A Perspective from Colha, Belize. In *Archaeological Views from the Countryside: Village Communities in Early Complex Societies*, edited by Glenn M. Schwartz and Steven E. Falconer, pp. 64–90. Smithsonian Institution Press, Washington, D.C.

Kunen, Julie

1999 Natural Resource Use and Socioeconomic Organization in an Ancient Maya Bajo Community. Paper presented at the 64th Annual Meeting of the Society for American Archaeology, Chicago.

Kunen, Julie, and T. Patrick Culbert

1997 Use of Seasonal Wetlands in the Maya Lowlands: Recent Research in the Bajo la Justa. Paper presented at the 62nd Annual Meeting of the Society for American Archaeology, Nashville.

Levi, Laura J.

1996 Sustainable Production and Residential Variation: A Historical Perspective on Prehispanic Domestic Economies in the Maya Lowlands. In *The Managed Mosaic: Ancient Maya Agriculture and Resource Use*, edited by Scott L. Fedick, pp. 92–106. University of Utah Press, Salt Lake City.

Liendo Stuardo, Rodrigo Rubén Gregorio
1999 The Organization of Agricultural Production at a Maya Center: Settlement Patterns in the Palenque Region, Chiapas, Mexico. Ph.D. diss., Department of Anthropology, University of Pittsburgh.

Lohse, Jon C.
1997 Results of 1996 Season of Mapping Investigations: An Interim View of Residential Organization at Dos Hombres, Belize. Report on file at the Mesoamerican Archaeology Research Laboratory, University of Texas at Austin.
1998 Interim Results from the 1997 Season of Household and Community Investigations at Dos Hombres. Report on file at the Mesoamerican Archaeology Research Laboratory, University of Texas at Austin.
2001 The Social Organization of a Late Classic Maya Community: Dos Hombres, Northwestern Belize. Ph.D. diss., Department of Anthropology, University of Texas at Austin.

Lohse, Jon C., and Patrick N. Findlay
2000 A Classic Maya House-Lot Drainage System in Northwestern Belize. *Latin American Antiquity* 11(2):175–185.

Mabry, Jonathan B.
1996 The Ethnology of Local Irrigation. In *Canals and Communities: Small-Scale Irrigation Systems*, edited by Jonathan B. Mabry, pp. 3–30. University of Arizona Press, Tucson.

McAnany, Patricia A.
1995 *Living with the Ancestors: Kinship and Kingship in Ancient Maya Society.* University of Texas Press, Austin.

McCay, Bonnie J., and James M. Acheson
1987 Human Ecology of the Commons. In *The Question of the Commons: The Culture and Ecology of Communal Resources*, edited by Bonnie J. McCay and James M. Acheson, pp. 1–34. University of Arizona Press, Tucson.

MacKinnon, J. Jefferson, and Susan M. Kepecs
1989 Prehispanic Saltmaking in Belize: New Evidence. *American Antiquity* 54(3):522–533.

Morley, Sylvanus
1946 *The Ancient Maya.* First edition. Stanford University Press, Stanford.

Neff, Theodore L., Cynthia Robin, Kevin Schwartz, and Mary K. Morrison
1995 The Xunantunich Settlement Survey. In *Xunantunich Archaeological Project: 1995 Field Season*, edited by Richard M. Leventhal and Wendy Ashmore, pp. 140–163. Unpublished report on file in the Belize Institute of Archaeology, Belmopan.

Netting, Robert McC.
1968 *Hill Farmers of Nigeria: Cultural Ecology of the Kofyar of the Jos Plateau.* University of Washington Press, Seattle.
1977 Maya Subsistence: Mythologies, Analogies, Possibilities. In *The Origins of Maya Civilization*, edited by Richard E. W. Adams, pp. 299–333. University of New Mexico Press, Albuquerque.

1993 *Smallholders, Householders: Farm Families and the Ecology of Intensive, Sustainable Agriculture.* Stanford University Press, Stanford.

Pohl, Mary D.

1990b Summary and Proposals for Future Excavation Research. In *Ancient Maya Wetland Agriculture: Excavations on Albion Island, Northern Belize,* edited by Mary D. Pohl, pp. 397–439. Westview Press, Boulder.

Pohl, Mary D. (editor)

1985 *Prehistoric Lowland Maya Environment and Subsistence Economy.* Papers of the Peabody Museum of Archaeology and Ethnology 77. Harvard University, Cambridge.

1990a *Ancient Maya Wetland Agriculture: Excavations on Albion Island, Northern Belize.* Westview Press, Boulder.

Potter, Daniel R., and Eleanor M. King

1995 A Heterarchical Approach to Lowland Maya Socioeconomies. In *Heterarchy and the Analysis of Complex Societies,* edited by Robert M. Ehrenreich, Carole L. Crumley, and Janet E. Levy, pp. 17–32. Archaeological Papers of the American Anthropological Association 6. Washington, D.C.

Rice, Don S.

1976 Middle Preclassic Maya Settlement in the Central Maya Lowlands. *Journal of Field Archaeology* 3(3):425–445.

Rice, Don S., and Prudence M. Rice

1990 Population Size and Population Change in the Central Petén Lakes Region, Guatemala. In *Precolumbian Population History in the Maya Lowlands,* edited by T. Patrick Culbert and Don S. Rice, pp. 123–148. University of New Mexico Press, Albuquerque.

Robichaux, Hubert Ray

1995 Ancient Maya Community Patterns in Northwestern Belize: Peripheral Zone Survey at La Milpa and Dos Hombres. Ph.D. diss., Department of Anthropology, University of Texas at Austin.

Sahlins, Marshall

1972 *Stone Age Economics.* Aldine, Atherton, Chicago.

Sanders, William T.

1977 Environmental Heterogeneity and the Evolution of Lowland Maya Civilization. In *The Origins of Maya Civilization,* edited by Richard E. W. Adams, pp. 287–297. University of New Mexico Press, Albuquerque.

Santley, Robert R., and Kenneth G. Hirth (editors)

1993 *Prehispanic Domestic Units in Western Mesoamerica: Studies of the Household, Compound, and Residence.* CRC Press, Boca Raton.

Scarborough, Vernon L.

1991 *Archaeology at Cerros, Belize, Central America, Volume III: The Settlement System in a Late Preclassic Maya Community.* Southern Methodist Press, Dallas.

1993 Water Management in the Southern Maya Lowlands: An Accretive Model for the Engineered Landscape. In *Economic Aspects of Water Man-*

agement in the Prehispanic New World, edited by Vernon L. Scarborough and Barry L. Isaac, pp. 17–68. Research in Economic Anthropology Supplement 7. JAI Press, Greenwich.

Scarborough, Vernon L., Matthew E. Becher, Jeffrey L. Baker, Garry Harris, and Fred Valdez, Jr.

1995 Water and Land at the Ancient Maya Community of La Milpa. *Latin American Antiquity* 6(2):98–119.

Scarborough, Vernon L., Fred Valdez, Jr., and Nicholas P. Dunning

1999 An Introduction to the Engineered Environment and Political Economy of the Three Rivers Area. Paper presented at the 64th Annual Meeting of the Society for American Archaeology, Chicago.

Schele, Linda, and David Freidel

1990 *A Forest of Kings: The Untold Story of the Ancient Maya*. William and Morrow, New York.

Schele, Linda, and Peter Mathews

1999 *The Code of Kings: The Language of Seven Sacred Maya Temples and Tombs*. Simon and Schuster, New York.

Shafer, Harry J., and Thomas R. Hester

1983 Ancient Maya Chert Workshops in Northern Belize, Central America. *American Antiquity* 48(3):519–543.

Sharer, Robert J.

1993 The Social Organization of the Late Classic Maya: Problems of Definition and Approaches. In *Lowland Maya Civilization in the Eighth Century A.D.*, edited by Jeremy A. Sabloff and John S. Henderson, pp. 91–109. Dumbarton Oaks, Washington, D.C.

Siemens, Alfred H., and Dennis E. Puleston

1972 Ridged Fields and Associated Features in Southern Campeche: New Perspectives on the Lowland Maya. *American Antiquity* 37(2):228–239.

Tourtellot, Gair, III

1988a *Peripheral Survey and Excavation Settlement and Community Patterns*. Memoirs of the Peabody Museum of Archaeology and Ethnology 16. Harvard University, Cambridge.

1988b Developmental Cycles of Households and Houses at Seibal. In *Household and Community in the Mesoamerican Past*, edited by Richard R. Wilk and Wendy Ashmore, pp. 97–120. University of New Mexico Press, Albuquerque.

Tourtellot, Gair, III, Gloria Everson, and Norman Hammond

2003 Suburban Organization: Minor Centers at La Milpa, Belize. In *Perspectives on Ancient Maya Rural Complexity*, edited by Gyles Iannone and Samuel V. Connell, pp. 95–107. Los Angeles: Cotsen Institute of Archaeology, UCLA. Monograph 49.

Tourtellot, Gair, III, Norman Hammond, and Shannon Plank

1997 The City on the Hill: Investigations at La Milpa, Northwestern Belize. Paper presented at the 62nd Annual Meeting of the Society for American Archaeology, Nashville.

Tozzer, Alfred (translator)

1941 *Landa's "Relación de las cosas de Yucatán."* Papers of the Peabody Museum 18. Harvard University, Cambridge.

Trachman, Rissa M.

2000 Household Investigations in the B-Transect, Dos Hombres: The 1999 Season. Report on file at Mesoamerican Archaeology Research Laboratory, University of Texas at Austin.

Turner, B. L., II

1974 Prehistoric Intensive Agriculture in the Mayan Lowlands. *Science* 185:118–124.

1983 *Once beneath the Forest: Prehistoric Terracing in the Río Bec Region of the Maya Lowlands.* Westview Press, Boulder.

Turner, B. L., II, and Peter D. Harrison (editors)

1983 *Pulltrouser Swamp: Ancient Maya Habitat, Agriculture, and Settlement in Northern Belize.* University of Texas Press, Austin.

Valdez, Fred, Jr., and Shirley B. Mock

1991 Additional Considerations for Prehispanic Saltmaking in Belize. *American Antiquity* 56(3):520–525.

Vogt, Evon Z.

1969 *Zinacantan: A Maya Community in the Highlands of Chiapas.* Belknap Press of Harvard University Press, Cambridge.

Walling, Stanley L.

1997 Economy and Social Organization in Prehispanic Maya Households: Insights from Recent Archaeological Investigations in the Orange Walk District of Northern Belize. Paper presented at the 62nd Annual Meeting of the Society for American Archaeology, Nashville.

1999 Living on the Edge: Classic Maya Settlement and Resource Use on the Río Bravo Escarpment, Belize, Central America. Paper presented at the 64th Annual Meeting of the Society for American Archaeology, Chicago.

Wilken, Gene C.

1987 *Good Farmers: Traditional Agricultural Resource Management in Mexico and Central America.* University of California Press, Berkeley.

Wolf, Eric R.

1966 *Peasants.* Prentice-Hall, Englewood Cliffs.

CHAPTER 7

Heterogeneous Hinterlands: The Social and Political Organization of Commoner Settlements near Xunantunich, Belize

JASON YAEGER AND CYNTHIA ROBIN

Scholars are moving toward ever more complex models of Classic period Maya society, models that include richly textured views of Maya commoners and their relationships to the Maya elite or nobility (Hendon 1996; Marcus 1995; McAnany 1993). These emerging models are the result of new empirical evidence from the Maya lowlands on the one hand and theoretical developments in anthropology and archaeology on the other.

The last two decades of the twentieth century witnessed the survey and excavation of many small settlements across the Maya lowlands. The data produced by these investigations demonstrate that the Maya countryside was a heterogeneous social landscape in at least two scales of analysis: within individual settlements (e.g., Ford and Fedick 1992; Haviland 1988; Levi 2003; Tourtellot 1988; Willey et al. 1965; Yaeger 2003a) and among settlements in a region (e.g., Ashmore et al. 2004; Haviland 1981; King and Potter 1994; Robin 2001, 2003a; Webster and Gonlin 1988; also see Lohse, this volume). In this chapter, we explore these two scales of heterogeneity using evidence from our investigations at two settlements in the hinterland of the Xunantunich polity in west-central Belize.

A second, equally important stimulus for the development of more complex models of Maya society has been the increasing interest in theoretical perspectives that focus our attention on interpersonal relations at a finer social scale than most previous archaeological paradigms (Canuto and Yaeger 2000; Dobres and Robb 2000; Hendon 1996; Meskell 1999; Robin 2003b; Robin and Rothschild 2002). We have found a range of post-structuralist and phenomenological theories to be useful tools for understanding the multifaceted ways in which people participate in their social world (e.g., Bourdieu 1977; de Certeau 1984; Garfinkel 1984; Giddens 1984). These perspectives have arisen in part as a response to social theo-

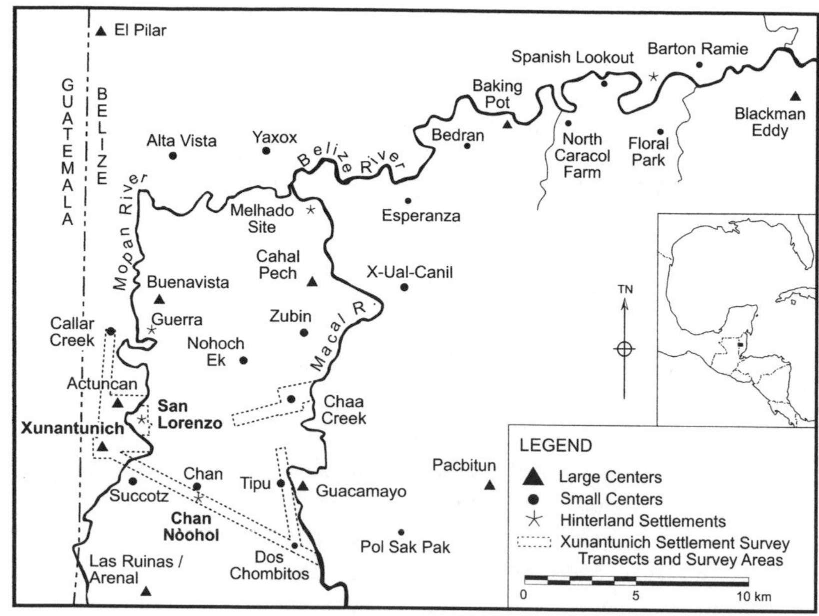

Figure 7.1. The Upper Belize River Valley, with areas mapped by the Xunantunich Settlement Survey (after Yaeger 2000a: Fig. 3.9)

ries that did not adequately address the role of individuals and their interactions in social processes. They reposition interactions at the intersection of enduring dispositions that guide and constrain action (structures) and the particular instances in which individuals make motivated or unmotivated choices (practices). Enduring structures and people's practices stand in a dialectic relationship in which structures influence practice and practice creates and re-creates structures. Although some of these theoreticians, particularly Pierre Bourdieu, lean toward a Marxian view of society, none of them prioritize economic factors above social and political ones. In this respect, we see poststructuralist and phenomenological theories as effective frameworks for integrating the various domains of social life in which structures and practices exist.

The two settlements that we discuss in this chapter, San Lorenzo and Chan Nòohol, were located only 4 km from one another (Figure 7.1), and their inhabitants had much in common. Despite that, the settlements show many differences: they had different historical trajectories, they were situated differently in the political organization of the Xunantunich polity, and each embraced an overlapping but noncoterminous diversity of commoner lifestyles. To understand these differences, we discuss Chan Nòohol and San Lorenzo in light of their social and historical development on the one hand and their members' political and economic relationships to the Xunantunich polity on the other. Although our discipline tends to distinguish social organization and political economy, the two are interwoven inextricably in these commoner settlements.

The data from Chan Nòohol and San Lorenzo demonstrate the complexity and heterogeneity inherent in the material record of pre-Columbian Maya settlements, a complexity that exists even in settlements as small as the ones we describe here. From the material record, we reconstruct the multifaceted interaction among the commoner residents of these settlements, as well as their interaction with diverse people from other settlements. The complex view of society forwarded by our case studies is multidirectional: not only do commoners react to elite strategies, but elites react to commoner strategies as well (see Inomata, this volume). Thus, social dynamics within the Xunantunich polity embrace simultaneously local and regional dynamics, commoners and elites, and social and political economic relations.

The Xunantunich Polity: Center and Hinterland

Several large sites dominated the upper Belize River valley in the Late Classic period, the largest of which was Xunantunich (Figure 7.1). The large public buildings and broad plazas of Xunantunich, arrayed around the 43 m tall complex called El Castillo, are situated on a limestone ridge that overlooks the fertile floodplain of the Mopan River. Investigations by the Xunantunich Archaeological Project between 1991 and 1997 detailed the site's rise to prominence, which was both rapid and late relative to other centers in the region (Ashmore 1998; Ashmore and Leventhal 1993; Fields 2004; LeCount et al. 2002; Leventhal and Ashmore 2004; also Ball and Taschek 1991; MacKie 1985; Pendergast and Graham 1981; Schmidt 1974; Thompson 1940). Although large-scale construction began on El Castillo early in the Late Classic, during the Samal phase (AD 600–670; dates after LeCount et al. 2002), the bulk of the site's architecture dates to the Hats' Chaak phase (AD 670–780). Despite rapid growth during the Hats' Chaak phase, several areas in Xunantunich were abandoned late in the phase. This process of abandonment of peripheral areas continued during the following Tsak' phase (AD 780–890) as the ritual life of the city became focused around El Castillo, Str A-1, and Plaza A-I (LeCount et al. 2002). Several structures were modified in the Tsak' phase, but these construction programs were neither large nor extensive, and they required significantly less labor than those of the Hats' Chaak phase. In this context of declining power, the Tsak'-phase leaders of Xunantunich sponsored the most explicit representations of individualized political authority found at Xunantunich: three carved stelae portraying nobles bedecked in ceremonial and military garb (Fields 1994; Graham 1978). Despite these claims, by the end of the Tsak' phase, Xunantunich and much of its sustaining hinterland was abandoned (Ashmore et al. 2004; LeCount et al. 2002).

A principal goal of the Xunantunich Archaeological Project was to understand the social processes that accompanied the florescence of Xunantunich. This goal required charting the dynamic relationships between hinterland settlements and institutions of political authority at Xunantunich (Ashmore and Leventhal 1993). Wendy Ashmore directed the Xunantunich Settlement Survey, which systematically recorded all archaeological features along three 400 m wide transects (Figure 7.1): T/A1 ran southeast from Xunantunich to the site of Dos Chombitos and the Macal River, traversing the Mopan Valley and the zone of low limestone hills that separates the Mopan and Macal Valleys; T/A2 ran north through the Mopan Valley from Xunantunich to the site of Callar Creek; and T/A3 extended north through the Macal River valley from Dos Chombitos. The survey personnel mapped several nontransect areas in the polity's hinterland, including the Rancho San Lorenzo Survey Area, and extensively excavated several small hinterland settlements, including San Lorenzo and Chan Nòohol.

Of the survey's many findings, two are most pertinent to this discussion. First, the Late-to-Terminal Classic population history in most parts of the Xunantunich hinterland paralleled the florescence and decline at Xunantunich, indicating a relatively tight relationship between the dynamics of local settlements and those of the regional polity (Ashmore et al. 1994; Ashmore et al. 2004; Neff 1998; Neff et al. 1995; Robin 2002a; Yaeger 2003b). Second, despite similarities in size and composition, the various settlements in the Xunantunich hinterland were not functionally, historically, or socially redundant (Ashmore et al. 2004; Yaeger 2003a). Our comparison below of Chan Nòohol and San Lorenzo illustrates these two findings in more detail.

Chan Nòohol and San Lorenzo

Chan Nòohol and San Lorenzo are two of the most studied settlements in the Xunantunich hinterland. Jason Yaeger (2000a) directed excavations at San Lorenzo between 1994 and 1996 to investigate the internal sociopolitical dynamics of Maya hinterland communities and the relationships of their members to larger social and political institutions. Cynthia Robin (1999) undertook excavations at Chan Nòohol in 1996 and 1997 to examine the complexities of the daily lives of its ordinary populace and the interconnections between life at the settlement and larger social, economic, and political developments in the Xunantunich area.

This research revealed that San Lorenzo and Chan Nòohol are both small settlements whose inhabitants shared an agrarian lifestyle. In the following sections, we first describe the location of each site and our reconstructions of their social composition, domestic economy and group identity, local ritual practices, and wider sociopolitical affiliations. We conclude with a comparative discussion of the implications that the data from these sites hold for social heterogeneity in the Xunantunich hinterland; this in turn has larger implications for models of Classic period Maya society.

We focus our discussion on the differences between the two settlements, but they share several characteristics that justify our comparative approach. First, San Lorenzo and Chan Nòohol were part of the same polity, and their residents would have interacted within the same networks of social and political relationships, distinct from those operating at nearby centers such as Baking Pot or Naranjo. They also would have been subject to the political strategies of the rulers of Xunantunich. Second, as members of the same polity, it is likely that the residents of these two settlements often came together at Xunantunich for polity-wide ceremonial celebrations and other activities. Of course, they also interacted outside the context of Xunantunich, as it is likely that they participated in many of the same decentralized economic networks, including networks for the distribution of many utilitarian items, such as granite manos and metates and Mount Maloney Black pottery, the most common pottery in the Xunantunich polity (LeCount 1996, 2001; Robin 1999; Yaeger 2000a).

San Lorenzo

Local Resources

San Lorenzo is situated adjacent to a fertile stretch of the floodplain of the Mopan River, 1.5 km northeast of Xunantunich (Yaeger 2000a). The settlement occupies the top and west side of a ridge that is blanketed by ancient alluvial soils. A flat zone of floodplain, marked by two paleochannels of the Mopan River, extends from the base of the ridge to the modern riverbed. Buried Preclassic features indicate that much of this flat area was an active floodplain sometime after the first human occupation of the region, probably during the Terminal Preclassic or Early Classic periods (Holley et al. 2000; Smith 1998; VandenBosch 1993).

The alluvial soils of the valley derive from different periods of the Mopan River's history, and they thus form a mosaic marked by differences in structure, fertility, and drainage. The largest expanses of soils around San Lorenzo are the Morning Star and Young Girl soil series, which are two of the most fertile and productive soils in the region (Fedick 1988:147; also Birchall and Jenkin 1979; King et al. 1991). Another important local alluvial resource is a series of thick channel deposits that include a high percentage of chert nodules (Smith 1998:33–34). The inhabitants of San Lorenzo utilized these deposits as a quarry for chert for stone tool production.

Chronology, Architecture, and Social Composition

The first settlers arrived in the San Lorenzo area during the Middle Preclassic Jenny Creek phase (600–300 BC), but the settlement was subsequently abandoned. The community under discussion here was established just before the Samal phase, apparently prior to the founding of Xunantunich. Paralleling Xunantunich's trajectory, however, it peaked in size in the Hats' Chaak phase and was abandoned sometime in the Tsak' phase after a history of approximately three centuries.

The site consists of twenty mound groups spaced every 25 to 50 m (Figure 7.2; mound groups are numbered using the prefix SL). These groups display significant variability in size and layout. They range from small single mounds that are under 20 m^2 in area and less than 25 cm in height, like SL-38, to large multistructure patio groups, the largest of which is SL-22, measuring over 32 m by 28 m in area and containing five structures, the largest of which measures over 2 m in height. The twenty mound groups can be divided into four different categories: three very small single mounds that are probably nonresidential; nine larger single mounds; one group of two mounds that are informally arranged; and seven patio groups containing between two and five structures formally arranged around an open patio. In several of these patio groups, the patio is raised above the surrounding ground surface with fill, whereas in others it is demarcated only by the adjacent structures. Although most of the

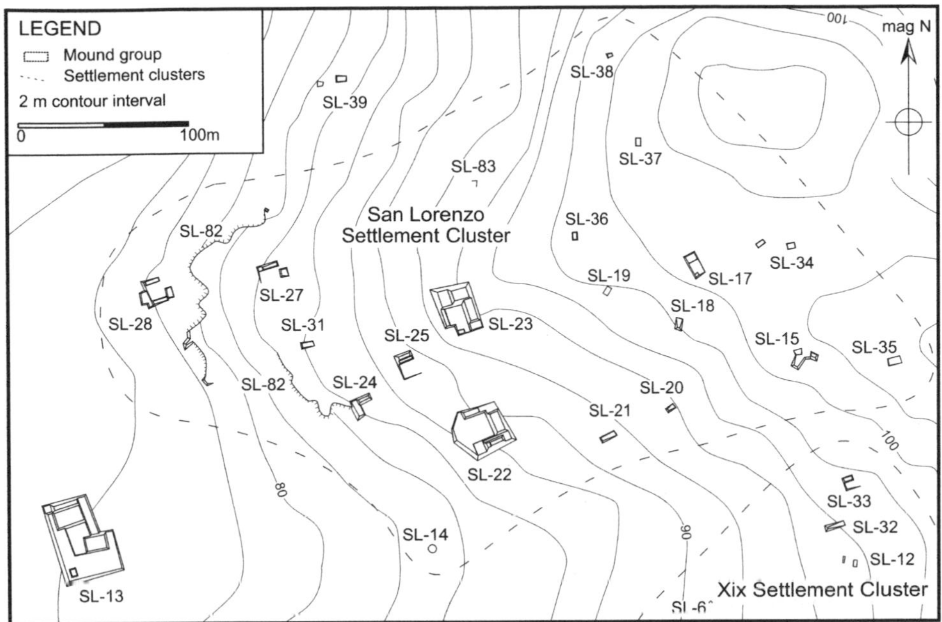

Figure 7.2. San Lorenzo (after Yaeger 2000a: Fig. 4.16)

structures in San Lorenzo were probably residences, some seem to have been favored for certain activities, based on their architecture and associated artifacts and ecofacts. For example, the low substructure of SL-22 Str 4 and a high frequency of plant remains and food storage and processing artifacts suggest it functioned in part as a kitchen. High benches in SL-24 Str 1 and SL-22 Str 3 suggest these structures were the seats, and homes, of local authority figures.

We infer, from the size and the nature of the associated buildings, that single mound and multimound groups were nuclear and extended family compounds respectively. The largest patio groups at San Lorenzo were among the earliest groups to be founded and the last to be abandoned. There is also a strong correlation between the date of a patio group's founding and the length of occupation of that group. In general, the largest patio groups were founded earliest and occupied the longest. In contrast, most smaller patio groups were occupied for only one phase, as they were established during the Hats' Chaak phase and abandoned during that same phase. Many of the single mounds were built first in the Samal phase and occupied into the Hats' Chaak phase.

Most of the structures at San Lorenzo consisted of small, wattle-and-daub superstructures sitting on low platforms faced with minimally modified river cobbles. Occasionally, these would have very low (5–10 cm) interior benches and, if their height required it, an outset stairway. There are, however, groups in which the substructure platforms are faced with limestone, in some cases finely cut blocks. This finer masonry is more common in the larger patio groups, although it occurs on a few single mounds as well. Restricted to the patio groups, however, are superstructures that employ foundation walls or braces of two-sided masonry that would have covered the base of the wattle-and-daub superstructure walls, sometimes to a height of over 1 m. In at least one case, a structure bore a corbel vaulted masonry roof. Although exact labor-investment calculations are difficult to determine because of the relatively limited architectural exposure in many structures and their complexity, some rough estimates can be made. Most of the structures in the settlement required very little labor to build (under one hundred person-days) and could have been completed easily by a single family. Others, however, required over one thousand person-days to build, suggesting the involvement of people outside the household in the construction process.

Domestic Economy and Group Identity

The five extensively excavated groups at San Lorenzo (SL-22, SL-24, SL-28, SL-31, and SL-34) all show evidence of a similar range of productive activities: granite manos and metates for grinding maize; large ceramic jars and bowls for storing and cooking food; lithic debitage indicating household-level stone tool production; and large chert bifaces used for farming. Most also had stone and ceramic spindle whorls and stone bark beaters. Yaeger has argued elsewhere (2000b) that these daily practices and the daily and seasonal scheduling they imply were important in forming a shared base of experience among the community members, while other practices helped forge a more explicit community identity.

There were, however, some economic differences between households. For example, the majority of cut marine shell fragments comes from the large patio group SL-22, suggesting that the residents of that group were engaging in shell artifact production, although we lack the blanks and preforms and manufacturing tools that would allow us to confirm this hypothesis. As discussed above, some households, including SL-22, clearly had more access to the labor of others in building their homes.

Most striking is the pattern indicated by the chert debitage. Although there is not a neatly compartmentalized system of lithic production at San Lorenzo, detailed analysis of lithic material from SL-22, SL-28, SL-

31, the quarry (SL-82), and the special-function SL-13 demonstrates a spatial and social division of labor in the manufacture of chipped stone (Yaeger 2000a). Comparisons of the mean size of lithic debitage in different groups, the mean state of reduction of that debitage, and the ratios of reduction by-products to formal and informal tools all demonstrate that the stone assemblages of SL-28, SL-31, and SL-82 derived more of their materials from the production of lithic tools and cores than those of SL-24, SL-22, and SL-13. The inhabitants of two more modest groups (SL-28 and SL-31) were more involved in lithic production, especially during the early stages of reduction, and the resulting products were taken elsewhere for use and discard.

Ritual Practices

Most of the domestic groups at San Lorenzo contained some evidence for domestic ritual activities, but a higher frequency of serving vessels and the nearly exclusive presence of faunal remains in the largest patio groups (SL-22, SL-23, and SL-24) indicate that feasting occurred much more frequently in those groups (Yaeger 2000a). Bone chemistry studies indicate that all residents at nearby Barton Ramie had equal access to meat (Gerry 1993); we suspect that, likewise, all of the San Lorenzo residents ate meat, but that this consumption largely occurred in ritually charged practices that took place only in the larger patio groups. The residents of San Lorenzo also buried a few of their deceased family members in their domestic compounds and sometimes placed caches of obsidian artifacts in the fill of their house platforms. These activities are only reflected in the material record of the larger patio groups, but they may have been more widespread.

Another important venue for ritual in the San Lorenzo area was SL-13, the area's largest group, which lies outside any of the settlement clusters. The layout of the group's buildings, the faunal assemblage, and the high frequency of ceremonial vessels suggest that SL-13 was the location for ritual celebrations. This complex was built at the time of Xunantunich's initial expansion, probably by its rulers, who presumably participated in the activities there.

Wider Sociopolitical Affiliations

Just as some households clearly had more access to the labor of others, the distribution of exotic raw materials indicates differential positioning of the community's households vis-à-vis the gifting networks that structured allegiances within the polity. We found worked marine shell in both single mounds and patio groups, but the simpler and more common *Oliva* shell tinklers make up a much greater proportion of the worked shell in the single mounds, whereas the larger patio groups had more elaborate shell artifacts. Furthermore, we recovered greenstone beads in only the larger patio groups, SL-22 and SL-24. In contrast, pendants and other objects of personal adornment made of slate, locally available, were widely distributed. Taken together, this evidence indicates that some householders had more privileged links with the polity elite, which they actively portrayed by wearing these objects made of exotic materials (Yaeger 2000b).

The domestic architecture at San Lorenzo reflects this same differentiation. As described above, the absolute labor investment in domestic architecture seems to form a continuum. Yet some architectural features (basal moldings, high interior benches, superstructures with walls partly or entirely made of masonry) are largely restricted to the larger patio groups, setting those groups apart from the rest of the community's residential compounds. Because these features are common in the monumental architecture at Xunantunich, the largest domestic compounds in San Lorenzo more closely resembled elite residential compounds at the polity's capital than they did the wattle-and-daub houses of their fellow community members. These San Lorenzo households were arguably claiming an affiliation with the polity's ruling elite, a connection that was probably important for maintaining and advancing their local positions (Yaeger 2000b).

Chan Nòohol

Local Resources

Chan Nòohol is a cluster of seven small mound groups situated in gently undulating limestone uplands in the Mopan and Macal river interfluvial zone 4 km east-southeast of Xunantunich (Robin 1999). The Chan Nòohol mound groups were part of a larger village called Chan (Ehret 1998; Robin et al. 2003) and were located south of the village center (*nòohol* is "south" in Yucatec Maya).[1]

From Chan Nòohol, residents would have been able to see Xunantunich atop its regionally imposing hilltop. The only natural water source at Chan Nòohol is a stream now running only intermittently. One artificial reservoir (*aguada*) may have augmented the water supply for at least some residents. As the Chan Nòohol area is 3–4 km away from a major waterway, these water resources would clearly have been of economic import for the farmers living there.

Chan Nòohol's Vaca suite, Cuxu subsuite soils are classed as having only limited agricultural potential under modern mechanized agricultural practices (Birchall and Jenkin 1979; King et al. 1991). Although modern assessments of agricultural potentials cannot be considered a proxy for ancient soil fertility, the inhabitants of Chan Nòohol considered it necessary to invest in terracing and fertilization, the latter evidenced through phosphorous enhancement, to enhance the land on which they lived (Robin 1999, 2002a). Whatever the ancient productivity quotients were, Chan Nòohol's farmers were not constrained by the same limitations that constrain modern mechanized farmers. They indeed transformed the land to create a productive agricultural landscape that supported over a century of habitation (also see Fedick 1988, 1995).

Chronology, Architecture, and Social Composition

Chan Nòohol's occupation was quite short-lived, restricted largely to the just-over-a-century-long Hats' Chaak phase, contemporary with the period of Xunantunich's apogee. Its occupation sequence is roughly parallel to what de Montmollin (1995) calls a boom-bust trajectory. The two episodes of Preclassic activity found in the Chan Nòohol area lack continuity with the Hats' Chaak phase community.

Locations such as Chan Nòohol that apparently were less desirable in terms of land and water seem to have been the areas into which expanding populations moved during the Hats' Chaak phase, the period of greatest hinterland settlement expansion in the Xunantunich polity. Chan Nòohol's short-term occupation and small-scale settlement are similar to those of the majority of other new settlements that emerged coincident with Xunantunich's political apogee (Ashmore et al. 2004; Robin 2002a).

Chan Nòohol's seven small mound groups were spaced every 50–100 m (Figure 7.3; each group is identified by the prefix CN). Each group consists of one or two mounds associated with one to three sets of agricultural terraces. An *aguada* is located at group CN1. Despite the seemingly simple and homogeneous nature of Chan Nòohol mound groups, based on number of mounds, there is a greater diversity in size and layout of structures at these groups, where excavations revealed ephemeral non-mound structures as well as those visible on the surface as mounds.

Mound and non-mound structures are morphologically distinctive.

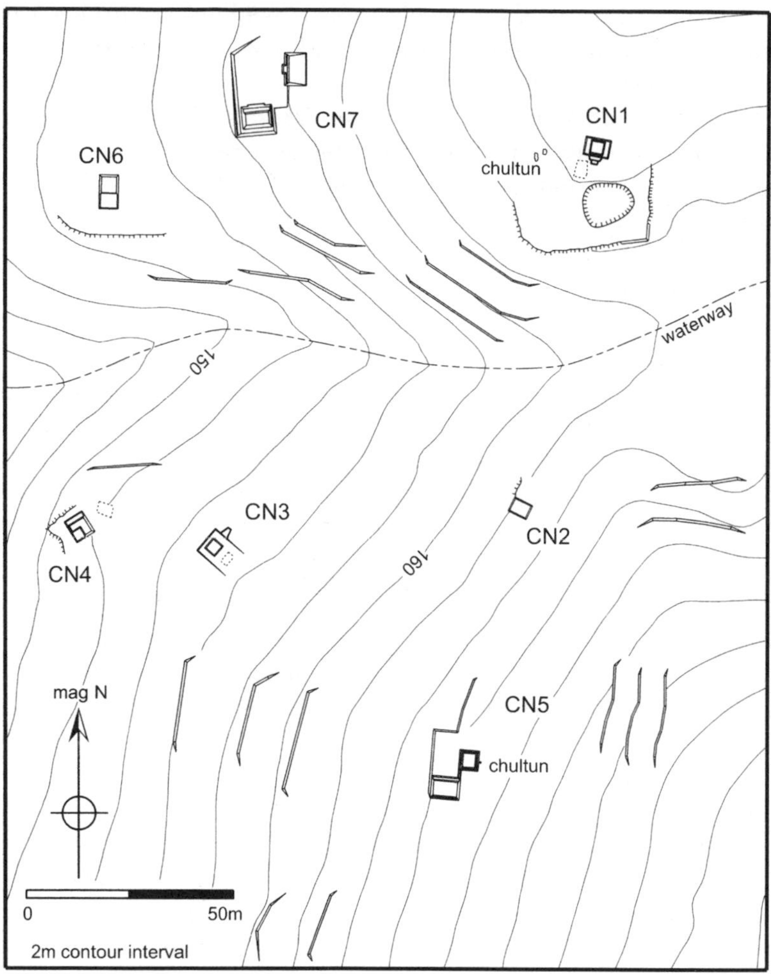

Figure 7.3. Chan Nòohol (after Robin 1999: Fig. 17)

Structures initially invisible on the surface are barely elevated above the surrounding ground (less than 20 cm), have basal areas under 10.5 m², and consist of a single level without benches, stairs, or sometimes even distinct facing stones. The structures that were visible on the surface were elevated between 50 cm and 1.1 m above the surrounding ground or patio surface and had basal areas of up to 42.4 m². They generally were bi-level, with low benches under 10 cm in elevation, had stairs where needed due to structure elevation, and always had distinctive facings. These combinations of architectural features, together with the structure's location in the group, associated artifacts, and chemical signatures from non-mound features, indicate that mound structures likely were residences, and non-mound structures probably served ancillary purposes.

Each mound group at Chan Nòohol is interpreted as a residential farmstead, comprising nuclear or extended two-family groups. Each contained one or two residential structures associated with agricultural terraces, a redundant range of domestic artifacts, and a redundant distribution of distinctive artifact and soil-chemistry signatures across the outdoor spaces around structures and terraces that define a house-lot activity area (Robin 2002a, 2002b, 2003b). Not surprisingly, single-residence groups (CN1, CN2, CN3, CN4, CN6) are smaller and less elaborate than double-residence groups (CN5, CN7). For instance, all dwelling structures at double-residence groups had cut-block limestone on all façades, but those at single-residence groups had cut-block limestone on only one façade, and in one case, CN3, there was no cut-block limestone. All superstructures at Chan Nòohol likely were pole and thatch, except at CN6, which was the only group where wattle and daub was found. None of the Chan Nòohol dwellings need have required additional specialized labor (e.g., Abrams 1994), assuming that the reciprocal labor arrangements among kinsfolk that contemporary Maya people draw upon to enable house construction were operative in the past (e.g., Redfield and Villa Rojas 1934). However, the dwellings of CN5 and CN7 did require more labor to construct.

Domestic Economy and Group Identity

In addition to having constructed a productive terraced agricultural landscape, all groups at Chan Nòohol show evidence of a similar range of productive activities as those aforementioned for San Lorenzo. High frequencies of artifacts and activity areas associated with the food-production process, from sowing to serving, coupled with low frequencies of artifacts associated with other activities, indicate that food production was the primary activity for Chan Nòohol residents. Additionally, agricultural produce was most likely the only item, beyond labor itself, exported from the settlement. As Chan Nòohol farmers conducted a similar set of basic domestic and agricultural tasks on a day-to-day basis, these activities framed the space and time of people's existence: the temporal rhythms of a day, the seasonal cycles of work, and the lived spaces of the land. The shared links to the land and water of their settlement may have been quite a tenuous tie, temporally and socially, for residents of the young Chan

Nòohol, and, as is discussed below, residents seem to have further concretized these relations through architecture and ritual. A group identity that focused on water is suggested by residents' construction of all but one of the groups to face the now intermittent stream (Robin 2002a).

The predominant tool found at Chan Nòohol is the chert utilized flake, followed by the chert general utility biface. Although microwear studies were not conducted on the Chan Nòohol chert material, extensive studies on morphologically similar tools at other Classic Maya sites have demonstrated that these items were multifunctional tools that would have served a wide range of domestic and agricultural tasks (e.g., Aldenderfer 1991; Lewenstein 1991; Mallory 1984). The debitage counts of 63.8 to 253.7 pieces per cubic meter of refuse suggest that Chan Nòohol residents only produced and re-sharpened their tools for household-level provisioning (compare the 200,000 pieces per cubic meter that VandenBosch [1997, 1999] finds at known tool-production households elsewhere in the Xunantunich area). Only late-stage lithic production was undertaken at Chan Nòohol.

Inequalities, albeit less marked than those at San Lorenzo, did exist within Chan Nòohol. Perhaps not surprisingly, the only Chan Nòohol residents to possess ornaments of greenstone and marine shell, mostly *Strombus* spp., were those living in the larger two-residence groups. The low frequencies of these items (2 and 4 respectively) and lack of production debris indicates that they were not produced at Chan Nòohol and that Chan Nòohol residents had relatively little access to these types of goods. More common forms of ornamentation found at both single- and double-residence groups at Chan Nòohol were slate ornaments, for which there is a source just 4 km to the east. Although Chan Nòohol residents had little access to ornaments made of nonlocal material, they all had access to items of everyday use made of nonlocal material, such as obsidian blades and granite and quartz manos and metates. Clearly they were not isolated from the larger political economy, only from particular types of items that circulated in the political economy, and these, in the Chan Nòohol case, were exotic ornaments, objects that probably derived some meaning from being indexed to nonlocal and elite ideals.

Ritual Practices

All domestic groups at Chan Nòohol show some evidence for domestic ritual activity. However, the only household at Chan Nòohol to hold small-scale feasts was the unassuming single-residence group CN1, the household situated next to the *aguada*. In addition to conventionally cited archaeological markers of feasting (higher frequencies of animal bone, ritual items, and serving vessels), Robin's (1999, 2002a) ethnoarchaeological study in a modern farming community in Yucatán[2] suggests that the size of cleared exterior work space in house-lots correlates with the frequency with which households hosted communal feasts, as these are events that require more outdoor work space than families typically use in day-to-day tasks. Distinctive combinations of artifact and soil-chemistry signatures were used at Chan Nòohol to define functional designations within house-lots, such as cleared outdoor work areas.

Given CN1's unassuming architecture, its proximity to the waterhole seems to be the key to the presence of ritual activities in only this particular group. As Evon Vogt (1969, 1976, this volume) has documented, waterholes in some modern Maya communities serve as focal points for integrating distinct social groups within the larger community and as such are sites of feasts. Modern waterhole rituals highlight people's incorporation into a group based on their links to water and land where they live and work, and the feasting next to the Chan Nòohol waterhole may have served a similar function. Nevertheless, the hosts of these feasts did not show any materialized social distinctions in terms of housing or exotic goods, as feasting hosts at San Lorenzo did. Seemingly, this ritual fostered intracommunity relationships more akin to that which some have called coordinate or heterarchical, as opposed to hierarchical.

Although many typical life-cycle events were enacted at Chan Nòohol, one important life-cycle event seems to be missing, the burial of the dead. Despite an excavation strategy that explored expected burial locations (e.g., Welsh 1988), only one interment was encountered, at CN5. It would seem that some aspects of ancestor veneration might have been largely missing from Chan Nòohol. Also missing from Chan Nòohol were venues for rituals involving outsiders or even the remains of large-scale competitively driven feasts, such as those performed in the houses of longer-established families at San Lorenzo. Perhaps the rituals associated with human interment and the more externally focused feasting events were conducted at households of more-established families in the larger Chan settlement (compare Robin 1989; Wilk and Wilhite 1991). If members of Chan Nòohol were in fact collectively burying their dead elsewhere in the Chan village and participating in larger-scale feasts and other ritual events at longer-standing households in Chan and occasionally at Xunantunich, these links would have enhanced solidarity within the larger social entities while simultaneously marking social differences within them.

Wider Sociopolitical Affiliations

Although inequalities were less marked at Chan Nòohol than at San Lorenzo, social distinctions were materialized, for some people (the residents of CN5 and CN7) had larger and more elaborate homes and relatively greater (in Chan Nòohol terms) access to exotic ornaments. Chan Nòohol residents' relatively lower access to exotic ornaments plausibly reflects the aforementioned more attenuated socioeconomic links to elite-controlled distribution, here filtered through Chan community leaders (e.g., Ehret 1998; Robin et al. 2003). In the local context of Chan Nòohol, the variation in the outward appearance of dwellings and people's dress could well have reflected and fostered a degree of social distinction that would have been visible and obvious to all at Chan Nòohol. The most obvious social distinctions that developed at Chan Nòohol arose in situations where the socioeconomic growth of extended families coincided with increasing access to political-economic links, most likely indirect links through Chan community leaders.

Discussion

San Lorenzo and Chan Nòohol clearly demonstrate a high degree of heterogeneity, both internally and in comparison to one another. Their constituent households participated in many similar domestic and agricultural practices, but they were quite diverse in many other respects. The households varied from nuclear to extended family groups, and their members had differential access to labor, engaged in diverse ritual practices, and portrayed their connections with outsiders in distinct ways. Chan Nòohol and San Lorenzo refute reconstructions of pre-Hispanic Maya society that envision commoners as a uniform, homogeneous peasantry. Explaining the internal heterogeneity and the differences between the two settlements requires addressing social, political, economic, and ecological factors that conditioned them and their members' practices.

In part, the differences between residences at San Lorenzo and Chan Nòohol can be explained by a social and historical model of settlement growth. Applying Fortes's (1958) and Goody's (1958) domestic developmental cycle to Classic Maya households and larger social groupings, we argue that households and rural settlements generally grew as consecutive generations, made up of children and immigrants, continued to reside within established households and communities, thus forming larger households and communities (for a discussion of applications of the developmental cycle model in the Maya area, see Ashmore et al. 2004; Haviland 1988; McAnany 1993; Robin 1996, 1999; Tourtellot 1988; Yaeger 1995, 2000a). Consequently, a correlation should exist between longevity and size and social composition in domestic groups. The longer-term occupation of the larger and more complex community at San Lorenzo and the shorter-term occupation of the smaller and simpler community at Chan Nòohol certainly support an association between length of occupation and social composition, but this association in and of itself cannot explain why San Lorenzo and Chan Nòohol are different.

One intriguing aspect of the Xunantunich hinterland is that, as in other nearby areas of the upper Belize River valley, most house mounds occur as isolates, suggesting some kind of truncation of developmental cycling (Ford 1990). At both Chan Nòohol and San Lorenzo, this is reflected in the preponderance of isolated residences, which at San Lorenzo are usually more long-lived than are small patio groups, precluding any simple unilinear correlation between longevity and household composition. Clearly, a domestic developmental cycle model represents only an "ideal model" that fits the broad regularities in settlement complexity, size, and longevity.

Equally important, as we discussed in our introduction, the social realm of family life is not isolated from other aspects of society. In this sense, "domestic growth" provides a framework within which we can begin to resituate past people into an otherwise vacant past settlement. As seen in the comparison of San Lorenzo and Chan Nòohol, domestic development is not invariant even within a given polity. Settings change through time in relation to the goals and strategies of the people inhabiting them, and the dynamics of family growth are inherently intertwined with the economic and political relations of people that constitute families (e.g., Blanton 1994; Goody 1958; Hanks 1990; Yanagisako 1979).

San Lorenzo was established several generations before Chan Nòohol, perhaps partially because of the diverse local resources along that stretch of the Mopan River. These resources were probably important factors in the greater realization of wealth accumulation at San Lorenzo, yet this wealth accumulation did not occur in a social or political vacuum. The three patio groups showing the greatest architectural investment at San Lorenzo were among the first groups established, suggesting that their status as founding households gave them some privileged access to local resources or authority as the community grew, a phenomenon that McAnany (1995) calls the "principle of first occupancy." Their founding roles and attendant local status positions likely made these households targets of strategies by the rulers of Xunantunich, and they show markedly greater evidence for interaction with the Xunantunich polity elite. They actively represented their ties to the elite through items of personal adornment and domestic architecture, suggesting a positive, reinforcing relationship between authority derived from internal factors such as primacy of occupation and perhaps place in local kin structures and that derived from external factors such as ties to the polity rulers. Ritual activity at San Lorenzo expressed the resulting hierarchical organization even as it simultaneously indexed the cohesion of the larger group in a manner seemingly similar to the rituals that Vogt (1976, this volume), among others, describes among contemporary Maya *cargo* holders.

In contrast, Chan Nòohol's apparently less desirable lands did not attract occupants until later in the region's occupation sequence and did not yield any great wealth for its inhabitants. The more limited potential of its land and lack of long-term history may be two of the reasons that social distinctions were less pronounced at Chan Nòohol than at San Lorenzo. Despite this, the largest households at Chan Nòohol, as at San Lorenzo, seemed to have greater access to goods made of exotic raw materials. Chan Nòohol's residents did express some affiliations with polity elite, albeit in less pronounced ways than San Lorenzo's residents. This difference plausibly reflects more attenuated links to elites at Chan Nòohol, links that were presumably filtered through the Chan community leaders. These attenuated links also probably reflect the timing of Chan Nòohol's founding, which was established during Xunantunich's heyday. Within the context of a well-established political economy, the residents of Chan Nòohol may not have had the long-term land tenure with which to negotiate tribute concessions from the polity rulers, nor the economic surpluses to interest the leaders of Xunantunich, as the Chan community leaders presumably negotiated these relations. Ultimately, for a range of social, political, and ecological reasons, materialized social distinctions were small at Chan Nòohol and plausibly minimally valued in either Chan Nòohol's world or that of polity elites. Commensurably, ritual within Chan Nòohol highlights the solidarity of the local group through its links to land and water.

While they certainly forged a local identity and derived most of what they consumed from local resources, Chan Nòohol farmers do not represent an autonomous unit existing outside of the political economy. Conversely, the co-occurrence of Chan Nòohol's occupation and Xunantunich's apogee and the nature of Chan Nòohol's production and consumption suggest clear, although likely indirect, links to polity elites and political economic networks, links that did not correspond with enhanced lifestyles for Chan Nòohol members.

Conclusions

Chan Nòohol and San Lorenzo were both part of the Xunantunich polity, simultaneously shaping and shaped by that polity's growth and expansion. Yet the way this occurred was specific to each site and conditioned by many factors, including each site's environment, economic strategies, history, and social organization. Each community played a different role in reciprocally influencing and conditioning the larger polity and the strategies of its rulers.

These conclusions could only be reached through a detailed comparative investigation. This fact illustrates the importance of intensive studies of Maya polities that integrate settlement surveys with more focused excavations of the settlement units within their settlement systems. Such excavations must sample a large number of settlement units, whether households, hamlets, or villages, as it is simply not valid to assume homogeneity within these analytical units (de Montmollin 1988, 1989, 1995; Pyburn 1998; Robin 2002a, 2003b; Yaeger 2000a).

Finally, to more fully understand social interaction and people's lived experience in the Maya countryside, smaller settlement units should be contextualized within larger settlement units (e.g., households within communities, communities within polities) and the material remains therein understood through an agent-oriented paradigm (Yaeger and Canuto 2000). From this perspective, we can better reconstruct the way daily practices and interactions structured people's positions in the various social and political institutions to which they belonged and also shaped larger processes of community and polity history.

Acknowledgments

We would like to thank the Belize Department of Archaeology and its Commissioners, the late Harriot Topsey, John Morris, Alan Moore, and Brian Woodye, for their support of the Xunantunich Archaeological Project (XAP). Rudy Juan, Dorrell Biddle, Mel Xix, David Magaña, Amelio Matus, and Oscar Montero gave us generous permission to work on their property and served as our hosts in Belize. We would also like to thank our project colleagues for the intellectually stimulating and supportive environment they created, with special thanks to project directors Richard M. Leventhal and Wendy Ashmore, and Michael Bletzer, Sabrina Chase, Ellie Harrison, Lisa LeCount, Aimee Preziosi, Jennifer Scarborough, and Laura Villamil.

We would also like to acknowledge Florentin Penados and the XAP crew members from San José Succotz and Benque Viejo del Carmen whose careful work provided the empirical basis for our understandings of the Xunantunich hinterland. Generous funds supporting the research reported here came from National Science Foundation grants to Ashmore (SBR9321503), Robin (SBR9618540), and Yaeger (SBR9530949), and awards to Robin and Yaeger by the Fulbright/II-E Program, the University of Pennsylvania Graduate School of Arts and Sciences, and the University of Pennsylvania Department of Anthropology. Yaeger developed many of the ideas presented here while a Junior Fellow in Precolumbian Studies at Dumbarton Oaks. Finally, we would like to thank Jon Lohse and Fred Valdez, Jr., for the invitation to contribute to this volume and for their patience during the process of revising our original symposium paper for publication.

Notes

1. The history and internal dynamics of the larger village is the current research project of Robin. http://chan.northwestern.edu

2. The name of this community is being withheld to protect the privacy of community members.

References

Abrams, Elliot M.

1994 *How the Maya Built Their World: Energetics and Ancient Architecture.* University of Texas Press, Austin.

Aldenderfer, Mark

1991 The Structure of Late Classic Lithic Assemblages in the Central Petén Lakes Region, Guatemala. In *Maya Stone Tools: Selected Papers from the Second Maya Lithic Conference,* edited by Thomas R. Hester and Harry J. Shafer, pp. 119–141. Monographs in World Archaeology 1. Prehistory Press, Madison.

Ashmore, Wendy

1998 Monumentos políticos: Sitio, asentamiento y paisaje alrededor de Xunantunich, Belice. In *Anatomía de una civilización: Aproximaciones interdisciplinarias a la cultura maya*, edited by Andrés Ciudad Ruiz, Yolanda Fernández Marquínez, María Josefa Ponce de León, Alfonso Lacadena García-Gallo, and Luis T. Sanz Castro, pp. 161–183. Sociedad Española de Estudios Mayas, Madrid.

Ashmore, Wendy, Samuel V. Connell, Jennifer J. Ehret, Chad H. Gifford, L. Theodore Neff, and Jon C. VandenBosch

1994 The Xunantunich Settlement Survey. In *Xunantunich Archaeological Project: 1994 Field Season*, edited by Richard M. Leventhal and Wendy Ashmore, pp. 248–289. Unpublished report on file in the Belize Institute of Archaeology, Belmopan.

Ashmore, Wendy, and Richard M. Leventhal

1993 Xunantunich Reconsidered. Paper presented at the Belize Conference, University of North Florida, Jacksonville.

Ashmore, Wendy, Jason Yaeger, and Cynthia Robin

2004 Commoner Sense: Late and Terminal Classic Social Strategies in the Xunantunich Area. In *The Terminal Classic in the Maya Lowlands: Collapse, Transition, and Transformation*, edited by Arthur A. Demarest, Don S. Rice, and Prudence M. Rice, pp. 302–323. University Press of Colorado, Boulder.

Ball, Joseph W., and Jennifer T. Taschek

1991 Late Classic Lowland Maya Political Organization and Central-Place Analysis: New Insights from the Upper Belize River Valley. *Ancient Mesoamerica* 2:149–165.

Birchall, C. J., and Richard N. Jenkin

1979 *The Soils of the Belize Valley, Belize, vol. 1.* Supplementary Report 15. Land Resources Development Centre, Overseas Development Administration, Surbiton, England.

Blanton, Richard E.

1994 *Houses and Households: A Comparative Study.* Plenum Press, New York.

Bourdieu, Pierre

1977 *Outline of a Theory of Practice.* Cambridge University Press, Cambridge.

Canuto, Marcello A., and Jason Yaeger (editors)

2000 *The Archaeology of Communities: A New World Perspective.* Routledge, London.

de Certeau, Michel

1984 *The Practice of Everyday Life.* University of California Press, Berkeley.

de Montmollin, Olivier

1988 Settlement Scale and Theory in Maya Archaeology. In *Recent Studies in Pre-Columbian Archaeology*, edited by Nicholas J. Saunders and Olivier de Montmollin, pp. 63–104. BAR International Series 431. British Archaeological Reports, Oxford.

1989 *The Archaeology of Political Structure: Settlement Analysis in a Classic Maya Polity.* Cambridge University Press, Cambridge.

1995 *Settlement and Politics in Three Classic Maya Polities.* Monographs in World Archaeology 24. Prehistory Press, Madison.

Dobres, Marcia-Anne, and John Robb (editors)

2000 *Agency in Archaeology.* Routledge, London.

Ehret, Jennifer J.

1998 Lineage, Land, and Loyalties: A Model for Rural, Mid-Level Settlement Variation in the Region of Xunantunich, Belize. Paper presented at the 63rd Annual Meeting of the Society for American Archaeology, Seattle.

Fedick, Scott L.

1988 Prehistoric Maya Settlement and Land Use Patterns in the Upper Belize River Area, Belize, Central America. Ph.D. diss., Arizona State University. University Microfilms, Ann Arbor.

1995 Land Evaluation and Ancient Maya Land Use in the Upper Belize River Area, Belize, Central America. *Latin American Antiquity* 6(1):16–34.

Fields, Virginia M.

1994 The Royal Charter at Xunantunich. In *Xunantunich Archaeological Project: 1994 Field Season*, edited by Richard M. Leventhal and Wendy Ashmore, pp. 65–74. Unpublished report on file in the Belize Institute of Archaeology, Belmopan.

2004 The Royal Charter at Xunantunich. In *The Ancient Maya of the Belize Valley: Half a Century of Archaeological Research*, edited by James F. Garber. University Press of Florida, Tallahassee.

Ford, Anabel

1990 Maya Settlement in the Belize River Area: Variations in Residence Patterns of the Central Maya Lowlands. In *Precolumbian Population History in the Maya Lowlands*, edited by T. Patrick Culbert and Don S. Rice, pp. 167–181. University of New Mexico Press, Albuquerque.

Ford, Anabel, and Scott L. Fedick

1992 Prehistoric Maya Settlement Patterns in the Upper Belize River Area: Initial Results of the Belize River Archaeological Settlement Survey. *Journal of Field Archaeology* 19(1):35–49.

Fortes, Meyer

1958 Introduction. In *The Developmental Cycle in Domestic Groups*, edited by Jack Goody, pp. 1–14. Cambridge University Press, Cambridge.

Garfinkel, Harold

1984 *Studies in Ethnomethodology.* Polity Press, Cambridge.

Gerry, John P.

1993 Diet and Status among the Classic Maya: An Isotopic Perspective. Ph.D. diss., Harvard University. University Microfilms, Ann Arbor.

Giddens, Anthony

1984 *The Constitution of Society: Outline of the Theory of Structuration.* Polity Press, Cambridge.

Goody, Jack

1958 The Fission of Domestic Groups among the LoDagaba. In *The Developmental Cycle in Domestic Groups*, edited by Jack Goody, pp. 53–91. Cambridge University Press, Cambridge.

Graham, Ian

1978 *Naranjo, Chunhuitz, Xunantunich*. Corpus of Maya Hieroglyphic Inscriptions, vol. 2, no. 2. Peabody Museum of Archaeology and Ethnology, Harvard University, Cambridge.

Hanks, William F.

1990 *Referential Practice: Language and Lived Space among the Maya*. University of Chicago Press, Chicago.

Haviland, William A.

1981 Dower Houses and Minor Centers at Tikal, Guatemala: An Investigation into the Identification of Valid Units in Settlement Hierarchies. In *Lowland Maya Settlement Patterns*, edited by Wendy Ashmore, pp. 89–117. University of New Mexico Press, Albuquerque.

1988 Musical Hammocks at Tikal: Problems with Reconstructing Household Composition. In *Household and Community in the Mesoamerican Past*, edited by Richard R. Wilk and Wendy Ashmore, pp. 121–134. University of New Mexico Press, Albuquerque.

Hendon, Julia A.

1996 Archaeological Approaches to the Organization of Domestic Labor: Household Practice and Domestic Relations. *Annual Review of Anthropology* 25:45–61.

Holley, George R., William I. Woods, Rinita A. Dalan, and Harold W. Watters, Jr.

2000 Implications of a Buried Preclassic Site in Western Belize. In *Mounds, Modoc, and Mesoamerica: Papers in Honor of Melvin L. Fowler*, edited by Steven R. Ahler, pp. 111–124. Illinois State Museum Scientific Papers 28. Springfield.

King, Eleanor, and Daniel R. Potter

1994 Small Sites in Prehistoric Maya Socioeconomic Organization: A Perspective from Colha, Belize. In *Archaeological Views from the Countryside*, edited by Glenn M. Schwartz and Steven E. Falconer, pp. 64–90. Smithsonian Institution Press, Washington, D.C.

King, Robert E., Ian C. Baillie, Trevor M. B. Abell, J. R. Dunsmore, David A. Gray, J. H. Pratt, Howard R. Versey, A. C. S. Wright, and Simon A. Zisman

1991 *Land Resource Assessment of Northern Belize, Volume 1*. Bulletin 43. Natural Resources Institute, Chatham Marine, Kent.

LeCount, Lisa J.

1996 Pottery and Power: Feasting, Gifting, and Displaying Wealth among the Late and Terminal Classic Lowland Maya. Ph.D. diss., University of California, Los Angeles. University Microfilms, Ann Arbor.

2001 Like Water for Chocolate: Feasting and Political Ritual among the Late Classic Maya at Xunantunich, Belize. *American Anthropologist* 103(4):935–953.

LeCount, Lisa J., Jason Yaeger, Richard M. Leventhal, and Wendy Ashmore

2002 Dating the Rise and Fall of Xunantunich, Belize: A Late and Terminal Classic Lowland Maya Regional Center. *Ancient Mesoamerica* 13(1):41–63.

Leventhal, Richard M., and Wendy Ashmore

2004 Xunantunich in a Belize Valley Context. In *The Ancient Maya of the Belize Valley: Half a Century of Archaeological Research*, edited by James F. Garber. University Press of Florida, Tallahassee.

Levi, Laura J.

2003 Space and the Limits to Community. In *Perspectives on Ancient Maya Rural Complexity*, edited by Gyles Iannone and Samuel V. Connell, pp. 82–93. Cotsen Institute of Archaeology Monograph 49, UCLA, Los Angeles.

Lewenstein, Suzanne

1991 Woodworking Tools at Cerros. In *Maya Stone Tools: Selected Papers from the Second Maya Lithic Conference*, edited by Thomas R. Hester and Harry J. Shafer, pp. 239–249. Monographs in World Prehistory 1. Prehistory Press, Madison.

MacKie, Euan W.

1985 *Excavations at Xunantunich and Pomona, Belize, in 1959–60*. BAR International Series 251. British Archaeological Reports, Oxford.

Mallory, John K.

1984 Late Classic Maya Economic Specialization: Evidence from the Copan Obsidian Assemblage (Honduras). Ph.D. diss., Pennsylvania State University. University Microfilms, Ann Arbor.

Marcus, Joyce

1995 Where Is Lowland Maya Archaeology Headed? *Journal of Archaeological Research* 3(1):3–53.

McAnany, Patricia A.

1993 The Economics of Social Power and Wealth among Eighth-Century Maya Households. In *Lowland Maya Civilization in the Eighth Century A.D.*, edited by Jeremy A. Sabloff and John S. Henderson, pp. 65–89. Dumbarton Oaks, Washington, D.C.

1995 *Living with the Ancestors: Kinship and Kingship in Ancient Maya Society*. University of Texas Press, Austin.

Meskell, Lynn

1999 *Archaeologies of Social Life: Age, Sex, Class et cetera in Ancient Egypt*. Blackwell, Oxford.

Neff, L. Theodore

1998 Precolumbian Lowland Maya Population Dynamics and Intensive Terrace Agriculture in the Xunantunich Area, Belize, Central America. Paper presented at the 97th Annual Meeting of the American Anthropological Association, Philadelphia.

Neff, L. Theodore, Cynthia Robin, Kevin Schwartz, and Mary K. Morrison

1995 The Xunantunich Settlement Survey. In *Xunantunich Archaeological Project: 1995 Field Season*, edited by Richard M. Leventhal and Wendy Ashmore, pp. 140–163. Unpublished report on file in the Belize Institute of Archaeology, Belmopan.

Pendergast, David M., and Elizabeth Graham

1981 Fighting a Looting Battle: Xunantunich, Belize. *Archaeology* 34(4):12–19.

Pyburn, K. Anne

1998 Smallholders in the Maya Lowlands: Homage to a Garden Variety Ethnographer. *Human Ecology* 26(2):267–286.

Redfield, Robert, and Alfonso Villa Rojas

1934 *Chan Kom: A Maya Village.* Carnegie Institution of Washington Publication 448. Washington, D.C.

Robin, Cynthia

1989 *Preclassic Maya Burials at Cuello, Belize.* BAR International Series 480. British Archaeological Reports, Oxford.

1996 Rural Household and Community Development in the Xunantunich Hinterlands during the Late and Terminal Classic. Dissertation Improvement Grant proposal submitted to the National Science Foundation. Manuscript in possession of author.

1999 Towards an Archaeology of Everyday Life: Maya Farmers of Chan Nòohol and Dos Chombitos Cik'in, Belize. Ph.D. diss., University of Pennsylvania. University Microfilms, Ann Arbor.

2001 Peopling the Past: New Perspectives on the Ancient Maya. *Proceedings of the National Academy of Sciences* 98(1):18–21.

2002a Outside of Houses: The Practices of Everyday Life at Chan Nòohol, Belize. *Journal of Social Archaeology* 2(2):245–268.

2002b Gender and Maya Farming: Chan Nòohol, Belize. In *Ancient Maya Women*, edited by Traci Ardren, pp. 12–30. Alta Mira Press, Walnut Creek.

2003a New Directions in Classic Maya Household Archaeology. *Journal of Archaeological Research* 11(4):307–356.

2003b Social Diversity and Everyday Life within Classic Maya Settlements. In *Mesoamerican Archaeology*, edited by Julia A. Hendon and Rosemary A. Joyce, pp. 148–168. Blackwell Publishers, Oxford.

Robin, Cynthia, William Middleton, Santiago Juárez, and Mary Morrison

2003 Surveying an Agrarian Community: The 2002 Season at the Chan Site, Belize. *Research Reports in Belizean Archaeology* 1(2):231–242.

Robin, Cynthia, and Nan Rothschild

2002 Archaeological Ethnographies: Social Dynamics of Outdoor Space. *Journal of Social Archaeology* 2(2):159–172.

Schmidt, Peter J.

1974 A New Map and Some Notes on Terminal Classic and Postclassic Activities at Xunantunich, Belize. Paper presented at the International Congress of Americanists, Mexico.

Smith, Jennifer R.

1998 Geology and Carbonate Hydrogeochemistry of the Lower Mopan and Macal River Valleys, Belize. Master's thesis, Department of Geology, University of Pennsylvania, Philadelphia.

Taschek, Jennifer T., and Joseph W. Ball

2004 Buenavista del Cayo, Cahal Pech, and Xunantunich: Three Centers, Three Histories, One Central Place. In *The Ancient Maya of the Belize Valley: Half a Century of Archaeological Research*, edited by James F. Garber. University Press of Florida, Tallahassee.

Thompson, J. Eric S.

1940 *Late Ceramic Horizons at Benque Viejo, British Honduras*. Contributions to American Anthropology and History, vol. 7, no. 35. Carnegie Institution of Washington Publication 528. Washington, D.C.

Tourtellot, Gair, III

1988 Developmental Cycles of Households and Houses at Seibal. In *Household and Community in the Mesoamerican Past*, edited by Richard R. Wilk and Wendy Ashmore, pp. 97–120. University of New Mexico Press, Albuquerque.

VandenBosch, Jon C.

1993 Investigations of San Lorenzo's Linear and Cobble Mounds. In *Xunantunich Archaeological Project: 1993 Field Season*, edited by Richard M. Leventhal, pp. 148–171. Unpublished report on file in the Belize Institute of Archaeology, Belmopan.

1997 Specialized Lithic Production in the Suburbs of a Late to Terminal Classic Center in Western Belize. Paper presented at the 20th Annual Midwest Conference on Mesoamerican Archaeology and Ethnohistory, Ann Arbor.

1999 Lithic Economy and Household Interdependence among the Late Classic Maya of Belize. Ph.D. diss., University of Pittsburgh. University Microfilms, Ann Arbor.

Vogt, Evon Z.

1969 *Zinacantan: A Maya Community in the Highlands of Chiapas*. Belknap Press of Harvard University Press, Cambridge.

1976 *Tortillas for the Gods: A Symbolic Analysis of Zinacanteco Rituals*. Harvard University Press, Cambridge.

Webster, David L., and Nancy Gonlin

1988 Household Remains of the Humblest Maya. *Journal of Field Archaeology* 15(2):169–190.

Welsh, W. Bruce M.

1988 *An Analysis of Classic Lowland Maya Burials*. BAR International Series 409. British Archaeological Reports, Oxford.

Wilk, Richard R., and Harold L. Wilhite

1991 The Community of Cuello: Patterns of Household and Settlement Change. In *Cuello, An Early Maya Community in Belize*, edited by Norman Hammond, pp. 118–133. Cambridge University Press, Cambridge.

Willey, Gordon R., William R. Bullard, Jr., John B. Glass, and James C. Gifford

1965 *Prehistoric Settlement in the Belize Valley*. Papers of the Peabody Museum of Archaeology and Ethnology 54. Harvard University, Cambridge.

Yaeger, Jason

1995 Changing Patterns of Community Structure and Organization: The End of the Classic Period at San Lorenzo, Cayo District, Belize. Dissertation Improvement Grant proposal submitted to the National Science Foundation. Manuscript in possession of author.

2000a Changing Patterns of Social Organization: The Late and Terminal Classic Communities at San Lorenzo, Cayo District, Belize. Ph.D. diss., University of Pennsylvania. University Microfilms, Ann Arbor.

2000b The Social Construction of Communities in the Classic Maya Countryside: Strategies of Affiliation in Western Belize. In *The Archaeology of Communities: A New World Perspective*, edited by Marcello A. Canuto and Jason Yaeger, pp. 123–142. Routledge, London.

2003a Small Settlements in the Upper Belize River Valley: Internal Complexity, Household Strategies of Affiliation, and Changing Organization. In *Perspectives on Ancient Maya Rural Complexity*, edited by Gyles Iannone and Samuel V. Connell, pp. 42–58. Cotsen Institute of Archaeology Monograph 49. University of California, Los Angeles.

2003b Untangling the Ties That Bind: The City, the Countryside, and the Nature of Maya Urbanism at Xunantunich, Belize. In *The Social Construction of Ancient Cities*, edited by Monica L. Smith, pp. 121–155. Smithsonian Institution Press, Washington, D.C.

Yaeger, Jason, and Marcello A. Canuto

2000 Introducing an Archaeology of Communities. In *The Archaeology of Communities: A New World Perspective*, edited by Marcello A. Canuto and Jason Yaeger, pp. 1–15. Routledge, London.

Yanagisako, Sylvia J.

1979 Family and Household: The Analysis of Household Groups. *Annual Review of Anthropology* 8:161–205.

CHAPTER 8

The Spatial Mobility of Non-Elite Populations in Classic Maya Society and Its Political Implications

TAKESHI INOMATA

Movements of non-elite populations over a landscape have significant implications in the study of political processes in a complex society. They are common means for non-elites to adjust to political and economic circumstances and to resist the oppression by the ruling class and state. The control of the subject population by the state tends to be more difficult when social, economic, and cultural factors allow non-elites to maintain a great degree of mobility. Conversely, non-elite populations with less mobility, particularly in aggregated settlements, are more amenable to state control. Thus, some states systematically try to limit the mobility of their population and to create aggregated settlements around their political centers. A well-known example is the Spanish strategy of *congregación* (congregating) applied to the indigenous population during the Colonial period. The Maya people under this policy still maintained a considerable level of mobility, and movements remained one of the most effective measures of resistance against colonial rule (Farris 1984:72–79, 199–223; Fox and Cook 1996). What was the degree of mobility of Maya non-elites during the Classic period? How and when did they move? I will discuss these problems by examining the settlement history of Aguateca, Guatemala.

Elites and Non-Elites

Before addressing the issue of mobility, it is necessary to discuss the question of who the Maya non-elites, or "commoners," were. Commoners are often contrasted with elites or nobles. Whereas elites or nobles are seen as distinct categories, commoners are often treated as "the rest of society," that is, not the elite. Jon Lohse and Fred Valdez (this volume) point out a lack of focus, definition, and adequate theoretical framework in the study of Maya commoners. These problems of research focus and definition are not due to the lack of interest in commoners. Instead, they probably reflect the diversity in the social reality of Maya commoners and the complexity of the theoretical problems involved.

A comparison with elites serves as a point of departure in defining the positions of non-elites in society. Elites may be defined as a minority of powerful people who, through their control of social institutions, bring about effects of broad significance for society at large (Giddens 1974:4; Marcus 1983:10–13; see Chase and Chase 1992; Houston and Stuart 2001; Inomata 2001a, 2001b for the discussion of Maya elites). Elites often share a common identity as members of the minority group, which may be expressed in an exclusive lifestyle and culture (Marcus 1983). My intention here is not to overemphasize the unity of elites; they are not internally homogeneous and are often characterized by factional conflicts (Brumfiel 1994). Yet the nature of the elite as a social group with a certain level of shared collective interests, lifestyle, and culture is more conspicuous than that of non-elites.

Commoners cannot be considered as the homogeneous masses. Those who engage in fishing, craft production, and trade may have lifestyles and value systems quite different from those of full-time farmers. Even among farmers, shared identity and collective interests are generally found mostly at the level of smaller groups, such as kin groups, local groups, and subclasses (see Dunning, this volume; Yaeger and Robin, this volume). It is important to remember that in European societies, the unity of commoners has been sought and expressed more strongly than in many other parts of the world. This tendency derives partly from the Greek and Roman traditions, in which an identity as commoners developed through political struggles with more privileged classes. Such patterns do not necessarily apply to non-Western societies.

In the case of the Contact period Maya, commoners were called *mazehualob* as opposed to *almehenob*, with the latter constituting the noble class. This native terminology does not necessarily indicate a lack of social mobility among two classes or the presence of a monolithic commoner class (Restall 1997). In addition, the identity as *mazehualob* was probably one imposed by the ruling classes, and did not derive from the social consciousness of the "*mazehualob*" themselves. Moreover, it is not clear how closely a Nahuatl-derived term such as *mazehual* reflects the social reality in Classic times. Thus, we need to be cautious in using Contact period analogies for the study of earlier periods (see Marcus, this volume, for a more detailed discussion of ethnohistoric terms of Mayan origin used to refer to various social statuses).

The term *commoner* implies that there may be even lower classes of slaves or serfs. The concept of non-elite is more comprehensive and relatively neutral to specific cultural traditions.[1] Non-elites, who may lack shared identities and interests, become the most distinguishable subjects of analysis in relation to and in comparison with elites. This does not mean that there is always a clear division between elites and non-elites. Configurations of social inequality and the degree of social mobility need to be examined empirically in each society (McGuire 1983; Palka 1995). An empirical study of non-elites in a given cultural and historical context needs to build on an understanding of the entire social organization and its relationship to elites.

Mobility of Non-Elites

The Concept of Mobility

The focus of this study is the mobility of non-elites over a political landscape. The concept of mobility is complex, involving multiple variables (Binford 1980, 1982; Eder 1984; Kelly 1992; Rafferty 1985; Rocek 1996; Varien 1999). Before I go on, a discussion of the conceptual framework used to examine mobility is in order. Below I address five theoretical issues concerning the concept of mobility.

The first issue relates to a change of the location of activities as a criterion of movement. This chapter focuses on movements that involve changes of location or area for routine domestic activities, as well as those for subsistence and occupational tasks. A change of residence as the main focus of domestic activities is an essential part of such moves. The fixed locations of residences can easily be targeted by the state for the purpose of controlling the subject population. Thus, movements of non-elites as means of resistance to state control usually involve a change of residence. This type of movement should be distinguished from moves of people out from and back to permanent or semipermanent residences for trade, subsistence work, pilgrimage, and social interactions (see Binford 1980). Residences, which are relatively easily recognizable as material remains, also figure as primary sources of data for archaeological studies of mobility. Movements that I discuss in this essay are also assumed to involve a change in the location of subsistence or occupational activities, although moves of such locations are difficult to detect in the archaeological record. We need to distinguish them, at least conceptually, from movements commonly seen in modern societies, in which individuals change residences but go to the same workplaces.

The second issue concerns the distinction between repetitive movements and moves to new localities. Some Classic Maya non-elites may have changed residences seasonally or cyclically between centers and peripheries and between different agricultural lands (Ford 1996; Lucero 1999a, 1999b:224–226; Tourtellot 1993). Such movements, if they occurred, would have been at least partially due to ecological reasons. Most archaeological studies of mobility have focused on such cyclical moves among hunter-gatherers and horticulturalists in relation to the development of sedentism (Binford 1980, 1982; Eder 1984; Kelly 1992; Rafferty 1985). Repetitive movements can also result from certain social institutions or customs, such as marriage. When different communities intermarry, the marrying individuals may move to "new" localities, which are new only from the point of view of the moving individuals. From the point of view of an observer, there may be recognizable repetitive patterns of movements of multiple marrying individuals over a long period of time within a set of communities.

These repetitive movements derived from ecological factors and social institutions would have significant political implications. They would constitute a precondition affecting the degree or effectiveness of political control over non-elites. Yet the primary focus of this chapter is on movements that involve the establishment of new sets of semipermanent loci or areas for domestic, occupational, and subsistence activities. Some scholars call this type of movement migration (Anthony 1990). In particular, I am interested in moves away from or into a sphere of control of a specific central authority or between different polities. Nonetheless, I should note that the distinction between repetitive movements and moves to new localities is not always clear. For example, swidden agriculturalists may move within the same set of agricultural fields according to their fallow schedule, but some may gradually move out to new fields when such lands are available.

The third issue is the spatial scale of movements. David Anthony (1990) distinguishes internal (short-distance) migrations and external (long-distance) movements (cf. Cadwallader 1992:4; Clark 1994). Internal migrations occur within a "local area" in which different social groups habitually interact. Thus, individuals or groups generally have a certain level of information on the destination locations, on which they base their decisions to migrate (Anthony 1990:901). External migrations beyond "local areas" did occur in pre-Hispanic Mesoamerica. Such movements over a long distance, however, were probably unusual and may have been caused by drastic changes in the social and natural environments. Here, I deal primarily with internal migrations within the Maya lowlands, which non-elites could more easily opt for under common social circumstances. Internal migrations should be movements out of the aforementioned range of cyclical moves derived from ecological factors, but may occur within the spatial domain of repetitive moves based on social institutions, such as marriage.

The fourth issue is the social scale of the moving or decision-making entity, varying from individuals to households to larger groups (Cameron 1995; Duff 1998). Factors underlying the mobility of individuals and households may be different from those of larger groups. All different scales are potentially relevant to this discussion, and the scale of moving entities needs to be narrowed down empirically.

The fifth issue is the conceptual distinction between movement and mobility. Movements and mobilities are often not clearly distinguished. For example, Martin Cadwallader (1992:4) called migrations within cities "residential mobility." In other words, mobility is considered a type of migration or movement. I argue that a clearer distinction between the two concepts is necessary for rigorous analysis. In archaeological studies focusing on hunter-gatherer groups, mobility generally refers to the frequency and distance of moves. In the analysis of mobility over a political landscape in sedentary societies, I prefer a more flexible definition. For me, movements—including migrations—refer to specific actions or sets of actions, while mobility means the likeliness or ability to make movements. In developed complex societies that are essentially sedentary, non-elites may stay in the same locations as long as political and economic conditions are favorable. But when political and economic circumstances change, populations with high mobility are more likely to move than those with low mobility. Thus, a fundamental definition of mobility should be the likeliness to make movements rather than the frequency of moves, although empirically, mobility still needs to be evaluated through the observation of the occurrence of moves during a certain period of time. Mobility is affected by various political, economic, social, and cultural factors. As discussed below in the analysis of factors, the distinction between migration and mobility is particularly important.

Factors Affecting Mobility

The analysis of factors affecting mobility should be structured differently from those affecting movements and migrations. In the study of migrations, scholars usually address negative "push" and positive "pull" factors at the place of origin and at the destination respectively (Anthony 1990:898). In other words, the factors influencing migrations are generally evaluated on the basis of the positive effects of moves as perceived by the moving entities. The focus is on "what they gain by moves." Positive effects include the avoidance or mitigation of negative "push" conditions at the place of origin and the benefits from positive "pull" conditions at the destination. It should also be noted that the factors of migrations are specific to a given empirical case of move.

In analyzing factors affecting mobility, one needs to focus on (1) more general conditions not bound to specific historical events, and (2) the negative effects of moves. The first class of factor includes the availability of economic resources, including agricultural lands, over a wide area in relation to the population density. Available means of transportation are also important. Social and cultural conditions include the structure of social networks and corporate groups, landholding patterns, the intensity of interactions and travels between different communities, the openness of communities to strangers, and the configuration of individual identities. It is also likely that those who move seasonally or cyclically are psychologically and economically more ready to migrate when needs or incentives arise than those who are more sedentary.

The second class of factor pertains to the negative effects of moves. For a sedentary population, any migrations involve the loss or abandonment of certain economic, social, and symbolic resources at the place of origin, in addition to emotional trauma. Migrations also require the reestablishment of such resources at the destination, as well as the economic and energetic expenditure directly related to transportation. Individuals or groups evaluate the perceived positive effects of a hypothetical move against the perceived negative effects as they decide whether to move. The smaller such perceived negative effects are, the more easily a move becomes a viable option in response to specific "push" and "pull" factors. Thus, in the analysis of factors affecting mobility, the focus should be more on "what they lose by moves."

An important economic factor in this respect is the level of labor and capital investment in the preparation of residences, agricultural fields, and other immovable assets. When such investments are large, people are less likely to move. A factor that is similar, but more social in its nature, is the degree of investment needed to build social networks or status in local groups. Also relevant are the quantity, value, exchangeability, and transportability of moveable possessions. The higher the value of the objects they have to leave because they are difficult to transport or to exchange into other forms of wealth, the less likely individuals or groups are to move. The ideological values of ancestral lands and houses or of religious loci may also be significant.

In this discussion, I have focused on social, economic, and cultural factors rather than on political concerns. This is because my focus is on mobility over a political landscape. In such a study, it is important, first, to examine factors that are less political in their nature and then to evaluate the political implications of mobility conditioned by such factors. This does not mean, however, that mobility shaped by social, economic, and cultural factors one-directionally influences administrative organization and political strategies of elites. In most cases, effects are two-directional, and various factors are closely intertwined with each other. On the one hand, the high mobility of non-elites tends to make political control by the ruling class more difficult. On the other hand, the strength of political control and the nature of political affiliation directly influence the degree of spatial mobility of non-elites. Elites and states may actively try to limit the mobility of their subjects and to create aggregated settlements. In this process, elites may even modify economic and ideological conditions that affect the mobility of non-elites. Such strategies include the concentration of economic activities and resources, the adoption or promotion of intensive agricultural methods, and the development of a state religion focused on the centers. It should also be noted that in the context of competition between elite groups, some elites may take advantage of non-elite mobility to lure away subjects of rival groups.

Factors Affecting the Mobility of Classic Maya Non-Elites

It is nearly impossible to evaluate from archaeological evidence the wide array of potential factors affecting mobility. I would assume, however, that in traditional agrarian societies, such as Classic Maya society, critical conditions are the degree of investment in the preparation of residences and agricultural fields, as well as the cultural and ideological factors that may bind people to fixed locations. In the case of the Classic Maya, the investment in the construction of non-elite houses is relatively small. Structures with wattle-and-daub walls and thatched roofs can be built relatively easily, and modern Maya farmers frequently rebuild such houses.

It is now clear that the Classic Maya engaged in diverse forms of intensive cultivation. Thus, the mobility of Classic Maya farmers may have been more limited than that of their Colonial period counterparts, who mainly practiced swidden agriculture. Yet, for a more precise evaluation of mobility, we need to distinguish initial investments of labor and capital in the preparation of fields, such as the construction of canals and terraces, from cyclical investments that are required season after season for their maintenance, seeding, weeding, and harvesting. While the notion of "intensive agriculture" comprises both types of investment, the question of mobility primarily concerns the former. In this regard, the preparation of wetland fields must have required significant initial investments, but the extent of these fields is still debated (Adams et al. 1990; Fedick 1996; Pope and Dahlin 1993). Where wetland agriculture is not possible, evidence of large-scale modifications of topography for agriculture is rather limited. Although terraced fields are common, initial investments in their construction do not appear to have been as great as those in elaborate terraces found in other premodern agrarian societies, such as the Andes, Bali, and Japan. For these reasons, limitations on mobility in terms of agricultural practice during the Classic period should not be exaggerated.

Cultural and ideological factors are far more difficult to address. The practices of burying the dead under house floors and of constant rebuilding over older structures may signal that the Classic Maya valued continuity in fixed localities (McAnany 1995). This ideology may have worked as a negative factor reducing mobility. Nonetheless, the Contact period Maya with similar practices exhibited a relatively high degree of mobility (see below). The nature of landholding patterns and of social organization is equally difficult to evaluate. Yet it is suggestive to note that in colonial Yucatán, patronymic groups were distributed over wide areas, crosscutting local groups (Roys 1943; Tozzer 1941:99). If such patterns existed in Classic times, they might have facilitated a high degree of mobility.

Mobility during the Contact and Colonial Periods

Before examining data from the Classic period, it is useful to briefly review the situations during the Contact and Colonial periods. Nancy Farris strongly emphasizes the high mobility of the lowland Maya during the Colonial period. She states that

> the colonial Maya changed residence with a facility and across distance . . . Members of premodern agrarian societies in general may have been much more geographically mobile than has ordinarily been as-

sumed . . . Even so, the lowland Maya seem to have been uncommonly restless for a people defined as "sedentary." (1984:19)

An important question is whether such mobility arose as a form of resistance to the colonial rule and as a sign of the disintegration of traditional Maya communities or whether it is rooted in an older, pre-Columbian tradition. Farris (1984:199) argues that "among the Maya a tendency toward physical fragmentation emerges whenever social cohesion weakens at the center," and suggests that colonial patterns parallel pre-Hispanic cycles of consolidation and dissolution, such as the "Classic collapse," suggested by the archaeological record. Matthew Restall (1997:174–175), however, contends that "Maya population movements . . . did not necessarily represent responses to extraordinary circumstances. A certain mobility, in fact, was the norm." He further argues that social cohesion was maintained despite the omnipresent tendency toward physical fragmentation. Implications are that the remarkable mobility of the Colonial period Maya has deep roots and that pre-Hispanic Maya may have been highly mobile throughout any time of political stability and upheaval.

Historical accounts on this aspect of pre-Hispanic Maya society are fragmentary. In a *Relación* written in 1582, Gaspar Antonio Chi stated that before the Spanish Conquest, vassals were not assigned to specific towns and were free to live wherever they wished (Tozzer 1941:230). Olivier de Montmollin (1989:91) cautions that the statement was meant to be an indirect condemnation of Spanish *congregación* and that it should not be taken at face value. An account of the origin of the powerful Chel family may be even more suggestive. According to Diego de Landa, after a son-in-law of a Mayapán high priest founded a new community, a large number of people came to live there because of his high reputation (Tozzer 1941:40). This account was not told in the context of criticism of Spanish policy. It implies that there was a certain level of spatial mobility and of the freedom to change political affiliation on the part of non-elites. It is also worth noting that, according to the account, the growth of the Chel family was achieved not through coercive power but through the high reputation associated with its prestigious ancestry. Though we do not have sufficient documentary sources to assert this, it appears quite likely that the high mobility seen among the Colonial period lowland Maya reflects a long-standing tradition.

Aguateca

In the following sections, I examine data related to the mobility of non-elites from the Classic Maya center of Aguateca, Guatemala. It is necessary to state that research at this center has been biased toward elites. Early studies conducted by Ian Graham (1967) and Stephen Houston (1993) focused on glyphic inscriptions. Investigations at Aguateca by the Petexbatún Regional Archaeological Project, supervised by Takeshi Inomata from 1990 to 1993, included survey and mapping of the center and its peripheries, as well as excavations in various parts of the site (Demarest et al. 1997; Inomata 1995, 1997; Inomata and Stiver 1998). This research provided important information on the settlement history. The Aguateca Archaeological Project, conducted from 1996 to 1999 under the direction of Inomata, Daniela Triadan, and Erick Ponciano, focused on the extensive excavation of rapidly abandoned elite residences at the site epicenter (Inomata et al. 1998, 2002). A few possible non-elite residences, which were smaller and less elaborate than elite residences, were also excavated during this project (see Inomata and Triadan 2003; Webster and Inomata 2003 for detailed discussions of elite and non-elite structures).

The results of excavations, along with epigraphic data, showed that Aguateca was occupied for a relatively short period. Aguateca became an important center probably at the beginning of the eighth century and was abandoned possibly at the beginning of the ninth century. Most structures had only one major construction episode. The direct cause of the abandonment was an attack by enemies. In the latter half of the eighth century, warfare intensified, and the residents of Aguateca tried to defend themselves by constructing a series of stone walls (Figure 8.1). Aguateca was finally attacked, and its epicenter was burned. The residents of the epicenter fled or were taken away, leaving a large number of their belongings behind. Despite the research bias toward the elite, the rise and fall of Aguateca in a relatively short period provide significant data on the mobility of non-elites.

Foundation of the Center: Where Did Non-Elites Come from and Why?

The occupation at Aguateca during the Early Classic period and the early part of the Late Classic was light or nearly absent. The Early Classic and early Late Classic stelae (St. 15, 16, 17, and 18) discovered in the 1990s in the middle of a steep escarpment away from the Main Plaza (Figure 8.1)

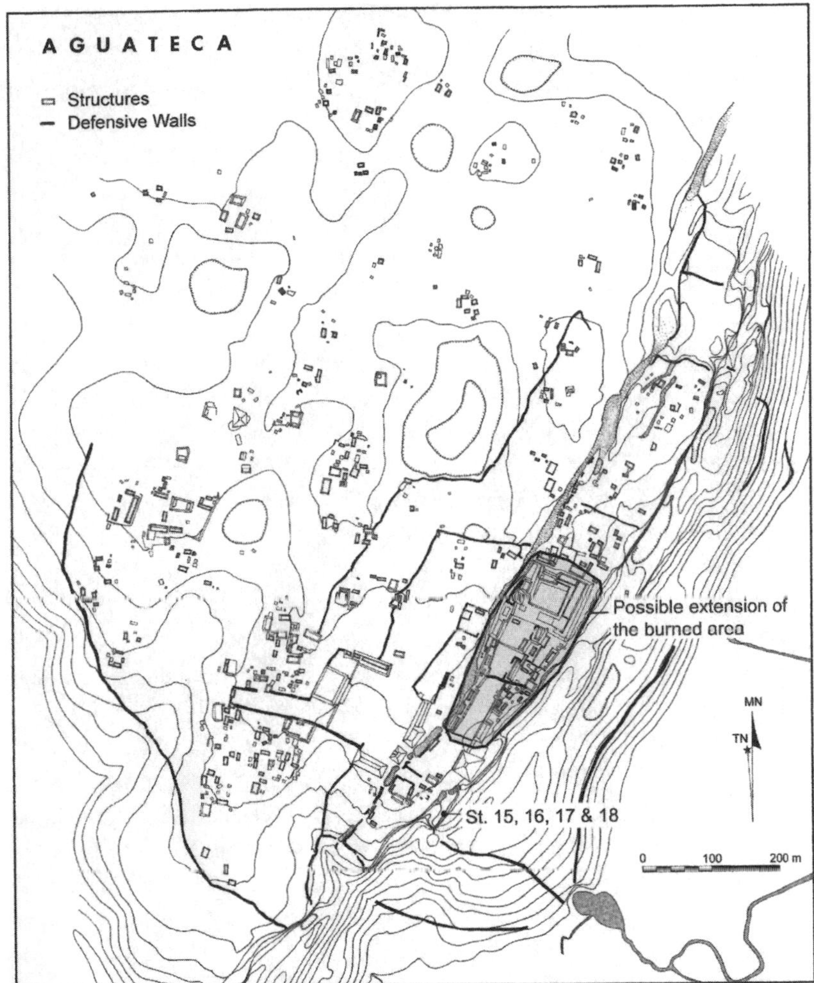

Figure 8.1. Map of Aguateca showing the location of the burned area and St. 15, 16, 17, and 18.

suggest that Aguateca was part of the Tamarindito polity and was used as a ritual place during these periods. Some scholars have suggested that in certain parts of the Maya lowlands, Preclassic ceramics continued to be used in Early Classic times and that the absence of Early Classic types does not necessarily mean a low population level (Brady et al. 1998; Laporte et al. 1993; Lincoln 1985). However, ceramics associated with Stelae 15, 16, 17, and 18 of Aguateca are clearly chronologically different from those found in other parts of the center. The low population level at Aguateca during the Early Classic period is also indicated by the change in settlement patterns from the Preclassic to the Late Classic and by a lack of buildup in Classic structures and plazas (Inomata 1995).

During the early Late Classic period, an intrusive dynasty, which probably originated from Tikal, founded its primary capital at Dos Pilas (Fahsen 2003; Houston 1993). The Dos Pilas dynasty established its second capital at Aguateca probably at the beginning of the eighth century. It is not clear how the Dos Pilas dynasty took over this place from the older Tamarindito polity. In any case, Aguateca grew rapidly into a densely occupied center. Where did the non-elite occupants of Aguateca come from? The population level in the Pasión region during the Early Classic period was generally low. Excavators of Seibal suggest that at the beginning of the Late Classic period a significant number of people migrated to this center, which was nearly depopulated in Early Classic times (Sabloff 1975; Tourtellot 1988). In the Pasión region, there are no obvious sources of migration to such centers as Dos Pilas, Aguateca, and Seibal. It is probable that at least some portion of new occupants came from outside the Pasión region.

An even more important question is why non-elites came to Aguateca. Was the non-elite population forced to move to Aguateca or did they come voluntarily? We do not have direct evidence regarding this question, but it is conceivable that the two mechanisms operated at the same time. It is worth reiterating that the population growth does not appear to have preceded the establishment of Aguateca as the secondary seat of the Dos Pilas dynasty; it probably occurred at the time of or after the takeover of Aguateca by the new dynasty. This pattern suggests that political factors may have been critical for the population aggregation. The foundation and development of a new center required a significant labor force for the construction of temples, palaces, and a causeway. For the royal family and other elites, securing a subject population must have been crucial. It seems unlikely that the newly established dynasty would have had enough coercive power to force such a large population to move to a new location. Like the Postclassic situation suggested by the episode of the Chel family, at least some non-elites probably moved to Aguateca voluntarily. This implies that the elite needed to provide some incentives to attract non-elites and that non-elites had a certain degree of mobility to move from the political sphere of one center to another. It is, however, difficult to conceive that all of the non-elite population came totally voluntarily. At least a certain number of non-elites, who worked as servants and close subjects of nobles, probably had little choice but to follow their masters. Moreover, even among the non-elites who moved voluntarily, some may have done so due to preexisting social and emotional ties to the migrating elite.

Warfare and Defensive Walls: Why Did Non-Elites Stay?

In the late eighth century, the royal family and other elites abandoned the principal capital of Dos Pilas, possibly as a result of military defeat (Demarest 1997; Houston 1993; Palka 1997). The royal family and other elites moved their primary seat of power to Aguateca, which occupied a more defensible location. Warfare in the region appears to have escalated significantly at this time, and the residents of Aguateca, as well as the small remaining population of Dos Pilas, built a series of defensive walls (Demarest et al. 1997; Inomata 1997; Palka 1997). What happened to the non-elite population? A significant number of them probably endured difficult times at Aguateca at least until near the final defeat of this center by enemies.

Defensive walls at the Aguateca center measure over 4 km in total and encircle a large part of the center. The walls have a roughly concentric pattern, centered on the Palace Group or a probable royal residence (see Figure 8.1). This pattern suggests that the main purpose of defensive wall construction was to protect the royal family. It appears that the construction of these walls was designed and supervised by the central authority. The labor of non-elites was probably mobilized for this construction. Various lines of evidence indicate that a significant population still remained in the center when the walls were constructed. First, most existing structures at Aguateca remained intact. At Dos Pilas, in contrast, excavators found clear evidence that some existing structures, including royal palaces and temples, were dismantled and their stones were used for the construction of defensive walls (Demarest 1997; Demarest et al. 1997; Palka 1995, 1997). This difference between Dos Pilas and Aguateca indicates that a significant number of residents left the former, whereas a large portion of the population remained in the latter. Second, walls at Aguateca are far more extensive than those at Dos Pilas, and the outermost wall surrounds a large part of the center (see Figure 8.1). Third, the layouts of walls where they connect with existing structures suggest that these buildings continued to be used. Fourth, excavators found a shallow midden deposited in a corner formed by the back wall of a residential structure (Str. L7-4) and a defensive wall. This midden was formed after the construction of the wall, indicating that the residential structure continued to be occupied. I should also mention that there is no clear evidence that the non-elite residents of Aguateca moved into the epicenter that was most heavily defended. Elites who lived in the epicenter appear to have maintained basically the same occupancy patterns (Inomata and Stiver 1998; Inomata et al. 1998, 2002).

The hasty construction of walls, along with the fact that a significant number of non-elites remained at the center, indicates that the walls were built as a desperate response to external threats. In other words, the walls were probably not built to protect against non-elite revolts. The elites still maintained the power to command non-elite labor, whether they achieved it through coercive, economic, or ideological sanctions. I should also note that some non-elites chose to stay at Dos Pilas rather than move to Aguateca. From the perspective of elites who were under the threat of an imminent enemy attack, it must have been desirable to have the largest subject population possible who would aid in their defense. The reason non-elites stayed at Dos Pilas was clearly not because they were commanded to by the royal dynasty. The remaining non-elites at Dos Pilas did not show any respect to royal palaces and temples (Demarest 1997; Demarest et al. 1997; Palka 1995).

Abandonment of the Center: What Happened to Non-Elites?

Despite this effort to defend the center, Aguateca was finally attacked by enemies, probably at the beginning of the ninth century. The elite residential area in the epicenter was burned, and elites left or were taken away, leaving a large number of their possessions behind. I have suggested that the primary target of the enemies was the elite, and that they intended to terminate Aguateca as a political and economic power (Inomata 1997). Soon after this event, the entire center was deserted. Again, the question is whether non-elites chose to abandon the center or were forced to do so. In addressing this question, the chronological sequence of events is critical. Did non-elites who lived outside the epicenter leave Aguateca before or after the attack? In both areas, excavated artifacts date to the end of the Late Classic period. Diagnostic artifacts include Chablekal Gray ceramics and vessels in transitional forms between Late Classic and Terminal Classic types (Foias 1996). Absent are typical Terminal Classic artifacts, such as Fine Orange and Tres Naciones Gray ceramics. These data indicate that non-elites left the center either immediately before or immediately after the attack.

If non-elites left the center before the attack, this may mean that they had the power and freedom to do so against the elite's will. For the elite, maintaining a large population must have been critical for the defense of the center and for their own survival. Under increasingly problematic social circumstances, elites may have lost their coercive power or may no longer have been able to offer economic or ideological incentives to their subjects. From the perspective of non-elites, being with the ruling class, which was the main target of enemies, may have posed a threat that weighed more than the potential protection from the elite. If it was after the attack that non-elites left the center, the coercion from the elite—in this case, the enemies—may have been the primary cause of their move. Otherwise, the abandonment of the center after the attack would probably have been more gradual.

Though we lack direct evidence, the second scenario appears more likely. Burned houses in the epicenter contained numerous still usable objects, such as grinding stones, but there are no clear indications that they were scavenged or that the residents tried to resettle. It appears that the residents of Aguateca were not allowed to go back to the center. In addition, data from Dos Pilas are suggestive. As mentioned above, a small non-elite population remained at Dos Pilas after it was abandoned by the dynasty. The presence of Fine Orange ceramics and other Terminal Classic materials suggests that this non-elite occupation at Dos Pilas continued even after the defeat of Aguateca (Foias 1996; Palka 1995). Non-elites gradually left Dos Pilas as the social and political environment of the region deteriorated. In contrast, the end of the occupation at Aguateca was abrupt, most likely due to political factors. Non-elites of Aguateca were probably forced to leave by the enemies (Inomata 2003).

Conclusion

It is plausible that the tradition of high mobility observed among the Colonial period Maya extends back to the Classic period. Common agricultural practices in the Maya lowlands, which involved seasonal or repetitive moves, may have constituted an underlying condition that allowed such mobility. The rapid rise of Aguateca possibly reflects the considerable mobility of the Classic Maya non-elite population.

The Late Classic period was a time when numerous centers grew throughout the Maya lowlands. At the beginning of the Late Classic period, various parts of the Maya lowlands still had relatively low population density. Gaining and securing their subjects must have been a major concern for competing elites, particularly for newly established dynasties. It is hard to imagine that Classic Maya elites tried to achieve this purpose solely through coercive force. If non-elites indeed had significant mobility, attraction through positive incentives may have been a more effective strategy to gain a larger subject population than coercion through negative sanctions. Possible elite strategies to draw subjects may have included the attractions of religious ceremonies and high culture that elites offered at the centers; economic incentives; and secured resources, such as water stored in reservoirs (Ford 1996; Lucero 1999a; Scarborough 1991). Other possible factors are the chance of social promotion through achievements in battles and defense against outsiders. The nature of elite-subject relations postulated here is analogous to the galactic-polity model developed for historical Thailand by Stanley Tambiah (1976) and applied to the Classic Maya by Arthur Demarest (1992) and Stephen Houston (1993). Demarest (1992) argues that ideological factors were particularly important in the relationship between elites and non-elites and that the political affiliation of subjects remained inherently unstable.

My intention here, however, is not to take one side in a dichotomous argument. It is probable that elites also had a certain level of coercive power. Elites at Aguateca were able to retain a considerable non-elite population under the deteriorating social and political circumstances and to mobilize their labor for the construction of defensive walls for the purpose of protecting the royal family. After the fall of Aguateca, elites—in this case, the victorious enemies—appear to have had the power to forcibly relocate non-elites and to forbid their return to this center.

Our understanding of the mobility of Classic Maya non-elites is quite limited, but it is necessary to recognize that non-elites were not always bound to fixed locations. It is even probable that high mobility analogous to that of the Colonial period conditioned the pattern of political organization and the nature of elite-subject relations. The further study of the degree of commoner mobility has important implications for the understanding of Classic Maya political processes.

Acknowledgments

I thank Jon Lohse, Fred Valdez, Lisa Lucero, and anonymous reviewers for thoughtful comments on earlier drafts. I am indebted to the Instituto de Antropología e Historia de Guatemala and its personnel for the permit and support. Investigations at Aguateca were supported by grants from the National Science Foundation, the National Geographic Society, the Mitsubishi Foundation, the Sumitomo Foundation, the Foundation for the Advancement of Mesoamerican Studies Inc., and the H. John Heinz III Charitable Trust.

Note

1. George Marcus (1992) warns us that elite studies developed in the analysis of European societies. In this regard, most anthropological and sociological studies of social organization and class systems are deeply embedded in the Western intellectual tradition, and we should be aware of this potential bias.

References

Adams, Richard E. W., T. Patrick Culbert, W. E. Brown, Peter D. Harrison, and Laura J. Levi

1990 Rebuttal to Pope and Dahlin. *Journal of Field Archaeology* 17:241–243.

Anthony, David W.

1990 Migration in Archaeology: The Baby and the Bathwater. *American Anthropologist* 92:895–914.

Binford, Lewis R.

1980 Willow Smoke and Dogs' Tails: Hunter-Gatherer Settlement Systems and Archaeological Site Formation. *American Antiquity* 45:4–20.

1982 The Archaeology of Place. *Journal of Anthropological Archaeology* 1:5–31.

Brady, James E., Joseph W. Ball, Ronald L. Bishop, Duncan C. Pring, Norman Hammond, and Rupert A. Housley

1998 The Lowland Maya "Protoclassic": A Reconsideration of Its Nature and Significance. *Ancient Mesoamerica* 9:17–38.

Brumfiel, Elizabeth M.

1994 Factional Competition and Political Development in the New World: An Introduction. In *Factional Competition and Political Development in the New World*, edited by Elizabeth M. Brumfiel and John W. Fox, pp. 3–13. Cambridge University Press, Cambridge.

Cadwallader, Martin

1992 *Migration and Residential Mobility, Macro and Micro Approaches.* University of Wisconsin Press, Madison.

Cameron, Catherine M.

1995 Migration and the Movement of Southwestern Peoples. *Journal of Anthropological Archaeology* 14:104–124.

Chase, Arlen F., and Diane Z. Chase

1992 Mesoamerican Elites: Assumptions, Definitions, and Models. In *Mesoamerican Elites: An Archaeological Assessment*, edited by Diane Z. Chase and Arlen F. Chase, pp. 3–17. University of Oklahoma Press, Norman.

Clark, Geoffrey A.

1994 Migration as an Explanatory Concept in Paleolithic Archaeology. In *Journal of Archaeological Method and Theory*, Vol. 1, No. 4 edited by Michael B. Schiffer, 305–343. University of Arizona Press, Tucson.

Demarest, Arthur A.

1992 Ideology in Ancient Maya Cultural Evolution: The Dynamics of Galactic Polities. In *Ideology and Pre-Columbian Civilizations*, edited by Arthur A. Demarest and Geoffrey W. Conrad, pp. 135–158. School of American Research Press, Santa Fe.

1997 The Vanderbilt Petexbatún Regional Archaeological Project 1989–1994: Overview, History, and Major Results of a Multidisciplinary Study of the Classic Maya Collapse. *Ancient Mesoamerica* 8:209–227.

Demarest, Arthur A., Matt O'Mansky, Claudia Wolley, Dirk Van Tuerenhout, Takeshi Inomata, Joel Palka, and Héctor Escobedo

1997 Classic Maya Defensive Systems and Warfare in the Petexbatún Region: Archaeological Evidence and Interpretations. *Ancient Mesoamerica* 8:229–253.

de Montmollin, Olivier

1989 *The Archaeology of Political Structure: Settlement Analysis in a Classic Maya Polity.* Cambridge University Press, Cambridge.

Duff, Andrew I.

1998 The Process of Migration in the Late Prehistoric Southwest. In *Migration and Reorganization: The Pueblo IV Period in the American Southwest*, edited by Katherine A. Spielmann, pp. 31–52. Anthropological Research Papers 51. Arizona State University, Tempe.

Eder, James F.

1984 The Impact of Subsistence Change on Mobility and Settlement Pattern in a Tropical Forest Foraging Economy: Some Implications for Archaeology. *American Anthropologist* 86:837–853.

Fahsen, Federico

2003 Rescuing the Origins of Dos Pilas Dynasty: A Salvage of Hieroglyphic Stairway #2, Structure L5-49. http//www.famsi.org/reports/01098

Farris, Nancy M.

1984 *Maya Society under Colonial Rule: The Collective Enterprise of Survival.* Princeton University Press, Princeton.

Fedick, Scott L. (editor)

1996 *The Managed Mosaic: Ancient Maya Agriculture and Resource Use.* University of Utah Press, Salt Lake City.

Foias, Antonia E.

1996 Changing Ceramic Production and Exchange Systems and the Classic

Maya Collapse in the Petexbatún Region. Ph.D. diss., Department of Anthropology, Vanderbilt University, Nashville.

Ford, Anabel
1996 Critical Resource Control and the Rise of the Classic Period Maya. In *The Managed Mosaic: Ancient Maya Agriculture and Resource Use*, edited by Scott L. Fedick, pp. 297–303. University of Utah Press, Salt Lake City.

Fox, John W., and Garrett W. Cook
1996 Constructing Maya Communities: Ethnography for Archaeology. *Current Anthropology* 37:795–801.

Giddens, Anthony
1974 Elites in the British Class Structure. In *Elites and Power in British Society*, edited by Phillip Stanworth and Anthony Giddens, pp. 1–21. Cambridge University Press, London.

Graham, Ian
1967 *Archaeological Explorations in El Peten, Guatemala.* Middle American Research Institute, Publications 33. Tulane University, New Orleans.

Houston, Stephen
1993 *Hieroglyphs and History at Dos Pilas: Dynastic Politics of the Classic Maya.* University of Texas Press, Austin.

Houston, Stephen, and David Stuart
2001 Peopling the Classic Maya Court. In *Royal Courts of the Ancient Maya*, edited by Takeshi Inomata and Stephen Houston, pp. 54–83. Westview Press, Boulder.

Inomata, Takeshi
1995 Archaeological Investigations at the Fortified Center of Aguateca, El Petén, Guatemala: Implication for the Study of the Classic Maya Collapse. Ph.D. diss., Department of Anthropology, Vanderbilt University, Nashville.
1997 The Last Day of a Fortified Classic Maya Center: Archaeological Investigations at Aguateca, Guatemala. *Ancient Mesoamerica* 8:337–351.
2001a King's People: Classic Maya Royal Courtiers in a Comparative Perspective. In *Royal Courts of the Ancient Maya, Volume 1: Theory, Comparison, and Synthesis*, edited by Takeshi Inomata and Stephen Houston, pp. 27–53. Westview Press, Boulder.
2001b The Power and Ideology of Artistic Creation: Elite Craft Specialists in Classic Maya Society. *Current Anthropology* 42(3): 321–349.
2003 War, Destruction, and Abandonment: The Fall of the Classic Maya Center of Aguateca, Guatemala. In *The Archaeology of Settlement Abandonment in Middle America*, edited by Takeshi Inomata and Ronald Webb, pp. 43–60. University of Utah Press, Salt Lake City.

Inomata, Takeshi, and Laura Stiver
1998 Floor Assemblages from Burned Structures at Aguateca, Guatemala: A Study of Classic Maya Households. *Journal of Field Archaeology* 25:431–452.

Inomata, Takeshi, and Daniela Triadan

2003 Where Did Elite Live? Possible Elite Residences at Aguateca, Guatemala. In *Maya Palaces and Elite Residences*, edited by Jessica Joyce Christie, pp. 154–183. University of Texas Press, Austin.

Inomata, Takeshi, Daniela Triadan, Erick Ponciano, Estela Pinto, Richard E. Terry, and Markus Eberl

2002 Domestic and Political Lives of Classic Maya Elites: The Excavation of Rapidly Abandoned Structures at Aguateca, Guatemala. *Latin American Antiquity* 13: 305–330.

Inomata, Takeshi, Daniela Triadan, Erick Ponciano, Richard E. Terry, Harriet F. Beaubien, Estela Pinto, and Shannon Coyston

1998 Residencias de la familia real y de la élite en Aguateca, Guatemala. *Mayab* 11:23–39.

Kelly, Robert L.

1992 Mobility/Sedentism: Concepts, Archaeological Measures, and Effects. *Annual Review of Anthropology* 21:41–66.

Laporte, Juan Pedro, Lilian A. Corzo, Héctor L. Escobedo, Rosa María Flores, K. Isabel Izaguirre, Nancy Monterroso, Paulino I. Morales, Carmen Ramos, Irma Rodas, Julio A. Roldán, Franklin Solares, and Bernard Hermes

1993 *La secuencia cerámica del valle de Dolores, Petén: Las unidades cerámicas.* Publicación 1. Altas Arqueológico de Guatemala. Ministerio de Cultura y Deportes e Instituto de Antropología e Historia, Guatemala.

Lincoln, Charles E.

1985 Ceramics and Ceramic Chronology. In *A Consideration of the Early Classic Period in the Maya Lowlands*, edited by Gordon R. Willey and Peter Mathews, pp. 55–94. Publication 10. Institute for Mesoamerican Studies, State University of New York, Albany.

Lucero, Lisa

1999a Water Control and Maya Politics in the Southern Maya Lowlands. In *Complex Polities in the Ancient Tropical World*, edited by Elizabeth A. Bacus and Lisa J. Lucero, pp. 35–49. Archaeological Papers of the American Anthropological Association 9, Arlington.

1999b Classic Lowland Maya Political Organization: A Review. *Journal of World Prehistory* 13:211–263.

Marcus, George E.

1983 A Review of Ethnographic Research on Elites in Complex Societies. In *Elites: Ethnographic Issues*, edited by George E. Marcus, pp. 29–39. University of New Mexico Press, Albuquerque.

1992 The Concern with Elites in Archaeological Reconstructions: Mesoamerican Materials. In *Mesoamerican Elites: An Archaeological Assessment*, edited by Diane Z. Chase and Arlen F. Chase, pp. 292–302. University of Oklahoma Press, Norman.

McAnany, Patricia A.

1995 *Living with the Ancestors: Kinship and Kingship in Ancient Maya Society.* University of Texas Press, Austin.

McGuire, Randall H.

1983 Breaking Down Cultural Complexity: Inequality and Heterogeneity. In *Advances in Archaeological Method and Theory*, Vol. 6, edited by Michael B. Schiffer, pp. 91–141. Academic Press, New York.

Palka, Joel W.

1995 Classic Maya Social Inequality and the Collapse at Dos Pilas, Petén, Guatemala. Ph.D. diss., Department of Anthropology, Vanderbilt University, Nashville.

1997 Reconstructing Classic Maya Socioeconomic Differentiation and the Collapse at Dos Pilas, Peten, Guatemala. *Ancient Mesoamerica* 8:293–306.

Pope, Kevin D., and Bruce H. Dahlin

1993 Radar Detection and Ecology of Ancient Maya Canal Systems. *Journal of Field Archaeology* 20:379–383.

Rafferty, Janet E.

1985 The Archaeological Record on Sedentariness: Recognition, Development, and Implications. In *Advances in Archaeological Method and Theory*, edited by Michael B. Schiffer, pp. 113–156. Academic Press, New York.

Restall, Matthew

1997 *The Maya World: Yucatec Culture and Society, 1550–1850.* Stanford University Press, Stanford.

Rocek, Thomas R.

1996 Sedentism and Mobility in the Southwest. In *Interpreting Southwestern Diversity: Underlying Principles and Overarching Patterns*, edited by Paul R. Fish and Jeffrey J. Reid, pp. 17–22. Anthropological Research Papers No. 48. Arizona State University, Tempe.

Roys, Ralph L.

1943 *The Indian Background of Colonial Yucatan.* Carnegie Institution of Washington Publication 543. Washington, D.C.

Sabloff, Jeremy A.

1975 *Excavations at Seibal: Ceramics.* Memoirs of the Peabody Museum of Archaeology and Ethnology, vol. 13, no. 2. Harvard University, Cambridge.

Scarborough, Vernon L.

1991 Water Management Adaptations in Non-Industrial Complex Societies: An Archaeological Perspective. *Archaeological Method and Theory* 3:101–154.

Stillwell, John, and Peter Congdon (editors)

1991 *Migration Models: Macro and Micro Approaches.* Belhaven Press, London.

Tambiah, Stanley J.

1976 *World Conqueror and World Renouncer.* Cambridge University Press, Cambridge.

Tourtellot, Gair, III

1988 *Excavations at Seibal: Peripheral Survey and Excavation: Settlement and*

Community Patterns. Memoirs of the Peabody Museum of Archaeology and Ethnology 16. Harvard University, Cambridge.

1993 A View of Ancient Maya Settlements in the Eighth Century. In *Lowland Maya Civilization in the Eighth Century A.D.*, edited by Jeremy A. Sabloff and John S. Henderson, pp. 219–242. Dumbarton Oaks, Washington, D.C.

Tozzer, Alfred M. (translator)

1941 *Landa's "Relación de las cosas de Yucatán."* Papers of the Peabody Museum of Archaeology and Ethnology 18. Harvard University, Cambridge.

Varien, Mark D.

1999 *Sedentism and Mobility in a Social Landscape: Mesa Verde and Beyond.* University of Arizona Press, Tucson.

Webster, David, and Takeshi Inomata

2003 Identifying Sub-royal Elite Palaces at Copán and Aguateca. In *Ancient Palaces of the New World: Form, Function, and Meaning*, edited by Susan Toby Evans and Joanne Pillsbury. Dumbarton Oaks, Washington, D.C. In press.

CHAPTER 9

Commoners in Postclassic Maya Society: Social versus Economic Class Constructs

MARILYN A. MASSON AND CARLOS PERAZA LOPE

The concept of a commoner class in Postclassic Maya society is an evasive one, suggesting that social status position does not vary evenly with conditions of economic life. As many of the contributors to this volume have demonstrated, when economic patterns of household production and local, regional, and distant exchange are compared, commoners are not always easily distinguished from elites. Elites are identified primarily from indicators of social status that are rooted in political and ritual activity. Such indicators include increased residential platform size, the monopolization of certain types of ritual events and paraphernalia, and the control of particular forms of production or exchange. These vary from site to site according to historical and geographic contexts that affected social and economic institutions at individual communities. From the perspective of material realities in the archaeological record, the continuum of social and economic indicators suggests that class structure was to some degree fluid. A single model of class relations within all Postclassic Maya communities is not reflected.

Although historic documents suggest that two distinct social classes of nobles and commoners were well defined within Mesoamerican society (Marcus 1992, 1993, this volume), others argue, based on archaeological evidence, for a middle class of individuals (A. Chase 1992). Archaeological data suggest a continuum of economic affluence at some sites based on architectural, mortuary, or artifact distributions that might indicate an upwardly mobile middle class (A. Chase 1992; King and Potter 1994)—though Joyce Marcus (1993) interprets such variation as evidence of differences within a commoner class (see also Smith and Masson 2000:20). Continuous settlement distributions have long been observed in the Maya area (Adams and Smith 1981:339). At many sites, even the humblest house mounds gained access to valuable materials, albeit in lesser quantities than found in elite contexts (Freidel 1986:414, 417; Haviland and Moholy-Nagy 1992:54).

Formal social classes, as defined emically by Maya noble families in historic records, represent a fundamentally different category than economic status groups that are materially expressed in the archaeological record. These two forms of power represent a dialectic not unique to Maya or Mesoamerican societies. In many complex societies, upper classes composed of those born wealthy are pervasively infiltrated by bourgeois entrepreneurs. A middle-class substrate of affluent "non-elites" carries within it members who strive to improve their economic or social status from generation to generation. Ralph Roys (1943:33) cites historic information to argue for the existence of three classes in Postclassic Maya society: nobles, commoners, and slaves, but Diane Chase (1986:362) describes the difficulty in identifying residences associated with such class differences. Archaeologically, she notes that a gradation in status is indicated that defies the rigid historical categories. Other historical sources point to considerable occupational heterogeneity in Postclassic Maya society, including lords, merchants, traders, priests, warriors, craft specialists, servants, and slaves (Barrera and Morley 1949; Roys 1962; Tozzer 1941), and the correspondence of these occupations to social standing probably varied for individuals at different communities. The debate about the number of formal social class categories rages on in Mesoamerican archaeology, and much of it surrounds the status of merchants in highland and lowland societies at various points in time (Adams and Smith 1981:347; Blanton et al. 1993; Sabloff and Rathje 1975a, 1975b; Smith and Masson 2000:20).

As Michael Mann's oft-cited (1986) work argues, there are different sources of social power, including ideological, economic, militaristic, and political networks. Archaeologists must evaluate the relative significance of these networks for specific societies through the material realm (Blanton 1998; Earle 1997). While extremes on either end of a continuum of architectural size and elaboration perhaps easily illustrate the commoner-versus-elite dichotomy, always problematic are those big small platforms or small big platforms found at the center of the distribution. As Diane Chase (1986:357) notes, "Such a continuum might indicate that commoners could accumulate wealth to the point that they were difficult to distinguish materially from the elite." Arlen Chase (1992) has argued for the likelihood of a Maya middle class based on such evidence. Household artifact distributions in many complex societies do exhibit a continuum that presents interpretive challenges to archaeologists. Superelites have more luxury items, secondary elites have less, affluent commoners less still, and last of all, true "have-not" commoners possess the least. These trends are states of material wealth, coinciding with at least two (nobles/commoners) socially conceived categories of social standing for the Maya area and perhaps more. Case-study examples of nobles who have lost their wealth but retained their titles, or of the nouveau riche who are loaded but who have no "class," are common in history. Marriages between these two groups often produce a blissful symbiosis—filling the bank accounts of the nobles and providing class legitimization to newly wealthy entrepreneurs. The Maya situation appears complicated by lineage group organization that crosscut social classes. Lineage groups, such as the patrilineal *chibal* institutions, included nobles as well as commoners (D. Chase 1986:349; Roys 1943:35). Patricia McAnany (1995) similarly rallies historical information regarding the social status heterogeneity of coresidential lineage group compounds.

This chapter focuses primarily on the notion of economic class in Postclassic Maya society. Evidence suggests that opportunities for entrepreneurship were abundant and that communities of all size scales participated in a burgeoning maritime market economy (Freidel and Sabloff 1984; Sabloff and Rathje 1975a, 1975b). Social mobility based on economic affluence was likely fluid. Many activities of economic production and exchange do not distinguish the households of elites and commoners. Social (rather than economic) elites maintained their distinctions much in the manner of Maya elites prior to the Postclassic period—through investment in domestic and ritual architecture and through the control of important calendrical ceremonies celebrated at Maya communities. Most probably, they also helped maintain their polities by hosting ritual activities essential to intercommunity integration, forging alliances external to their polities, and perhaps organizing major market events. As summarized by Diane Chase (1986:349), "The nobles [of Postclassic Yucatán society] were not only the ruling class, but were also the most important and/or wealthiest warriors, priests, farmers, and merchants. While commoners could be wealthy too, they were reportedly separated from the true nobility by their lack of knowledge concerning ritual." This trend is exactly that identified at Caye Coco and Laguna de On, described below.

It is not known to what extent affluent commoners could have crossed the line to become social elites with enough wealth or military support, and this process is worthy of consideration and further investigation. Social and economic capital are complementary resources that define class, and possession of economic capital can often open a back door toward upward mobility or form a dialectical relationship to upper social classes. The rise of merchant elites posed a challenge to the sociopolitical nobility of ancient Europe (Eisenstadt 1981; Gailey and Patterson 1987; Wolf 1982). As Christine Gailey and Thomas Patterson (1987:8) explicitly state, ". . . in state societies where several unproductive classes emerge, e.g., merchants and landowners, their continued existence may challenge the interests of the ruling class." A dialectic approach identifies such contradictions and relations that produce social forms (McGuire 1992). At various points in Maya history, similar conflicts likely existed among interest groups of varying social and economic standing.

Maya Economic Organization

Much has been written about the organization of Maya economy during the Classic period, though more research is needed to clarify lingering controversies. Recently, scholars (A. Chase 1998; Masson and Freidel 2002; Sheets 2000) have argued for a greater degree of integration of the "utilitarian economies" of smaller settlements in the countryside with central cities in their midst. In contrast, other scholars have argued for a relatively autonomous countryside economy, in which villages and towns engaged in production of the commodities of daily life (such as ceramics or lithic tools) for their own use and for exchange with other nearby small communities. This utilitarian realm is thought by some to have been relatively separate from a realm of elite exchange that supported Maya kingdoms (McAnany 1993; Rice 1987). An elite exchange network was based on gifts and tribute of fine, exotic crafts. Although elites are viewed as consumers of utilitarian production (McAnany 1989; Rice 1987), their role in the distribution of these commodities is not well understood.

Some models of Maya economy continue to stress exchange or tribute of elite prestige goods as the primary economic foundation of political centers (Ball 1993; Blanton et al. 1996; Reents-Budet 1994). Elite exchange is considered separate and distinct from utilitarian exchange, involving the production of specific commodities for different consumer-class destinations (Hester and Shafer 1994; McAnany 1993; Rice 1987). While luxury and utilitarian commodities may have had different value, and some of the former were obtained as gifts or tribute, it is likely that exchange among elites, commoners, and those in between involved both categories of items (Freidel 1986; Sheets 2000). David Freidel et al. (2002) argue that luxury items simply had greater value within a currency system of goods in Maya society. These scholars follow up on Freidel's earlier arguments to this effect. Referring to cacao, salt, and cotton, Freidel (1986: 414–415) notes, "These goods provide a material link between the household and the palace, the village and the center. If these goods served as currencies in earlier periods, as most of them did at the time of contact, they would have provided a practical means of controlling a very much wider range of goods and services connected to them by equivalency." Prudence Rice (1987) has discussed the changes in value that long-distance items undergo over time, based on factors such as changing availability. Locally made luxury items also can exhibit distributional transformations based on changing social and economic conditions (LeCount 1999; Rice 1987). Geographic location is also a variable that affects value, as has long been noted (Graham 2002; Renfrew 1975). For example, marine shell commodities likely held a lower place in commercial value systems of coastal areas than in systems deep in the interior. Similarly, Colha chert may have been much more highly valued at interior sites than in northern Belize (Gibson 1989; Potter 1993).

Alternatively, the same distributional evidence that has been used for the autonomous commoner production model can be used to argue for a highly integrated political economy for Classic period Maya kingdoms. Since members of all social tiers, from political center to agrarian hamlet, possess those utilitarian items made in the countryside, centralized market exchange is one mechanism that could have facilitated such generalized distributions (A. Chase 1998; West 2002). Richard Blanton et al. (1993:182, 221) argue for the probability of a market economy within Maya kingdoms during the Classic period, and they suggest that interregional commercialized market economies develop in the Postclassic period.

State economies in the Maya region have been evaluated according to a highland Mexico model in which evidence for the control of utilitarian production is weighed heavily in considering the economic foundation of central kingdoms. Evidence does not suggest that Maya kings were overseeing the production of daily items en masse for all members of society in their neighborhoods (McAnany 1993; Rice 1987). They may, however, have organized markets that facilitated the exchange of utilitarian wares and provided a venue for tribute collection (A. Chase 1998; Dahlin and Ardren 2002; Freidel 1986). In essence, they may have controlled gateways to distribution, in the form of markets, rather than production itself. The scale of one highland model at Teotihuacán for centralized production has been challenged (Clark 1986), and much production associated with the Aztec Empire also occurred in the countryside and was articulated through overlapping distributional mechanisms such as tribute and markets (Berdan 1988). David Freidel (1981) suggested this alternative for the Classic period Maya two decades ago. He argued that the control of regional markets, where products made throughout the countryside were exchanged, represented a far more complex economic organization for Maya kingdoms than other Mesoamerican case studies where production was more nucleated at central cities. Such markets may have been strategically timed with ritual calendrical celebrations (Freidel 1981). Arlen Chase (1998) and Georgia West (2002) have recently revisited this model, rallying settlement and artifactual evidence respectively for a "solar" marketing system for Classic period Maya economy. Bruce Dahlin and Traci Ardren (2002) use similar settlement evidence to that of Caracol (A. Chase 1998) to propose that Chunchucmil of northwest Yucatán was a Classic period market town.

The evidence for such organization is circumstantial. Although sourcing studies of Maya utilitarian ceramics do indicate dispersed community production in the hinterlands of major centers (Fry 1980; Rands and Bishop 1980; Rice 1987), consumer contexts of these items indicate that they were widely distributed throughout households of all social tiers in communities of varying political importance. The degree of distribution through market exchange can be measured by the comparison of household inventories (Hirth 1998; Smith 1999), practically irrespective of production location. More evidence is needed to evaluate these distributions so that the mechanisms of their exchange can be reconstructed. One hindrance to the identification of markets is the lack of references to them in Classic period political texts and images, which primarily describe the receipt of tribute or royal gifts at Maya courts (Foias 2002; McAnany et al. 2002; Reents-Budet 1994). However, household distributional studies can provide an independent archaeological method for evaluating economic exchange systems, and much work remains to be done in this area.

In the history of the social sciences, the notion of autonomous commoners (or utilitarian producers, in our case) played a vital role in distinguishing folk/urban and traditional/modern characteristics (Wolf 1982: 12–13). Eric Wolf has argued that the identification of autonomous cultural sectors is artificial and fails to take into account the complexity of greater world contexts of individual societies, communities, or social classes and their systemic interactions and connections with other social entities (1982:19). This argument rings true for the autonomous commoner model for the Maya.

Wolf (1982:19–23) and Randall McGuire (1992), following Karl Marx, take a historical approach and advocate that we toss out universal models of a single mode of production and instead investigate variation in local configurations of material relationships. The processes of class formation and maintenance in states are dialectically opposed to the autonomous integrity of kin-based communities, as states strive to extract support for nonproducing classes (Gailey and Patterson 1987:8). This dialectic represents the struggle of interests between members of state societies, with varying degrees of subordinate, exploitative relations between classes or resistance to such relations. As Gailey and Patterson (1987:10) note, "Subject classes are only partly in control of the conditions in which they conduct their lives. This does not mean, however, that they are completely without power or control over their existence." Applying this advice to the Maya case, some commoners may have been more autonomous than others, and we must examine local degrees of integration into tiers of local political networks (e.g., Yaeger and Robin, this volume), broader networks over the Maya area, and networks connecting the Maya area with other interacting polities. Our challenge is to quantify and explain these differences in light of the temporal and geographic dynamics of political economies.

The analysis of households, as a fundamental unit in Maya economic and social production, can provide clues toward the organization of class and economy (Arnold 1991; Hirth 1998; Rathje 1983; Santley and Hirth 1993; Smith 1999; Smith and Heath-Smith 1994; Wilk and Ashmore 1988). Two classes of settlement data are traditionally used to evaluate social or political standing: the relative size of structures within a site and the relative size of settlements within a region. Smaller dwellings or dwellings at smaller settlements in the Maya area sometimes have inventory lists that overlap with those at certain larger dwellings or dwellings at larger settlements (Gonlin, this volume). Shared inventory lists suggest that valuables trickled down to members of lower classes (Freidel 1986), but the key question in a diachronic analysis of Maya economy is, how many of the highly valued items are present across social tiers? Kenneth Hirth's (1998) distributional model suggests that the greater the amount of highly valued items that are found in houses of all sizes (reflecting members of all social status groups) within a community (or region), then the greater the development of their market economy. The reasoning behind this proposition is that market development is a major mechanism that makes luxury or long-distance items generally available to individuals of any social class. Through market development, such products can also be more affordable and in greater supply. Quantitative differences are still to be expected, with upper social classes possessing the means to acquire greater quantities of highly valued items. However, where market development is significant, these quantitative differences are substantially reduced (Hirth 1998; Smith 1999).

In recent works, Richard Blanton and colleagues (Blanton 1998; Blanton et al. 1996) identify alternative forms of state political economies, termed *network* and *corporate* formations. These models revise previous evolutionary anthropology models for measuring societal complexity. Network societies described by Blanton et al. (1996), like the Classic period Maya, have political economies that rely to a greater extent on luxury-item exchange and the use of luxury items to symbolize the prestige of political leaders. Corporate societies, sometimes correlated with more open market economies, tend to de-emphasize charismatic characteristics of individual political leaders and opt instead for institutional or group-oriented symbols of power. In such corporate formations, luxury items may thus be less strictly monopolized through elite exchange networks and may be more readily obtained by members of all social tiers (Blanton 1998; Blanton et al. 1996). Some aspects of the corporate model appear to fit the Postclassic period Maya political doctrine and political economy (Blanton et al. 1996; Masson 2000).

We suspect that household inventories from the Classic to Postclassic periods (in general) reflect a qualitative and quantitative shift, with more highly valued items appearing in households of all sizes (and social classes) during the Postclassic period compared to the Classic period. Jeremy Sabloff and William Rathje (Rathje 1975; Rathje et al. 1978; Sabloff and Rathje 1975a, 1975b), in their initial outline of the mercantile model, suggest that producers kept more of the surplus (profit) of their labor in the absence of tyrannical kingly wars to fight or massive temples to build during the Postclassic period. Such surplus was thus reinvested into economic institutions such as market exchange (for a more recent discussion, see Kepecs 1998, 2003). This trend, coupled with the amplification of a maritime trade network that created markets for utilitarian and subsistence items across a wider Yucatecan sphere—with the means to transport them in bulk via maritime canoes—culminated in greater overall social affluence and prospects for upward mobility, according to these authors. Thus, "commoner" producers had greater means to acquire highly valued items and to accumulate wealth than their predecessors who lived under the authority of powerful Classic period city-states.

Class Expression at Postclassic Maya Sites

Evidence from the Postclassic Maya sites of Laguna de On, Caye Coco, and Mayapán supports and refines the arguments of Sabloff and Rathje (Rathje 1975; Rathje et al. 1978; Sabloff and Rathje 1975a, 1975b). These sites represent three different scales of site sizes of varying political significance from the eastern and northwestern Maya lowlands. Laguna de On and Caye Coco are located in northeastern Belize. Laguna de On represents a small settlement of lesser political significance, as no mounded architecture or stone monuments were found at this site. This lagoon settlement consists of an island site (175 × 60 m) at the lagoon's north end and associated lagoon-side occupations extending for 1 km on the lagoon's west shore. Caye Coco is an island political center (200 × 400 m) located 20 km to the north of Laguna de On at Progresso Lagoon. It is also associated with a shore settlement that extends for 3 km along the west shore of the lagoon, and smaller occupied islands on Progresso Lagoon are also contemporary with Caye Coco (Masson 1999b). Mayapán, located in northwestern Yucatán, represents the largest urban center of the Postclassic Maya world. This well-known site was the political capital of a polity located in this region that retained alliances with east coast polities of the Yucatán Peninsula (Pollock 1962; Roys 1962). The northeastern Belize region was part of one of these allied polities, the Chetumal Province (Roys 1957).

Social status is expressed at all three of these sites in the form of more elaborate and larger residential architecture and the monopolization of particular ritual paraphernalia, as discussed in previous publications (Masson 1999a, 1999b, 1999c, 2000). This trend closely follows that observed by Diane Chase (1986:356) at Santa Rita, who states, "There is no direct archaeological evidence for occupational difference between classes at Santa Rita Corozal with the exception of ritual activity."

Laguna de On

The island settlements of Laguna de On and Caye Coco were probably the political nuclei of their associated lagoon communities, as the greatest evidence for construction projects and ritual activity is found on these islands. At Laguna de On, a platform shrine and patio complex is located at the island's highest point (Structure II). A three-sided residential structure (Structure I) was located a few meters to the south of this shrine.

A possible sunken ballcourt cut into limestone bedrock is at the north end of the island (Masson 2000). Much of the eastern edge of the island represents an artificially constructed terrace of soil fill (brought by canoe from the lagoon shore) that is retained by a stone wall. Two other islands on the lagoon are the locations of mounds constructed of lagoon sand. Evidence of smashed censers and sacrificed animals was found at Structure I, and Thomas Gann (1928) collected numerous similar offerings from the surface of Structure II. A small shrine was also located on the lagoon's west shore (Suboperation 11). These three contexts were the only locations where censer ceramics were found, suggesting control of ritual by a few individuals (Masson 1999b, 1999c). The inventory of elite residential Structure I is otherwise quite similar to all other domestic zones tested on the island and shore, with the exception of marine shell debris, which is more abundant than at other contexts. The limited distributions of ritual artifacts (including sacrificed animal remains) and shrine structures distinguish a potential social class of elites at Laguna de On from other family groups.

Marine shell ornament-making debris and obsidian arrow points also are located in larger quantities in the vicinity of Structure I than at other locations (Masson 2000: Table 5.22, 130). Despite this fact, marine shell debris represents only 2 percent of the sample of artifacts at the site (this percentage was calculated from the total number of artifacts occurring in low numbers, which excludes ceramics, lithic flakes, and faunal bones, Masson 2000: Figure 5.21). Luxury items such as miniature greenstone axes, exotic mineral beads, and long-distance goods such as obsidian are evenly distributed among all domestic zones and do not distinguish elite residential areas (Masson 2000: Table 5.23, Figure 5.15).

Domestic industries such as weaving, pottery making, fish and meat processing, food production, and flintknapping also occurred at all locations tested. At Laguna de On, obsidian forms 71 percent of the Postclassic lithic tool assemblage (including both obsidian and non-obsidian tools; Masson 2002; Masson and Chaya 2000). This fact suggests that residents of this island relied heavily on long-distance items for daily tasks and that these items were readily accessible and affordable.

Caye Coco

Residential architecture is quite large at Caye Coco compared to Laguna de On, with structures measuring up to 4 m high and 20 m wide at the base

(Rosenswig and Masson 2002). In contrast, Structure II at Laguna de On is only 50 cm in height, and Structure I is a single course wall alignment (Masson 1999c, 2000). Elite structures at Laguna de On are dwarfed by those at Caye Coco, with the exception of lagoon sand island platforms at Laguna de On that are around 3 m in height. This analysis of elite versus commoner signatures is thus a relative one, considering the relationships between community leaders and other family groups within each site respectively. This approach is perhaps justified according to ethnohistorical information regarding Maya political structure. Political hierarchies were distributed horizontally across communities, with larger centers hosting regional lords and supporting communities hosting tribute collectors or other forms of lower-tier administrators that integrated them into polity centers (Adams and Smith 1981:338–339; D. Chase 1986; Marcus 1993; Roys 1957).

Despite the differences in scale, the same general patterns that distinguish elite community leaders are observed at Caye Coco as at Laguna de On. Larger and more elaborate residential architecture is the most obvious criterion. Small shrine rooms are located at elite residences at Caye Coco, suggesting control of ritual (Masson 1999b). Marine shell ornament-making debris is also far more common at elite residences or middens associated with them than at other off-mound locations at the site (Masson 1999b, 2002, 2003). Far more marine shell is observed at Caye Coco than at Laguna de On. At Caye Coco, marine shell forms 12 percent of the late-facet assemblage of artifacts occurring in low numbers at the site (all artifact categories excluding ceramics, lithic flakes, and faunal bone; Masson 2002: Figure 12.8), compared to only 2 percent at Laguna de On (discussed above). Marine shell working is thus associated with elites at the more politically significant center of Caye Coco than at the less significant Laguna de On (Masson 2002: Figure 12.9). Obsidian arrow points are almost exclusively found at the site's one public building, a long structure at the top of the island that was probably a council house for the elite family groups occupying the island. Diane Chase (1986) similarly notes the association of ritual features with high-status families at Santa Rita, and she draws analogies to Landa's account of the hosting of ritual festivities at various homes of upper-class individuals within Colonial period Maya communities. Obsidian blades form 64 percent of all obsidian and non-obsidian lithic tools of Caye Coco. As for Laguna de On, this proportion indicates heavy reliance on a long-distance resource for household activities at Caye Coco. Little variation is observed in the proportion of obsidian among households at either site, suggesting all community members could easily obtain this item, probably through markets (Masson 2002; Masson and Chaya 2000).

Mayapán

At Mayapán, it has long been noted that monumental political and ritual architecture is concentrated near the site's center, in Square Q of the Carnegie Map (D. Chase 1992: Figure 8.4; Jones 1962; Smith 1962:265). Large elite residential platforms and large ritual architecture are located in this vicinity and in adjacent 500 m squares to the east, west, and south. Some anomalous large elite groups (residential and ritual) are located outside the core of this city, notably the Itzmal Chen group. Scholars have argued over the organization of this city, debating Bishop Landa's concentric model that the elites were clustered within the city's core (D. Chase 1992; Marcus 1983). Diane Chase (1992) argues effectively for the presence of additional elite barrios outside Square Q, along with ritual features. Ruling families of northwest Yucatán kept residences within this city, and it was home to other elite specialists such as priests, merchants, and military leaders (Roys 1962). The presence of substantial quantities of large architecture and ritual features across the city attests to the status of such individuals and the city's complex organization. The association of ritual activities with the highest social tiers of this city is not an exclusive one. Carnegie scholars (Smith 1962) noted the presence of smaller ritual features at residences throughout the city. In this general sense, ritual practice is not confined to Mayapán's core-dwelling elites. However, deposits with the largest numbers of censers recovered by the Carnegie were always associated with upper-status houses (e.g., Group R-86, Q-208), temples (e.g., Q-214, Q-126), or colonnaded halls (e.g., Q-81, Q-151) or features in their affiliated compounds (Proskouriakoff and Temple 1955 [R-86]; Shook 1954, 1955 [Q-214, Q-126]; Shook and Irving 1955 [Q-151]; Thompson 1954 [Q-208]; Winters 1955 [Q-81]. Mayapán did house a large proportion of the privileged sector of the population, and it is thought to have been the nucleus of religious teachings for the peninsula (Roys 1962; Tozzer 1941:25–26). Thus, far more ritual features might be expected to occur at this site than in smaller communities of the Postclassic world. Chase (1986) also discusses the anomalous organization of Mayapán compared to smaller Maya centers such as Santa Rita, specifically its distinctive monumental core.

A closer look at the kinds of ritual paraphernalia associated with the site core (Square Q) and other areas of the site does suggest important spatial thematic differences. Sculptures depicting feline figures, human portraits (probably lineage figures), serpents, and stelae are far more common in Square Q than in other parts of the city (Masson 2000:198–210). Outside Square Q, miniature shrines, turtle sculptures, diving figures, and burden-bearing figures are more common. Over half of the turtle sculptures in squares external to Square Q are from the outlying elite group of Itzmal Chen (Masson 2000:211). Elites at Mayapán may thus have controlled most types of religious symbols and rituals, and religious integration may have been achieved by celebration of other types of ritual throughout the city (Masson 2000:198–210).

Preliminary information is available for artifact distributions associated with Mayapán's monumental center and other parts of the city. Clifford Brown (1999) provides important house-group data from outlying areas of the city that reflect occupational specialization in aspects of lithic or ceramic production. Functional and stylistic variation at Mayapán residential groups documented by Brown suggest that household settlement groups were the primary locus of economic production. In 2001, we conducted a subsequent surface survey and collection of residential zones in seven areas of the city (Masson and Peraza 2002). This work provides the basis for some preliminary observations. Surface survey of nine cleared milpa zones across the city revealed sixty-one artifact concentrations associated with residential structures or associated *albarrada* (house-lot wall) enclosures. A 100 percent surface collection was taken from a 28.26 m^2 sample of each concentration, in the form of a dog-leash collection area of 6 m in diameter. These surface materials suggest variation in production and exchange activities across the city.

The most general results of this survey indicate quantitative differences in the amount of artifact debris in residential zones near the city's monumental core (Squares Q, P, R) compared to other neighborhoods near the city's center (Squares Z, AA) and areas more distant from it (Squares EE, X, Y). Far more artifact concentrations, and greater density within artifact concentrations, are found in the Q and P squares near the monumental core compared to other parts of the city (Masson and Peraza 2002). These distributions may signal areas of more intense production or consumption near the city's center, or perhaps market activities. They may also reflect the greater density of occupation in this area. Greater quantities of luxury items such as greenstone and copper are found on the surface of Square Q structures compared to those of other areas, which may identify the greater wealth of city-core-dwelling elites. The largest residential structures and yards were located in Squares Q, P, and R, presumably homes of the most elite members of the city represented within the sampled areas of the 2001 season. One square from outside the city walls is excluded from the artifact frequency comparisons below, as only ceramics were recovered in its concentrations of material.

Obsidian from the total sample of all areas surveyed represents 37.3 percent of all obsidian and non-obsidian (chert) lithic tools recovered. Considerable variation in the distribution of obsidian is observed among the collection areas, in contrast to the trends described above for Laguna de On and Caye Coco. Squares Q and R, in areas quite near the monumental core, had the most obsidian (68.3 percent and 88.9 percent, respectively, of all obsidian and non-obsidian tools). Four other areas were closer to the site average, with obsidian percentages ranging between 31.6 and 50 percent at Squares X, Y, AA, and P. Squares EE and Z had obsidian in proportions ranging from 16.7 to 17.1 percent of all lithic tools, much lower than other areas sampled. Square Z's low percentage is not explained by its distance from the center, as this residential zone is located just south of the monumental core. This pattern may indicate that members of different social standing or occupational specialization dwelt near the city's center.

Two areas in Squares Y and Z had higher proportions of chert flakes (31.4 and 35 percent, respectively) compared to all other areas sampled (between 3.2 and 7.9 percent). Chert flake percentages here are calculated as a proportion of all materials collected from concentrations in each square. Square Z also had higher proportions of chert tools (5.4 percent of all materials collected from this square) compared to all other areas sampled in which chert tools formed between 0.3 and 2.0 percent of the total sample of materials. These data, along with high numbers of chert flakes, may suggest specialization in chert tool manufacture at households in Squares Z and Y, a pattern not uniformly observed across the site (also noted by Brown 1999:582).

Marine shell debris, indicative of shell-ornament manufacture, is present in greater proportions (between 21 and 33 percent) in some squares, including squares near the center (Squares Q, P, AA, with 21, 26, and 33 percent, respectively), and one area that is more distant from the monumental core (Square EE, with 25 percent). Marine shell proportions are calculated here as a percentage of low-frequency artifact classes (such as obsidian, chert tools, and marine shell) that are not abundant in the concentrations. This calculation highlights their relative abundance, as their proportions are dwarfed when expressed as a percentage of all categories of materials, since ceramics form over 58 percent of all surface collections, and over 89 percent of all collections except in Squares Y and Z, which had large numbers of chert flakes. This relative percentage also parallels that calculated for marine shell proportions at Laguna de On and Caye Coco (described above). While central Squares Q and P have some of the largest proportions of marine shell, high proportions are also noted in EE and AA. Marine shell working does not exclusively correlate with those areas presumed to have housed elite families, as it does at the sites in Belize discussed above.

Almost no spindle whorls were recovered in the dog-leash surface concentrations of this study, although they are occasionally found at the site. This pattern suggests this industry was less significant at Mayapán than at northern Belize sites, though larger samples are needed to evaluate the validity of this comparison.

These preliminary data suggest that greater differences in economic production and consumption are observed between residents of varying social standing at Mayapán than at Postclassic sites in northern Belize. Such a trend might be expected for a core capital city. At Mayapán, certain production and exchange activities may have been more tightly controlled by elites than others. The large urban population of this city housed families of considerably greater occupational diversity, which may be reflected in the variation among domestic assemblages discussed above. Perhaps the most striking difference from the northeastern Belize sites is the overall lower proportion of obsidian compared to chert tools at Mayapán. Obsidian forms just over one-third of the lithic assemblage of this sample, compared to almost two-thirds of the Caye Coco assemblage and almost three-fourths of the Laguna de On assemblage. Perhaps Mayapán's more distant location from the highland source of Ixtepeque (Braswell 2003; Masson and Chaya 2000) affected the availability of obsidian to various occupants of this site. However, some residential zones near the city core had over twice the proportion of obsidian as other areas, suggesting that families of means were able to obtain this preferred resource for use in household activities. Chert tool making, not monopolized by elites at Mayapán, was apparently a significant local industry there. Marine shell is present in higher proportions at Mayapán than at the Belize sites, despite Mayapán's greater distance from the coast. Perhaps members of this city were more extensively involved in manufacturing currency-type items such as shell jewelry than their hinterland cohorts. Our preliminary evidence does not exclusively correlate this activity with the site core, however, and more work is needed to investigate this and other spatial trends outlined here.

Discussion and Conclusions

The identification of commoners versus elites in this study is undertaken on a site-by-site basis. Commoners did not host community rituals at their dwellings at Laguna de On and Caye Coco, though they likely participated in calendrical festivities organized and hosted by elites. D. Chase's (1986) observation that elite social status is most strongly indicated archaeologically by its association with ritual is confirmed by the patterns observed at Laguna de On and Caye Coco. This archaeological pattern does not mean that commoners were not reverent or may not have performed small-scale rituals with perishable materials, as observed in some ethnographic cases today (Gossen and Leventhal 1993; Vogt 1976). The control of constructed ritual features and certain types of paraphernalia by Postclassic Maya elites is indicated at the northeastern Belize sites and at Mayapán (D. Chase 1992; Masson 2000; Proskouriakoff 1962). Ritual was not practiced primarily at the household level, as scholars once thought (Pollock 1962:17; Proskouriakoff 1962:136; Thompson 1957:624), as the smallest, most ubiquitous dwelling types at Mayapán seldom have altars or censers. This assumption was also challenged by investigations at Cozumel, where evidence suggests that ritual features were carefully placed for public use (Freidel and Sabloff 1984:183–184). Although the Carnegie project gained an important place in history for its dwelling excavations, the majority of houses investigated were not those of the poorest residents of the city. Smith's and Ruppert's investigations more commonly targeted larger multiroom dwellings or oratories (Ruppert and Smith 1952, 1954; Smith and Ruppert 1953, 1956; Chowning and Thompson 1956; Thompson 1954).

Evidence for autonomous commoner production and exchange is not observed at Postclassic Maya sites, as some of the most common long-distance commodities were those destined for household consumption. Historic sources suggest that members of all communities geared their production toward local and regional markets throughout Yucatán (Pina Chan 1978). In exchange, they obtained goods used in daily life from communities located a long distance away. Commoners at northeastern Belize sites appear to conform to an entrepreneurial model in which they likely participated directly in regional market exchange with the surplus of their labors that remained after fulfilling the tribute demands of local polities. Commoners contributed significantly to a Pan-Yucatecan exchange system that was facilitated through elite diplomatic and organizational efforts (Roys 1962). Their contributions lie in the production of valuable exchange commodities, such as cotton and cacao that were coveted in distant parts of the Maya area, as well as materials destined for their own consumption and exchange with neighboring sites, such as pottery, stone tools, raw materials, or subsistence goods (Masson 2003). Substantial perishable commodities that are difficult to detect in the archaeological record were shipped out of northeast Belize/southeast Quintana Roo; these include cotton, cacao, honey, forest products (such as canoes from Bacalar), and other items (Jones 1989; Pina Chan 1978). In exchange, they relied on maritime trading networks for abundant quantities of obsidian (clearly visible archaeologically) and probably salt and other perishables (Kepecs 1998, 2003). The long-distance exchange of everyday items that profoundly affected commoner households is a singular hallmark of the Postclassic period. This maritime capacity for bulk transport of utilitarian goods is perhaps the most important variable in the development of a widely integrated mercantile economy that is characteristic of this period (Blanton et al. 1993; Rathje 1975; Rathje et al. 1978; Sabloff and Rathje 1975a, 1975b). In this sense, the production of utilitarian commodities and market valuables (cotton and cacao) by Postclassic commoners was an integral, essential component to the Maya economic world.

The association of Belize subregion elites with shell jewelry production may attest to their occupations as merchants, since shell items were one form of currency used in Postclassic markets (Freidel 1986; Freidel et al. 2002). Perhaps elite shell manufacture was one form of making money. Southern Yucatecan provinces such as those in northeastern Belize also made money grow on trees, quite literally, in the form of cacao production. Historic references cite the cacao orchard holdings by social elites in this area at Contact period (Jones 1989; McAnany 1995; Pina Chan 1978; Roys 1962).

The existence of a Postclassic Maya elite social class whose members maintained themselves through diplomatic activities (Roys 1962), integrative festival/market enterprises (Freidel 1981, 1986), and money manufacture (Freidel et al. 2002; Masson 2003) is supported by historical and archaeological evidence, as summarized above. A definition of a Postclassic commoner class as those "other" individuals who did not engage in such activities is unsatisfying and simplistic. The archaeological record reflects greater complexity of economic, occupational, and social standing, and we need a better understanding of the possibilities for mobility in Postclassic society within different polities across the lowlands.

The distribution of many classes of material in households of all sizes implies that opportunities for economic affluence may have been fluid for some non-elites. Along with such affluence, perhaps the prospects of upward social mobility that often accompany mercantile development in cross-cultural cases (Eisenstadt 1981) were also promising for some Postclassic Maya entrepreneurs.

At Mayapán, a heterogeneous set of production and exchange activities across the city is suggested by a preliminary look at spatial artifact distributions. The proportion of obsidian at the site as a whole implies obsidian was less important in the daily activities of every domestic context at the site compared to households in Belize. It was present, however, in significant quantities and formed a major component of household inventories at many areas sampled. Privileged citizens of the city were able to obtain nearly triple the quantities of this distant material than other residents. Some, but not all, residential zones near the city have more obsidian, and this trend supports Diane Chase's (1986) suggestion that the presence of lineage groups composed of members of different social or economic status is observed in the archaeological neighborhoods (house-lot clusters, barrios) at Mayapán and other Postclassic sites. Marine shell working and shell ornaments are more common at Mayapán than at our Belize sites, a pattern that may reflect its use as a currency in the city's markets referred to in historic accounts. If the patterns described here are accurate, the manufacture of shell ornaments was not exclusively controlled by elites dwelling at the city's core. This trend provides further support for the view that Mayapán's settlement organization was not simply concentric (D. Chase 1986), and it may imply that the industry of shell working was not fully centralized. Among the city's occupants were craft specialists, including chert tool makers (see also Brown 1999), and the ubiquitous nature of chert debris at some residential groups in the city suggests that this was one of its important local industries. The association of elites with ritual features, as observed at other Postclassic Maya sites, is indicated by the correlation of certain sculptural themes, murals, and massive censer deposits with the site center or outlying high-ranking contexts.

The activities of Maya commoners described here for Laguna de On, Caye Coco, and Mayapán represent a limited view of social and economic realities for the Postclassic period. Examining the interplay between occupational specialization, economic affluence, and social status is an important question raised by the editors of this volume. The trends described here find important similarities in economic and social-class indicators at two sites in Belize, where elites elevated themselves through a bottleneck of privileged knowledge and information. The control of knowledge by Postclassic elites preserved for them the prerogative to organize ritual, diplomatic, and probably mercantile events that justified their tribute demands and claims to resources such as lavish orchards or farmlands. Other than ritual features and larger residences, the material threshold that separated one class from the other was blurred. More work is needed to examine how affluent commoners might have crossed this social boundary. Mayapán's preliminary data suggest a more complex picture. The city was home to many elites and specialists of varying status levels, and the site's material record suggests greater inequalities among residents of the city and, perhaps, a more rigorous class structure based on amplified control of ritual, diplomatic, and mercantile networks. Identifying the dialectical conditions of Postclassic Maya class structure at this site will take many more years of careful investigation.

References

Adams, Richard E. W., and Woodruff D. Smith

1981 Feudal Models for Classic Maya Civilization. In *Lowland Maya Settlement Patterns*, edited by Wendy Ashmore, pp. 335–350. University of New Mexico Press, Albuquerque.

Arnold, Phillip J., III

1991 *Domestic Ceramic Production and Spatial Organization.* Cambridge University Press, Cambridge.

Ball, Joseph W.

1993 Pottery, Potters, Palaces, and Polities: Some Socioeconomic and Political Implications of Late Classic Maya Ceramic Industries. In *Lowland Maya Civilization in the Eighth Century A.D.*, edited by Jeremy A. Sabloff and John S. Henderson, pp. 243–272. Dumbarton Oaks, Washington, D.C.

Barrera Vásquez, Alfredo, and Sylvanus Griswold Morley

1949 *The Maya Chronicles.* Contributions to American Anthropology and History, vol. 10, no. 48. Carnegie Institution of Washington Publication 585. Washington, D.C.

Berdan, Frances F.

1988 Principles of Regional and Long-Distance Trade in the Aztec Empire. In *Smoke and Mist: Mesoamerican Studies in Memory of Thelma D. Sulli-*

van, edited by J. Kathryn Josserand and Karen Dakin, pp. 639–656. BAR International Series 402. British Archaeological Reports, Oxford.

Blanton, Richard E.

1998 Beyond Centralization: Steps toward a Theory of Egalitarian Behavior in Archaic States. In *Archaic States*, edited by Gary M. Feinman and Joyce Marcus, pp. 135–172. School of American Research Press, Santa Fe.

Blanton, Richard E., Gary M. Feinman, Stephen A. Kowalewski, and Peter N. Peregrine

1996 A Dual-Processual Theory for the Evolution of Mesoamerican Civilization. *Current Anthropology* 37(1):1–14.

Blanton, Richard E., Stephen A. Kowalewski, Gary M. Feinman, and Laura M. Finsten

1993 *Ancient Mesoamerica: A Comparison of Change in Three Regions*. 2nd ed. Cambridge University Press, Cambridge.

Braswell, Geoffrey E.

2003 Obsidian Exchange Spheres. In *The Postclassic Mesoamerican World*, edited by Michael E. Smith and Frances Berdan, pp. 131–158. University of Utah Press, Salt Lake City.

Brown, Clifford T.

1999 Mayapán Society and Ancient Maya Social Organization. Ph.D. diss., Department of Anthropology, Tulane University, New Orleans.

Chase, Arlen F.

1992 Elites and the Changing Organization of Classic Maya Society. In *Mesoamerican Elites: An Archaeological Assessment*, edited by Diane Z. Chase and Arlen F. Chase, pp. 30–49. University of Oklahoma Press, Norman.

1998 Planeación cívica e integración de sitio en Caracol, Belize: Definiendo una economía administrada del período Clásico maya. *Los investigaciones de la cultura maya* 6 (Tomo 1), pp. 26–44. Secud, Universidad Autónoma de Campeche, Campeche, Mexico.

Chase, Diane Z.

1986 Social and Political Organization in the Land of Cacao and Honey: Correlating the Archaeology and Ethnohistory of the Postclassic Lowland Maya. In *Late Lowland Maya Civilization: Classic to Postclassic*, edited by Jeremy A. Sabloff and E. Wyllys Andrews V, pp. 347–377. University of New Mexico Press, Albuquerque.

1992 Postclassic Maya Elites: Ethnohistory and Archaeology. In *Mesoamerican Elites: An Archaeological Assessment*, edited by Diane Z. Chase and Arlen F. Chase, pp. 118–134. University of Oklahoma Press, Norman.

Chowning, Ann, and Donald E. Thompson

1956 A Dwelling and Shrine at Mayapán. *Current Reports* 33:425–442. Carnegie Institution of Washington, Department of Archaeology, Washington, D.C.

Clark, John E.

1986 From Mountains to Molehills: A Critical Review of Teotihuacán's Obsidian Industry. In *Research in Economic Anthropology Supplement 2*, edited by Barry L. Isaac, pp. 23–74. JAI Press, Greenwich.

Dahlin, Bruce, and Traci Ardren
2002 Modes of Exchange and Their Effects on Regional and Urban Patterns at Chunchucmil, Yucatán, Mexico. In *Ancient Maya Political Economies*, edited by Marilyn A. Masson and David A. Freidel, pp. 249–284. Altamira Press, Walnut Creek, California.

Earle, Timothy
1997 *How Chiefs Come to Power: The Political Economy in Prehistory.* Stanford University Press, Stanford.

Eisenstadt, Shmuel N.
1981 Cultural Traditions and Political Dynamics: The Origins and Modes of Ideological Politics. *British Journal of Sociology* 32:155–181.

Foias, Antonia E.
2002 At the Crossroads: The Economic Basis of Political Power in the Petexbatún Region, Southwest Petén, Guatemala. In *Ancient Maya Political Economies*, edited by Marilyn A. Masson and David Freidel, pp. 223–248. Altamira Press, Walnut Creek, California.

Freidel, David A.
1981 The Political Economics of Residential Dispersion among the Lowland Maya. In *Lowland Maya Settlement Patterns*, edited by Wendy Ashmore, pp. 371–382. University of New Mexico Press, Albuquerque.
1986 Terminal Classic Lowland Maya: Successes, Failures, and Aftermaths. In *Late Lowland Maya Civilization: Classic to Postclassic*, edited by Jeremy A. Sabloff and E. Wyllys Andrews V, pp. 409–430. University of New Mexico Press, Albuquerque.

Freidel, David A., and Jeremy A. Sabloff
1984 *Cozumel: Late Maya Settlement Patterns.* Academic Press, New York.

Freidel, David A., Kathryn Reese-Taylor, and David Mora Marin
2002 The Old Shell Game: Commodity, Treasure, and Kingship in the Origins of Maya Civilization. In *Ancient Maya Political Economies*, edited by Marilyn A. Masson and David Freidel, pp. 41–86. Altamira Press, Walnut Creek, California.

Fry, Robert E.
1980 Models of Exchange for Major Shape Classes of Lowland Maya Pottery. In *Models and Methods in Regional Exchange*, edited by Robert E. Fry, pp. 3–18. SAA Papers 1. Society for American Archaeology, Washington, D.C.

Gailey, Christine W., and Thomas C. Patterson
1987 *Power Relations and State Formation.* American Anthropological Association, Washington, D.C.

Gann, Thomas
1928 *Maya Cities.* Self-published, London and New York.

Gibson, Eric C.
1989 The Organization of Late Preclassic Maya Lithic Economy in the Eastern Lowlands. In *Prehistoric Maya Economies of Belize*, edited by Patri-

cia A. McAnany and Barry L. Isaac, pp. 115–138. Research in Economic Anthropology Supplement 4. JAI Press, Greenwich.

Gossen, Gary H., and Richard M. Leventhal

1993 The Topography of Ancient Maya Religious Pluralism. In *Lowland Maya Archaeology in the Eighth Century A.D.*, edited by Jeremy A. Sabloff and John S. Henderson, pp. 185–218. Dumbarton Oaks, Washington, D.C.

Graham, Elizabeth

2002 Perspectives on Economy and Theory. In *Ancient Maya Political Economies*, edited by Marilyn A. Masson and Favid A. Freidel, pp. 398–418. Altamira Press, Walnut Creek, California.

Haviland, William A., and Hattula Moholy-Nagy

1992 Distinguishing the High and Mighty from the Hoi Polloi at Tikal, Guatemala. In *Mesoamerican Elites: An Archaeological Assessment*, edited by Diane Z. Chase and Arlen F. Chase, pp. 50–60. University of Oklahoma Press, Norman.

Hester, Thomas R., and Harry J. Shafer

1994 The Ancient Maya Craft Community at Colha, Belize, and Its External Relationships. In *Archaeological Views from the Countryside: Village Communities in Early Complex Societies*, edited by Glenn M. Schwartz and Steven E. Falconer, pp. 48–63. Smithsonian Institution Press, Washington, D.C.

Hirth, Kenneth

1998 The Distributional Approach. *Current Anthropology* 40:520–527.

Jones, Grant D.

1989 *Maya Resistance to Spanish Rule: Time and History on a Colonial Frontier.* University of New Mexico Press, Albuquerque.

Jones, Morris

1962 Map of Mayapán. In *Mayapan, Yucatan, Mexico*, edited by Harry E. D. Pollock, Ralph L. Roys, Tatiana Proskouriakoff, and A. Ledyard Smith. Carnegie Institution of Washington Publication 619. Washington, D.C.

Kepecs, Susan

1998 Diachronic Ceramic Evidence and Its Social Implications in the Chikinchel Region, Northeast Yucatán, Mexico. *Ancient Mesoamerica* 9(1):121–136.

2003 Chikinchel. In *The Postclassic Mesoamerican World*, edited by Michael E. Smith and Frances F. Berdan, pp. 259–268. University of Utah Press, Salt Lake City.

King, Eleanor, and Daniel R. Potter

1994 Small Sites in Prehistoric Maya Socioeconomic Organization: A Perspective from Colha, Belize. In *Archaeological Views from the Countryside: Village Communities in Early Complex Societies*, edited by Glenn M. Schwartz and Steven E. Falconer, pp. 64–90. Smithsonian Institution Press, Washington, D.C.

LeCount, Lisa
1999 Polychrome Pottery and Political Strategies in Late and Terminal Classic Lowland Maya Society. *Latin American Antiquity* 10(3):239–258.

Mann, Michael
1986 *The Sources of Social Power, Volume I: A History of Power from the Beginning to A.D. 1760.* Cambridge University Press, Cambridge.

Marcus, Joyce
1983 On the Nature of the Mesoamerican City. In *Prehistoric Settlement Patterns: Essays in Honor of Gordon R. Willey*, edited by Evon Z. Vogt and Richard M. Leventhal, pp. 195–242. University of New Mexico Press, Albuquerque.
1992 Royal Families, Royal Texts: Examples from the Zapotec and Maya. In *Mesoamerican Elites: An Archaeological Assessment*, edited by Diane Z. Chase and Arlen F. Chase, pp. 221–241. University of Oklahoma Press, Norman.
1993 Ancient Maya Political Organization. In *Lowland Maya Civilization in the Eighth Century A.D.*, edited by Jeremy Sabloff and John S. Henderson, pp. 111–184. Dumbarton Oaks, Washington, D.C.

Masson, Marilyn A.
1999a The Manipulation of "Staple" and "Status" Faunas at Postclassic Maya Communities. *World Archaeology* 31:93–120.
1999b Postclassic Maya Communities at Progresso Lagoon and Laguna Seca, Northern Belize. *Journal of Field Archaeology* 25:285–306.
1999c Postclassic Maya Ritual at Laguna de On Island, Belize. *Ancient Mesoamerica* 10: 51–68.
2000 *In the Realm of Nachan Kan: Postclassic Maya Archaeology at Laguna de On, Belize.* University of Colorado Press, Boulder.
2002 Postclassic Maya Community Economy and the Mercantile Transformation in Northeastern Belize. In *Ancient Maya Political Economies*, edited by Marilyn A. Masson and David A. Freidel, pp. 335–359. Altamira Press, Walnut Creek, California.
2003 Postclassic Economic Patterns in Northern Belize. In *The Postclassic Mesoamerican World*, edited by Michael E. Smith and Frances F. Berdan, pp. 269–281. University of Utah Press, Salt Lake City.

Masson, Marilyn A., and Henry Chaya
2000 Obsidian Trade Connections at the Postclassic Maya Site of Laguna de On, Belize. *Lithic Technology* 25:135–144.

Masson, Marilyn A., and David Freidel (editors)
2002 *Ancient Maya Political Economies.* Altamira Press, Walnut Creek, California.

Masson, Marilyn A., and Carlos Peraza
2002 Proyecto económica de Mayapán: Informe de la Primera Temporada, 2001. In preparation for submission to Centro INAH, Yucatán.

McAnany, Patricia A.
1989 Economic Foundations of Prehistoric Maya Society: Paradigms and

Concepts. In *Prehistoric Maya Economies of Belize*, edited by Patricia A. McAnany and Barry L. Isaac, pp. 347–372. Research in Economic Anthropology Supplement 4. JAI Press, Greenwich.

1993 The Economics of Social Power and Wealth among Eighth-Century Maya Households. In *Lowland Maya Civilization in the Eighth Century A.D.*, edited by Jeremy Sabloff and John Henderson, pp. 65–90. Dumbarton Oaks, Washington, D.C.

1995 *Living with the Ancestors: Kinship and Kingship in Ancient Maya Society.* University of Texas Press, Austin.

McAnany, Patricia A., Ben S. Thomas, Steven Morandi, Polly A. Peterson, and Eleanor Harrison

2002 Praise the Ajaw and Pass the Kakaw: Xibun Maya and the Political Economy of Cacao. In *Ancient Maya Political Economies*, edited by Marilyn A. Masson and David A. Freidel, pp. 123–139. Altamira Press, Walnut Creek, California.

McGuire, Randall H.

1992 *A Marxist Archaeology.* Academic Press, San Diego.

Pina Chan, Román

1978 Commerce in the Yucatec Peninsula: The Conquest and Colonial Period. In *Mesoamerican Communication Routes and Culture Contacts*, edited by Thomas A. Lee and Carlos Navarrete, pp. 37–48. Papers of the New World Archaeological Foundation 40. Brigham Young University, Provo.

Pollock, Harry E. D.

1962 Introduction. In *Mayapan, Yucatan, Mexico*, edited by Harry E. D. Pollock, Ralph L. Roys, Tatiana Proskouriakoff, and A. Ledyard Smith, pp. 1–23. Carnegie Institution of Washington Publication 619. Washington, D.C.

Potter, Daniel R.

1993 Analytical Approaches to Late Classic Maya Industries. In *Lowland Maya Civilization in the Eighth Century A.D.*, edited by Jeremy Sabloff and John Henderson, pp. 273–298. Dumbarton Oaks, Washington, D.C.

Proskouriakoff, Tatiana

1962 Civic and Religious Structures of Mayapán. In *Mayapan, Yucatan, Mexico*, edited by Harry E. D. Pollock, Ralph L. Roys, Tatiana Proskouriakoff, and A. Ledyard Smith, pp. 87–164. Carnegie Institution of Washington Publication 619. Washington, D.C.

Proskouriakoff, Tatiana, and Charles R. Temple

1955 A Residential Quadrangle—Structures R-85 to R-90. *Current Reports* 29:289–362. Carnegie Institution of Washington, Department of Archaeology, Washington, D.C.

Rands, Robert L., and Ronald L. Bishop

1980 Resource Procurement Zones and Patterns of Ceramic Exchange in the Palenque Region, Mexico. In *Models and Methods in Regional Exchange*, edited By Robert E. Fry, pp. 19–46. SAA Papers 1. Society for American Archaeology, Washington, D.C.

Rathje, William L.

1975 The Last Tango in Mayapán: A Tentative Trajectory of Production-Distribution Systems. In *Ancient Civilization and Trade*, edited by Jeremy A. Sabloff and C. C. Lamberg-Karlovsky, pp. 409–448. University of New Mexico Press, Albuquerque.

1983 To the Salt of the Earth: Some Comments on Household Archaeology among the Maya. In *Prehistoric Settlement Patterns: Essays in Honor of Gordon R. Willey*, edited by Evon Vogt and Richard Leventhal, pp. 23–34. University of New Mexico Press, Albuquerque, and the Peabody Museum of Archaeology and Ethnology, Harvard University, Cambridge.

Rathje, William L., David. A. Gregory, and Frederick M. Wiseman

1978 Trade Models and Archaeological Problems: Classic Maya Examples. In *Mesoamerican Communication Routes and Culture Contacts*, edited by Thomas A. Lee and Carlos Navarrete, pp. 147–175. Papers of the New World Archaeological Foundation 40. Brigham Young University, Provo.

Reents-Budet, Dorie

1994 *Painting the Maya Universe: Royal Ceramics of the Classic Period*. Duke University Press, Durham.

Renfrew, Colin

1975 Trade as Action at a Distance: Questions of Integration and Communication. In *Ancient Civilization and Trade*, edited by Jeremy A. Sabloff and C. C. Lamberg-Karlovsky, pp. 3–59. University of New Mexico Press, Albuquerque.

Rice, Prudence M.

1987 Economic Change in the Lowland Maya Late Classic Period. In *Specialization, Exchange, and Complex Societies*, edited by Elizabeth M. Brumfiel and Timothy K. Earle, pp. 76–85. Cambridge University Press, Cambridge.

Rosenswig, Robert M., and Marilyn A. Masson

2002 Postclassic Maya Monumental Architecture from Caye Coco, Northern Belize. *Ancient Mesoamerica* 13:213–236.

Roys, Ralph L.

1943 *The Indian Background of Colonial Yucatán*. Carnegie Institution of Washington Publication 548. Washington, D.C.

1957 *The Political Geography of the Yucatán Maya*. Carnegie Institution of Washington Publication 613. Washington, D.C.

1962 A Review of Historic Sources for Mayapán. In *Mayapan, Yucatan, Mexico*, edited by Harry E. D. Pollock, Ralph L. Roys, Tatiana Proskouriakoff, and A. Ledyard Smith, pp. 25–86. Carnegie Institution of Washington Publication 619. Washington D.C.

Ruppert, Karl, and A. Ledyard Smith

1952 Excavations in House Mounds at Mayapan. *Current Reports* 4:45–66.

Carnegie Institution of Washington, Department of Archaeology, Washington, D.C.

1954 Excavations in House Mounds at Mayapan: III. *Current Reports* 17:27–52. Carnegie Institution of Washington, Department of Archaeology, Washington, D.C.

Sabloff, Jeremy A., and William L. Rathje (editors)

1975a *Changing Precolumbian Commercial Systems, the 1972–1973 Seasons at Cozumel, Mexico.* Monographs of the Peabody Museum 3. Harvard University Press, Cambridge.

Sabloff, Jeremy A., and William L. Rathje

1975b The Rise of a Maya Merchant Class. *Scientific American* 233:72–82.

Santley, Robert S., and Kenneth G. Hirth (editors)

1993 *Pre-Hispanic Domestic Units in Western Mesoamerica: Studies of the Household, Compound, and Residence.* CRC Press, Boca Raton.

Sheets, Payson

2000 Provisioning the Cerén Household: The Vertical Economy, Village Economy, and Household Economy in the Southeast Maya Periphery. *Ancient Mesoamerica* 11:217–230.

Shook, Edwin M.

1954 Three Temples and Their Associated Structures at Mayapán. *Current Reports* 14: 254–291. Carnegie Institution of Washington, Department of Archaeology, Washington, D.C.

1955 Another Round Temple at Mayapán. *Current Reports* 27:267–280. Carnegie Institution of Washington, Department of Archaeology, Washington, D.C.

Shook, Edwin M., and William N. Irving

1955 Colonnaded Buildings at Mayapán. *Current Reports* 22:127–224. Carnegie Institution of Washington, Department of Archaeology, Washington, D.C.

Smith, A. Ledyard

1962 Residential and Associated Structures at Mayapan. In *Mayapan, Yucatan, Mexico*, edited by Harry E. D. Pollock, Ralph L. Roys, Tatiana Proskouriakoff, and A. Ledyard Smith, pp. 165–320. Carnegie Institution of Washington Publication 619, Washington, D.C.

Smith, A. Ledyard, and Karl Ruppert

1953 Excavations in House Mounds at Mayapan: II. *Current Reports* 10:180–206. Carnegie Institution of Washington, Department of Archaeology, Washington, D.C.

1956 Excavations in House Mounds at Mayapan: IV. *Current Reports* 36:471–528. Carnegie Institution of Washington, Department of Archaeology, Washington, D.C.

Smith, Michael E.

1999 Comment on Hirth's "The Distributional Approach." *Current Anthropology* 40:528–529.

Smith, Michael E., and Cynthia Heath-Smith

1994 Rural Economy in Late Postclassic Morelos. In *Economies and Polities in the Aztec Realm*, edited by Mary G. Hodge and Michael E. Smith, pp. 349–376. Institute for Mesoamerican Studies, State University of New York, Albany.

Smith, Michael E., and Marilyn A. Masson

2000 *The Ancient Civilizations of Mesoamerica: A Reader.* Blackwell Publishers, Malden.

Thompson, J. Eric S.

1954 A Presumed Residence of the Nobility at Mayapan. *Current Reports* 19:71–88. Carnegie Institution of Washington, Department of Archaeology, Washington, D.C.

1957 Deities Portrayed at Mayapan. *Current Reports* 40. Carnegie Institution of Washington, Department of Archaeology, Washington, D.C.

Tozzer, Alfred M.

1941 *Landa's "Relación de las cosas de Yucatan": A Translation* Papers of the Peabody Museum of Archaeology and Ethnology 18. Harvard University, Cambridge.

Vogt, Evon Z.

1976 *Tortillas for the Gods: A Symbolic Analysis of Zinacanteco Rituals.* University of Oklahoma Press, Norman.

West, Georgia

2002 Ceramic Exchange in the Late Classic and Postclassic Maya Lowlands: A Diachronic Approach. In *Ancient Maya Political Economies*, edited by Marilyn A. Masson and David Freidel, pp. 140–196. Altamira Press, Walnut Creek, California.

Wilk, Richard R., and Wendy Ashmore (editors)

1988 *Household and Community in the Mesoamerican Past.* University of New Mexico Press, Albuquerque.

Winters, Howard D.

1955 A Vaulted Temple at Mayapán. *Current Reports* 30:363–379. Carnegie Institution of Washington, Department of Archaeology, Washington, D.C.

Wolf, Eric R.

1982 *Europe and the People without History.* University of California Press, Berkeley.

CHAPTER 10

Methods for Understanding Classic Maya Commoners: Structure Function, Energetics, and More

NANCY GONLIN

In recent years of Maya archaeology, we have witnessed an unprecedented focus on Classic Maya commoners through the excavations of numerous humble house mounds all over the lowlands (Gonlin 1993; Johnston 1994; Kovak n.d.; Lohse 2001; Robin 1999; Sheets 1992). These excavations not only represent another dimension of Classic Maya society but provide the long-needed emphasis on the commoner segment and understanding of the general population, which can reveal much about sociocultural evolution (Freter 1988). Even twenty years ago, an entire volume dedicated to this topic would not have been possible, given the same geographical and theoretical coverage. This new body of data augments classic studies conducted several decades ago (Smith 1962; Wauchope 1934; Willey et al. 1965). However, as much as we now know about Classic Maya commoners, what Edward Thompson (1892:265) said over a century ago—"Of the home life of the humble dwellers there is much yet to be learned"—still applies.

Below are presented some points for consideration for those of us who have enthusiastically embraced excavations of the low-status Classic Maya. There are many approaches to studying Classic Maya commoners (Johnston and Gonlin 1998; see also Lohse and Valdez and Marcus, this volume). But to try to understand the household and the activities within it, the larger community of which the household is a part, socioeconomic organization in general, and the agents of the past, a fundamental pursuit in archaeology remains that of determining structure function (Houston 1998). Whether archaeologists admit it today, we still want to know the answer to the question, What was the function of that building? This question is inherently a part of many excavation strategies, and the pursuit of an answer to it still has relevance, even though we may not approach it as directly as in the past. Whether we are trying to decipher the use of a royal palace (Martin 2001; Webster 2001), the function of a building with a unique architectural signature (Stomper 2001), or the layout of a lonely farmstead (Gonlin 1993)—all of which contain encoded information about Classic Maya culture—we find the question compelling enough to search for an answer. The following discussion will highlight the four Classic Maya sites of Copán, Cerén, Tikal, and Cobá; how researchers at each of these locations have determined the use of architecture; and how the ancient Maya may have used their built environment.

In addition to the main section on the determination of structure function, discussions of the courtyard and the hearth are included in this chapter to emphasize the point that, apart from architecture, much can be learned from features such as these that represent other aspects of the built environment. We still focus on architecture, even though recognition of the importance of ambient space, that is, the house-lot (Killion 1992a, 1992b; Santley and Hirth 1993), and consideration of the larger community (Canuto and Yaeger 2000) are gaining momentum. Other types of approaches discussed here, such as boundary and access analyses, show the insights that can be gained from considering alternate research strategies not commonly employed by Mayanists.

Excavations of Classic Maya commoner houses that were conducted during the 1980s (Gonlin 1993, 1994; Webster et al. 2000; Webster and Gonlin 1988; Webster et al. 1997) form the primary reference point for the present analysis. From 1984 to 1986, eight small rural sites in the Copán Valley, Honduras, were extensively excavated through lateral exposure of architecture and ambient space. While it may be more common to think of low-status sites as physically discrete entities dotting the landscape—the abodes of the farming population—numerous commoners inhabited elite compounds, such as at Copán's urban core, where they probably were employed in a service capacity. Several house mounds of low-status occupants directly connected to elite compounds within the urban core of Copán were excavated by a number of researchers (Diamanti 1991; Gerstle 1987; Hendon 1987; Sheehy 1991; Webster et al. 1998), providing information from both rural and urban contexts.

Information Encoded in Houses

The function and symbol of the house are inseparable, although, analytically, these domains are often treated separately by archaeologists specializing in one theoretical perspective or another. Archaeologists assume that form reflects desired activities (Rapoport 1990:11), and we *expect* to see differences in buildings and their functions. Hence, there are labels such as "temple," "palace," "sweathouse," "kitchen," "residence," and so on. The expectation of finding compartmentalized structures must be met with the reality that, in many cultures, structures are multifunctional. To what extent do we have control over functional overlap of space? The strongest signature of structure function will occur when the building's function has remained the same through time. Since the continuity of function may not be a realistic assumption (e.g., David 1971; Widmer and Sheehy 1990), we must consider the possibility that the first purpose for which a building was constructed is reflected in its architectural signature, and subsequent functions of a structure may be reflected in the artifactual record (Deal 1985) or in architectural modifications. Architecture may be the most lasting artifact, but it may reveal only the purpose for which the structure was originally built.

Some of the more traditional approaches to the study of Maya domestic architecture include examination of size, shape, and construction materials. But many of these analyses also take account of information about artifact content, since the two bodies of data must be considered to create an accurate reconstruction. Fortunately for the archaeologist, the nature of a structure often *does* relate to its function. By examining differences in architecture, we may be able to determine why the structure was built, and if the functions have remained the same through time, this behavior may be reflected in its artifact history. The present discussion will not address the consideration that functional labels may hinder other types of analyses, but this point is well recognized.

Structure Function and Its Importance in Maya Archaeology

Archaeology in general, and household archaeology in particular, has stressed the determination of structure function (Becker 1982; Harrison 1986; Stenholm 1979). Why is structure function so important to Maya studies and archaeological studies in general, and how do we go about determining it? This determination has ramifications on many levels of sociopolitical complexity, as discussed below.

One of the most obvious uses to which structure function studies have been applied is the estimation of population size. The counting of house mounds is a popular method for making demographic estimates (Culbert and Rice 1990; de Roche 1983; Haviland 1972; Smith and Lewis 1980). The number of rooms in a structure has also been used to infer population (Webster and Freter 1990), but this method also relies on initial mound counts. Others have used more innovative methods, such as Richard Adams's (1974) study of palace population based on bench space, or Patricia McAnany's (1990) use of water storage potential in the Puuc region. As Julia Hendon (1987:7) states, there is no one-to-one correlation between the number of mounds and the number of structures used for sleeping, so the total number of mounds cannot be used exactly to infer population. This fact makes the determination of structure function a necessary step. Population size has in turn been used to estimate sociopolitical complexity (Carneiro 1967), and population growth has been attributed a prime importance by some researchers in cultural evolution (Sanders and Price 1968; however, cf. Cowgill 1975a, 1975b).

The deduction of structure function has been used for the analysis and understanding of group size, the determination of engendered use of space, and insights into other aspects of social organization. There is a simple assumption that one group equals one household, particularly for small, low-status groups of the Maya lowlands. This proposition needs to be tested explicitly in each case, but even in the best of preservation conditions (e.g., Cerén), exact identification of the social group is difficult. However, the resolution of structure function will remain an important issue in archaeology, whether it is done explicitly, as in the past, or implicitly, as in more recent work.

Examples of Structure Function from Four Classic Maya Sites

Copán, Honduras

In a zone of urban habitation at Copán called Las Sepulturas, a high-status neighborhood located a few hundred meters away from the site core, Hendon (1991) identified three distinct building types (not including those located in the Acropolis). Ancillary structures, residential structures, and ritual structures are recognizable by specific architectural features and unique artifact signatures. Most of the ancillary structures are small in size, measuring under 25 m^2 in area. The platforms had either a perishable superstructure or none at all and were used for storage or as cooking/food-preparation areas. The artifact signature of such platforms includes a significant number of large and small jars and small bowls (jars) with restricted necks. Other artifacts in association with ancillary structures include grinding stones and three-prong braziers. The deposits are lacking in fineware bowls, plates, and cylinders; censers used in ritual activities; and manufacturing items (i.e., bone needles). Additionally, middens are associated with most of the platforms.

Residential structures are the most numerous type of building in Copán's urban neighborhoods, especially in Las Sepulturas, and they are identified as structures with either a partial or complete stone superstructure built on top of a raised substructure. A variety of activities took place at residences, including cooking, food preparation and serving, ritual activities, storage, and manufacture. The number of rooms per substructure varies, but many of them have stone benches, some of which were probably used for sleeping. Terraces are an important component of residential architecture, and they were used for activities such as weaving or cooking that required good lighting or ventilation. Residential structures may also contain caches.

Ritual structures are the fewest in the excavated groups of Copán's urban neighborhoods, apart from the Acropolis. Such a nonroyal structure is identified architecturally as a perishable superstructure sitting atop a high square substructure. Artifacts are few in comparison with residences and often relate to ritual activities, and there are no middens. Caches and burials are rarely associated with ritual structures, and benches, if present, are small.

The conclusions reached from a functional approach to architecture at Copán have been extremely productive, due to Hendon's (1987) use of both architecture and artifacts, including midden analysis. I also used this approach (Gonlin 1993) with productive results in the analysis of low-status rural architecture. However, all urban groups, including both low- and high-status households, examined by Hendon had buildings that stood out as one form or another, and the use of space seemed to be compartmentalized. This amount of functional differentiation is not present in the low-status rural Copán groups or is not detectable, although we know that similarity in activities existed because of similarity in overall artifact assemblages. For example, ritual objects are present in both rural and urban groups, but household rituals in the rural area may have been performed within a residence rather than in a specially constructed temple/*oratorio*. Differential use of space may have to do with energy procurement and status in both rural and urban contexts rather than with differences in household activities (Becker 1986). Michael Deal's (1987) work with the highland Maya shows that the family altar is the focus of household ritual. From ethnohistoric sources, Deal (1987:177) notes that ". . . native priests and nobility had private *oratorios* within their household compound, while few poorer families could afford them." Modern family altars within domiciles are constructed of perishable material, as is much of the associated paraphernalia. If similar materials were used in archaeological contexts, recovery of such ritual areas will be extremely challenging.

Joya de Cerén, El Salvador

A unique project in the Maya region is the excavation of Cerén, El Salvador (Kievit 1994; Sheets 1992, 1994, 2000; Sheets et al. 1990; Sheets and McKee 1989, 1990; Sheets and Simmons 1993). At Cerén, in situ material and buildings preserved in volcanic ash greatly aid in the identification of structure function. Perhaps here we have the only case in Mesoamerica where the systemic context is very nearly reflected in the distribution of artifacts. As a result, we have identified structures that are known to be domiciles, storehouses, and kitchens, in addition to a sweathouse (Tucker 1992) and communal buildings. Since both domiciles and *bodegas* are used for storage, it will be helpful to determine the attributes of storage structures versus domiciles. Using this site as a model, we can summarize what we would expect to find in storehouses, for which the data have been analyzed (Gerstle 1992; Sheets et al. 1990). Both artifactual and architectural information have been utilized in this procedure.

There are three storehouses (Structures 4, 6, 7) among the eleven buildings excavated, defined by a number of criteria. These criteria include: (1) large number of ceramics and other artifacts compared with other structures of the household, (2) slightly smaller size than houses, (3) consistent number of ceramic vessels (25 to 28 vessels each), (4) no bench, and (5) location behind a domicile structure. Storage structure architecture is similar to that of the domicile, indicating that the same materials were used for both types of buildings. Houses have variable numbers of vessels, whereas storehouses tend to have similar numbers of vessels. Since houses are also used for storage, some of the same vessel types will be present in both residences and storehouses. There is variation in the nonceramic contents of storehouses. For example, the inventory of Structure 4 at Cerén included cacao beans and cacao, but this was not found in the other storage structures. Storehouses also contain broken artifacts, such as grinding-stone fragments and sherds, presumably being kept for recycling purposes.

Andrea Gerstle (1992) emphasizes that the bulk of the family's possessions are found in a storehouse, making them very important units of analysis for household archaeology (see also Hendon 2000). Materials are stored in bins on the floor and on shelves constructed for small and lightweight items, such as jars of dried chiles. Not all items were placed there for long-term storage, and those items to which quick access was needed were placed in the front of the structure.

How do we apply these criteria in an area where preservation is poor and where postdepositional processes (other than volcanism) have affected the distribution of artifacts? It may be possible to determine which buildings contained large numbers of ceramics and other artifacts if we look at the interiors of structures and deposits surrounding the buildings. These approaches, however, are problematical, since most in situ material has been removed either by the inhabitants themselves upon moving or from the sweeping of floors, so that a study of floor contents may not produce useful information. Deposits surrounding buildings may or may not pertain to the function.

The second attribute of storehouses is that they are of slightly smaller size than residences. This characteristic can be directly observed in the archaeological record for those buildings with complete or reconstructable dimensions. A comparison of structure area may provide insights for the determination of function. Third, storehouses at Cerén had a consistent number of storage vessels, but this criterion proves to be extremely challenging on the excavation data composed of sherd counts from midden contexts. The fourth criterion used to determine storehouses at Cerén is that they have no benches, whereas houses sometimes do. This characteristic may provide a strong, but not a definitive, clue.

The fifth criterion, that storehouses are located behind domicile structures, may be applied to both courtyard groupings and less formal arrangements of Maya structures. Storehouses may be on the fringes of the patio rather than central to it, or adjacent to houses rather than behind them.

From the Cerén material, it seems that architectural information may be of most help in determining structure function at poorly preserved sites, along with gross observations of artifact distributions. Much of the in situ material and organic artifacts found at Cerén, such as dried chiles on a shelf, will not likely be recovered at most sites. However, the larger observations from Cerén are valuable and applicable.

Large numbers of ceramic artifacts may be associated with buildings for reasons other than storage. The possibility of cooking and food-preparation activities must also be considered, because the distribution of ceramics may be highlighting kitchen areas as well as storage places.

Houses are also places of storage and use, so it is not surprising that heavy deposits of sherds (presumably representing original house contents or activities) surround some of the larger buildings in a group. Additionally, discarded artifacts may be thrown in the vicinity of a building. The Cerén data is valuable in itself because of the picture of the richness of life that it provides, but it is also useful for comparative purposes. David Webster et al. (1997) have already elaborated on the comparisons from Cerén to Copán.

Tikal, Guatemala

Extensive archaeological work at Tikal, Guatemala, has included the excavation of two groups, 4F-1 and 4F-2, which are located in the 16 km^2 mapped area surrounding Tikal (Haviland 1985). The groups are geographically close to the urban area of Tikal, and some of the buildings are well-built, complex domiciles. Artifactual remains are similar to other domestic compounds throughout the Maya lowlands. Determination of structure function of the more than sixteen buildings in the two groups at Tikal was accomplished by William Haviland in various ways. Among the analytical methods used was the examination of architectural type and the distribution of artifacts. Discussed below is the architectural analysis.

Buildings that are too small to have been inhabited must be ancillary in nature (Haviland 1985:120), such as the small, square one-level structures. The Copán (Hendon 1987) and Cerén (Sheets 1992) data agree with these observations on structure size. The habitability factor at Tikal, however, is not the same for every Maya site. For example, small rural buildings at Copán, which were probably residences, are smaller than the smallest ancillary structures at Tikal from Groups 4F-1 and 4F-2 (Gonlin 1993:629). (This observation may be due to a sampling issue at Tikal, where low-status rural groups farther from the site core have not been investigated, or the information has not been published.)

At the two Tikal groups, the criterion of "squareness" has been utilized to define some basic aspects of construction. Square buildings generally tend to be smaller than rectangular ones, providing a general clue to the function. The length and width are used to produce ratios, with those buildings tending toward a square shape having a ratio approaching 1, when width is divided by length (Haviland 1985: Table 84). In the Copán rural area, most of the square buildings are smaller in size than rectangular structures, and square buildings are associated with heavy deposits of ceramics (Gonlin 1993:631). Haviland further divides architecture at Tikal according to other attributes, such as platform levels, masonry form, wall style, and so on. If we examine the square buildings in rural Copán, the one-level platforms separate out from the two-level square platforms in terms of function.

Haviland (1985:120) observes for Tikal that two-level square platforms are similar to two-level rectangular platforms that were likely residences but may still be ancillary in nature. The two-level square platforms (mean area = 26.75 m^2) in the rural Copán sample are larger overall than the one-level square platforms (16.2 m^2). This difference in size further reinforces the interpretation for Copán that the smallest and simplest structures are usually ancillary (Gonlin 1993:631).

Cobá, Quintana Roo, Mexico

At Cobá, Quintana Roo, Mexico, two small compounds (Groups 2-14 and 15-37) have been intensively excavated (Manzanilla 1987). Architecture in both is quite similar to other low-status buildings throughout the Maya region (Benavides and Manzanilla 1985; Manzanilla and Benavides 1985), though in this part of the Yucatán Peninsula, oval structures are more common (Burgos and Palomo 1984), and some of the buildings at Cobá rest on basal platforms.

The abundance of ceramics, along with other markers, has been used to identify kitchens (Benavides-Castillo 1987:56). At Cobá, the polythetic identifiers of kitchens include small structure size, association of metates, ash zones, presence of lithics used for scraping and crushing, and occasionally the remains of animal bones and shell. A combination of both architectural and artifactual data is necessary to define structure function, as has been the case in the above examples.

Some of the Cobá groups appear to have had their own altars or shrines (Benavides-Castillo 1987:58), collectively identified as a small square building with an interior space too small to be habitable. A shrine is also differentiated by its location on the east side of the plaza, with a western orientation of its central space. Small shrines at Cobá are not associated with construction offerings, burials, or metates—artifacts that might perhaps confer a different use. The Cobá criteria suggest particular buildings that may have been used as kitchens or for ritual activity.

Summary of Structure Function at Copán, Cerén, Tikal, and Cobá

Even in this small sample of domestic architecture, there are more similarities between Copán, Cerén, Tikal, and Cobá than there are differences. The similarities in the distribution of activities are striking, and the remains of these small households provide evidence of the general Maya culture shared by these people throughout the Maya region. Many of the criteria from these sites are overlapping and serve to reinforce each other. Small, square one-level platforms are more likely to be ancillary structures than larger rectangular buildings or two-level square platforms. Smaller buildings on a site may have functioned as storehouses or kitchens or, more rarely, as shrines/ritual structures. Both kitchens and storehouses are associated with large numbers of ceramics, so that the types of vessels may be more important in determining function when two structures both have an overall high quantity of artifacts. Polythetic characteristics of ancillary structures both aid and hinder functional identification, reflecting the complex set of events that occurred at many of the groups during and after habitation.

A few words of caution should accompany these observations. Ancillary structures are not always the smallest buildings, as they are at Cerén and Tikal. Square platforms do not always indicate an ancillary function, especially for those that have two levels. Artifact concentrations are more likely produced from a variety of activities rather than just one, such as cooking. The differences, however, may indicate that there is variation in settlement and domestic organization of small households in the Maya region.

One should also keep in mind that some of the observations used above to deduce structure function come from studies of elite architecture, such as at Copán, where Hendon (1987, 1991) analyzed the elite urban core zone, and I in turn used those criteria to examine low-status rural buildings (Gonlin 1993, 1994). However, at Copán, it is well documented that many types of household behaviors are common to all domestic compounds, regardless of status (Gonlin 1993). Therefore, it is not unwarranted to use patterns from elite contexts to illuminate patterns of behavior among commoners, and vice-versa, as each may help paint a fuller picture of Maya culture when used together.

Using Energetic Calculations as Clues to Structure Function

Another approach to the determination of structure function is the use of energetics. Edward H. Thompson (1892:264–265) observed over one hundred years ago that "authorities commanding less valuable labor had to be content with terraces of less altitude and stone structures less imposing." Today, these differences in construction costs have been quantified (Abrams 1984, 1987, 1989, 1994, 1998) and can be tied to structure function and status. Elliot Abrams's cluster analysis of energetic costs at Copán reinforces the supposition that size and quality of architecture are tied to status differences. Abrams emphasizes that energetic calculations are very site specific, and this thought is echoed by Gair Tourtellot et al. (1992:88), who observe that ". . . discrepancies in local resources further complicate site-to-site comparisons of elite when identifications of the elite are made on only an architectural basis."

Work at Copán has shown that ancillary structures require less energy to build, as measured in person-days, than do domiciles (Gonlin 1993), largely because of the lower substructure height and smaller size of the former compared to the latter. There is some variability in energetic costs for ancillary structures, and the best method for using energetics to determine structure function is to calculate costs of all the buildings in a group and then make intragroup comparisons. For example, the cost of an ancillary structure in the urban core of Copán may well exceed the cost of a domicile in rural Copán. Ethnographic observations provide analogous information.

There are a number of ways to keep construction costs to a minimum. For most Classic Maya commoners, Kathryn Kamp's observations on building in a Syrian village may apply. Kamp (1993:305–306) states that building costs are kept relatively low for most members of society by not using costly or exotic materials, and that fairly standardized building practices are the result of local unspecialized labor. She further states that construction costs can be kept to a minimum by making room use as flexible as possible (Kamp 1993:306). This flexibility, observed ethnographically for the Maya, is exactly what confuses the archaeologist studying the Classic Maya.

Even without making explicit energetic comparisons, architectural properties can be used in the determination of structure function. This observation is best exemplified at Cerén, El Salvador, where Karen Kievit (1994:202) has worked toward an archaeology of Maya architecture by comparing thickness of walls to building type and site distribution at Cerén. Furthermore, she uses wall type to deduce structure function, as in her reinterpretation of Structure 3 as a civic structure rather than a dwelling, "based in part on the fact that it had solid walls as well as on the fact that other structures with *bajareque* walls also had more convincing domestic-artifact assemblages" (Gerstle 1989:79, cited in Kievit 1994:201). Kievit (1994:200) also compares height to function, noting that storehouses (Structures 6 and 7 at Cerén) generally are situated on shorter and smaller platforms than their respective dwellings.

The sturdiness of a structure may also lend clues to structure function. Nicholas David's (1971) work with the Fulani and Randolph Widmer and James Sheehy's (1990) work in a modern potting compound of San Sebastián, Mexico, near Teotihuacán show that architecture and function are more likely to match when the use-life of the structure is short. Less energy would be invested in a short use-life structure, and there is a greater likelihood that the structure would have fewer functions over its short life. Frequent re-use or functional changes occur more often when buildings are more permanent. And as Kamp (1993:310) has observed, "In general, then, major effort is not expended to alter the architectural characteristics of a room when its function is altered. With the exception of roofs, whose basic materials are expensive and can be scavenged, structural attributes are allowed to progress unopposed. Room contents, however, are altered to correspond to the new requirements of the room type."

Dana Oswald (1987:322) has noted that a family performs more different types and numbers of activities in a generation than it does in one year. Does this show up archaeologically, in that longer-lived Maya courtyard groups have more differentiation of architecture or activity areas and artifacts than does a shorter-lived group? This information generally coincides with observations that pioneering families may build a single multifunctional structure and then add specific-function buildings later in time.

Beyond Buildings: The Maya Courtyard

Though there is much we can learn from architecture, we can also learn a great deal if we de-emphasize its importance when we try to decipher household activities. Students of architectural studies know that the concept of the home includes much more than the house itself (Pearson and Richards 1994:5–6). For the Maya, too, then, we must consider more than architecture in the analysis of the domicile. We must include the ambient space around such buildings that were inhabited by the ancients, as well as symbolic information encoded in the structure and layout of the homestead (Hirth 1993:24), for architecture is but a small part of culture (Rapoport 1990:10). Far more structures than courtyards have been excavated, and courtyards have not received the same degree of attention in many kinds of analyses as buildings have.

Small, dimly lit interiors of Maya dwellings are not well suited for many activities. Ethnographic observations of Maya groups (e.g., Wisdom 1940) tell us that the exterior space of a house and the courtyard are important activity areas and that many of the waking hours are spent in these places. For example, Charles Wisdom (1940:99) records that the Chorti eat their meals either in the kitchen or on a bench in the courtyard. Additionally, "Within the courtyard are some of the family's fruit trees and shrubs, medicinal plants, and a number of large trees used for shading the workers during the warm months. Under these are set up poles on which agave fiber is cleaned and made into articles" (Wisdom 1940:120). In smaller households, Wisdom (1940:120) notes that the courtyard is used by the household to "lounge during the day when there is no rain, talk with neighbors and relatives, and entertain visitors with coffee, *atol*, and hot *tortillas*. It contains several *butaca* chairs and two wooden benches which are built against the facing walls of the two houses." The courtyard is used as a place for social and ceremonial gatherings, a place of entertainment as well as work.

Archaeologically, what could we expect to find that parallels ethnographic use of the courtyard? Logically, we know that numerous activities occurred in ancient courtyards, but we should not expect the remains of such activities to stay in their same spatial locations through time. Nevertheless, from the excavations of courtyards at Copán in both rural and urban locations (Gonlin 1993; Hendon 1987), we know that many artifacts are recovered from such contexts. An exceptional example comes from Cerén. The Cerén structures generally have small interiors, but roofed-over space outside the walls often exceeds interior space (Sheets 1992:56). Some extramural roofed areas were kept clean of broken artifacts, and the soil in these areas is highly compacted, indicating heavy use. Other courtyard areas at Cerén are full of artifacts. Outside the eaves of Structure 1, the forked sticks that supported a metate were found, and small fragments of artifacts were found that had been ground into the earthen courtyard. In the open area (i.e., courtyard) of Gr. 15-37 at Cobá, Manzanilla hypothesized from chemical analysis that it was likely used for a variety of activities, including food processing, cooking, and consumption (Manzanilla and Barba 1990:43).

At Copán, where preservation is more typical of tropical sites, the excavation of courtyards in both rural and urban areas provides an interesting illustration. Melissa Diamanti (1991) found that most patio floors were paved with either cobbles or plaster in the urban core groups of Las Sepulturas, and as at Cerén, there were some areas that were kept relatively clean of broken artifacts, whereas other areas were littered. Extramural areas are also extremely important places for burials at Las Sepulturas, with dozens of interments located in either the patio or along structure walls (Diamanti 1991: Table 3.24). Hendon (1987) has found metates and manos to occur most frequently on structure terraces, patio floors in front of buildings, and occasionally inside buildings. Low-status rural Copán groups have many similarities with urban groups in terms of courtyard artifact distribution and burial location (Gonlin 1993). Grinding-stone fragments are more often found than whole artifacts, and these fragments are rarely located in structures. Of ten rural grave locations recovered in the Rural Sites Project, nine of these were either in the patio or adjacent to outside structure walls (Gonlin 1993: Table 3.16). Hearths were most often recovered in patio areas just outside structure walls.

Areas adjacent to structures were also important for a variety of activities. At Cerén, just centimeters beyond the edge of the thatch roof of Structure 6 (the storehouse), evidence for a kitchen garden was found. The garden gave the appearance of being carefully attended: the three species of plants were neatly organized into two separate rows (Sheets 1992:58). Farther south of Household 1, a milpa had been planted, as evidenced by the remains of young corn. This pattern of planting is what William Sanders and Thomas Killion (1992:14) call "settlement agriculture." The chapters of Killion's book (1992a) discuss the form, function, and ramifications of this type of agriculture for Mesoamerica and its prime importance in the evolution of ancient agriculture.

Home Is Where the Hearth Is

The hearth, used for warmth, cooking, and gathering, is a pivotal point, its derivation coming from the Latin "focus" (Pearson and Richards 1994: 12). The hearth probably reflected the center of many activities for the Maya, but it was also much more than that. David Freidel, Linda Schele, and Joy Parker (1993) explain the centrality of the three-stone hearth in Maya religion and cosmology (see Taube 1998 for additional information on the meaning of the hearth). Functionally, the three-stone configuration is ideal for confining the fire and for supporting cooking vessels (Wauchope 1938:126). The hearth, as a material correlate for the activity of cooking, may reflect status differences within Maya society. Different types of hearths may be used to cook different types of foods, an observation that has wider economic implications (Pyburn 1989).

The three-stone hearth is popular today in the Maya region, however many other options for cooking may have existed in the past. For example, at the Postclassic highland Maya site of Cauinal, Robert Hill (1982:43) identified the remains of three possible types of hearths: a patch of burnt earth, burnt clay laid upon a stone foundation in the shape of a ring, and a ring of stones around a burnt-clay base. Other types of hearths may be located on benches or cooking tables, or perhaps braziers were used for cooking (Pyburn 1989:334). The list of types of hearths given here is not exhaustive, and as Pyburn (1989:338) points out, "there are other types of cooking arrangements that we are not finding or not recognizing."

Ethnographic observation of hearths is more easily accomplished than archaeological observation of this feature (see Vogt, this volume). Its physical location can vary considerably: Robert Wauchope (1938:117) reports that it is located at one end or corner of the house or kitchen, if the kitchen is a separate structure. In Yucatán, the hearth may be placed near the main post. It has been reported that sometimes two fireplaces are set at the same end of the house, one for cooking tortillas and regular meals and the other for simmering stew or water all day long (Wauchope 1938). The location of a hearth may lend clues to social status, as Kamp (1993:300) states: "Activities such as cooking may exhibit more variability in status. Thus, the difference between backstage and frontstage activities seems to depend on both the relative importance of the activity as a public display and the cultural mandate for privacy."

Not all hearths occur inside structures. Many hearths are located in the courtyard of Maya groups, observed both ethnographically (Smyth 1990) and archaeologically (Gonlin 1993; Pyburn 1989). The location of outside hearths signals that activities occurred outside of structures, reinforcing the thought that external space figured importantly in domestic activities. David (1971:120) has noted for the Fulani that during the dry season, cooking is done outside, but during the wet season, cooking is done inside on the hearth in the kitchen. If this were the case for the Classic Maya, we would expect to find both indoor and outdoor hearths within the same group. However, few hearths have been recovered archaeologically (Haviland 1963; Pyburn 1989), in part because of the fragility of some types of this feature, but perhaps also because of the failure to recognize a hearth in the excavation process. Anne Pyburn (1989) discusses the problem of identifying hearths in the field and the proper recording of such features, which is sometimes neglected by archaeologists.

The three-stone hearth would be easy to identify archaeologically *if* the stones were left in place, undisturbed over the millennia. Because of the symbolic and practical aspects of the stones themselves, it is more than likely that the ancient Maya removed the hearthstones upon relocating their residences, a practice that has been observed ethnographically by Wauchope (1938:117). This act of removal underscores the importance of the hearthstones, which are rarely found in domestic archaeological contexts, but instances of cached hearthstones or their symbolic equivalents are sometimes recovered archaeologically (Taube 1998).

Apart from confirming the functional aspect of cooking, hearths have been used by anthropologists to estimate the number of women in a compound. In the Fulani case, David (1971:121) notes that since only women cook, there is a correlation between the number of hearths in a compound and the number of adult females. David cautions, however, that population estimation is a more complicated procedure than simply counting hearths, and his formula failed in 25 percent of his sample. If demographers were to rely on such a method for the Classic Maya, population estimates would be extremely low.

Other Ways of Looking at Commoner Sites: Cultural Conventions and Boundaries

Cultural conventions will have an impact on the ultimate shape of the built environment. However, the perspective of cultural determinism should be avoided as much as environmental determinism. Donald Sanders (1990) discusses cultural conventions as they relate to domestic space, and boundaries may be particularly amenable to archaeological analysis. Four types of boundaries are defined: psychological, personal space, social, and sociophysical (Lavin 1981, cited in Sanders 1990:51).

What kinds of cultural conventions are manifested in Maya architecture, and how do we recover them? We can examine boundaries used by low-status Maya in their domestic architecture and compare these markers to those used in high-status architecture for insights into Maya social structure. One problem that excavators of perishable structures face is that some boundary markers have disappeared or are harder to read in this type of low-status architecture as compared to elite stone structures that have survived through the centuries. Internal divisions in stone structures are often preserved, whereas we must only surmise at the internal divisions that may have existed in perishable structures. Differences in the use and placement of boundaries may signify ethnic differences. Gerstle (1987) has hypothesized that a Lenca enclave resided in the urban core of Copán in one patio of Group 9N-8, in part based on variation in architectural configuration.

The Maya of all statuses used steps as boundaries. In domestic architecture, most steps are placed on the front side of the building, facing the courtyard. Some steps are also found inside structures when more than one level is present. Steps are of varying numbers, depending on platform height, with higher platforms obviously needing more steps and leading to more private buildings. What else do steps do? Functionally, they make it easier to get into and out of a building, but ideologically, steps, along with their associated platforms, serve to elevate the human being to a higher level, with the platform eventually superseding the house itself (Miller 1998).

The placement of architectural features such as benches, walls, and steps provides clues to privacy. For example, benches at Cerén were found in the innermost rooms of dwellings and in the outer room of communal or civic structures (see Kievit 1994:203–204 and Johnston and Gonlin 1998:149). This pattern for dwellings is repeated at many other sites throughout the Maya lowlands. Stone benches are normally placed against the back or side wall, in areas that would provide the most privacy and be the least visible from the courtyard. Internal stone walls serve to compartmentalize rooms, communication, and activities.

In a larger setting, we can examine boundaries within a courtyard and those that exist between groups. Do the boundary markers differ between urban and rural groups or between low-status and high-status groups? It appears that rural areas offer open spaces that separate groups from one another, whereas boundaries in urban contexts may have been more pronounced. However, what we conceive of today as open space between rural groups may not have been a reality of the past. For example, the Chorti are reported to have used fences to enclose milpas, gardens, house groups, and sometimes orchards, and these fences are built of limbs, growing plants, and stone (Wisdom 1940:129). In some instances, this expression of territoriality can be observed archaeologically. Stone fences that are still visible at some Maya sites, such as at Cobá (Manzanilla 1987) and in the Río Bec region (Eaton 1975), serve as boundary markers between groups (also see Dunning, this volume). It is possible that perishable fences made of growing plants, especially thorny species or spiny plants (Wisdom 1940:119), served the same purpose. Likewise, kitchen gardens may have aided in the separation of groups from one another.

How sharp are boundaries, and are sharp boundaries more archaeologically visible? Sharp boundaries are those that functioned to effectively divide and direct traffic and control privacy and territoriality. The most archaeologically visible boundaries are those that have survived through time, which may or may not correspond to the attribute of sharpness. Looking for boundary markers can be quite productive and may lead to new insights, such as those achieved through access analysis (see below). However, as Susan Kent (1990:148) notes, "Architecture can be segmented or divided conceptually, physically, or both." If Maya architecture is divided conceptually without a corresponding material expression, how do we detect these divisions?

The division of space within the house according to gender has been discussed by Michael Pearson and Colin Richards (1994:19–20), among many other more recent analyses. Although gender boundaries may truly exist, we should be careful when making normative statements about such places and activities, as cautioned by Richard Wilk (1990:42). A degree of flexibility should be expected when such behavioral statements are made. For example, Wisdom (1940:120) reports that the kitchen is the house of the females for the Chorti; however, he also observes that meals are sometimes taken in the kitchen (Wisdom 1940:99) by both sexes. Evon Vogt (1990, this volume) has also noted the presence of gender-specific work areas and places in the household among the Zinacantecos. Archaeologically, at Cerén, Payson Sheets (1992) notes a similar division of work areas according to gender. The domicile, kitchen, and storehouses were probably female associated, whereas the maize fields and the ramada-like building (Structure 5) are likely to have been male domains. What needs to be established is whether material correlates of male and female activities exist, what their spatial distribution is, and how these relate to boundaries.

Wisdom (1940) reports the existence of a pronounced inside/outside dichotomy for the Chorti, with the house associated primarily with females and the outside world with males. However, women and men both attend the market to buy and sell goods, and men as well as women have domestic chores in the compound. Observations of the Zinacantecos (Vogt 1990, this volume) show that the agricultural fields are primarily a male domain. If this general observation holds for the Classic Maya, then we might expect field huts, when recovered archaeologically, to reveal clues about gender boundaries. If field huts were the exclusive domain of males, an absence of female-related artifacts might be expected.

Personal possessions may indicate the location of private areas and may represent a strong territorial marker (Sanders 1990:69). Our ability to recover and define personal possessions may be difficult under normal conditions of preservation, and the definition of "personal property" may vary cross-culturally. It is suggested that items such as clothing and jewelry may qualify as personal possessions in many societies. Some of these materials have long since perished in the archaeological record, but other more durable materials, such as jewelry made of precious stones, have been removed from their original contexts. For example, of the twenty-three loci of ornaments recorded from features and middens at Las Sepulturas, Copán, from Groups 9N-8, 9M-22, and 9M-24, only three of them occur within a room, with most ornaments recovered from middens (Diamanti 1991: Table 3.21). The distribution of jewelry at Copán is correlated with status differences: ornaments are more numerous in higher-status urban compounds (i.e., Type 4) than in lower-status (i.e., Type 1) compounds in either rural or urban locations.

The recovery of ornaments may not always denote private space, however. One of the ornament locations within a room at 9N-8 corresponds to a workshop/residence that produced shell gorgets, identical to the gorgets carved in the hieroglyphic bench of Structure 82 of Gr. 9N-8. Obviously, this ornament does not denote personal space, but craft activity, the end product of which was intended for another's possession. At Aguateca (Inomata 1995), in situ materials indicate that craft/scribal activity occurred in Structure M8-10. Several tools and finished products of shells and bones were recovered. One of the shell ornaments contains a personal name among the glyphs inscribed on it. By analogy with the Copán example, this ornament may actually have been intended for another's use, or, alternatively, it may have belonged to the resident of M8-10, inferred to have been a scribe, based on the remains of tools and on the *its'at* (sage) title inscribed on the shell ornament.

Access Analysis

The use of architectural features to understand the degree of privacy or protection and social control may be achieved through access analysis, which is a versatile analytical technique that can be used on architecture from any period or cultural affiliation (Fairclough 1992; Foster 1989; Hopkins 1979; Sanders 1990; see Hillier and Hanson 1984 for a full explanation of this technique).

What was the access and vision of a low-status domestic Maya compound? The courtyard provides high vision for "public" activities and equal access from all structures around it, emphasizing the importance of the courtyard to the Maya. However, this observation is already heavily documented ethnographically. From a position in the middle of the courtyard, the view into the interior of a structure depends upon the height of its substructure or platform. If a platform is high enough, the structure's interior may not be seen at all. When platforms are low enough so that one may peer into a building, vision may depend upon the width of the doorway. Doorways that are around one meter wide will provide a limited vision inside. The most private parts of the structure would be the interior corners of a rectilinear building and the back of the structure. We might expect that sleeping and other personal activities occurred in these areas.

Ritual paraphernalia is located in more private areas of the house. Deal (1987:178) reports for contemporary Maya and for the Postclassic archaeological site of Mayapán that altars "were set against the back walls of dwellings, opposite the main entrance of the living structure, in tiny chambers extended from the back wall of the living structure, or against the rear wall of the center room of a three-room house." There are no windows to provide vision onto the courtyard and the activities that may be taking place there. Thus, when one leaves the building, a total transition from private to public sphere is made.

In Maya domiciles that are multiroom structures, the access to each of the rooms provides details about function and social control. The multiroom structure M8-10 at Aguateca has three rooms linearly placed, none of which is accessible to the other, meaning that one must go outside in order to enter another room. Why are these divisions so common in higher-ranking and urban Classic Maya domiciles? And did similar perishable divisions exist in single-room houses? As Sanders (1990:63), commenting on early Bronze Age settlement at Myrtos, Crete, has noted, "The restriction of access and vision suggests that privacy was a factor determining the functional organization of the house." Components of social organization may help to explain such arrangements in higher-class Maya architecture. Polygamy existed in some of the households, and in extended family households, the size of the resident group was probably large and included several nuclear families, each of which may have required private quarters.

However, access to Maya compounds can be controlled through architecture regardless of status. For example, Jack Eaton (1975:59) has recorded at Operation 10, Suboperation C, in the Río Bec region, an entrance passageway no wider than 90 cm that leads into a small compound. Everyone must go through this passage to enter the domicile. Examples of much more controlled access are readily seen in the literature, especially for higher-ranking elite compounds in the Maya region. Some courtyards are nearly entirely closed off to outsiders. Those areas that are least accessible may represent the most sacred places or areas associated with high-ranking individuals. Graham Fairclough's (1992:364) findings on medieval castles caution us, however, that "there may be situations in which the correlation of depth with high status is reversed as a means of hiding service areas," an observation to be kept in mind for the Maya when we are examining highly inaccessible areas. Jerry Moore (1992), in his study of U-shaped rooms in palace complexes in Chan Chan, Peru, concludes that the reasons for restricted access may be multicausal: to protect storehouses, to symbolically guard sacred space, or to reinforce the division between elites and commoners. Therefore, when access analysis is used, the results need to be judiciously interpreted.

Summary

Many different approaches to the archaeological record of Classic Maya commoners have been discussed above. Although we no longer excavate to find only the functions of a building—because we expect much more from our data—we are expected to know what those functions were. I am not suggesting that we focus exclusively or explicitly on structure function, but that we admit when we are using structure function conclusions in our analyses of the household and community. Energetic studies will provide important comparative information about variability within and between major sites when architecture is the focus. Following the caveats stated above, it would be enlightening to see more work done in this area.

De-emphasizing architecture in Maya archaeology has taken many directions, including more excavations of courtyards and other areas adjacent to structures, which have led to a greater awareness of the house-lot. Though we may not recover abundant artifacts or architecture in such areas, other methods of data recovery, such as chemical analysis, can be employed to determine the use, if any, of such areas (see Dunning, this volume). The recovery of hearths is a prime example of the importance of excavating extramural space. Examining boundaries and access to sites provides information about privacy and cultural norms. Many researchers look at the lack of information in low-status houses, especially when compared to high-status palaces, rather than examining the richness before us.

As the present volume attests, information about the Classic Maya is now becoming more complete because of the current emphasis on the low-status segment of society. A theme reiterated throughout this volume, and underscored again here, is that Classic Maya commoners were not a monolithic entity and should not be treated as such. Only when we have a large sample of commoner sites can we begin to understand the majority of people who constituted the glorious kingdoms of the past. Combining the new information with the abundant data on elites, we can more fully understand Classic Maya culture in its entirety.

Acknowledgments

I would like to acknowledge the many archaeologists who influenced and broadened my thinking on the topics in this chapter. Many discussions with Stephen Houston, Patricia McAnany, Karl Taube, and David Webster during the summer of 1994 at Dumbarton Oaks were very valuable, and I was fortunate to have access to the excellent research facilities of D.O. Gratitude is due to the Instituto Hondureño de Antropología e Historia for allowing me to present material on Copán. I have benefited greatly from the invaluable technical advice of Frances Peppard and from the interlibrary loan expertise of Benayah Israel, both of Bellevue Community College. Thanks are due to David Webster, K. Viswanathan, and the anonymous reviewers for commenting on earlier drafts of this chapter. I thank the editors of this volume, Jon Lohse and Fred Valdez, Jr., for inviting me to participate in this work and for their insightful comments.

References

Abrams, Elliot M.

1984 Systems of Labor Organization in Late Classic Copán, Honduras: The Energetics of Construction. Ph.D. diss., Department of Anthropology, Pennsylvania State University, University Park.

1987 Economic Specialization and Construction Personnel in Classic Period Copán, Honduras. *American Antiquity* 52:485–499.

1989 Architecture and Energy: An Evolutionary Approach. In *Archaeological Method and Theory, Volume 1,* edited by Michael B. Schiffer, pp. 47–87. University of Arizona Press, Tucson.

1994 *How the Maya Built Their World.* University of Texas Press, Austin.

1998 Structures as Sites: The Construction Process and Maya Architecture. In *Function and Meaning in Classic Maya Architecture*, edited by Stephen D. Houston, pp. 123–140. Dumbarton Oaks, Washington, D.C.

Adams, Richard E. W.

1974 A Trial Estimation of Classic Maya Palace Populations at Uaxactun. In *Mesoamerican Archaeology: New Approaches*, edited by Norman Hammond, pp. 285–296. University of Texas Press, Austin.

Becker, Marshall J.

1982 Ancient Maya Houses and Their Identification: An Evaluation of Architectural Groups at Tikal and Inferences Regarding Their Functions. *Revista Española de Antropología Americana* 12:111–129.

1986 Household Shrines at Tikal, Guatemala: Size as a Reflection of Economic Status. *Revista Española de Antropología Americana* 14:81–85.

Benavides-Castillo, Antonio

1987 Arquitectura doméstica en Cobá. In *Cobá, Quintana Roo*, edited by Linda Manzanilla, pp. 25–68. Universidad Nacional Autónoma de México, Mexico City.

Benavides-Castillo, Antonio, and Linda Manzanilla

1985 Unidades habitacionales excavadas en Cobá, Q.R. Arquitectura y arqueología: Metodologías en la cronología de Yucatán. *Collection Etudes Mesoaméricaines* 11-8:69–76.

Burgos V., Rafael, and Yoly Palomo C.

1981 Salvamento arqueológico en Pixoy, Yucatán. *Boletín de la Escuela de Ciencias Antropológicas de la Universidad de Yucatán* 12:23–37.

Canuto, Marcello A., and Jason Yaeger (editors)

2000 *The Archaeology of Communities: A New World Perspective.* Routledge Press, London.

Carneiro, Robert L.

1967 On the Relationship between Size of Population and Complexity of Social Organization. *Southwest Journal of Anthropology* 23:234–243.

Cowgill, George L.

1975a On the Causes and Consequences of Ancient and Modern Population Changes. *American Anthropologist* 77:505–525.

1975b Population Pressure as a Non-explanation. *Memoirs of the Society for American Archaeology* 30:127–131.

Culbert, T. Patrick, and Don S. Rice (editors)

1990 *Precolumbian Population History in the Maya Lowlands.* University of New Mexico Press, Albuquerque.

David, Nicholas

1971 The Fulani Compound and the Archaeologist. *World Archaeology* 3:111–131.

Deal, Michael

1985 Household Pottery Disposal in the Maya Highlands: An Ethnoarchaeological Interpretation. *Journal of Anthropological Archaeology* 4:243–291.

1987 Ritual Space and Architecture in the Highland Maya Household. In *Mirror and Metaphor: Material and Social Constructions of Reality*, edited by Daniel W. Ingersoll and Gordon Bronitsky, pp. 171–198. University Press of America, Lanham.

de Roche, C. D.
1983 Population Estimates from Settlement Area and Number of Residences. *Journal of Field Archaeology* 10:187–192.

Diamanti, Melissa
1991 Domestic Organization at Copán: Reconstruction of Maya Elite Households through Ethnographic Analogy. Ph.D. diss., Department of Anthropology, Pennsylvania State University, University Park.

Eaton, Jack D.
1975 Ancient Agricultural Farmsteads in the Río Bec Region of Yucatán. In *Contributions of the University of California Archaeological Research Facility* 27:56–82. University of California, Berkeley.

Fairclough, Graham
1992 Meaningful Constructions—Spatial and Functional Analysis of Medieval Buildings. *Antiquity* 66:348–366.

Foster, Sally M.
1989 Analysis of Spatial Patterns in Buildings (Access Analysis) as an Insight into Social Structure: Examples from the Scottish Atlantic Iron Age. *Antiquity* 63:40–50.

Freidel, David, Linda Schele, and Joy Parker
1993 *Maya Cosmos: Three Thousand Years on the Shaman's Path.* William Morrow, New York.

Freter, AnnCorinne
1988 The Classic Maya Collapse at Copán, Honduras: A Regional Perspective. Ph.D. diss., Department of Anthropology, Pennsylvania State University, University Park.

Gerstle, Andrea
1987 Maya-Lenca Relations in Late Classic Period Copán, Honduras. Ph.D. diss., Department of Anthropology, University of California, Santa Barbara.
1989 Excavation at Structure 3, Cerén, 1989. In *1989 Archaeological Investigations at the Cerén Site, El Salvador: A Preliminary Report,* edited by Payson D. Sheets and Brian R. McKee, pp. 59–80. Report on file, Department of Anthropology, University of Colorado, Boulder.
1992 The Storehouses of Cerén. Paper presented at the 57th Annual Meeting of the Society for American Archaeology, Pittsburgh.

Gonlin, Nancy
1993 Rural Household Archaeology at Copán, Honduras. Ph.D. diss., Department of Anthropology, Pennsylvania State University, University Park.
1994 Rural Household Diversity in Late Classic Copán, Honduras. In *Archaeological Views from the Countryside: Village Communities in Early Complex Societies,* edited by Glenn M. Schwartz and Steven E. Falconer, pp. 177–197. Smithsonian Institution Press, Washington, D.C.

Harrison, Peter
1986 Form and Function in a Maya "Palace" Group. *Proceedings of the 38th International Congress of the Americanists*, Stuttgart-Munchen I:165–172.

Haviland, William A.
1963 Excavations of Small Structures in the Northeast Quadrant of Tikal, Guatemala. Ph.D. diss., Department of Anthropology, University of Pennsylvania, Philadelphia.
1972 Family Size, Prehistoric Population Estimates and the Ancient Maya. *American Antiquity* 37:135–139.
1985 *Excavations in Small Residential Groups at Tikal, Groups 4F-1 and 4F-2.* Tikal Report 19. University Museum, University of Pennsylvania, Philadelphia.

Hendon, Julia A.
1987 The Uses of Maya Structures: A Study of Architecture and Artifact Distribution at Sepulturas, Copán, Honduras. Ph.D. diss., Department of Anthropology, Harvard University, Cambridge.
1991 Status and Power in Classic Maya Society: An Archaeological Study. *American Anthropologist* 93:894–918.
2000 Having and Holding: Storage, Memory Knowledge, and Social Relations. *American Anthropologist* 102:42–53.

Hill, Robert M
1982 Ancient Maya Houses at Cauinal and Pueblo Viejo Chixoy el Quiché, Guatemala. *Expedition* 24:40–48.

Hillier, Bill, and Julienne Hanson
1984 *The Social Logic of Space.* Cambridge University Press, Cambridge.

Hirth, Kenneth G.
1993 The Household as an Analytical Unit: Problems in Method and Theory. In *Prehispanic Domestic Units in Western Mesoamerica: Studies of the Household, Compound, and Residence*, edited by Robert Santley and Kenneth G. Hirth, pp. 21–36. CRC Press, Boca Raton.

Hopkins, Mary
1979 Teotihuacán: An Explication of the Plans of Some Compounds. Bachelor of Arts thesis, Department of Anthropology, Harvard University, Cambridge.

Houston, Stephen D. (editor)
1998 *Function and Meaning in Classic Maya Architecture.* Dumbarton Oaks, Washington, D.C.

Inomata, Takeshi
1995 Archaeological Investigations at the Fortified Center of Aguateca, El Petén, Guatemala: Implications for the Study of the Classic Maya Collapse. Ph.D. diss., Department of Anthropology, Vanderbilt University, Nashville.

Johnston, Kevin J.
1994 The "Invisible" Maya: Late Classic Minimally Platformed Residential

Settlement at Itzán, Guatemala. Ph.D. diss., Department of Anthropology, Yale University, New Haven.

Johnston, Kevin J., and Nancy Gonlin
1998 What Do Houses Mean? Approaches to the Analysis of Classic Maya Commoner Residences. In *Function and Meaning in Classic Maya Architecture*, edited by Stephen D. Houston, pp. 141–185. Dumbarton Oaks, Washington, D.C.

Kamp, Kathryn A.
1993 Towards an Archaeology of Architecture: Clues from a Modern Syrian Village. *Journal of Anthropological Research* 49:293–317.

Kent, Susan
1990 A Cross-Cultural Study of Segmentation, Architecture, and the Use of Space. In *Domestic Architecture and the Use of Space: An Interdisciplinary Cross-Cultural Study*, edited by Susan Kent, pp. 127–152. Cambridge University Press, Cambridge.

Kievit, Karen A.
1994 Jewels of Cerén: Form and Function Comparisons for the Earthen Structures of Joya de Cerén, El Salvador. *Ancient Mesoamerica* 5:193–208.

Killion, Thomas W. (editor)
1992a *Gardens of Prehistory: The Archaeology of Settlement Agriculture in Greater Mesoamerica*. University of Alabama Press, Tuscaloosa.

Killion, Thomas W.
1992b Residential Ethnoarchaeology and Site Structure: Contemporary Farming and Prehistoric Settlement Agriculture at Matacapan, Veracruz, Mexico. In *Gardens of Prehistory: The Archaeology of Settlement Agriculture in Greater Mesoamerica*, edited by Thomas W. Killion, pp. 119–149. University of Alabama Press, Tuscaloosa.

Kovak, Amy
n.d. Household and Neighborhood Studies on the Periphery of Piedras Negras, Guatemala. Ph.D. diss., in progress, Department of Anthropology, Pennsylvania State University, University Park.

Lavin, Marjorie Woods
1981 Boundaries in the Built Environment: Concepts and Examples. *Man-Environment Systems* 11:195–206.

Lohse, Jonathan Campbell
2001 The Social Organization of a Late Classic Maya Community: Dos Hombres, Northwestern Belize. Ph.D. diss., Department of Anthropology, University of Texas at Austin.

Manzanilla, Linda (editor)
1987 *Cobá, Quintana Roo: Análisis de dos unidades de habitaciones mayas*. Instituto de Investigaciones Antropológicas, Serie Antropológica 82. Universidad Nacional Autónoma de México, Mexico City.

Manzanilla, Linda, and Luis Barba
1990 The Study of Activities in Classic Households: Two Case Studies from Coba and Teotihuacan. *Ancient Mesoamerica* 1:41–49.

Manzanilla, Linda, and Antonio Benavides
1985 Arquitectura doméstica en el área maya: El Formativo Tardío y el Clásico. *Cuadernos de Arquitectura Mesoamericana* 5:3–16.

Martin, Simon
2001 Court and Realm. In *Royal Courts of the Ancient Maya, Volume 1, Theory Comparison, and Synthesis*, edited by Takeshi Inomata and Stephen D. Houston, pp. 168–194. Westview Press, Boulder.

McAnany, Patricia A.
1990 Water Storage in the Puuc Region of the Northern Maya Lowlands: A Key to Population Estimates and Architectural Variability. In *Precolumbian Population History in the Maya Lowlands*, edited by T. Patrick Culbert and Don S. Rice, pp. 263–284. University of New Mexico Press, Albuquerque.

Miller, Mary
1998 A Design for Meaning in Maya Architecture. In *Function and Meaning in Classic Maya Architecture*, edited by Stephen D. Houston, pp. 187–222. Dumbarton Oaks, Washington, D.C.

Moore, Jerry D.
1992 Pattern and Meaning in Prehistoric Peruvian Architecture: The Architecture of Social Control in the Chimu State. *Latin American Antiquity* 3:95–113.

Oswald, Dana Beth
1987 The Organization of Space in Residential Buildings: A Cross-Cultural Perspective. In *Method and Theory for Activity Area Research, an Ethnoarchaeological Approach*, edited by Susan Kent, pp. 295–344. Columbia University Press, New York.

Pearson, Michael Parker, and Colin Richards
1994 Ordering the World: Perceptions of Architecture, Space, and Time. In *Architecture and Order*, edited by Michael P. Pearson and Colin Richards, pp. 1–37. Routledge Press, New York.

Pyburn, K. Anne
1989 Maya Cuisine: Hearths and the Lowland Economy. In *Prehistoric Maya Economies of Belize*, edited by Patricia A. McAnany and Barry L. Isaac, pp. 325–344. Research in Economic Anthropology, Supplement 4. JAI Press, Greenwich.

Rapoport, Amos
1990 Systems of Activities and Systems of Settings. In *Domestic Architecture and the Use of Space*, edited by Susan Kent, pp. 9–20. New Directions in Archaeology. Cambridge University Press, Cambridge.

Robin, Cynthia
1999 Towards an Archaeology of Everyday Life: Maya Farmers of Chan Noo-

hol and Dos Chombitos Cikin, Belize. Ph.D. diss., Department of Anthropology, University of Pennsylvania, Philadelphia.

Sanders, Donald

1990 Behavioral Conventions and Archaeology: Methods for the Analysis of Ancient Architecture. In *Domestic Architecture and the Use of Space: An Interdisciplinary Cross-Cultural Study*, edited by Susan Kent, pp. 43–72. Cambridge University Press, Cambridge.

Sanders, William T., and Thomas W. Killion

1992 Factors Affecting Settlement Agriculture in the Ethnographic and Historic Record of Mesoamerica. In *Gardens in Prehistory: The Archaeology of Settlement Agriculture in Greater Mesoamerica*, edited by Thomas W. Killion, pp. 14–31. University of Alabama Press, Tuscaloosa.

Sanders, William T., and Barbara J. Price

1968 *Mesoamerica: The Evolution of a Civilization*. Random House, New York.

Santley, Robert S., and Kenneth G. Hirth (editors)

1993 *Prehispanic Domestic Units in Western Mesoamerica: Studies of the Household, Compound, and Residence*. CRC Press, Boca Raton.

Sheehy, James J.

1991 Structure and Change in a Late Classic Maya Domestic Group at Copán, Honduras. *Ancient Mesoamerica* 2:1–19.

Sheets, Payson

1992 *The Cerén Site: A Prehistoric Village Buried by Volcanic Ash in Central America*. Harcourt Brace Jovanovich, Fort Worth.

1994 Tropical Time Capsule. *Archaeology* 47:30–33.

2000 Provisioning the Cerén Household: The Vertical Economy, Village Economy, and Household Economy in the Southeastern Maya Periphery. *Ancient Mesoamerica* 11:217–230.

Sheets, Payson D., Harriet F. Beaubien, Marilyn Beaudry, Andrea Gerstle, Brian McKee, C. Dan Miller, Hartmut Spetzler, and David B. Tucker

1990 Household Archaeology at Cerén, El Salvador. *Ancient Mesoamerica* 1:81–90.

Sheets, Payson D., and Brian McKee (editors)

1989 *1989 Archaeological Investigations at the Cerén Site, El Salvador: A Preliminary Report*. Report on file, Department of Anthropology, University of Colorado, Boulder.

1990 *1990 Investigations at the Cerén Site, El Salvador: A Preliminary Report*. Report on file, Department of Anthropology, University of Colorado, Boulder.

Sheets, Payson D., and Scott E. Simmons (editors)

1993 *Preliminary Report of the Cerén Research Project, 1993 Season*. Report on file, Department of Anthropology, University of Colorado, Boulder.

Smith, A. Ledyard

1962 Residential and Associated Structures at Mayapan. In *Mayapan, Yucatan, Mexico*, edited by Harry E. D. Pollock, Ralph L. Roys, Tatiana Proskouriakoff, and A. Ledyard Smith, pp. 165–320. Carnegie Institution of Washington Publication 619. Washington, D.C.

Smith, S. K., and Bart B. Lewis
1980 Some New Techniques for Applying the Housing Unit Method of Local Population Estimation. *Demography* 17:323–339.

Smyth, Michael P.
1990 Maize Storage among the Puuc Maya: The Development of an Archaeological Method. *Ancient Mesoamerica* 1:51–70.

Stenholm, Nancy A.
1979 Identification of House Structures in Mayan Archaeology: A Case Study at Kaminaljuyu. In *Settlement Pattern Excavations at Kaminaljuyu, Guatemala*, edited by Joseph W. Michels, pp. 31–182. Pennsylvania State University Press, University Park.

Stomper, Jeffrey Alan
2001 A Model for Late Classic Community Structures at Copán, Honduras. In *Landscape and Power in Ancient Mesoamerica*, edited by Rex Koontz, Kathryn Reese-Taylor, and Annabeth Headrick, pp. 197–229. Westview Press, Boulder.

Taube, Karl
1998 The Jade Hearth: Centrality, Rulership, and the Classic Maya Temple. In *Function and Meaning in Classic Maya Architecture*, edited by Stephen D. Houston, pp. 427–478. Dumbarton Oaks, Washington, D.C.

Thompson, Edward H.
1892 The Ancient Structures of Yucatan Not Communal Dwellings. *Proceedings of the American Antiquarian Society* 8(2):262–269.

Tourtellot, Gair, Jeremy A. Sabloff, and Kelli Carmean
1992 "Will the Real Elites Please Stand Up?": An Archaeological Assessment of Maya Elite Behavior in the Terminal Classic Period. In *Mesoamerican Elites: An Archaeological Assessment*, edited by Diane Z. Chase and Arlen F. Chase, pp. 80–98. University of Oklahoma Press, Norman.

Tucker, David B.
1992 Structure Function Interpretation and Ethnographic Analogy: Enigmatic Structures at Cerén. Paper presented at the 57th Annual Meeting of the Society for American Archaeology, Pittsburgh.

Vogt, Evon Z.
1990 *The Zinacantecos of Mexico: A Modern Maya Way of Life.* 2nd ed. Holt, Rinehart, and Winston, Fort Worth.

Wauchope, Robert
1934 *House Mounds of Uaxactun, Guatemala.* Carnegie Institution of Washington Publication 436. Washington, D.C.
1938 *Modern Maya Houses: A Study of Their Archaeological Significance.* Carnegie Institution of Washington Publication 502. Washington, D.C.

Webster, David
2001 Spatial Dimensions of Maya Courtly Life. In *Royal Courts of the Ancient*

Maya, Volume 1, Theory, Comparison, and Synthesis, edited by Takeshi Inomata and Stephen D. Houston, pp. 130–167. Westview Press, Boulder.

Webster, David, Barbara Fash, Randolph Widmer, and Scott Zeleznik
1998 The Skyband House: Investigations of a Classic Maya Elite Residential Complex at Copán, Honduras. *Journal of Field Archaeology* 25:319–343.

Webster, David, and AnnCorinne Freter
1990 The Demography of Late Classic Copán. In *Precolumbian Population History in the Maya Lowlands*, edited by T. Patrick Culbert and Don S. Rice, pp. 37–62. University of New Mexico Press, Albuquerque.

Webster, David, AnnCorinne Freter, and Nancy Gonlin
2000 *Copán: The Rise and Fall of an Ancient Maya Kingdom.* Harcourt College Publishers, Fort Worth.

Webster, David, and Nancy Gonlin
1988 Household Remains of the Humblest Maya. *Journal of Field Archaeology* 15:169–190.

Webster, David, Nancy Gonlin, and Payson D. Sheets
1997 Copán and Cerén: Two Perspectives on Ancient Mesoamerican Households. *Ancient Mesoamerica* 8:43–61.

Widmer, Randolph J., and James J. Sheehy
1990 Archaeological Implications of Architectural Changes in the Development Cycle of a Modern Pottery Workshop in Teotihuacán. Paper presented at the 50th Annual Meeting of the Society for American Archaeology, Las Vegas.

Wilk, Richard R.
1990 The Built Environment and Consumer Decisions. In *Domestic Architecture and the Use of Space: An Interdisciplinary Cross-Cultural Study*, edited by Susan Kent, pp. 34–42. Cambridge University Press, Cambridge.

Willey, Gordon R., William R. Bullard, Jr., John B. Glass, and James C. Gifford
1965 *Prehistoric Maya Settlements in the Belize Valley.* Papers of the Peabody Museum of Archaeology and Ethnology 54. Harvard University, Cambridge.

Wisdom, Charles
1940 *The Chorti Indians of Guatemala.* University of Chicago Press, Chicago.

CHAPTER 11

Maya Commoners: The Stereotype and the Reality

JOYCE MARCUS

Commoners made up the bulk of Maya society, though for various reasons, I suspect the percentage was closer to 90 percent than to the 98 percent proposed by some authors.[1] Ironically, commoners have received relatively little attention in spite of frequent suggestions that we should study Maya economics "from the bottom up," building from the household to the palace, from the commoner to the king. All scholars recognize that the labor of commoners was essential to the construction of major public works, to the maintenance of diverse agricultural strategies, to the movement of goods between sites, to craft production, and, in general, to the creation of a thriving economy. Nevertheless, attention to commoners' daily round of activities throughout the community still lags, as does a strong focus on their role in intersite trade, joint military efforts, and labor projects that united manpower from several different sites.

All archaeologists agree that commoners affected the economy and urban structure in each Maya city. It seems likely that hard-working commoners would become influential actors, particularly those individuals who showed initiative and great skills. The articulation between the commoner household economy and the community's economic and political standing vis-à-vis other Maya cities is also a link we need to understand. This is not a new chord to strike in Maya archaeology. Seventy years ago, Robert Wauchope (1934:113) stated: "We know very little of the great residue of the Maya, the people who were numerous enough to provide the sheer man-power that made possible the pyramids and the palaces."

Where did these commoners live? In the 1890s, Edward H. Thompson (1892:262, 266–267) noted numerous house mounds in the vicinity of Labná in northern Yucatán. At the turn of the twentieth century, excavations were being made in individual "house mounds" at various sites,

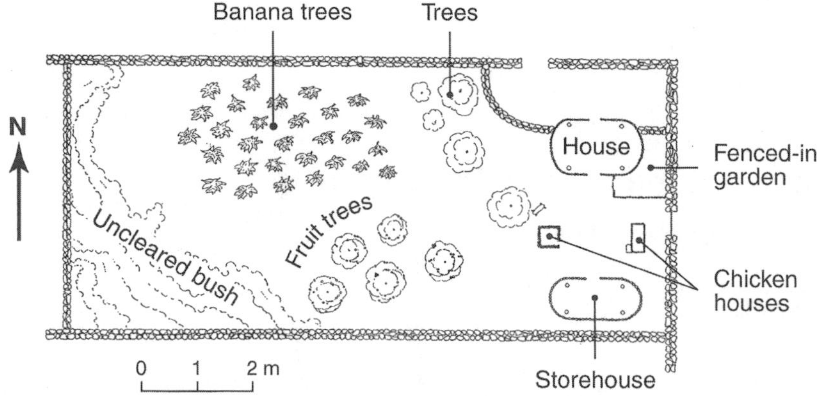

Figure 11.1. A house and associated structures from the Maya village of Chan Kom. Although both the house and storehouse are apsidal in shape, the house is larger. The house-lot includes a fenced-in garden, square chicken houses, orchards, and uncleared bush (redrawn from Wauchope 1938: Fig. 47b).

including Copán (Gordon 1896:26), Uaxac Canal (Seler 1901:43–44), and Quiriguá (Hewett 1912:242–243). And, in the 1920s and 1930s, other scholars (Gann 1925:228–229; Schufeldt 1950:226; Tozzer 1913:149–150) remarked on the omnipresence of "house mounds" around and between Maya cities.

The first major publication devoted to ordinary Maya residences was *House Mounds of Uaxactun, Guatemala*, published in 1934 by Robert Wauchope. A few years later, in 1938, Wauchope published another landmark, *Modern Maya Houses: A Study of Their Archaeological Significance*, the first ethnoarchaeological study of Maya commoners and their houses (Figures 11.1–11.3). Given these pioneering studies on houses and house mounds, it is surprising that commoners did not become a major focus of Maya archaeology until the 1950s, when Gordon Willey, William Bullard, John Glass, and James Gifford (1965) began their project in the Belize River Valley.

Later, in the 1960s, archaeologists such as William Haviland (at Tikal) and Gair Tourtellot (at Seibal) focused on low mounds and produced new excavation data to show that not all "house mounds" were actually houses. Their work did much to modify the "principle of abundance"—the assumption that since (1) commoners constituted most of Maya society, (2) the family was the most numerous component of Maya society, (3) low mounds were everywhere, and (4) low mounds were the most numerous kind of mound, it followed that those mounds must have been houses.

Haviland (1965, 1966, 1988), Tourtellot (1988a, 1988b), and Linda Manzanilla and Luis Barba (1990) have shown that although some low mounds were dwellings (the sleeping quarters of a family), other mounds had different functions (serving as altars, shrines, storage areas, work platforms, and kitchens; Figure 11.4). Haviland and Tourtellot showed that in cases where three or four mounds formed a patio or courtyard group, sometimes only one of the four mounds was an actual dwelling. This discovery has implications for population estimates (Haviland 1967, 1972a, 1972b, 1982; J. E. S. Thompson 1971).

Tourtellot (1988b:264) says, "As many as one-third of the small struc-

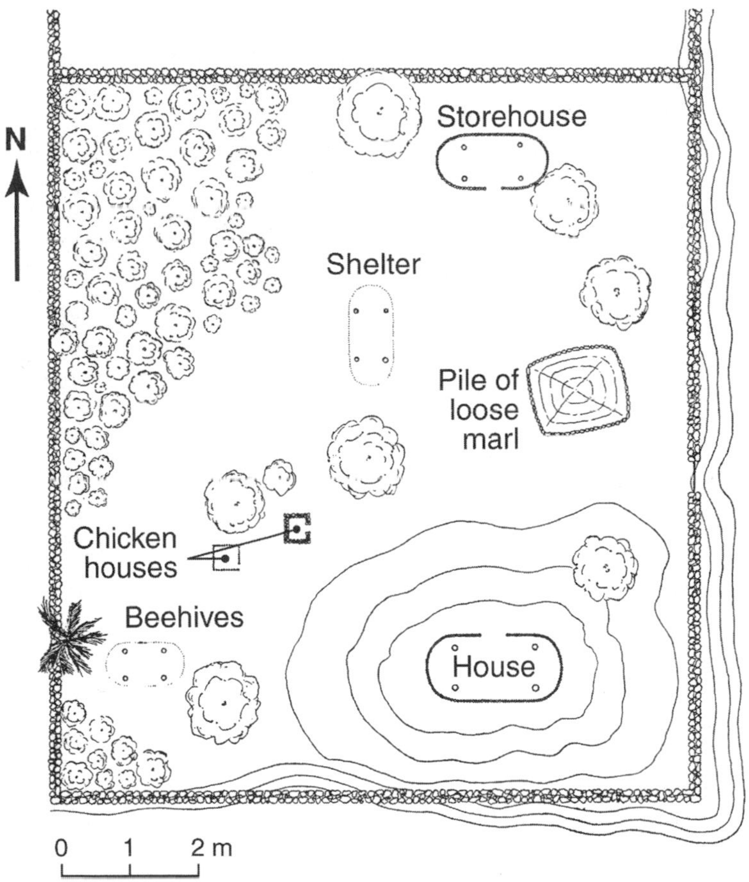

Figure 11.2. A house and associated structures from Chan Kom. In addition to the house, there is a beehive shelter, chicken houses, and a storehouse (redrawn from Wauchope 1938: Fig. 47a).

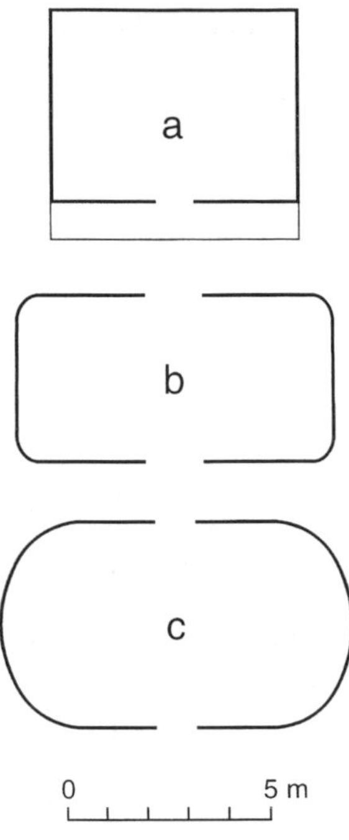

Figure 11.3. The ground plan of a Maya house usually has one of three shapes: (a) *square*, such as this house from San Pedro de Laguna, Guatemala; (b) *rectangular with rounded corners*, such as this one from Tizimín, Yucatán, and (c) *apsidal*, such as this one from Chan Kom (redrawn from Wauchope 1938: Fig. 6).

tures in the central area [of Seibal] are not likely to be dwellings, even though over half of these nondwellings are in domestic units. . . . For comparison, about 83.5% of small structures in units (not overall) at Tikal are not dwelling structures (Haviland 1965:19)." In the case of Mayapán (Pollock et al. 1962), perhaps 2,300 to 3,200 (57–80%) of the 4,000 structures were dwellings. Tourtellot (1988b:265) concludes that "the 'principle of abundance' alone is indeed a poor guide to counts of 'houses,' but it is proved a theoretically and empirically valid observation on counts of dwellings *when those are defined by multiple independent criteria*" (emphasis in original).

Thus three major problems persist: (1) identifying which low mounds were dwellings and which had nonresidential functions, (2) demonstrating what those nonresidential functions were, and (3) distinguishing "elite houses" from "commoner houses."

Because many stereotypes about "commoners" and "elites" abound, I will discuss a few of them here. (Those I do not discuss are addressed elsewhere in this volume, by authors who present new field data to dispel them.) My next task is to separate stereotypes from reality and to suggest potentially productive avenues for future research.

Stereotype 1: Commoners Constitute a Homogeneous Group

One of the biggest stereotypes is that all commoners were alike; it parallels another stereotype, that all elites were alike. Each group, in fact, has been stereotyped to facilitate making contrasts. Although such stereotyping serves to reinforce the dichotomy, actual archaeological data suggest that the remains of "elites" and "commoners" can be difficult to distinguish as two completely discrete categories with clear-cut boundaries. Therefore, the task of assigning one of the two terms—*elite* or *commoner*—to specific houses, features, patios, middens, graves, platforms, and other buildings can be a real challenge. Such a task often ends up being subjective and intuitive. If the conceptual dichotomy we use is overly simplified and does

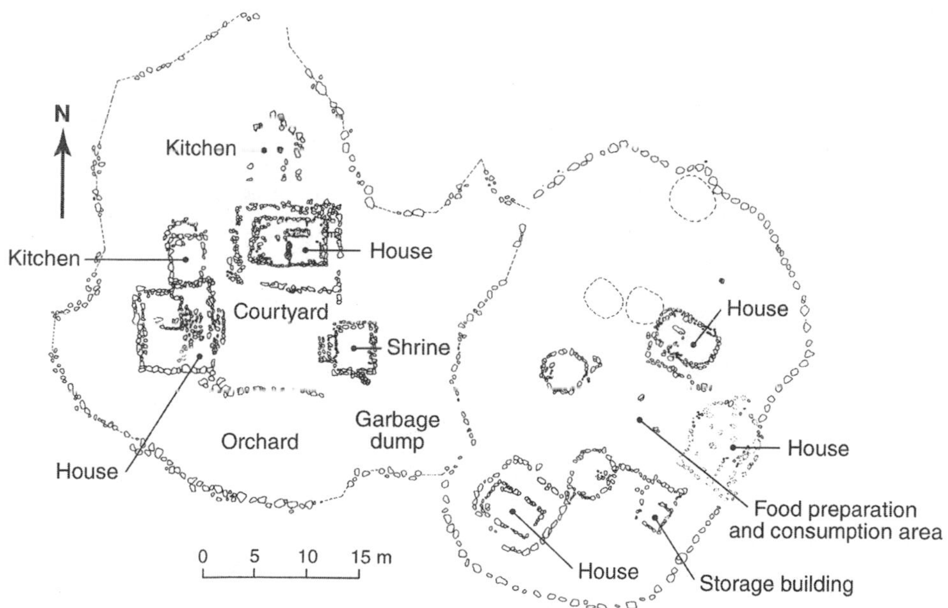

Figure 11.4. Two domestic units from Cobá, Mexico. The western unit had two stuccoed houses, two kitchens, a shrine, and an orchard. The eastern unit included two wattle-and-daub houses, five circular structures (possibly kitchens or storage units), and one square building (possibly used for storage). Manzanilla and Barba suggest that the western unit was built between AD 600 and 700 by the initial "founding" family, and when their offspring married, the eastern unit was added to meet the needs of a growing family (redrawn from Manzanilla and Barba 1990: Fig. 2).

not fit archaeological reality, where did it come from, and why don't we create a conceptual framework that is more in line with Maya reality?

The Maya Conceptual Framework

The sixteenth-century Maya divided their world into two groups: commoners (*ah pach kab, ah chembal winikob*) and nobles by lineage (*almehenob, ah chibal;* Martínez Hernández 1929:116, 119, 623). Nobles had offspring with known descent in both the male and female line (Roys 1933:178). Nobles were associated with generosity, and the expression *almehen ol* referred to the "warm-hearted," "good-hearted," and "generous" nature of a Maya noble (Martínez Hernández 1929:119). Nobles constituted a group that could only be perpetuated by class endogamy; when nobles married nobles, they passed on the privileges they had inherited to their offspring.

From Classic and Postclassic texts and documents, we learn the terms the Maya used for their kings and lords (*ajaw, k'uhul ajaw, kaloomte'*) and for their sublords and subordinate officers (*b'aah sajal, sajal, aj kul, aj kulel, aj k'uhun*). Such terms clearly indicate the presence of a political hierarchy, since the leaders of capitals were referred to as "kings" or "lords," and leaders of subordinate sites were referred to as "sublords" and the holders of other titles. Access to these titles and offices was hereditary, and most (if not all) were restricted to nobles. The distribution and use of these titles over time and space reveal that the ancient Maya had both a hierarchy and a heterarchy of titles; in other words, some terms specified different hierarchical posts, but others referred to offices on the same rung of the ladder. Furthermore, as more Classic period (AD 250–900) texts are deciphered, the number of such titles and offices (both hierarchical and heterarchical) are likely to increase. Since these hieroglyphic texts were commissioned by nobles to legitimize and label important things in their elite world, they are a poor source of information on commoners. For more detailed information on commoners, we need to turn to archaeological, ethnographic, and ethnohistoric data.

What terms did the sixteenth-century Maya use for commoners? One term was *yalba winik*, which meant "small or short in stature, a common and plebeian man" (Martínez Hernández 1929:440–441). Another term, *pach kah winikob*, can be glossed as "townspeople." Commoners were thought to have been made from clay or earth (*Relaciones de Yucatán* 1898–1900, Vol. 11:79) or born out of earth that was mixed with grass (López de Cogolludo 1867–1868, Book 4, Ch. 7). Such lowly terrestrial origins of commoners were an explicit contrast with the celestial origins of Maya nobles.

I have argued elsewhere (Marcus 1992:225–226) that there was no Maya "middle class," at least in the sense of a third, class-endogamous stratum. However, the Spaniards collected the term *açmen winik*, which they translated as "a man between *principal* [noble] and plebeian, a man of middling status" (Martínez Hernández 1929:69). It is likely that such men were commoners who had increased their wealth through achievement or been appointed to an office such as ward head or tribute collector, causing them to stand out from the mass of subsistence farmers. Virtually all ancient states had commoners who were appointed to bureaucratic positions or had become successful merchants or military men. They could not aspire to noble titles, but their houses and burials might appear intermediate in richness between those of the nobility and those of the bulk of the commoners. Such houses and burials make it all the more difficult to draw sharp lines between "elite" and "commoner."

It seems clear from both Colonial documents and Classic period hieroglyphic texts that the ancient Maya had much less trouble than we do in recognizing who was a noble and who was a commoner. Archaeologists have little trouble identifying the burials of kings and poor commoners. The trouble lies with the boundary between minor nobles and wealthy commoners. The ancient Maya had one continuum of statuses within the commoner stratum and another continuum of statuses within the elite stratum. Unfortunately, the sixteenth-century Spaniards do not supply us with details on how the houses and burials of minor nobles differed from those of wealthy commoners or those with bureaucratic appointments.

Nor do the middens we excavate necessarily provide us with clear-cut data on social class. Middens cannot always be traced to one household, but may belong to an entire neighborhood that changed in composition over time.[2] An additional problem is that many nobles had servants living in and around their residential structures; such households would generate a midden that included both high-status and low-status items.

In life, each Maya would have communicated something of his or her status through personal clothing and adornment, including hairstyle, headdress, sandals, and personal ornaments. So much of this adornment perishes in the tropical lowlands that we are forced to put an enormous interpretive burden on nonperishable items like jade, polychrome pottery, obsidian and chert eccentrics, and stone vessels. When it comes to commoners, we usually define their burials in terms of the *absence* of anything imperishable we consider elite rather than the *presence* of anything we consider low status. Deprived of the full inventory of perishable and nonperishable items, we tend to rely on more ambiguous clues to status, such as (1) the labor investment and quality of materials used in the structure or tomb and (2) its proximity to the center of the site or to some major architectural/public building group(s).

Although some Mayanists assume they are working on commoners when they dig low house mounds, even this strategy may not bring to light the humblest form of architecture: simple wattle-and-daub houses with thatched roofs, built directly on the soil. Our sample of residential architecture is still strongly skewed to structures with stone walls or foundations, to structures set on platforms that were often rebuilt several times on that spot. The ephemeral hut, occupied for one generation by a low-status family, is largely missing from our Maya database. This is a significant body of missing data because the contents of such houses should show us the nonperishable inventory of the lowliest commoners.

There are other ramifications of the notion that all commoners are alike. Among other things, that notion encourages archaeologists to believe that one household can stand for *all* households—as if the house of a subsistence farmer and a craftsman would be identical. How many houses would we need to dig to say confidently that we had recovered the *full range of variability among commoner houses?* Since Maya sites seem to include thousands of "house mounds" and perhaps an even greater number of thatched huts without platforms, it will be difficult to recover the full range of variation. What we are likely to get are, let us say, four "house mounds" excavated from one site, with two of them classified as "low status/commoner" and two as "high status/elite." If it were possible to excavate one hundred houses, we might find that we had a long continuum rather than the two-part dichotomy mentioned above, and that the material culture and household inventories showed more variation than we had expected.

Stereotype 2: Commoners Were Passive Recipients of Elite Directives, Not Active Agents

Some scholars regard the individual commoner household as the essential unit for understanding the Maya economy. Others regard elite control of household labor (and the products manufactured by that labor) as the essential ingredient for understanding the economy. A frequent assumption is that the elite not only directed the commoners but also led all aspects of the economy. We should not discount the likelihood that commoners had some degree of control over certain items, made active choices, created innovations, and displayed significant decision making in producing a product. Relationships between commoners and elite were no doubt dynamic, changing from period to period, differing by commodity and by site. What we need to determine is the degree of elite control and commoner autonomy rather than *assuming* absolute elite control. The elite may have controlled the distribution and access to some finished products, but commoners probably had opportunities to innovate during various steps in the chain of production. Commoner households should not simply be assumed to be passive recipients of elite directives.

Stereotype 3: Commoners Were Largely Conservative

Some household activities are admittedly basic—grinding corn, storing water, making chipped-stone and ground-stone tools—and were engaged in by all the households in a village, perhaps for centuries. The ubiquity of the artifacts associated with these tasks (manos, metates, waste flakes, storage jars, and so on) tend to make commoners *look* unchanging through time and space. The presence of this conservative set of utilitarian artifacts does not mean, however, that commoners were so conservative that household behaviors and practices never changed.

Let us look at an example of food preparation, one of the most conservative household tasks. Since the contemporary Maya make tortillas every day, we might expect that ancient Maya commoners did the same thing. Tortillas today are cooked on a *comal*, or clay griddle, called *xamach* in Yucatec and *semet* in Tzotzil. Such clay griddles, however, have not been found in the earliest Maya villages (Marcus 1982:248).

Comales were manufactured in Middle to Late Preclassic times in highland Maya sites (e.g., Kaminaljuyú [Popenoe de Hatch 1997:86, 119] and Chalchuapa [Sharer 1978, Vol. 3:87]), but they do not appear until much later—in Classic or Postclassic times—at many lowland Maya sites (e.g., Brainerd 1958; R. E. Smith 1971; J. E. S. Thompson 1938). Even when *comales* are found in late deposits in lowland Maya sites, they seem to be rare finds.

Both George Brainerd (1958:312, Fig. 97k) and Robert Smith (1971:84) noted how rare *comales* were, even in Postclassic sites such as Mayapán. The few *comales* found at Mayapán could have been used for cooking tortillas, but Smith suggests that they could just as easily have been used to toast cacao beans, seeds, or nuts. Smith (1971:84) adds, "However, if this toasting function was of real concern to these Maya people it would seem logical for them to have manufactured more than the very few sherds encountered."

The available data suggest that for much of lowland Maya prehistory, tortillas were unknown and corn was prepared in other ways (Marcus 1982:248). For example, many lowland households serve corn in the form of *atole* (*'ul, sa'*), as a gruel made from green corn (*is 'ul*), as pozole (*k'eyem*), or as beverages (for example, as *pinole* [*kah*], made from corn toasted with cinnamon or other ingredients, or as a drink made from corn cooked without lime [*saca*]). Corn may also be prepared as tamales (*wah, waah*) or as thick cakes (*pimpim wah*) cooked in a subterranean earth oven called a *pib* (Tozzer 1941:89–90; Villa Rojas 1945:54). Because of changes in food preparation over time, the term *wah* has become increasingly inclusive—it initially seems to have referred only to tamales, then was applied to both tamales and tortillas, and today refers to tamales, tortillas, and other kinds of bread introduced from the Old World.

We have seen that *comales* were manufactured in the Maya highlands earlier than in the Maya lowlands. *Comales* seem to appear during Middle Preclassic times at several sites throughout the Mexican highlands. In Oaxaca, for example, *comales* first appear around 500 BC at the urban center of Monte Albán, and we suspect that their appearance there had something to do with the need to mass-produce food for the thousands of urban laborers. Lowland Maya cities presumably had to feed thousands of laborers, too, and evidently found a different way to do it. Based on ethnographic analogy, it is possible that each Maya laborer carried a ball of uncooked maize dough to his workplace, where he mixed it with water for nourishment at mealtime.

The progression from corn gruel to dough balls to tortillas tells us that even the most common tasks of food preparation did not remain static over time, and commoners were probably as instrumental in innovation and change in such tasks as the elite.

Stereotype 4: Commoner Households Are Likely to Show Considerable Uniformity

Mesoamericanists have been strongly influenced by ethnographic studies of contemporary indigenous households, many of which have relatively uniform contents. For example, Alan Sandstrom (1991:111–113), speaking about a modern Nahua community, reports:

> A survey of household items that I conducted found that the average house contained between 45 and 55 different items. Surprisingly, the household possessions of wealthier families are practically indistinguishable from those of poorer families in either quality and quantity. Consumption patterns do not seem to be significantly affected by the level of wealth of the household.

What we sometimes forget is that today's Indian society is no longer stratified along the lines of class-endogamous nobles versus commoners. Today's villagers are peasants in a money-based national economy, where terms such as "upper," "middle," and "lower" refer to arbitrary divisions of an economic continuum rather than hereditary social strata. While certain aspects of their life are relevant to the past, others are not.

Both ethnohistoric accounts and archaeological evidence suggest that there was less uniformity in the pre-Hispanic era.[3] We know that commoners could be masons, potters, mat makers, weavers, traders, hunters, fishers, plant collectors, snail collectors, beekeepers, salt makers, charcoal burners, dyers, sandal makers, tanners, and so forth (Martínez Hernández 1929:74–111), and such diverse activities were associated with equipment that may have been used in the courtyards of commoners or brought to their houses after work for safekeeping. The problem arises when we ingenuously try to measure such diversity by relying on a single conveniently abundant and nonperishable artifact category, such as pottery. The result, as Ken Hirth reports from Xochicalco in Morelos, can be disappointing:

> The analysis of ceramic assemblages did not reveal as many differences between segments of the society as the architectural information suggested might exist. . . . The single most important conclusion of this study has been that individual artifact categories should not be relied upon to make socioeconomic inferences about the past. Ceramic, chipped stone, ground stone, and architectural data each reflect different aspects of socioeconomic condition. As a result, the reliability of the conclusions about socioeconomic status increases in direct proportion to the number of artifact classes and data sets included in the analysis. (Hirth 1993:140, 143)

One project to tackle the problem of household diversity through the use of multiple artifact classes and data sets was that of David Webster and Nancy Gonlin in the Copán Valley (Webster and Gonlin 1988; Webster et al. 1997). They utilized complete household inventories, complete courtyard inventories, and a wide range of excavated courtyard features and activity areas, and their data reveal considerably more heterogeneity than we usually see (Gonlin 1994, this volume).

Webster and Gonlin excavated eight rural sites in the Copán Valley, exposing hundreds of square meters in each case. Such horizontal exposures yielded both the residential structures and the associated outdoor spaces. In some cases, the house itself constituted only 10 percent of the area excavated, with more than 90 percent being the dooryard or outdoor work space. This excavation strategy was extremely effective, standing in marked contrast with previous projects that had simply test-pitted a house mound or excavated only the interior of the house. (In fairness to most earlier projects, it should be stressed that they had different goals. They simply wanted to date "house mounds" and gauge population growth, not obtain household inventories, find activity areas, and reveal the status of each and every commoner household.)

In Webster and Gonlin's sample of Copán Valley houses, the average size of the stone platform that supported a perishable house was 30 m^2. One rural site yielded a fine example of a small domestic structure on a rectangular platform, which measured 3.8 × 2.3 m, or 8.74 m^2 (Webster and Gonlin 1988: Figure 8). This one-room dwelling was accompanied by a flimsy addition. Webster and Gonlin (1988:186) noted that "many of the poorer inhabitants in the modern [Copán] valley live in houses of comparable size." They went on to say, "We must point out, though, that at Copán platform area, or interior living space, is a much less sensitive indicator of social status than is the height and quality of buildings." They noted that rural houses rarely had cut stone, as was typical of the houses in the city of Copán. Nor did rural houses show evidence of plaster or paint, "which were conspicuously used on structures of all ranks in the urban core."

The residences of rural commoners throughout the Copán Valley consisted of 3–5 mounds around a courtyard, with all mounds less than one meter in height (these mound groups were classified as Type 1; see Willey et al. 1978; Willey and Leventhal 1979). Such mounds contained cobblestone platforms that had originally supported perishable structures (Figure 11.5). Commoner residences in the city of Copán, on the other hand, were larger than those in the countryside. Urban houses of commoners averaged 45.5 m^2 (ca. 5 × 9 m), while those in rural areas averaged 34 m^2 (ca. 5 × 6.8 m). Archaeologists interested in the houses of commoners might do well to excavate more Type 1 groups, expanding the database developed by Webster and Gonlin (1988).

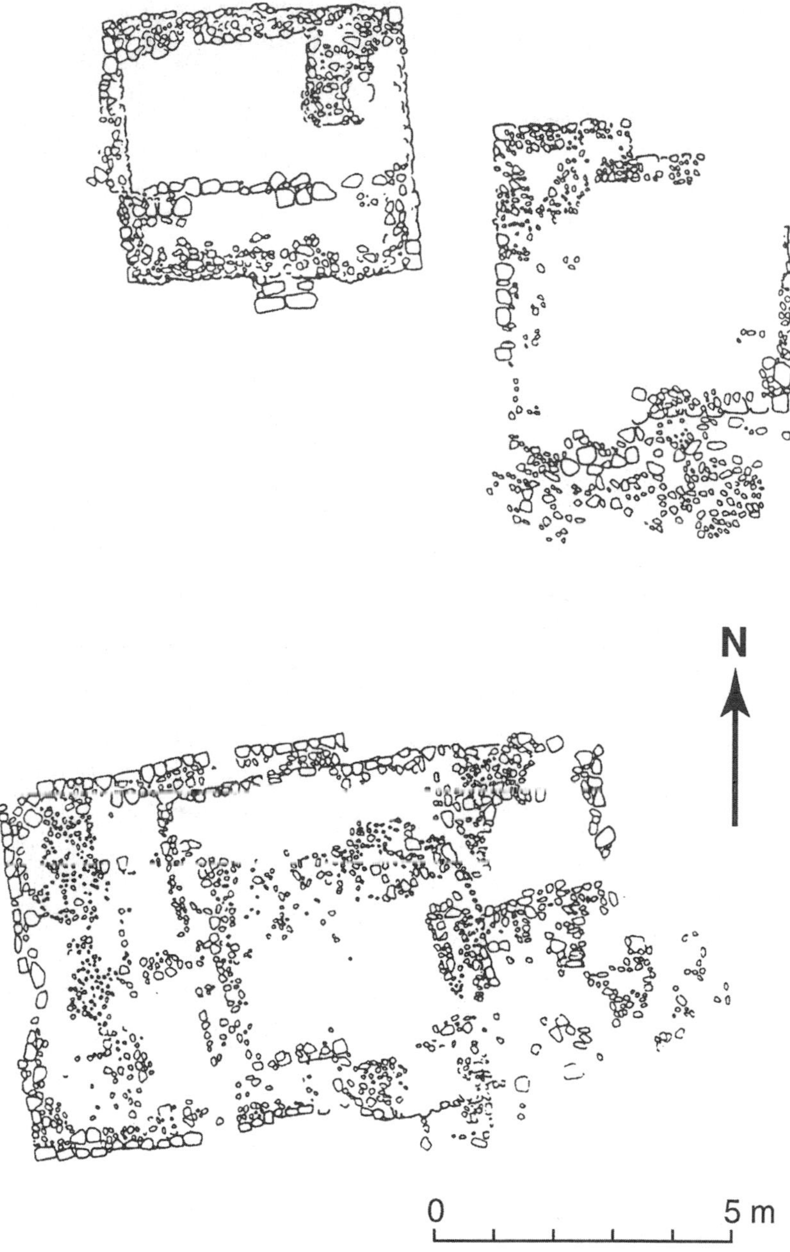

Figure 11.5. This Copán Valley household, known as 7D-6-2, includes three structures: a house (to the north), a kitchen (to the east), and possibly another large house (to the south) (redrawn from Gonlin 1994: Fig. 88).

Significantly, the Copán Valley sample showed that commoners were not a uniform group. For example, Gonlin (1994:195) says:

> What is unexpected is the diversity revealed in small rural households. Although, in general, the rural type 1 groups had simpler architecture, simpler graves, less fineware, fewer exotic goods, and restricted access to prime agricultural land, there were wide wealth differences within this category. It should no longer be assumed that rural areas of complex societies are homogeneous in either chronology, function, or sociocultural dimensions.

In addition, the excavation of middens around households at other Maya sites like Tikal now makes it clear that commoners *did* obtain some of the goods formerly labeled "high status" or "exotic," such as obsidian and shell. Whether those commoner households were the initial destination for some of these items, or whether such goods "trickled down" to them after being discarded by higher-status families, is not clear (Haviland and Moholy-Nagy 1992:54).

It is worth noting that in the past, when our data came from more limited testpits in house mounds, commoner households looked more similar than they do today. Small testpits yield incomplete inventories, no information on spatial clustering of artifacts and activity areas, and few data on the size of the house and labor investment in its construction. They also tend to force us to rely on just one category of material—ceramics. As Hirth points out, it is necessary to take into account as many classes of material as we can. Like Webster and Gonlin, Hirth stresses that the complete architectural unit (its size, height, elaboration, quality of materials, and number of built-in features, such as benches) may be even more important as an indicator of socioeconomic status than the associated artifacts.

The inhabitants of many sites—including Copán, Cerén, Cobá, and Don Martín—built multistructure units in which various buildings had different functions. Of the twenty-three structures excavated at rural sites in the Copán Valley, some thirteen (or 57%) were probably residences. For example, at Site 7D-6-2 is a household group that consisted of three structures—a house to the north, a kitchen to the east, and possibly another house to the south (see Figure 11.5).

At Cerén, each cluster of "household structures" included a house, a storehouse, a kitchen, and occasionally a ramada used as a workshop (Figure 11.6). Special buildings at Cerén included two that had religious

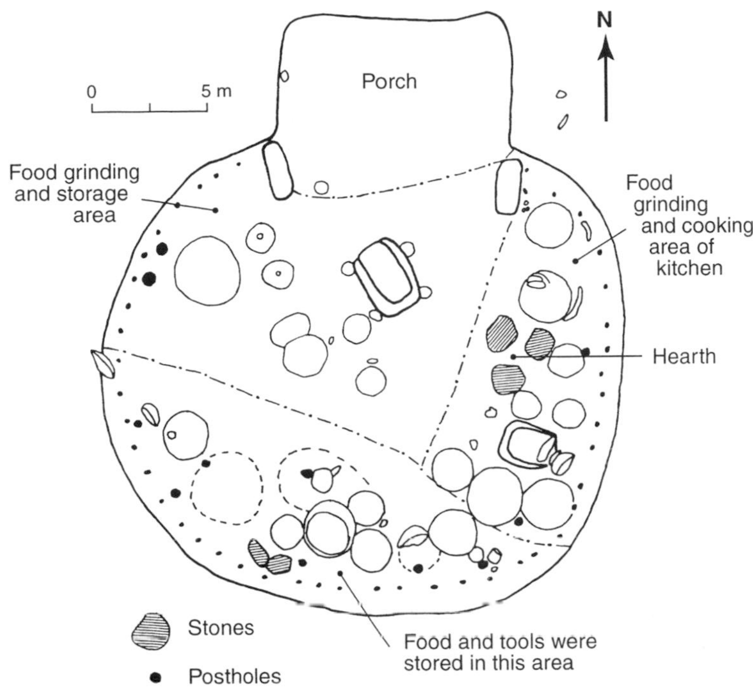

Figure 11.6. Some kitchens were circular, like this one at Cerén, which measures 17.2 m^2 (compare with those from Cobá in Figure 11.4). Careful piece-plotting allowed Payson Sheets, the excavator, to divide the Cerén kitchen into different activity areas (redrawn from Webster et al. 1997: Fig. 8a).

functions, one that was a sweatbath, and one that served a civic function (Webster et al. 1997:50). Of the seven household structures excavated at Cerén (Sheets 1992:39), only two are identified as a *domicile*, i.e., the "eating, sleeping, and daytime activity structure of the household." One good indicator of a domicile was the presence of interior benches, presumably used for sleeping or storage. Cerén, of course, had atypical preservation of artifacts, and the excavators were impressed with the richness of inventories found in houses, kitchens, and storerooms. Included were polychrome pottery, painted gourds, and pigments such as cinnabar, achiote, and hematite (Webster et al. 1997:58). Many Cerén buildings show high concentrations of artifacts on the floor; in fact, "interiors are so packed with possessions that it is hard to imagine how people moved about or habitually used interior spaces . . ." (Webster et al. 1997:55).

At Cobá in Quintana Roo, two contiguous units included not only domiciles for sleeping but also separate buildings that served as kitchens, storage structures, shrines, and other functions (see Figure 11.4). At the site of Don Martín in Chiapas, a domestic unit that covered 640 m^2 consisted of four stone platforms around a patio with an altar (Figure 11.7). Given the poor preservation, the destruction of both the perishable artifacts and perishable structures, and the relative homogeneity of the artifacts on those platforms, Alejandro Martínez (1986:432–435) was unable to identify specific activity areas, so he simply labeled each platform "casa" and placed that word in quotation marks. If he had had better preservation and discovered activity areas, he would have been able to say something more about building functions.

In sum, when the excavations are extensive enough or the preservation is very good, the households of Maya commoners do show considerable variation. This variation is sufficient to show a continuum from wealthy craft specialists to poor subsistence farmers, and it is likely that the true variation was even greater than the glimpses archaeology gives us.

Units of Analysis in the Study of Commoners

The Mayanist Robert Wauchope (1934, 1938) believed that the *house* was the unit where the study of Maya commoners should begin (Figure 11.8). It is clear that the house was also an important unit for the Maya themselves, since terms such as *nah* or *otoch* were widely used. *Nah* could be used to designate a house or a building whose owner was not specified, as in *nikte'il nah*, "meeting house." In contrast, *otoch* or *otot* always has a prefix to show it is possessed, as in *yotoch* (Yucatec) and *yotot* (Chol), "his house" (Schele and Mathews 1998:43). These root words for "house" were even extended to palaces (*ka'anal nah*), to royal houses (*ajawlil nah*), to temples (*yotoch k'u*, *k'unah*, *k'ul nah*), and to other public buildings (*popol nah*, *k'ak'al nah*, *nikte'il nah;* see Barrera et al. 1980 for other examples).

The Maya had both huts (*xa'nil nah*, *k'axbil nah*, or *kumkab nah*) and stone houses (*nokak nah;* Figure 11.9). It is tempting to assume that huts were for commoners and stone houses were for nobles, but it was not as simple as that. After the old class-endogamous strata were removed by the Spanish Conquest, contemporary and Colonial Maya had stone houses, depending on the family's wealth.

The house was an important building block of Maya society, but we know from various researchers that there were both smaller units (such as activity areas within the house) and larger units (such as the

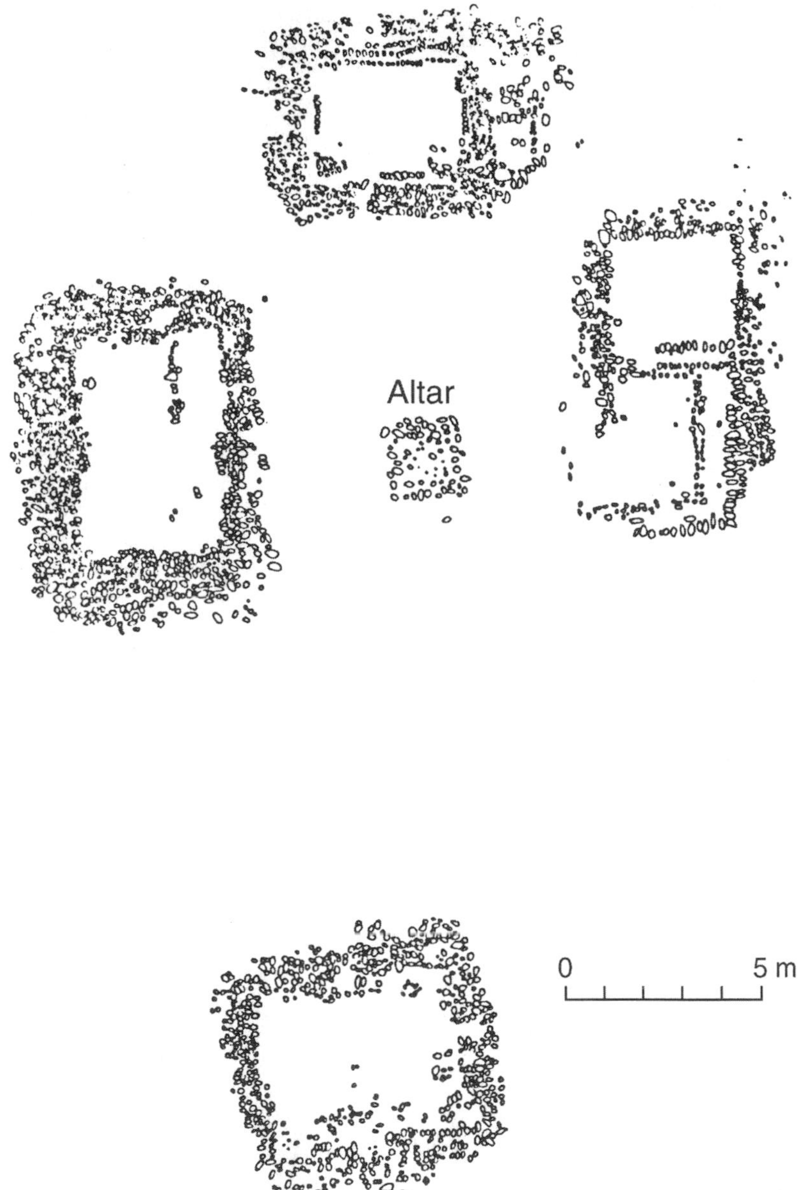

Figure 11.7. Four platforms surround a patio with a central altar at Don Martín, Chiapas. The differences in size and layout suggest that each structure may have had a different function. The eastern structure has two rooms, one 9 m^2 and the other 11.25 m^2. The northern structure has one room that is 10 m^2, the western structure has one room that is 19.25 m^2, and the southern structure has one room that is 17.5 m^2 (redrawn from Martínez 1986: Fig. 4).

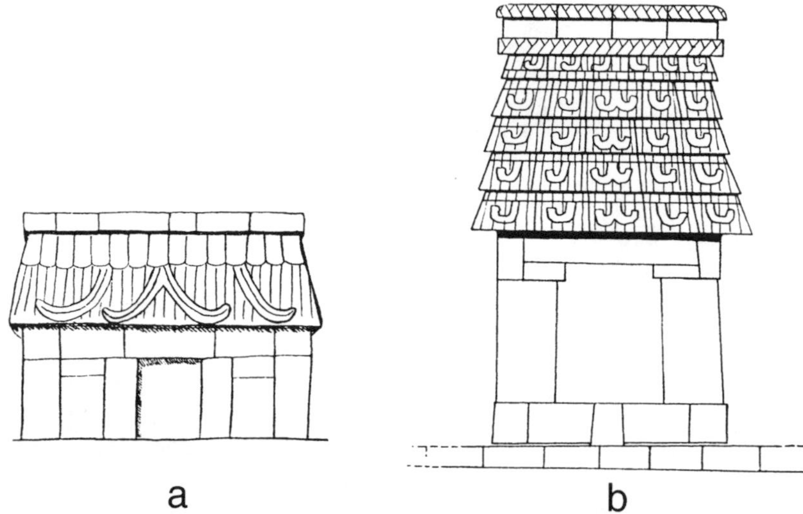

Figure 11.8. Humble Maya houses with thatched roofs could be depicted on the façade of stone palaces and public buildings. Examples occur on (a) the north side of the Nunnery Quadrangle at Uxmal and on (b) Building 5 at Labná (redrawn from Wauchope 1934: Figs. 7c, 7b).

integrated groups of structures found by Gonlin, Webster, Manzanilla, Barba, A. Martínez, Sheets, and others). In his ethnographic work in highland Chiapas, Evon Vogt (1969:83–85) showed that Maya houses were conceptually divided into separate living spaces for men and women (Figure 11.10). The woman's side of the house had her three-stone hearth (*'oshyoket*) and cooking pots, her manos and metates, water jars, ladles, looms, and baskets. The man's side of the house had his tools and digging stick and the censer and altar.

As for the larger unit, or multistructure house-lot, it is possible that it was not only recognized as a unit but also given a specific name. This practice was widespread in pre-Hispanic Mexico; the Nahua speakers of Tepoztlán in Morelos named both individual houses[4] and house compounds (Redfield 1930). In the Huasteca, Sandstrom (1991:106–107) studied a Nahua-speaking community in which each house or house cluster was given a name, a *caltocayotl* (from *calli*, "house," and *tocayotl*, "nickname"). Specific house names were based on the same type of environmental features used to label village subareas. The house name itself was sometimes taken on by the individuals who lived in that house. The ancient Maya may have shared some of these naming practices, because we know that they gave names to many stone buildings (Figure 11.11). Some buildings were called "big white house," "6 Sky sacred building," "serpent house," "flower building," "house of the nine bushes,"[5] and "his temple, his house" (Freidel and Schele 1989; Schele 1990; Schele and Freidel 1990; Schele and Mathews 1998). What we do not know is whether the Maya, like the Nahua of Tepoztlán and Amatlán, also named the houses of commoners.

Wards and Still Larger Units

Our discussion of multistructure households and dooryards brings us to the threshold of the next larger unit of analysis: the residential ward. The ward was of significance to the ancient Maya, and such clusters of households or neighborhoods may be depicted in murals at Chichén Itzá (Figures 11.12, 11.13). The excavation of a ward would require even more extensive work than that expended by Payson Sheets on the households of

Figure 11.9. A Maya house from Telchac Pueblo in Yucatán has an apsidal plan, dry rubble masonry walls, and a thatched roof (redrawn from Wauchope 1938: Fig. 25).

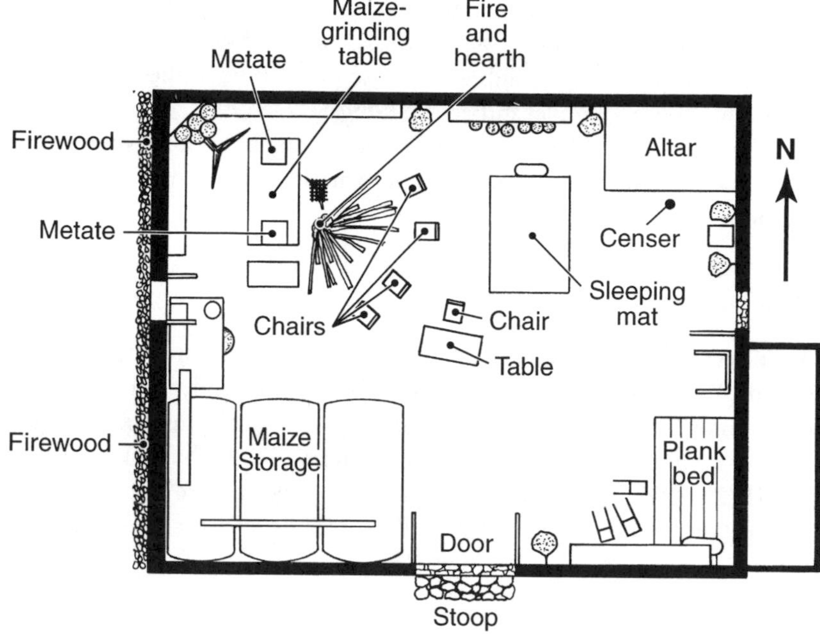

Figure 11.10. This Tzotzil Maya house (measuring 6 × 7 m) is divided into (1) a *woman's area* to the left, where we see the hearth, stored maize, and kitchen implements, and (2) a *man's area* to the right, where the altar and objects owned and used by men are located (redrawn from Vogt 1969: Fig. 32).

Cerén and that by Webster and Gonlin on the households of the Copán Valley. The potential payoffs might include (1) even greater diversity in commoner activities and (2) a sample of all those features that occur out in the open, in the space between houses.

Ethnohistoric and ethnographic data[6] suggest the following continuum of analytical units, from smallest to largest:

1. At the level of the individual commoner, the man's or woman's activity area
2. At the level of the family, the house (*nah*, *otoch*) and dooryard
3. At the level of the domestic group (*otochnal*), a series of structures around a shared patio
4. At the level of the lineage (*chibal*), a residential ward (*cuchteel*, *chi'na*)
5. At the level of an entire lineage sharing the same Maya patronymic, a hamlet or village (*cah*, *chancah*)
6. At the level of multiple patrilineages, a town (*noh cah*)

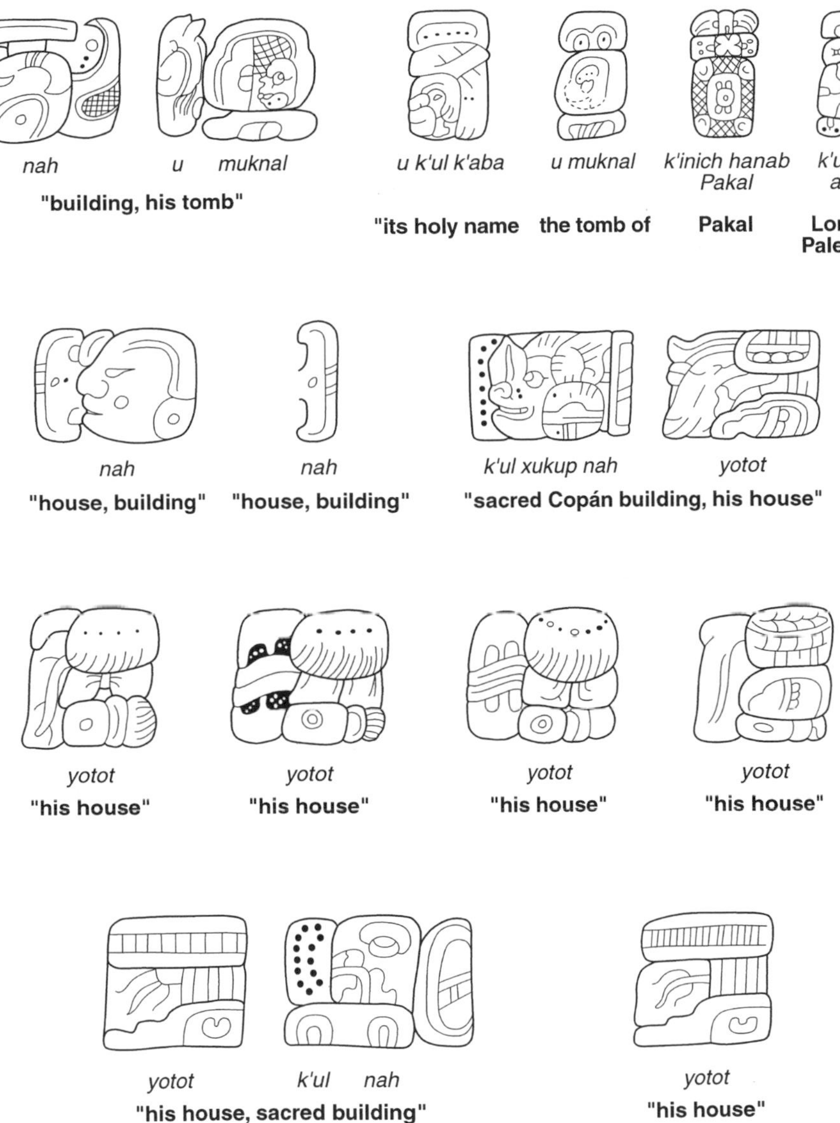

Figure 11.11. The hieroglyphs for *nah* and *otot,* words meaning "house" and "structure," were used by the ancient Maya to label public buildings, including royal temples and palaces (redrawn from Marcus n.d.: Fig. 5; Schele and Freidel 1990: Figs. 6.14, 6.15, 6.16; Schele and Mathews 1998: Fig. 1.15).

Figure 11.12. Groups of thatched-roof houses are depicted in Late Classic murals in the Temple of the Warriors at Chichén Itzá (redrawn from Wauchope 1934: Fig. 3b).

Note that the ward falls somewhere near the midpoint of this continuum.[7] Excavating larger units such as "village" and "town" is likely to be logistically impossible for even the most dedicated archaeologist, and such a large task would have to be approached through a sampling program. Sampling several residential wards within the same village, however, is feasible and could reveal additional variation in the activities of commoners.

Conclusions

In his pioneering study of house mounds at Uaxactún, Wauchope (1934: 160) expressed admiration for the archaeological work being done in the Aegean and Egypt on "commoners" and hope that we would one day gain "a complete knowledge of the life and customs of the 'average man'" in the Maya area.

Wauchope's hope remains as laudable as ever, but we now know that the situation is more complex than he imagined. Finding house mounds is only a beginning, since they contain house platforms but usually lack wattle-and-daub huts built directly on the ground. Test-pitting house mounds is only a beginning, too, because test-pitting exposes so little of each house that it reinforces a stereotype of homogeneity. The complete excavation of multimound domestic groups in their entirety has begun to show us the diversity of commoners' lives (e.g., Gonlin 1994; Webster and Gonlin 1988; Webster et al. 1997).

Since "commoner" simply means anyone who is not of noble birth, it includes everyone from impoverished subsistence farmers to wealthy craftsmen, or even trusted commoners appointed to bureaucratic offices by nobles. Wealthy commoners may have commanded as many resources, and built houses just as impressive, as some of the minor nobility—those who were genealogically most distant from the ruler. This is why I have real reservations about using the term "middle class" for the Maya. It can refer only to an *economic bracket* (not to a third class-endogamous social stratum), and as such it is likely to conflate minor nobles and wealthy commoners.

Ethnohistory tells us that commoners competed with each other for bureaucratic positions and often used achievement as a means to social and economic mobility. Unfortunately, ethnohistory does not tell us how to

Figure 11.13. Groups of thatched-roof houses are depicted in Late Classic murals in the Temple of the Warriors at Chichén Itzá (redrawn from Wauchope 1934: Fig. 3a).

distinguish the house of a wealthy commoner craftsman from the house of a successful commoner bureaucrat. Archaeologists will have to do more than test-pit house mounds if they seek to distinguish the different kinds of residents who occupied the houses of an ancient Maya city. Ethnohistory reminds us that commoners and nobles did not necessarily come neatly packaged in two kinds of houses. Many nobles had commoner assistants, servants, and even slaves, some of whom lived in the noble residence; thus, the refuse from a palace or noble residence is not necessarily all "elite refuse." Even wealthy commoner merchants or craftsmen may have had servants or slaves. In fact, one can imagine an artisan with his own servants, attached to the household of a noble patron with his own servants. Although our archaeological units of analysis may be houses and wards, we are trying to get at people, and complicating that effort is the fact that some households may have included several kinds of people (e.g., Robin 2001). A major challenge is to put faces on the faceless, to convert a stereotyped group of commoners into individuals.

Notes

1. Adams and Smith (1981:338) and Webster (1992:146–147) discuss the ways that such percentages have been estimated and calculated.

2. For discussions of developmental cycling in the domestic group, see Ashmore 1981, Fortes 1958, Haviland 1988, and Tourtellot 1988a.

3. Even in 1940, Wauchope (1940:233) says that "all Maya houses, contrary to an assumption at one time, are not alike; we are beginning to realize that the differences between them are significant from historical, economic, and social points of view."

4. "In most cases people live on the sites in which lived their ancestors for many generations. These house sites bear individual Nahuatl names by which addresses are given . . ." (Redfield 1930:72–73). Their names include Tecuantlan, "place of wolves"; Tlaxcalchican, "place of tortillas"; Iztapa, "place of salt"; Pulquetlan, "place of pulque"; Totoc, "place of birds"; and Tlateliticpac, "on top of the slope."

5. *Bolon-haaban yotoch* (Roys 1933:33)

6. Barrera et al. 1980; Marcus 1983:468–469.

7. Similarly, for the Aztec, four levels emerged from archaeology: Level 1, the house; Level 2, the Patio Group; Level 3, the House Cluster; and Level 4, the Macrocluster. From Aztec ethnohistory we see the following: Level 1, Calli (House); Level 2, Ithualli (House Compound); Level 3, Chinamitl or Small *calpulli;* Level 4, the Macrocluster or the Calpulli (Smith 1993:193–202).

References

Adams, Richard E. W., and Woodruff D. Smith

1981 Feudal Models for Classic Maya Civilization. In *Lowland Maya Settlement Patterns*, edited by Wendy Ashmore, pp. 335–349. University of New Mexico Press, Albuquerque.

Ashmore, Wendy

1981 Some Issues of Method and Theory in Lowland Maya Settlement Archaeology. In *Lowland Maya Settlement Patterns*, edited by Wendy Ashmore, pp. 37–69. University of New Mexico Press, Albuquerque.

Barrera Vásquez, Alfredo, et al.

1980 *Diccionario Cordemex: Maya-Español, Español-Maya.* Ediciones Cordemex, Mérida.

Brainerd, George W.

1958 *The Archaeological Ceramics of Yucatan.* Anthropological Records 19. University of California Press, Berkeley.

Fortes, Meyer

1958 Introduction. In *The Developmental Cycle in Domestic Groups*, edited by Jack Goody, pp. 1–14. Cambridge University Press, Cambridge.

Freidel, David A., and Linda Schele

1989 Dead Kings and Living Temples: Dedication and Termination Rituals among the Ancient Maya. In *Word and Image in Maya Culture*, edited by William Hanks and Don Rice, pp. 233–243. University of Utah Press, Salt Lake City.

Gann, Thomas

1925 *Mystery Cities.* Scribner's Sons, New York.

Gonlin, Nancy

1994 Rural Household Diversity in Late Classic Copan, Honduras. In *Archaeological Views from the Countryside: Village Communities in Early Complex Societies*, edited by Glenn M. Schwartz and Steven E. Falconer, pp. 177–197. Smithsonian Institution Press, Washington D.C.

Gordon, George Byron

1896 *The Prehistoric Ruins of Copan, Honduras.* Memoirs of the Peabody Museum of Archaeology and Ethnology, vol. 1, no. 1. Harvard University, Cambridge.

Haviland, William A.

1965 Prehistoric Settlement at Tikal, Guatemala. *Expedition* 7 (3):14–23.

1966 *Maya Settlement Patterns: A Critical Review.* Middle American Research Institute Publication 26. Tulane University, New Orleans.

1967 Stature at Tikal, Guatemala: Implications for Ancient Maya Demography and Social Organization. *American Antiquity* 32 (3):316–325.

1972a Family Size, Prehistoric Population Estimates, and the Ancient Maya. *American Antiquity* 37:135–139.

1972b Estimates of Maya Population: Comments on Thompson's Comments. *American Antiquity* 37:261–262.

1982 Where the Rich Folks Lived: Deranging Factors in the Statistical Analysis of Tikal Settlement. *American Antiquity* 47:427–429.

1988 Musical Hammocks at Tikal: Problems with Reconstructing Household Composition. In *Household and Community in the Mesoamerican Past*, edited by Richard R. Wilk and Wendy Ashmore, pp. 121–134. University of New Mexico Press, Albuquerque.

Haviland, William A., and Hattula Moholy-Nagy

1992 Distinguishing the High and Mighty from the Hoi Polloi at Tikal, Guatemala. In *Mesoamerican Elites: An Archaeological Assessment*, edited by Diane Z. Chase and Arlen F. Chase, pp. 50–60. University of Oklahoma Press, Norman.

Hewett, Edgar L.

1912 The Excavation of Quirigua, Guatemala, by the School of American Archaeology. *Proceedings of the 18th International Congress of Americanists*, pp. 241–248. N.p., London.

Hirth, Kenneth G.

1993 Identifying Rank and Socioeconomic Status in Domestic Contexts: An Example from Central Mexico. In *Prehispanic Domestic Units in Western Mesoamerica: Studies of the Household, Compound, and Residence*, edited by Robert S. Santley and Kenneth G. Hirth, pp. 121–146. CRC Press, Boca Raton.

Landa, Diego de (see Tozzer 1941)

López de Cogolludo, Diego

1867–1868 [1688] *Historia de Yucatán*. 3rd ed. 2 vols., Mérida.

Manzanilla, Linda (editor)

1986 *Unidades habitacionales mesoamericanas y sus áreas de actividad*. Universidad Nacional Autónoma de México, Mexico City.

Manzanilla, Linda, and Luis Barba

1990 The Study of Activities in Classic Households: Two Case Studies from Coba and Teotihuacan. *Ancient Mesoamerica* 1:41–49.

Marcus, Joyce

1982 The Plant World of the Sixteenth- and Seventeenth-Century Lowland Maya. In *Maya Subsistence: Studies in Memory of Dennis E. Puleston*, edited by Kent V. Flannery, pp. 239–273. Academic Press, New York.

1983 Lowland Maya Archaeology at the Crossroads. *American Antiquity* 48:454–488.

1992 Royal Families, Royal Texts: Examples from the Zapotec and Maya. In *Mesoamerican Elites: An Archaeological Assessment*, edited by Diane Z. Chase and Arlen F. Chase, pp. 221–241. University of Oklahoma Press, Norman.

n.d. The Inscriptions of Calakmul, Part II. 1987 manuscript in possession of the author.

Martínez Hernández, Juan (editor)
1929 *Diccionario de Motul: Maya-Español.* Compañía Tipográfica Yucateca, Mérida.

Martínez Muriel, Alejandro
1986 Unidades domésticas prehispánicas en el centro de Chiapas. In *Unidades habitacionales mesoamericanas y sus áreas de actividad*, edited by Linda Manzanilla, pp. 425–446. Universidad Nacional Autónoma de México, Mexico City.

Pollock, Harry E. D., Ralph L. Roys, Tatiana Proskouriakoff, and A. Ledyard Smith
1962 *Mayapan, Yucatan, Mexico.* Carnegie Institution of Washington Publication 619. Washington, D.C.

Popenoe de Hatch, Marion
1997 *Kaminaljuyú/San Jorge: Evidencia arqueológica de la actividad económica en el Valle de Guatemala, 300 a.C. a 300 d.C.* Universidad del Valle de Guatemala, Guatemala City[?].

Redfield, Robert
1930 *Tepoztlán, A Mexican Village: A Study of Folk Life.* University of Chicago Press, Chicago.

Relaciones de Yucatán
1898–1900 *Colección de Documentos Inéditos Relativos al Descubrimiento, Conquista y Organización de las Antiguas Posesiones Españolas de Ultramar*, 2nd series. Vols. 11, 13. Sucesores de Rivadeneyra, Madrid.

Robin, Cynthia
2001 Peopling the Past: New Perspectives on the Ancient Maya. *Proceedings of the National Academy of Sciences* 98(1): 18–21.

Roys, Ralph L.
1933 *The Book of Chilam Balam of Chumayel.* Carnegie Institution of Washington Publication 438. Washington, D.C.

Ruppert, Karl, and A. Ledyard Smith
1957 House Types in the Environs of Mayapan and at Uxmal, Kabah, Sayil, Chichen Itza, and Chacchob. *Current Reports* 39:573–597. Carnegie Institution of Washington, Department of Archaeology, Washington, D.C.

Sandstrom, Alan R.
1991 *Corn Is Our Blood: Culture and Ethnic Identity in a Contemporary Aztec Indian Village.* University of Oklahoma Press, Norman.

Schele, Linda
1990 House Names and Dedication Rituals at Palenque. In *Vision and Revision in Maya Studies*, edited by Flora Clancy and Peter Harrison, pp. 143–157. University of New Mexico Press, Albuquerque.

Schele, Linda, and David A. Freidel
1990 *The Forest of Kings.* William Morrow, New York.

Schele, Linda, and Peter Mathews
1998 *The Code of Kings.* Simon and Schuster, New York.

Schufeldt, P. W.
1950 Reminiscences of a Chiclero. In *Morleyana*, edited by Arthur J. O. Anderson, pp. 224–229. The Museum of New Mexico and the School of American Research, Santa Fe.

Seler, Eduard
1901 *Die alten Ansiedelungen von Chaculá.* Dietrich Reimer, Berlin.

Sharer, Robert J. (editor)
1978 *The Prehistory of Chalchuapa, El Salvador, Vol. 3: Pottery and Conclusions.* University of Pennsylvania Press, Philadelphia.

Sheets, Payson D.
1992 *The Cerén Site: A Prehistoric Village Buried by Volcanic Ash in Central America.* Harcourt Brace Jovanovich, Fort Worth.

Smith, Michael E.
1993 Houses and the Settlement Hierarchy in Late Postclassic Morelos: A Comparison of Archaeology and Ethnohistory. In *Prehispanic Domestic Units in Western Mesoamerica: Studies of the Household, Compound, and Residence*, edited by Robert S. Santley and Kenneth G. Hirth, pp. 191–206. CRC Press, Boca Raton.

Smith, Robert Eliot
1971 *The Pottery of Mayapan.* Papers of the Peabody Museum of Archaeology and Ethnology 66. Harvard University, Cambridge.

Thompson, Edward Herbert
1892 The Ancient Structures of Yucatan Not Communal Dwellings. *Proceedings of the American Antiquarian Society* 8(2): 262–269.

Thompson, John Eric Sidney
1938 Sixteenth and Seventeenth Century Reports on the Chol Mayas. *American Anthropologist* 40:584–604.
1971 Estimates of Maya Population: Deranging Factors. *American Antiquity* 36:214–216.

Tourtellot, Gair, III
1988a Developmental Cycles of Households and Houses at Seibal. In *Household and Community in the Mesoamerican Past*, edited by Richard R. Wilk and Wendy Ashmore, pp. 97–120. University of New Mexico Press, Albuquerque.
1988b *Excavations at Seibal, Department of Peten, Guatemala.* Memoirs of the Peabody Museum of Archaeology and Ethnology 16. Harvard University, Cambridge.

Tozzer, Alfred M.
1913 *A Preliminary Study of the Prehistoric Ruins of Nakum, Guatemala.* Memoirs of the Peabody Museum of Archaeology and Ethnology, vol. 5, no. 3. Harvard University, Cambridge.
1941 *Landa's "Relación de las cosas de Yucatan": A Translation.* Papers of the Peabody Museum of Archaeology and Ethnology 18. Harvard University, Cambridge.

Villa Rojas, Alfonso

1945 *The Maya of East Central Quintana Roo.* Carnegie Institution of Washington Publication 559. Washington, D.C.

Vogt, Evon Z.

1969 *Zinacantan: A Maya Community in the Highlands of Chiapas.* Harvard University Press, Cambridge.

Wauchope, Robert

1934 *House Mounds of Uaxactun, Guatemala.* Carnegie Institution of Washington Publication 436. Contributions to American Archaeology, vol. 2, no. 7:107–171. Washington, D.C.

1938 *Modern Maya Houses: A Study of Their Archaeological Significance.* Carnegie Institution of Washington Publication 502. Washington, D.C.

1940 Domestic Architecture of the Maya. In *The Maya and Their Neighbors,* edited by Clarence L. Hay et al., pp. 232–241. D. Appleton-Century, New York.

Webster, David

1992 Maya Elites: The Perspective from Copan. In *Mesoamerican Elites: An Archaeological Assessment,* edited by Diane Z. Chase and Arlen F. Chase, pp. 135–156. University of Oklahoma Press, Norman.

Webster, David, and Nancy Gonlin

1988 Household Remains of the Humblest Maya. *Journal of Field Archaeology* 15(2):169–190.

Webster, David, Nancy Gonlin, and Payson Sheets

1997 Copan and Cerén: Two Perspectives on Ancient Mesoamerican Households. *Ancient Mesoamerica* 8(1):43–61.

Willey, Gordon R., William R. Bullard, Jr., John B. Glass, and James C. Gifford

1965 *Prehistoric Maya Settlements in the Belize Valley.* Papers of the Peabody Museum of Archaeology and Ethnology 54. Harvard University, Cambridge.

Willey, Gordon R., and Richard M. Leventhal

1979 Prehistoric Settlement at Copan. In *Maya Archaeology and Ethnohistory,* edited by Norman Hammond and Gordon R. Willey, pp. 75–102. University of Texas Press, Austin.

Willey, Gordon R., Richard M. Leventhal, and William L. Fash, Jr.

1978 Maya Settlement in the Copan Valley. *Archaeology* 31:32–43.

Contributors

BARBARA ARROYO, *Research Associate*
Universidad del Valle de Guatemala

NICHOLAS P. DUNNING, *Professor, Department of Geography*
University of Cincinnati

NANCY GONLIN, *Instructor of Anthropology*
Bellevue Community College

TAKESHI INOMATA, *Associate Professor, Department of Anthropology*
University of Arizona

JON C. LOHSE, *Research Associate*
University of Texas at Austin

JOYCE MARCUS, *Elman R. Service Professor of Cultural Evolution*
Museum of Anthropology, University of Michigan

MARILYN MASSON, *Associate Professor, Department of Anthropology*
University at Albany–SUNY

CARLOS PERAZA LOPE, *Archaeologist*
Centro-INAH Yucatán, Mérida

TERRY G. POWIS, *Assistant Professor, Department of Anthropology*
Kennesaw State University, Georgia

CYNTHIA ROBIN, *Assistant Professor, Department of Anthropology*
Northwestern University

FRED VALDEZ, JR., *Associate Professor, Department of Anthropology*
University of Texas at Austin

EVON Z. VOGT, *Professor of Anthropology*
Harvard University

JASON YAEGER, *Assistant Professor, Department of Anthropology*
University of Wisconsin–Madison

Index

Abaj Takalik, 77
Abrams, Elliot, 235
Abundance, principle of, 256, 258
Access analysis, 243–245
Achiote, 269
Adams, Richard E. W., 55–56, 228, 278n.1
Aegean, 276
Agriculture: adaptive responses by farmers, 108–109; and box terraces, 129, 131, 132; in Chan Nòohol, 157, 159; cotton production, 82; in Dos Hombres, 120–137; dry-slope or contour terracing in, 123; and fertilizers, 157; in Guatemala, 75, 77, 82–83, 100, 102–104; and irrigation, 126; in La Milpa and environs, 99–104; maize production, 25, 26–27, 124–125, 242; Maya homesteads as farmsteads, 97–109, 159; milpa production, 97; mobility of Classic Maya farmers, 181–182, 189; in Petexbatún/Río de la Pasión region, 100, 102–104, 129; in Puuc region, 104–106; regional-level analyses of, 119; at San Lorenzo, 154; scholarship on environmental diversity and, 118–120; seedbeds for, 129, 131; settlement agriculture, 238; slash-and-burn agriculture, 117; small-scale analyses of, 119; and study of subsistence economy, 8–9; and terracing, 123, 129, 131, 132, 157, 159; and water management, 100, 123–126; in Zinacantan, 25, 26–27. *See also* Cacao; Cotton; Soils
Aguada Margins, 128–130, 131, 133–134
Aguadas (enclosed depressions), 128–130, 133–134, 136, 156–157, 161
Aguateca: abandonment of, 188–189; architecture of, 244; as capital of Dos Pilas dynasty at, 102, 186–187; elites in, 184, 188–190; foundation and development of, 184–187; map of, 185; pottery in, 185–186, 188, 189; and spatial mobility of Maya commoners, 175, 184–189; warfare and defensive walls in, 102, 184, 187–189
Aguateca Archaeological Project, 184
Albarrada (house-lot wall) enclosures, 209
Albion Island, 108
Alcaldes, 43, 44
Alcalde viejo, 44
Alcalde xuves, 44
Alféreces, 43, 44
Almehenob (nobility), 97, 176
Altar de Sacrificios, 51
Altars, 229–230, 233, 244, 257, 270, 271, 272, 274. *See also* Ritual ceremonies

Amatlán, 273
Ancestors, of Zinacantecos, 29–31
Ancient Maya commoners. *See* Maya commoners
Animal sacrifice, 206
Animal spirit companions, 30
Anthony, David, 178–179
Archaeological record, for identification of Maya commoners, 5, 73
Architecture: and access analysis, 243–245; of Aguateca, 244; of Caye Coco, 206–207; of Cerén, 92, 230–238, 241, 268–269; of Chan Nòohol, 157–159, 163; of Classic period, 98, 109; of Cobá, Quintana Roo, 233; Conchas houses, 77–78; of Copán, 228–230, 232–235, 237–238, 240–241, 256, 266; of Copán Valley, 265–268; of courtyards, 236–238, 239, 241, 243–245, 257, 259, 266, 270, 271; and cultural conventions and boundaries, 240–243, 245; deemphasis of, in Maya archaeology, 245; of Dos Hombres, 130–137; ground plans of houses and associated structures, 85, 256, 257, 258, 259; of Guatemala Pacific coast, 80–87, 90–92; and hearths, 238–240, 245, 274; and "house mounds" of commoners, 255–258, 262, 276, 278; of Laguna de On, 205–206; of Mayapán, 208; meaning of, 98; pole-and-thatch structures, 159, 276, 277; and privacy, 241, 242, 243–244; of San Lorenzo, 152–154, 156, 163–164; size of houses, 266, 274; square buildings, 232–233; and steps, 241; stone buildings and houses, 270, 272, 273; and structure function, 226–236; of Tikal, 232–233; wattle-and-daub houses, 153–154, 156, 159, 181, 262, 276; of Xunantunich, 149–150, 156; of Zinacantan, 27, 28, 32–35
Ardren, Traci, 202
Arroyo, Bárbara, 10, 73–93
Ashmore, Wendy, 7, 150
Atol, 237
Atole, 264
Autonomous commoner production model, 201, 202–203, 212
Azmen uinic (middle or medium men), 5
Aztecs, 202, 278n.7

Bajareque (construction material), 83, 84, 90, 91, 235
Bajos (karst depressions), 99, 100, 121, 126, 129
Baking Pot, 151
Balberta, 80–83
Ballcourt, 206
Barba, Luis, 257, 259, 272
Barba Group, 100, 102
Bark beaters, 85, 154
Barton Ramie, 54, 66, 155
Beach, Timothy, 129–130
Belize: irrigation in, 126; map of, 50; marine shell working in, 211; obsidian in, 214; Protoclassic pottery in, 55, 65, 67. *See also* Caye Coco; Dos Hombres; Laguna de On; Lamanai; Xunantunich
Belize River valley, 9, 129, 148, 149, 163, 256. *See also* Xunantunich
Benches, 241
Bilbao, 86, 88, 90
Blanton, Richard, 201, 204
Blue Creek, 55
Bodegas, 230
Boom-bust trajectory, 157
Borreria, 125
Boston University, 130
Boundaries, architectural, 240–243, 245
Bourdieu, Pierre, 148
Bove, Frederick, 77, 80, 82, 83, 90
Box terraces, 129, 131, 132
Brainerd, George, 263
Brokaw, Nicholas, 121, 123, 127
Broken Ridges zone, 126–127, 131
Bronze Age, 244
Brown, Clifford, 209

Buenavista, 67
Bullard, William, 256
Burials: in Chan Nòohol, 161; of commoners, 261–262; in Copán, 229, 238; of elites, 261; on Guatemala Pacific coast, 79, 82–83, 91; in San Lorenzo, 155
Butaca chairs, 237

Cacao, 62, 82, 90, 201, 213, 230, 264
Cadwallader, Martin, 179
Cah (community), 107, 274
Cahal Pech, 92
Callar Creek, 150
Campeche, Mexico, 104–106
Cannon, Aubrey, 6
Caracol, 4–5, 108, 131, 202
Cargo system, 26, 30, 38, 42–46, 164
Carmean, Kelli, 135
Carnegie project, 208, 212
Castles, medieval, 245
Cauinal, 239
Caye Coco, 199, 205, 206–208, 211, 212, 214–215
Ceramics. *See* Pottery
Ceremonial and status pottery, 55
Ceremonies. *See* Ritual ceremonies
Cerén: archaeological excavation of, 273–274; architecture of, 92, 228, 230–238, 241, 268–269; benches at, 241; food at, 231; kitchens in, 269; pottery in, 66, 230–232, 269; structure function at, 230–236; women's and men's areas in houses in, 242
Cerros, 51, 92
Cerro Zaro, 132, 133
Chalchuapa, 51, 263
Chamarras (ponchos), 24
Chan Chan, 245
Chan Kom, 257
Chan Nòohol: agriculture in, 157, 159; archaeological studies of, 150–151; architecture of, 157–159, 163; burials in, 161; chronology of, 157; conclusions on, 165; domestic economy and group identity in, 159–160; local resources of, 156–157, 164; location of, 156; map location of, 148; ritual practices at, 160–162; social and political organization of, 148–149, 150–151, 156–165; social composition of, 159; soils of, 157; water supply of, 156–157, 160; wider sociopolitical affiliations of, 162
Chan village, 156, 161, 162, 164
Chase, Arlen, 2, 4, 56, 73, 76, 198, 202
Chase, Diane, 2, 4, 56, 73, 198, 199, 205, 207, 208, 212, 214
Chel family, 183
Chenopodium ambrosioides, 30
Chert, 154–155, 160, 201, 210, 211, 214
Chi, Gaspar Antonio, 183
Chiapas, 10, 67, 272
Chiapas Project (Harvard), 10
Chibal (lineage), 107, 199, 274
Chichén Itzá, 273, 275, 276, 277
Children, 25, 26
Chinchilla, Oswaldo, 86
Chocolate, 62
Chorti, 237, 241, 242
Christmas–New Year, 44
Chultun (subterranean storage feature), 52, 62, 65, 105
Chunchucmil, 108
Cinnabar, 269
Classic period: architecture of, 98, 109; cacao during, 62; economic organization in, 200–204; of Guatemala Pacific coast, 83–92; homesteads as farmsteads during, 97–109; motifs in art of, 60; pottery in elite households during, 49, 51, 64, 66; social and political organization during, 147–165; spatial mobility of Maya commoners during, 184–190; traits of pottery from, 56
Clothes washing, 25–26
Clothing and adornment, 261
Coastal commoners. *See* Guatemala
Cobá, 9, 233–234, 241, 259, 268, 269–270
Coe, Michael, 75
Colha, 55, 62

Collier, George, 6
Colonial period, 97, 107, 175, 182–183, 261, 270
Comales (griddles), 23, 24, 263–264
Commoners: characteristics of, 2–4, 175–177; definition of, 73; difficulties in identification of, 73, 259–260; distinctions between elite and, 2, 175–177, 259–260; upward mobility of, 199–200. *See also* Maya commoners
Community organization. *See* Social and political organization
Conchas houses, 77–78
Congregación (congregating), 175, 183
Contact period, 176, 182–183
Contour or dry-slope terracing, 123
Cooking. *See* Food
Copán: architecture of, 226, 228–230, 232–235, 237–238, 240–241, 256, 266; economic production at, 5; food at, 9, 228–229; ornaments at, 243; pottery in, 66; ritual ceremonies at, 229; structure function at, 228–230, 232–235
Copán Valley, 265–268
Copper, 209
Corn. *See* Maize production; Tortillas
Corporate group pattern, 100, 118, 130–133, 135
Corporate societies, 204
Cotton, 82, 201, 213
Cotzumalguapa, 86–90, 92
Courtyards, 236–238, 239, 241, 243–245, 257, 259, 266, 270, 271
Cozumel, 9, 212
Cristóbal, 77
Cross shrines, 36, 37
Cuello, 51, 55
Culbert, T. Patrick, 66
Cultural conventions and boundaries, 240–243, 245
Cunil phase, 92
Curing ceremonies, 38–42

Dahlin, Bruce, 202
David, Nicholas, 236, 239, 240
Deal, Michael, 229–230, 244
Decorated vessels, 59, 62
Defensive walls, 184, 187–188
Demarest, Arthur, 190
De Montmollin, Olivier, 157, 183
Diamanti, Melissa, 237–238
Diet. *See* Food
Domestic architecture. *See* Architecture
Domestic developmental cycle, 162–163
Domestic economy. *See* Economic organization
Domestic group hierarchy, 35–38
Don Martín, 268, 270, 271
Dos Chombitos, 150
Dos Hombres: agriculture in, 5, 120–137; Aguada Margins in, 128–130, 131, 133–134; Broken Ridges zone in, 126–127, 131; corporate group pattern of settlement in, 130–133, 135; environmental setting of study area at, 120–130; Escoba Bajo in, 127–128, 131, 132; micro-community pattern of settlement in, 133–135; project area of settlement survey of, 120; regional trade and exchange system at, 5; residences at, 130, 131; Riverine Floodplain in, 124–126, 131; settlement patterns in, 100, 130–137; summary discussions and conclusions on, 135–137; Transitional Uplands in, 122–124, 130, 131; Upland Bajo in, 122, 131
Dos Pilas, 102, 186, 187–189
Dreams, 28, 38, 39
Dry-slope or contour terracing, 123
Dunning, Nicholas, 3, 7, 9, 10, 97–110
Dwellings. *See* Architecture

Early Classic period, 79–83, 184–186
Early Formative period, 74–76, 91, 92
Eaton, Jack D., 98, 244
Economic class: in Caye Coco, 199, 205, 206–208, 211, 212, 214–215; and entrepreneurship, 199; in Laguna de On, 199, 205–206, 211, 212, 214–

215; in Mayapán, 205, 208–212, 214–215; merchant elites, 200; in Postclassic Maya society, 197–200, 205–215; and settlement studies, 203; and social mobility, 199–200; versus social classes, 198. *See also* Economic organization
Economic organization: autonomous commoner production model, 201, 202–203, 212; in Caye Coco, 199, 205, 206–208, 211, 212, 214–215; in Chan Nòohol, 159–160; in Classic period, 200–204; elite exchange, 200–201; elites' role in, 262–263; and household distributional studies, 203, 204; in Laguna de On, 199, 205, 205–206, 211, 212, 214–215; and luxury items, 200–201, 203–204, 209–210; Maya commoners' contributions to generally, 255; in Mayapán, 205, 208–212, 214–215; and occupations of commoners, 198, 206, 210–211, 213, 215, 265; in Postclassic Maya society, 197–200, 205–215; and regional markets, 5, 202, 212–213; in San Lorenzo, 154–155; and settlement studies, 203; and solar marketing system, 202; utilitarian production and exchange, 200, 201–202, 213. *See also* Agriculture; Economic class
Effigy bowls, 59, 62
Egypt, 276
El Bálsamo, 77
El Baúl, 86, 88, 89, 90
El Castillo, 86, 88, 90, 149
Elite exchange, 200–201, 202
Elites: in Aguateca, 184, 188–190; burials of, 261; at Caye Coco, 207; characteristics of, 260; in colonial Yucatán, 97; definition of, 2, 176; distinctions between commoners and, 2, 175–177, 259–260; and economic organization, 262–263; and elite exchange, 200–201, 202; on Guatemala Pacific coast, 76, 77, 79, 82; and indicators of social status, 197, 261; at Laguna de On, 206; and lineage, 260; and luxury items, 200–201, 203–204, 209–210; in Mayapán, 208–209, 212, 215; merchant elites, 200; and obsidian, 79, 82; and *oratorios*, 229–230; personal clothing and adornment of, 261; in Postclassic period, 199, 206–209, 212, 213; pottery of, 49, 51, 55–56, 64, 66, 67; relationships between commoners and, 190, 262–263; and ritual ceremonies, 199, 206, 207, 208–209, 212, 215; rural, 4; stereotypes of, 259; structures associated with, 56; terms and titles for, 260
El Mesak, 74, 75
El Mirador, 100
El Posito, 55
El Salvador. *See* Cerén; Joya de Cerén
El Ujuxte, 79, 80, 92
Energetic studies of structure function, 231–236, 245
Entrepreneurship, 199
Epazote (Mexican tea), 30
Escoba Bajo, 127–128, 131, 132
Escoba palms, 127
Escuintla, 75–76, 77, 80–83, 83
Ethnoarchaeology, 6, 67–68, 161
Ethnographic studies, 5–6, 237, 239, 244, 264, 272, 274, 276
Ethnohistory, 5, 207, 265, 274, 276, 277–278
Europe, ancient, 200
Extended families: in Chan Nòohol, 159, 162–163; in Classic period, 107–108; private quarters for each nuclear family within, 244; in San Lorenzo, 153, 162–163; in Zinacantan, 35–38
External versus internal migrations, 178–179

Fairclough, Graham, 245
Families: in Chan Nòohol, 159, 162–163; in Classic period, 107–108; in San Lorenzo, 153, 162–163; in Zinacantan, 35–38

Family altars. *See* Altars
Farmsteads, 97–109, 159. *See also* Agriculture
Farris, Nancy, 182–183
Feasts. *See* Ritual meals
Female figurines, 76, 77, 79
Fences, 241
Fertilizers, 157
Figurines, 75, 76, 77, 79, 85, 91–92, 209
First occupancy, principle of, 163–164
Flakes, 76, 263
Flamenco, 83–86, 87, 92
Flannery, Kent, 75
Folan, William, 9
Food: at Cerén, 231; at Copán, 9, 228–229; and courtyards, 237, 238, 239; on Guatemala Pacific coast, 75; and hearth, 238–240; preparation of, 23–27, 263–264; and ritual meals, 28–32, 155, 160–161; in San Lorenzo, 154, 155; tortillas, 23–27, 30–32, 237, 239, 263–264; in Zinacantan, 23–27. *See also* Agriculture; Kitchens
Fortes, Meyer, 162
France, 3
Freidel, David, 200–202, 238
Fulani, 239, 240
Function of structures. *See* Structure function
Furniture, 24, 237

Gailey, Christine, 200, 203
Gardens, 26, 238, 241, 256
Gender boundaries and division of labor, 23–28, 240, 242, 272, 274
Gerstle, Andrea, 230–231, 240–241
Gifford, James, 256
Glass, John, 256
Goldberg, Paul, 130
Gonlin, Nancy, 5, 6, 8, 12, 92, 107, 225–246, 265–266, 268, 272, 274
Goody, Jack, 162
Graham, Elizabeth, 52, 65
Graham, Ian, 184
Graves. *See* Burials
Greenstone, 156, 160, 206, 209
Guatemala: agriculture in, 75, 77, 82–83, 100, 102–104; ancient Maya commoners on Pacific coast of, 73–93; burials on Pacific coast of, 79, 82–83, 91; Early Formative commoners in, 74–76, 91, 92; elites on Pacific coast of, 76, 77, 79, 82; houses on Pacific coast of, 80–87, 90–92; irrigation in, 126; Late Preclassic and Early Classic commoners in, 79–83; map of Pacific coast of, 74; Middle Classic, Late Classic, and Postclassic commoners in, 83–92; Middle Formative commoners in, 76–79, 91; Petexbatún/Río de la Pasión region of, 100, 102–104, 108, 129; pottery from highlands of, 60; research on Pacific coast commoners in, 73–74. *See also* Aguateca; Tikal

Hageman, Jon B., 107
Hall, Barbara, 5
Hamblin, Nancy, 9
Hanks, William F., 98
Harvard Chiapas Project, 10
Hats' Chaak phase, 149, 150, 152, 153, 157
Haviland, William, 232–233, 256, 257
Hayden, Brian, 6
Healing. *See* Curing ceremonies
Hearths, 238–240, 245, 274
Hematite, 269
Hendon, Julia, 228, 229, 234, 238
Hill, Robert, 6, 239
Hirth, Kenneth, 5, 203, 265, 268
Hobel, 32
Honduras. *See* Copán
"House mounds," 255–258, 262, 276, 278
House Mounds of Uaxactun, Guatemala (Wauchope), 256
Household archaeology, 7–8, 119, 227–228, 262, 264–276
Household distributional studies, 203, 204
Houses: Conchas, 77–78; ground plans of, 85, 256, 257, 258, 259; hieroglyphs for words for, 275; and "house mounds" of commoners,

255–258, 262, 276, 278; men's and women's areas in, 242, 272, 274; names and root words for, 270, 272–273, 278n.4; new house dedication ceremonies, 32–35; on Pacific coast of Guatemala, 80–87, 90–92; size of, 266, 274; structure function information encoded in, 226–227; wattle-and-daub, 153–154, 156, 159, 181, 262, 276. *See also* Architecture; Household archaeology
Houston, Stephen D., 98, 184, 190
Huasteca, 272

Illness. *See* Curing ceremonies
Inomata, Takeshi, 7, 10, 12, 175–190
Internal versus external migrations, 178–179
Irrigation, 126. *See also* Water supply and management
Its'at (sage), 243
Itzán, 92
Itzmal Chen, 208, 209
Ixtepeque, 211

Jade, 79
Jenny Creek phase, 152
Jewelry. *See* Ornaments
Johnson, Mark, 83
Johnston, Kevin, 92, 107
Joya de Cerén, 230–236
Joyce, Rosemary, 2

Kaminaljuyú, 263
Kamp, Kathryn A., 235, 236, 239
K'axob, 51, 55, 60
Kent, Susan, 242
Kichpanha, 55
Kievit, Karen, 235–236
Killion, Thomas, 238
Kitchen gardens. *See* Gardens
Kitchens, 231–232, 233, 234, 237, 242, 259, 267, 269, 270. *See also* Food
Koral (corral), 41

La Blanca, 77, 79
Labná, 255, 272
Laguna de Juan Piojo, 124
Laguna de On, 199, 205–206, 211, 214–215
Lamanai: ceramic types and ceramic groups at, 57, 58, 59; decorated vessels at, 59, 62; domestic and ritual activity areas for elite and commoner structures at, 54; facets represented in ceramic assemblage at, 52, 54–55; identification of "elite" versus "commoner" contexts for pottery from, 55–56; map location of, 50, 52; number of ceramic vessels recovered from, 52; plan of central portion of, 53; pottery and Late Preclassic Maya commoners at, 49–68; Protoclassic pottery from, 55, 65, 67; size of vessels at, 57, 60, 61; Terminal Preclassic at, 4; vessel forms at, 57, 60, 61
La Milpa and environs, 99–104, 131
Landa, Diego de, 82, 183, 208
Land claims and land wealth, 105, 107
Las Morenas, 77
Las Sepulturas, 228–229, 238, 243
Las Terrazas, 129, 131
Late Classic period: agriculture during, 99, 102, 104–106; of Aguateca, 184–186, 188; Albion Island settlement pattern during, 108; at Dos Hombres, 117–137; of Guatemala Pacific coast, 83–92; population growth during, 99, 100, 102, 189–190; at Sayil, Yucatán, 135; warfare during, 102–103; of Xunantunich, 149, 150
Late Formative period, 91
Late Preclassic period: in Pacific coast of Guatemala, 79–83; pottery of Maya commoners at Lamanai during, 49–68; resource-specialized communities during, 136
Laundry, 25–26
La Victoria, 74, 75, 77–79
Lentz, David, 9
Lineage ceremony, 36
Lineages, 107, 199, 209, 260
Liquor, 29, 30–31
Lithics, 154–155, 160, 210, 233

Lohse, Jon C., 1–12, 100, 117–137, 175–176
Los Cerritos-Sur, 77
Los Chatos–Texas–Manantial site, 83, 84
Love, Michael, 77, 79
Lowland Maya Settlement Patterns (Ashmore), 7
Luxury items, 26, 109–110, 200–201, 203–204

Macal River, 150, 156
Macal Valley, 150
Maize production, 25, 26–27, 124–125, 242
Mallory, Elizabeth, 121, 122, 127
Mann, Michael, 198
Manos and metates, 85, 151, 154, 238, 263, 272, 274
Manzanilla, Linda, 257, 259, 272
Marcus, George, 191n.1
Marcus, Joyce, 5, 6, 7, 8, 11, 12, 92, 197, 255–278
Marine shells, 154, 156, 160, 201, 206, 207, 210–211, 213, 214, 233, 243
Markets, regional, 5, 202, 212–213
Martínez, Alejandro, 270, 272
Marx, Karl, 3, 203
Masson, Marilyn, 5, 10, 11, 197–215
Maya area: map of, 11. *See also* specific sites
Maya commoners: and access analysis, 243–245; archaeological record used for identification of, 4–5; burials of, 261–262; characteristics of, 175–177; and courtyards, 236–238, 239, 241, 243–245, 257, 259, 266, 270, 271; cultural conventions and boundaries at commoner sites, 240–243, 245; difficulties in identification of, 73, 259–260; distinctions between elite and, 175–177, 259–260; in Dos Hombres, 117–137; elite-subject relationship, 190, 262–263; and food preparation, 23–27, 263–264; and hearths, 238–240, 245, 274; as heterogeneous group, 259–262; and homesteads as farmsteads, 97–109, 159; and household diversity, 264–276; importance of labor of, 255; occupations of, 198, 206, 210–211, 213, 215, 265; overview of scholarship on, 1–12, 225–226, 255–258; on Pacific coast of Guatemala, 73–93; in Postclassic period, 197–215; pottery and food consumption among, at Lamanai, 49–68; social and political organization of, near Xunantunich, 147–165; spatial mobility of, 175–190; statistics on, 2, 256; stereotypes of, 259–278; and structure function, 226–236; terms and titles for, 260; units of analysis in study of, 270, 272–276; upward mobility of, 199–200. *See also* Architecture; Food; Pottery; *specific sites*
Mayapán, 183, 205, 208–212, 214–215, 258
Mayordomos, 43–44
Mayores, 43
Mazehualob (commoners), 97, 176
McAnany, Patricia A., 59, 107, 163, 199, 228
McGuire, Randall, 203
Meals. *See* Food
Medrano, Sonia, 91
Men's work and living areas, 23–28, 242, 272, 274
Mercantile model, 204
Merchant elites, 200
Mesoamerican Elites (Chase and Chase), 4
Metates and manos, 85, 151, 154, 233, 238, 263, 272, 274
Mexico. *See* Chiapas; Chunchucmil; Cobá; Cozumel; Mayapán; San Sebastián; Sayil; Yucatán; Zinacantan
Micro-community pattern, 100, 118, 133–135
Middle class, 5, 197–199, 261, 277
Middle Classic period, 83–91, 264
Middle Formative period, 76–79, 91
Middle Preclassic period, 52, 62, 152
Migration. *See* Spatial mobility

Milpa, 97, 98, 209, 238, 241
Mobility. *See* Social mobility; Spatial mobility
Moletik, 44
Monaghan, John, 6
Montana-Paraíso-Manantial complex, 84
Monte Albán, 264
Monte Alto, 77
Moore, Jerry, 245
Mopan River, 149, 152, 156, 163
Mopan Valley, 150
Morelos, 272
Morley, Sylvanus, 117
Muhlenbergia macroura, 32
Municipio of Zinacantan, 38
Musical instruments, 85
Myrtos, Crete, 244

Nah (house or building), 270, 274, 275
Nahua, 264–265, 272–273
Nakbe, 100
Naranjo, 151
Network societies, 204
New house dedication ceremonies, 32–35
Nobles. *See* Elites
Nohmul, 55
Non-elites. *See* Maya commoners

Oaxaca, 264
Obsidian, 79, 82, 85, 155, 206, 207–208, 210, 211, 214
Occupations of commoners, 198, 206, 210–211, 213, 215, 265
Oliva shells, 156
Olmec, 73
Olmeca reflexa, 39
Oratorio, 229–230
Ornaments, 156, 162, 243, 261
Oswald, Dana, 236
Otatea fimbriata, 39
Otoch, otot (house), 270, 274, 275

Pacific coast of Guatemala. *See* Guatemala
Parker, Joy, 238
Pasión region, 186
Pataxte, 90
Patios. *See* Courtyards
Patterson, Thomas, 200, 203
Pearson, Michael, 242
Pendergast, David, 52, 66
Peraza Lope, Carlos, 10, 11, 197–215
Personal property, 242–243
Peta, 74, 76
Petates (reed mats), 24
Petén, 100, 102–104
Petexbatún, 100, 102–104, 108, 129
Petexbatún Regional Archaeological Project, 184
Pib (subterranean earth oven), 264
Pilar, 77
Pinole, 264
Plants. *See* Agriculture; Vegetation
Platforms, 170, 233, 234, 257, 259, 266, 270, 271, 276
Pole-and-thatch structures, 159, 276, 277
Political organization. *See* Social and political organization
Pollen record, 124–125
Polygamy, 244
Ponciano, Erick, 83, 85, 184
Population growth in Late Classic period, 99, 100, 102, 189–190
Population size, 227–228, 240, 257
Posh (sugarcane liquor), 29, 30–31
Postclassic period: in Caye Coco, 199, 205, 206–208, 211, 212, 214–215; commoner class in, 197–215; economic class in, 197–215; elites in, 199; of Guatemala Pacific coast, 83–92; in Laguna de On, 199, 205–206, 211, 214–215; in Mayapán, 205, 208–212, 214–215; occupations in, 198, 206, 210–211, 213, 215; social classes during, 198–199; social mobility during, 199–200
Pottery: in Aguateca, 185–186, 188, 189; basins, 63; buckets, 63–64; ceramic types and ceramic groups at Lamanai, 57, 58, 59; ceremonial and status pottery, 55; in Cerén, 66, 230–232, 269; conclusions on, 67–68; crude open bowls, 64–65;

decorations on, 59, 62; effigy bowls, 59, 62; in elite households, 49, 51, 55–56, 64, 66, 67; functional studies and functional categories of, 51, 57–65; future research on, 68; on Guatemala Pacific coast, 85; for holding liquids, 61–64; household analysis through, 265, 268; in houses and kitchen areas, 231–232, 233, 234; identification of "elite" versus "commoner" contexts for, 55–56; at Laguna de On, 206; and Late Preclassic Maya commoners at Lamanai, 49–68; polychrome pottery, 64–67; of Preclassic period, 185; Protoclassic pottery, 54–55, 65, 67; size of vessels at Lamanai, 57, 60, 61; spouted vessels, 62, 63; in storehouses, 230–231, 234; vases, 63–64; vessel forms at Lamanai, 57, 60, 61; in Xunantunich, 151, 154
Powis, Terry, 4, 10, 49–68
Pozole, 264
Principle of abundance, 256, 258
Principle of first occupancy, 163–164
Privacy, 241, 242, 243–244
Protoclassic pottery, 54–55, 65, 67
Puuc region, 104–106, 228
Pyburn, K. Anne, 239

Quiriguá, 256

Ramada, 268, 269
Ramón, 127
Rancho San Lorenzo Survey Area, 150
Rapoport, Amos, 98
Rathje, William, 204, 205
Regidores, 43, 44
Regional markets, 5, 202, 212–213
Relación, 183
Reservoirs, 100
Residences. *See* Architecture; Houses
Residential wards, 273–276, 278
Restall, Matthew, 107, 183
Retalhuleu, 83–86, 90–91
Reynosa, 77
Rice, Prudence, 201
Richard, Colin, 242
Río Bec region, 98, 241, 244
Río Bravo, 124, 127
Río Bravo Embayment zone, 120–122, 123
Río Bravo Escarpment, 100, 121, 122
Río Bravo Terrace Uplands, 122
Río de la Pasión region, 100, 102–104
Río Hondo, 126
Ritual ceremonies: and altars, 229–230, 233, 244, 257, 270, 271, 272, 274; burials, 79, 82–83, 91, 155, 161, 229, 238, 261–262; and *cargo* system, 26, 30, 42–46; at Caye Coco, 207, 212; in Chan Nòohol, 160–162; at Cobá, 233; at Copán, 229; at Cozumel, 212; curing ceremonies, 38–42; and domestic group hierarchy, 35–38; and elites, 199, 206, 207, 208–209, 212, 215; on Guatemala Pacific coast, 75, 76, 77, 85; at Laguna de On, 206, 211; lineage ceremony, 36; at Mayapán, 208–209; new house dedication ceremonies, 32–35; and *oratorios*, 229–230; repeating ritual sequences, 32, 44; ritual meals, 28–32, 155, 160–161; and saints' days, 44; in San Lorenzo, 155, 161, 164; and shamans, 33, 36, 38–42, 45–46; waterhole ceremony, 37–38, 161; witchcraft rituals, 44; Year Renewal Ceremonies, 45–46; in Zinacantan, 28–46
Ritual meals, 28–32, 155, 160–161
Riverine Floodplain, 124–126, 131
Robertson, Robin, 51
Robin, Cynthia, 7, 10, 147–165
Royal Ontario Museum, 52
Roys, Ralph, 198
Ruppert, Karl, 212
Rural elite, 4
Rural Sites Project, 238

Sabloff, Jeremy, 204, 205
Saca, 264
Sacrifice, 206
Salinas La Blanca, 74, 75

Salinas Sinaloa, 74, 76
Salt, 201, 213
Samal phase, 149, 152
San Cristóbal Las Casas, 25
San Lorenzo: archaeological studies of, 150–151; architecture of, 152–154, 156, 163–164; chronology of, 152–153; conclusions on, 165; domestic economy and group identity in, 154–155; local resources of, 151–152, 163; location of, 151–152; map location of, 148; ritual practices in, 155, 161, 164; social and political organization of, 148–156, 162–165; social composition of, 153; soils of, 152; wider sociopolitical affiliations of, 155–156
San Lorenzo Fiesta, 44
San Pedro de Laguna, 258
San Sebastián, Mexico, 236
San Sebastián Fiesta, 32, 44
Sanders, Donald, 240, 244
Sanders, William, 238
Sandstrom, Alan, 264–265, 272
Santa Elisa Pacacó, 90–91
Santa Rita, 55, 205, 207, 208
Sayil, Yucatán, 5, 105, 135
Scarborough, Vernon, 136
Schele, Linda, 238
Seedbeds, 129, 131
Seibal, 131, 186, 256, 258
Settlement agriculture, 238
Settlement studies: and agglomeration into multifamily compounds, 107–108; corporate group pattern in, 100, 118, 130–133, 135; description of, 7; and dispersal into nuclear family units, 107–108; of Dos Hombres, 100, 118, 130–137; of La Milpa and environs, 100; of Mayapán, 209; micro-community pattern in, 100, 118, 133–135; and social or political standing, 203; Xunantunich Settlement Survey, 150
Shamans, 33, 36, 38–42, 45–46
Sharer, Robert, 4
Shaw, Leslie, 9–10
Sheehy, James, 236
Sheets, Payson, 242, 269, 272, 273–274
Shells. *See* Marine shells
Shrines, 36, 37, 257, 259, 270. *See also* Ritual ceremonies
Sin Cabezas, 83
Slash-and-burn agriculture, 117
Slate, 156, 160
Slaves, 198, 278
Smith, A. Ledyard, 212
Smith, Michael E., 5, 67–68
Smith, Robert, 263–264
Smith, Woodruff D., 278n.1
Social and political organization: corporate formations, 204; in Late Classic period in Dos Hombres, 117–137; network formations, 204; scholarship on, 147–150; in Xunantunich, 147–165
Social classes: and burials, 261–262; and luxury items, 200–201, 203–204, 209–210; versus autonomous integrity of kin-based communities, 203; versus economic status groups, 198. *See also* Commoners; Elites; Maya commoners; Middle class
Social mobility, 199–200
Social non-elites. *See* Maya commoners
Social power, 198–199
Soils: of *aguadas*, 128–130; of Broken Ridges zone, 127; of Chan Nòohol, 157; in Dos Hombres, 122–130; of Escoba Bajo, 127–128, 132; of Riverine Floodplain, 124–126; of San Lorenzo, 152; of Transitional Uplands, 122–124; of Upland Bajo, 122. *See also* Agriculture
Solar marketing system, 202
Soul and soul loss, 29–30, 41–42
Spanish Conquest, 270
Spatial mobility: and Aguateca, 175, 184–189; in Colonial period, 182–183; concept of, 177–179; conclusions on, 189–190; in Contact period, 182–183; definition of, 179; distinction between movement and,

179; distinction between repetitive movements and moves to new localities, 178; factors affecting generally, 180–181; factors affecting mobility of Classic Maya non-elites, 181–182; of farmers, 181–182, 189; and internal versus external migrations, 178–179; and location of activities as criterion for movement, 177–178; of Maya commoners in Classic period, 175–190; and social scale of moving or decision-making entity, 179; and spatial scale of movements, 178–179
Spindle whorls, 82, 85, 154, 211
Spouted vessels, 62, 63
Square buildings, 232–233
Stann Creek region, Central Belize, 65
Stark, Barbara, 5
Steps, 241
Stereotypes: commoners as homogeneous group, 259–262; commoners as passive recipients of elite directives, 262–263; conclusions on, 276–278; conservative nature of commoners, 263–264; of elites, 259; uniformity of commoner households, 264–276
Stone buildings and houses, 270, 272, 273
Storehouses, 230–231, 234, 236, 238, 242, 256, 257, 259, 270
Strombus spp., 160
Structure function: and architectural properties, 235–236; at Cerén, 230–236; at Cobá, Quintana Roo, 233–234; at Copán, 228–230, 232–235; energetic studies of, 234–236, 245; importance of, in Maya archaeology, 227–228; information encoded in houses, 226–227; and population size, 227–228; at Tikal, 232–234. *See also* Architecture
Subsistence economy, 8–10
Suchitepéquez, 74, 75–76, 76
Sugarcane liquor (*posh*), 29, 30–31
Surplus, 204
Sweatbath and sweathouse, 230, 269
Syria, 235

Tamales, 264
Tamarindito, Petén, 104
Tambiah, Stanley, 190
Tax, Sol, 6
Telchac Pueblo, 273
Teotihuacán, 73, 201, 236
Tepoztlán, 272–273
Terminal Classic period: agriculture during, 99, 104–106; at Sayil, Yucatán, 135; of Xunantunich hinterland, 150
Terminal Preclassic at Lamanai, 4
Terracing, 123, 129, 131, 132, 157, 159
Test pitting of house mounds, 276, 278
Thailand, 190
Thatched-roof houses, 159, 276, 277
Theobroma bicolor, 90
Thompson, Edward H., 225, 234–235, 255–256
Tikal, 5, 66, 108, 131, 186, 232–234, 256, 258, 268
Tiquisate, 83
Tools, 85, 151, 154, 160, 206, 210, 211, 213, 214, 243, 263, 272
Tortillas, 23–27, 30–32, 237, 239, 263–264
Tot'il-me'iletik (fathers-mothers), 29, 31
Tourtellot, Gair, 235, 256, 257–258
Trade. *See* Regional markets
Transitional Uplands, 122–124, 130, 131
Trees, 9, 122, 124, 127, 237
Triadan, Daniela, 184
Tringham, Ruth E., 3
Tsak' phase, 149–150, 152
Tzotzil, 107, 263, 274

Uaxac, 256
Uaxactún, 276
University College London, 52
Upland Bajo, 122, 131
Upland Forest, 122

Upper class. *See* Elites
Urban centers, in Late Classic period, 108
U-shaped rooms, 245
Utilitarian production and exchange, 200, 201–202, 213
Uxmal, 272

Vakash na (cow houses), 32
Valdez, Fred, Jr., 1–12, 175–176
Vegetation, 124–125, 127, 241
Vessels. *See* Pottery
Virgen de Rosario Fiesta, 44
Vista Hermosa, 77
Vogt, Evon Z., 4, 10, 23–46, 161, 164, 272

Wards, 273–276, 278
Warfare, 102–103, 184, 187–189
Waterhole ceremony, 37–38, 161
Water supply and water management, 100, 123–126, 156–157, 160
Wattle-and-daub houses, 153–154, 156, 159, 181, 262, 276
Wauchope, Robert, 239, 240, 255, 256, 270, 276, 278n.3
Weaving, 206, 229
Webster, David, 109, 232, 265–266, 268, 272, 274, 278n.1
West, Georgia, 202
Widmer, Fulani, 236
Widmer, Randolph, 236
Wilk, Richard, 242
Willey, Gordon, 7, 10, 256
Wisdom, Charles, 6, 237, 242
Witchcraft rituals, 44
Wolf, Eric, 3, 202–203
Women's work and living areas, 23–28, 240, 242, 272, 274

Xkipché Project Regional Extended Settlement Survey (XPRESS), 106
Xochicalco, 265
XPRESS (Xkipché Project Regional Extended Settlement Survey), 106
Xunantunich: architecture of, 149–150, 156; Chan Nòohol in, 148–149, 150–151, 156–165; conclusions on, 165; El Castillo in, 149; map of, 148; San Lorenzo in, 148–156, 162–165; social and political organization of commoner settlements near, 147–165
Xunantunich Archaeological Project, 149, 150

Yaeger, Jason, 7, 10, 147–165
Year Renewal Ceremonies, 45–46
Yucatán: agriculture in, 104–106; Colonial period of, 97, 107; hearths in, 239; house in, 273; local and regional markets in, 212–213; market towns in, 202; modern farming community in, 161; pottery in, 60. *See also* Chunchucmil; Mayapán; Sayil
Yucatec, 263

Zinacantan: agriculture in, 25, 26–27; *cargo* system in, 26, 30, 38, 42–46; Ceremonial Center in, 42–46; climate of, 24; curing ceremonies in, 38–42; daily life of, in mid-1900s, 10, 23–28; domestic group hierarchy and related ceremonies in, 35–38; food and food preparation in, 23–27; furniture in, 24; gender division of labor in, 23–28, 242; house compound in, 27, 28; lineage ceremony in, 36; new house dedication ceremonies in, 32–35; ritual ceremonies in, 28–46; ritual meals in, 28–32; waterhole group in, 35, 36–38